Principles of agricultural economics

WYE STUDIES IN AGRICULTURAL AND RURAL DEVELOPMENT

Solving the problems of agricultural and rural development in poorer countries requires, among other things, sufficient numbers of well-trained and skilled professionals. To help meet the need for topical and effective teaching materials in this area, the books in the series are designed for use by teachers, students and practitioners of the planning and management of agricultural and rural development. The series is being developed in association with the innovative postgraduate programme in Agricultural Development for external students of the University of London.

The series concentrates on the principles, techniques and applications of policy analysis, planning and implementation of agricultural and rural development. Texts review and synthesise existing knowledge and highlight current issues, combining academic rigour and topicality with a concern for practical applications. Most importantly, the series provides simultaneously a systematic basis for teaching and study, a means of updating the knowledge of workers in the field, and a source of ideas for those involved in planning development.

Other titles in this series

Peasant Economics
Frank Ellis
Extension Science
Niels Röling

Principles of agricultural economics

MARKETS AND PRICES IN LESS DEVELOPED COUNTRIES

DAVID COLMAN AND TREVOR YOUNG
Department of Agricultural Economics, University of Manchester

Published by the Press Syndicate of the University of Cambridge
The Pitt Building, Trumpington Street, Cambridge CB2 1RP
40 West 20th Street, New York, NY 10011-4211 USA
10 Stamford Road, Oakleigh, Melbourne 3166, Australia

First published 1989
Reprinted 1990, 1992, 1993, 1995

Printed in Great Britain by
Athenæum Press Ltd, Gateshead, Tyne & Wear

British Library cataloguing in publication data

Colman, David, 1928-
Principles of agricultural economics:
markets and prices in less developed countries. -
(Wye studies in agricultural and rural development).
1. Developing countries. Agricultural industries
I. Title II. Young, Trevor
338.1'09172'4

Library of Congress cataloguing in publication data

Colman, David.
Principles of agricultural economics:
markets and prices in less developed countries.
David Colman and Trevor Young.
p. cm.-(Wye studies in agricultural and rural development)
Bibliography: p.
Includes index.
ISBN 0 521 33430 6. ISBN 0 521 33664 3 (paperback)
1. Agriculture-Economic aspects-Developing countries.
2. Agriculture prices-Developing countries.
I. Young, Trevor. II. Titles. III. Series.
HD1417.C63 1989
338.1'09172'4-dc19 88-10297 CIP

ISBN 0 521 33664 3 paperback

UP

Contents

Acknowledgements

Our warm appreciation is offered to the many colleagues who attempted to keep us on a straight and narrow path in the preparation of this book. Derek Ray, at Wye College, deserves particular mention for his advice on structural and presentational issues. Also at Wye we would like to thank both Henry Bernstein and Jonathan Kydd for their continual support and advice. Among our immediate colleagues at Manchester University, Martin Currie, Noel Russell, Ian Steedman and Colin Thirtle all made telling and much appreciated responses to drafts of different chapters of the book. Our thanks are also extended to Hartwig de Haen at the University of Gottingen and Joachim von Braun at the International Food Policy Research Institute for their correspondence in connection with material presented in Chapter 12. Needless to say none of those mentioned is in any way responsible for any tendencies to stray that the book exhibits or for any of the errors that we may have committed. We accept full responsibility for those.

To illustrate the significance of various concepts we have drawn upon the work of others. The authors and publishers would therefore like to thank the following who have kindly given permission for the use of copyright material:

The Controller of Her Majesty's Stationery Office for a table from *Household Food Consumption and Expenditure 1985*; the International Bank for Reconstruction and Development for (i) a table from *A Survey of Agricultural Household Models* by I. Singh, L. Squire and J. Strauss (1986), (ii) a table from *Agricultural Price Policies and the Developing Countries* by G. S. Tolley, V. Thomas and Chung Ming Wong (1982), and (iii) a table from *World Development Report 1986*; the International Food Policy Research Institute for diagrams and tables from *The Effect of Food*

Price and Subsidy Policies on Egyptian Agriculture by J. von Braun and H. de Haen (1983); the International Rice Research Institute for tables from *Adoption, Spread and Production Impact of Modern Rice Varieties in Asia* by R. W. Herdt and C. Capule (1983); Praeger for an extract from a table in *Agricultural Supply Response: A Survey of the Econometric Evidence* (1976); and to the United Nations Food and Agriculture Organisation for a table in *Agricultural Price Policies* (C85/19) (1985).

A special debt of thanks is owed to Jennifer Vaughan and Judy Darnton for their heroic efforts in typing and processing the various drafts and many revisions of the book; this they did with unfailing grace and humour. As always, however, much of the strain was transmitted to our immediate families who had to cope with the bouts of moody introspection that accompany a venture such as this. In what can only be a token recognition of their generous support, this book is lovingly dedicated to Sandy, Sue, Lucy and Sophie.

D. Colman
T. Young

1

Introduction

Economists emphasise the importance of the agricultural sector in the development process and there is wide agreement that a necessary condition for economic growth is an agricultural transformation which ensures a large and increasing domestic agricultural surplus. However, it has not always been the case that agriculture has been seen to play such a significant role. In the 1950s the emphasis in development policy was placed on urban industrial growth, with the agricultural sector being regarded as a residual source of inputs (mainly labour) for the manufacturing sector. There was a shift of emphasis in the 1960s when the importance of 'balanced growth' was stressed, which entailed recognition of the need for a certain pattern of agricultural growth to complement that of other sectors. It was also at this time that the contributions of agriculture to the development process were more sharply identified in the work of Kuznets (1961), Mellor (1966) and others, and the positive role of agriculture as an engine of development became accepted. Subsequent events in the 1970s and 1980s have reinforced the need for more attention to be paid to agricultural development policy. The series of 'oil shocks' which raised oil prices had serious consequences for the trade balances of non-oil exporting countries and caused them to focus attention on their trading accounts in agricultural products. This necessity was intensified by a growing tendency in some Less Developed Countries (LDCs) to increase food imports as demand growth outstripped that of supply. It has forced countries to take a positive view of the benefits of increased agricultural production for both export and domestic consumption, and to focus more attention upon the factors determining supply and demand growth. This has necessitated increasingly sophisticated analysis of the operation of agricultural markets, and of the impacts and effectiveness of government policies for the sector. Particular emphasis has been given to the economics of production and supply, an area in which agricultural economics has a major contribution to make.

It is our intention to equip the reader with the analytical tools which agricultural economists need for the study of supply, demand and agricultural markets in developing countries. The importance of an analytical framework is stressed since the main contribution of agricultural economists working on development issues lies in their ability to provide a consistent, logical basis for the study of complex policy problems. This framework provides the basis for the systematic quantitative analysis which is a major input into agricultural political decision-making.

Because agriculture is special (almost unique) in a number of ways a specialised branch of economics has developed to address the problems associated with it. In this agricultural economists make extensive use of 'micro-economics' or 'price theory', in which propositions on the functioning of markets, in terms of production, consumption and exchange, are developed from hypotheses about the behaviour of individual producers and consumers.[1] The central theme is that resources – land, labour, capital, time etc. – are limited, or too few to satisfy all human wants, and that as a consequence of this scarcity choices must be made. The problems which we will study are ones of 'constrained choice', that is of how limited quantities of inputs are allocated between alternative production uses and of how limited incomes are allocated between the many products consumers may buy.

In essence, our approach to the subject is neoclassical, mainstream or orthodox.[2] The distinguishing feature of this school of thought is the emphasis placed on market forces and on prices as signals to appropriate resource allocation. This approach is very topical in that the role of markets in developing countries' agriculture and the (possibly detrimental) impact of government policy on agricultural resource use are issues with which much of the current development literature has been concerned.[3] However, we would wish to make it clear that we are not arguing that all markets function well, adjusting instantaneously and fully to changing circumstances, or that government intervention is always undesirable. Rather we will be discussing at some length instances when inertia and lags in adjustment by both producers and consumers of agricultural products are to be expected and we will be outlining a framework for the analysis of activities (such as subsistence farming, home crafts, fuel gathering) for which no market exists. Moreover, it is evident that markets in the private sectors are not, and cannot be, organised for the adequate provision of physical infrastructure in roads and other communication channels, electricity supply, irrigation, etc., and of 'human capital' infrastructure in agricultural research and extension services. It is also to be expected that there will be cases in which the market works well but to the disadvantage of some group and where society views the outcome as intolerable. The adoption of a neoclassical approach in no way denies the importance of these considerations. As Little (1982, pp. 25, 26) has put it:

> 'Neoclassical economics can thus be described as a paradigm that tells one to investigate markets and prices, perhaps expecting them often to work well but also to be on the watch for aberrations and ways of correcting them. Perhaps the single best touchstone is a concern for prices and their role'.

The book proceeds by considering the three main strands in the theoretical analysis of agricultural product markets – production, consumption, and exchange which is the interaction of consumption and production. Production and consumption are each dealt with in blocks of three chapters. In the first chapter of each block the basic economic theory of the independent decision-making unit is presented; these are the firm in the case of production (Chapter 2) and the individual consumer in matters of consumption (Chapter 5). A second chapter in each block presents the economic theory at the market level; thus Chapter 3 deals with supply and Chapter 6 with demand. The third chapter in each triad deals with special and more advanced topics in supply and demand. Chapter 4 examines the economics of technological change and the concept of economic efficiency, as well as explaining the importance of the concept of 'duality' in the economic relationships of production. Chapter 7 likewise considers economic duality in demand relationships (which some readers may find overly technical, and wish to skip), and also outlines some new, recent approaches to demand analysis.

Chapter 8, on Equilibrium and Exchange, explores the way in which supply and demand interact to determine prices. The treatment goes beyond the scope of standard agricultural economics textbooks by examining market disequilibrium and the behaviour of prices through time. It also includes a body of analysis which recognises the special place of the semi-subsistence 'agricultural household' in developing countries, in which production and consumption activities are combined under one roof. The special functions and structure of agricultural markets are discussed in more detail in Chapter 9. It is our intention that Chapters 2 to 9 taken together should provide a solid foundation for an understanding of the workings of the agricultural sector within the economic system.

The remainder of the book is more concerned with assessing the merits of alternative economic situations. Chapter 10 provides the analytical tools for such an assessment, namely theoretical 'welfare economics', which Arrow and Scitovsky (1969) define as 'the theory of how and by what criteria economists and policy-makers make or ought to make their choice between alternative policies and between good and bad institutions'. A major policy issue for the developing countries is the distribution of the benefits from international trade in primary products. The theoretical underpinnings for this debate are presented in Chapter 11, 'Economics of Trade'. In the final chapter, many of the economic concepts introduced in earlier sections are applied to the evaluation of domestic food and agricultural policy. Through the careful analysis of these complex issues, which permits better informed judgements to be made by politicians, the agricultural economist can make a valuable contribution to policy debates.

The microeconomic principles of agricultural economics are universal, and to that extent it is hoped that this book will appeal to a wide audience. It is primarily written for postgraduate students in agricultural development, who although they may not be economics specialists are adopting economics as a major discipline in their studies. It is also intended to be suitable for economics and agricultural economics undergraduates with interests in the problems of developing countries.

2

Economics of agricultural production: theoretical foundations

2.1 *Introduction*

Growth in agricultural production is necessary not only to increase food availability and raise nutrition levels of the population; it is essential to the development process. Indeed it is accepted that a prerequisite for rapid economic growth is the channelling of agricultural surplus (production in excess of own consumption) to the non-farm sector. It will not however be our purpose to analyse the way in which the agricultural sector can make a contribution to development.[1] Rather the importance of agricultural production will be taken as given and we will focus instead on the determinants of agricultural output. In this and the following two chapters particular attention will be given to (i) the factors which influence the supply of agricultural product, (ii) the factors which govern the usage of productive inputs (labour, fertiliser, machinery etc.), (iii) the efficiency of resource use and (iv) the impact of technological change. These topics are central to the analysis of agricultural markets and in particular to the design of effective development policies aimed at motivating agricultural producers, mobilising resources in the sector and spreading new technologies.

In this chapter we present the main elements of the theory of production economics which have proved useful in the study of agricultural markets. As with all branches of economics, production economics is concerned with the allocation of scarce resources to alternative uses. In production theory the main choices centre upon what to produce (which product or combination of products), how much to produce (the level of output) and how to produce (the combination of inputs to use). The decision making unit is the *firm* which is defined as a 'distinct agent specialised in the conversion of inputs into desired goods as outputs' (Hirshleifer (1976)).

(The aggregate of all firms in a given market is termed the *industry*.) Whilst not reflecting the full complexities of productive activity in an economy, this definition is a useful simplification for economic analysis. In the agricultural sectors of developing and developed countries, there are farms, producing cash crops for the domestic or foreign market, which fall within the definition of a firm. In the developing countries there may also be a number of subsistence farms in which all production is consumed and none passes through the market. However, pure subsistence farming is rare (Wharton (1970)) and it is more common that farms produce some amount of *marketable surplus*. We would therefore argue that the theory presented in this chapter has direct relevance to the analysis of agricultural markets in both developed and developing countries. Indeed the main drawback of the theory when applied to the developing countries is not its focus on commercial aspects of production but rather on the distinction between firms and consumers. Many farms are both production and consuming units (in the sense that a proportion of their output is consumed on the farm) and so for some analyses a synthesis of the production theory of this chapter and the consumer theory of Chapter 5 is required. Recent attempts at such a synthesis are discussed in Chapter 8.

This is the first of a set of three chapters concerned with the economics of production, supply and input demand. It presents the principles or foundations underlying the theory of profit maximising firms and of market level supply. For those readers who have previously taken an introductory course in economics, the chapter is intended to provide a concise review of the elements of production economics. For those who are less familiar with economic analysis it is intended as a guide to those principles which it is important to grasp before proceeding to Chapters 3 and 4. It is shown how, starting only with a simple technological relationship (called a *production function*) between a number of inputs and a single output, rules for determining the optimum level of output and input use for the profit-maximising firm can be established.

2.2 *Physical relationships*

Production is the process of combining and coordinating inputs (resources or factors of production) in the creation of a good or service. Producing a ton of wheat, for example, requires, in addition to suitable climatic conditions, some amount of arable land, seed, fertiliser, the services of equipment such as ploughs and harvesters, and human labour. It seems reasonable to assume that production will vary in a systematic way with the levels of input usage and, as a shorthand device, economists often express this relationship between inputs and outputs in mathematical symbols. Hence a *production function* is defined as:

$$Q = f(X_1, X_2, \ldots, X_n) \tag{2.1}$$

where Q denotes the quantity of a specific product (wheat in the example above) produced in a given time period; and $X_1, \ldots, X_n$ represent the quantities of an unspecified number (n) of inputs employed in the production process (for example X_1 might denote the usage of fertiliser, X_2 the usage of seed, and so on). The expression 2.1 merely states that output is related to (i.e. is a function of) the levels of input usage. The precise form of the relationship is not specified, since most of our analytical conclusions can be derived from the general function.[2]

The production function is a purely physical concept: it depicts the *maximum output* in physical terms for each and every combination of specified inputs in physical terms. It relates to a given state of technology. As should become clear, the production function is the core concept in the economic theory of production.

For ease of exposition, the technical aspects of production will be discussed (i) in terms of the factor–product relationship, where there is one variable input in a production process creating a single output, and (ii) the factor–factor relationship, where there are two or more variable inputs. In addition we will outline (iii) the product–product relationship in which more than one product may be produced from the available stock of inputs.

2.2.1 *The factor–product relationship*

If it is assumed that all inputs except one (say, fertiliser, denoted as X_1) are held fixed at some level, the relationship between output[3] and the single variable factor can be derived. This *factor product* relationship is denoted as

$$Q = f(X_1 \mid X_2, \ldots, X_n) \tag{2.2}$$

where $X_2, \ldots, X_n$ are the fixed factors; X_1 is the variable factor. Graphically the relationship is represented by the *total product* (*TP*) curve of Fig. 2.1(*a*). In this case, as more fertiliser (X_1) is applied, output (Q) increases until a maximum, associated with input usage X_1'', is reached. Further applications of fertiliser will only serve to reduce the total quantity produced. Note that the *TP* curve is drawn for a given level of the fixed factors and for a given state of technology. For a numerical illustration of this relationship refer to Table 2.1.

Two other aspects of the factor–product relationship will be of interest. These are

(i) the *marginal product* (*MP*) of the variable input. This is defined as the change in output resulting from a small change in the variable input expressed per unit of the input. The symbol Δ is commonly used to denote a change. Thus the marginal product of a small change, ΔX_1, in input X_1 can be obtained from the following expression:

$$MP_{X_1} = \frac{\Delta Q}{\Delta X_1}$$

For an infinitesimal change (∂X_1) in the factor, $MP_{X_1} = \partial Q/\partial X_1$ = the slope of the total product curve at the relevant point.[4] Thus in Fig. 2.1, *MP* is at a maximum (the slope of *TP* is greatest) at the point of inflection of the curve (at input level X'), it is zero at the point of maximum total product (at input level X'') and it becomes negative at input levels beyond X''.

(ii) the *average product* (*AP*) of the variable input. This is defined as total product divided by the amount of variable input i.e.

$$AP_{X_1} = \frac{Q}{X_1}$$

Diagrammatically, average product at a particular level of input use is given as the slope of a line from the origin at point *O* to the relevant point on the total product curve. Thus, for example,[5] in Fig. 2.1(*a*) the slope of line *OA* gives the average product of X_1 at input level X_1^0.

It should be clear from these definitions why $AP_{X_1} = MP_{X_1}$ at X_1^0 in Fig. 2.1 (the slope of the *TP* curve = the slope of a line from the origin at X_1^0), and why AP_{X_1} is at a maximum at this point (a line from the origin to the *TP* curve has greatest slope there).

The product curves in Fig. 2.1 satisfy the almost universal *law of diminishing marginal returns*. This states that as more and more of a variable input is used, with other inputs held constant, eventually the increases to total product will become smaller and smaller i.e. after some point the marginal product of the variable input will decline. In Fig. 2.1, the factor–product relationship is one of increasing returns up to X_1', but diminishing marginal returns set in beyond this level of input usage.

As we have already noted, the total product is a purely physical relationship; economic considerations involving prices of inputs and outputs are not part of the analysis. Yet it is possible to determine, on technical grounds alone, a range of input usage in which the rational producer will operate. This point may be illustrated with the aid of Fig. 2.1 where the *TP*, *MP* and *AP* curves have been divided into *stages of production. Stage 1* is defined to be that in which the average product of X_1, AP_{X_1}, is rising; in *Stage 2* both marginal (MP_{X_1}) and average product are falling but both are positive; *Stage 3* is that in which marginal product, MP_{X_1}, is actually negative. In the following discussion, it will be helpful to bear in mind that the producer is using at least two inputs: a variable input, say fertiliser, and a second which represents a set of fixed factors of production (land, labour, seed etc.).

Fig. 2.1. (*a*) The total product curve.

(*a*)

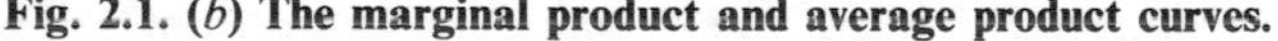

Fig. 2.1. (*b*) The marginal product and average product curves.

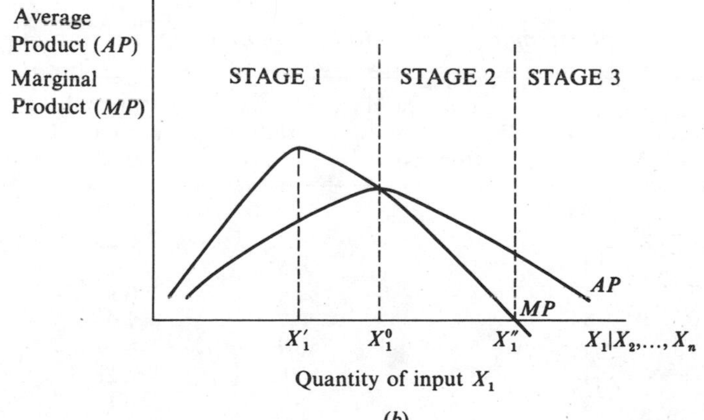

(*b*)

In Stage 3, additional units of fertiliser *reduce* total product i.e. the marginal product of fertiliser is negative. The fixed inputs, notably land, are overloaded and the producer's interest would be better served (output would increase) by using less fertiliser and in so doing, by moving back, out of Stage 3. In other words it is irrational to choose a level of fertiliser in Stage 3. Whereas in Stage 3 the producer uses too much fertiliser, by contrast in Stage 1 not enough of the input is being applied, given the level of the fixed factors. In Stage 1, the average product of the variable input is rising and throughout this stage *MP* lies above *AP*. With each additional unit of fertiliser, more is being added to total product than was added on average by the previous units of fertiliser. Therefore if it is profitable to produce any output, the farmer can make more profit by using more fertiliser at least up to the end of Stage 1. It would therefore be predicted that the optimum position in terms of variable input usage will lie somewhere in Stage 2. The precise position can only be determined by incorporating the prices of inputs and of the final product into the analysis.

A numerical illustration of the factor–product relationships for a simple production function are presented in Table 2.1. Three inputs, fertiliser, land and labour are used to produce maize. Naturally if none of these inputs is employed total product is zero. With one unit of all three inputs total product rises to 0.25 tonnes. Thereafter column 4 shows how total product of maize changes as successive units of fertiliser are employed while land and labour are both fixed at one unit each. As an exercise readers might care to check that they can calculate the average and marginal product values in columns 5 and 6. They might also usefully graph the data in Table 2.1 and examine its relationship to Fig. 2.1.

Table 2.1. *Hypothetical example: factor–product relationships*

Units of fertiliser	Units of land	Units of labour	Total product of maize (tonnes)	Average product of fertiliser	Marginal product of fertiliser
0	0	0	0	—	—
1	1	1	0.25	0.25	0.25
2	1	1	1.0	0.5	0.75
3	1	1	1.8	0.6	0.8
4	1	1	2.8	0.7	1.0
5	1	1	3.5	0.7	0.7
6	1	1	3.7	0.62	0.2
7	1	1	3.8	0.54	0.1
8	1	1	3.6	0.45	−0.2

BOX 2.1
Total product relationships in peasant agriculture

The 'textbook' representation of the total product curve is the one given in Fig. 2.1. In particular empirical settings, the response of output to input usage may however take a number of alternative forms. Here we will consider two cases which may be more relevant in the study of developing countries' agriculture: the 'surplus labour' case and the 'hard-working peasant' case (using Mellor's (1985) terminology).

Fig. 2.2 depicts the 'surplus labour' case.[6] The amount of output required for one person to exist (the 'subsistence wage') is denoted as *Oa* but, as production response is quite rapid, the labour input of one worker (say, L_1) provides much more than this level. However as labour usage increases beyond this point, total output soon reaches its maximum (given the state of technology) and the marginal product of labour falls to zero. Moreover as the labour input on the farm increases, the average product per person approaches the subsistence level. Given this general characterisation of agricultural production, Mellor (1985) considers a number of possible

Fig. 2.2. The surplus labour case.

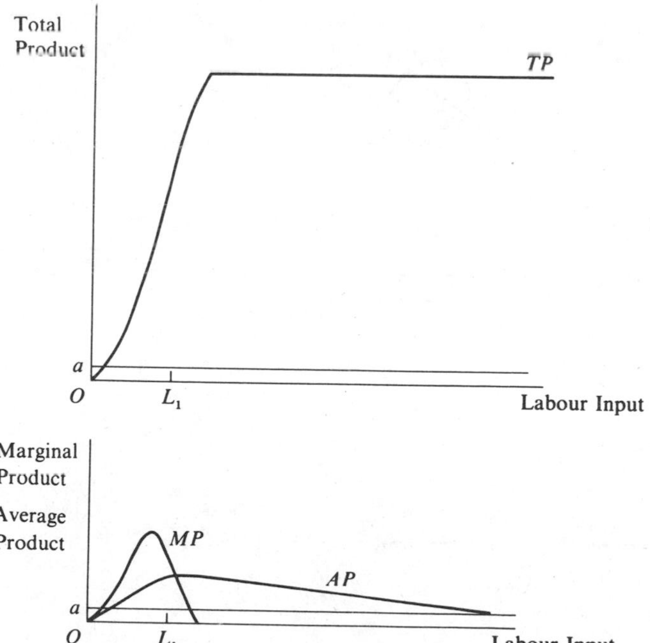

outcomes with respect to the incidence of rural poverty. For example, if all available land is already in use, population growth in the agricultural sector will push average incomes to the minimum subsistence level. Indeed this is the case on which a number of 'dual economy' models of the 1950s and 1960s were based (e.g. Lewis (1954) and Fei and Ranis (1961)). These models, focusing on the economic implications of transferring labour from agriculture to industry, generated a great deal of controversy in terms of their theoretical and empirical soundness. Much of the heat, however, has gone out of the issue.

An alternative characterisation, the 'hard-working peasant' case, is illustrated in Fig. 2.3. Here the total product curve is a straight line from the origin, with a slope which implies that increased labour input provides only basic subsistence. Marginal product, as well as average product, will be just equal to the subsistence wage; no surplus output will be forthcoming. Once the maximum output level is reached, the farm cannot support further increases in labour, and indeed additional labour is portrayed as reducing total product thus causing average product to fall and marginal product to be negative. Beyond this point (L' in the figure), alternative employment (on

Fig. 2.3. The hard working peasant case.

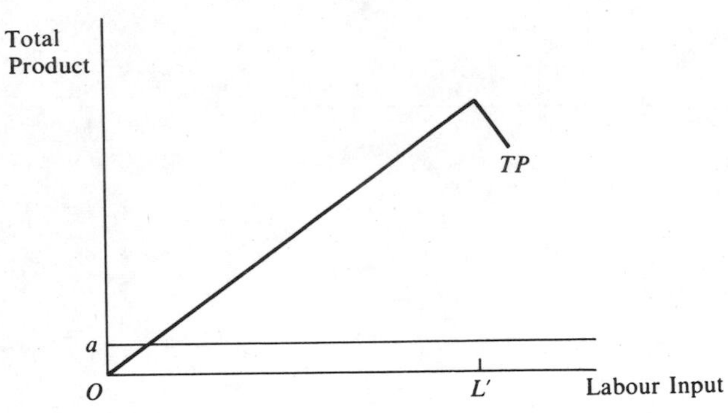

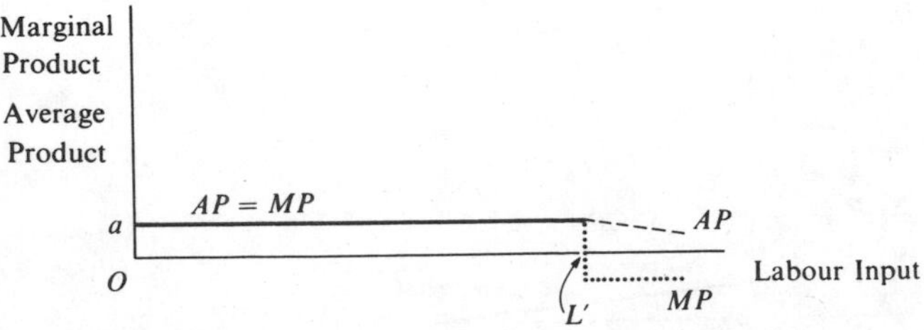

uncultivated land, if any exists) outside the farm must be sought by the surplus labour.

Mellor suggests that the 'hard working peasant' case might be typical of large parts of sub-Saharan Africa, for example, and that the 'surplus labour' case might be common in parts of India, Bangladesh and the Philippines. However the two cases are presented here as hypothetical relationships; how prevalent they actually are is an empirical question.

2.2.2 *The factor–factor relationship*

Typically in a given production period of say a year, there would be more than one variable factor of production. For example, in the production of wheat, fertiliser, seed and labour services may be variable, while the land and machinery inputs remain fixed. In this case, we are interested both in the relationship between output and the set of variable inputs and the extent to which one variable factor may be substituted for another. Discussion of these factor-factor relationships is often confined to the two variable inputs case, but the results can be generalised to the case of three or more variables.

Assuming two variable inputs, the production function is denoted as:

$$Q = f(X_1, X_2 \mid X_3, \ldots, X_n) \tag{2.3}$$

where the vertical line before X_3 indicates that all inputs other than X_1 and X_2 are fixed. This relationship can be conveniently illustrated by an *isoquant* map such as the one in Fig. 2.4. An isoquant is a 'contour' line or locus of different combinations of the two inputs which yield the same

Fig. 2.4. The isoquant map.

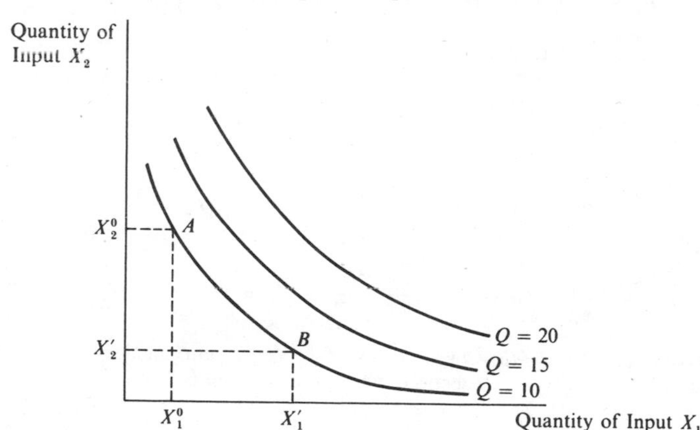

level of output. Thus, for example, ten units of output can be produced by both the input combination at point *A* and that at point *B* in Fig. 2.4. In moving from *A* to *B* the amount of X_1 is increased from X_1^0 to X_1' and that of X_2 is reduced from X_2^0 to X_2'; that is X_1 substitutes for X_2. The rate at which one input substitutes for another at any point on the isoquant is called the *marginal rate of substitution* (*MRS*) and it can be measured as the slope of the isoquant. It measures the rate at which one input must be substituted for the other if output is to remain constant. In notational form it may be written as

$$MRS \text{ of } X_1 \text{ for } X_2 = \frac{\Delta X_2}{\Delta X_1} = \frac{\partial X_2}{\partial X_1},$$

where Δ signifies a change, and ∂ the derivative for an infinitesimally small change. In general, *MRS* is negative[7] since more usage of one input is associated with less of another i.e. the isoquant is downward sloping. However the negative sign is often omitted and this will be the convention adopted here.

Examples of different rates of substitution between inputs, for a given output level ($\bar{Q}$) are depicted in Fig. 2.5. In panel *a*, the input being increased substitutes for successively smaller amounts of the input being replaced i.e. the *MRS* of X_1 for X_2 (in absolute terms) at *A* is greater than at *B*. This is the 'textbook' form of the isoquant. In panel *b*, the amount of X_1 required to replace a unit of X_2 remains the same, as usage of X_1 increases; the marginal rate of substitution is constant. In panel *c*, there are no substitution possibilities, since the inputs must be used in fixed proportions.[8]

However, the *MRS* as a measure of the degree of substitutability of inputs has a serious defect in that it depends on the units of measurement

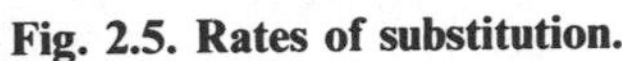

Fig. 2.5. Rates of substitution.

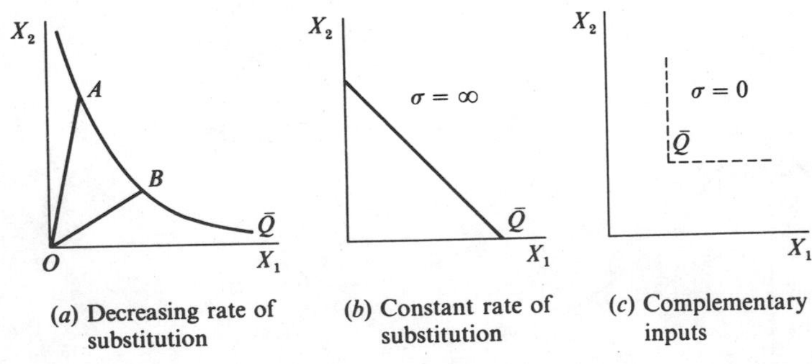

(*a*) Decreasing rate of substitution

(*b*) Constant rate of substitution

(*c*) Complementary inputs

of the inputs.[9] A better measure is provided by the *elasticity of substitution* (σ), which is defined as:

$$\sigma = \frac{\text{Percentage change in } \dfrac{X_2}{X_1}}{\text{Percentage change in } MRS} \tag{2.4}$$

This is a 'pure number', that is one which is independent of units of measurement. The numerator is the percentage change in the *input ratio* or *factor intensity*. Referring back to Fig. 2.5(*a*), the factor intensity at A is given by the slope of the ray ($0A$) from the origin to the isoquant. In moving from A to B, the ratio of X_2/X_1 falls; an X_2-intensive production plan is replaced by an X_1-intensive one. The denominator in equation 2.4 is the percentage change in the marginal rate of substitution as we move along the isoquant.

In Fig. 2.5(*b*), where inputs are perfect substitutes, $\sigma = \infty$ since, as the MRS is constant, the denominator in 2.4 is zero. In the case of fixed proportions (Fig. 2.5(*c*)), $\sigma = 0$, since the numerator in 2.4 is zero. We would expect that in most production settings, σ will lie within these two extremes. The larger the value of σ, the greater the ease of substitution will be. Diagrammatically, the value of σ increases as the curvature of the isoquant decreases, i.e. the elasticity of substitution is inversely proportional to the curvature of the isoquant.

Thus far, our discussion has concerned the production setting in which some factors of production are variable, while other factors are fixed. In economic terminology, we have been dealing with *the short run* i.e. a period when the set of inputs available to the producer is not wholly adjustable. In *the long run* changes in output can be achieved by varying *all* factors. Thus, in the long run, the farmer may vary all available resources including the size of the farm, the number of farm buildings and the type of machinery.

The long run factor–factor relationship which receives most attention is that known as *the returns to scale*. In the long run output may be increased by changing all factors by the same proportion i.e. by altering the scale of the operation. The response of output to scale changes in inputs will depend on the technical characteristics of the production function. A classification of possible outcomes is useful: If, when all inputs are increased by the same proportion (say, by 50%), output increases by the same proportion (i.e. 50%), then we say there are *constant returns to scale*.

If output increases less than in proportion (say, by 25%) with the same (50%) increase in all factors, we have *decreasing returns to scale*.

If output increases more than in proportion (say, by 75%) when we increase all factors by 50%, we have *increasing returns to scale*.

The assumption that the production technology exhibits constant returns to scale is frequently made in the economics literature.

2.2.3 *The product–product relationship*

In this section, the analysis is extended to the multiproduct firm, since most farmers have a range of alternative crops they could grow on the same land and of livestock they could rear.

To simplify the exposition, it is assumed that the producer can produce two products, wheat and maize, each output being produced by a set of *n* inputs. Production functions for wheat and maize respectively can be specified:

$$Q_W = f_1(X_1, \ldots, X_n)$$
$$Q_M = f_2(X_1, \ldots, X_n)$$

The form of these production relationships, together with the level of the (limited) resources available, will determine the production possibilities facing the producer. The production options which are technically feasible can be illustrated by a *production-possibility frontier* (or *transformation curve*), Fig. 2.6. This curve is the locus of combinations of wheat and maize which can be produced with a set of given inputs and assuming a particular state of technology. If all available resources were used in the production of wheat, w_0 units of wheat could be grown; if all inputs were diverted to maize production, m_0 units of maize could be produced. Alternative combinations of the two products are depicted by points along the curve w_0m_0.

The slope of the production-possibility frontier represents the *marginal rate of transformation* (*MRT*) of maize for wheat:

$$MRT = \frac{\Delta Q_W}{\Delta Q_M}$$

This measures the *opportunity cost* of producing maize in terms of wheat i.e. how much wheat must be sacrificed in order to obtain an additional unit of maize. In Fig. 2.6, the slope of the curve (or *MRT*) increases, in absolute terms, as more maize is produced. This is an example of increasing opportunity costs i.e. increasing amounts of wheat output must be sacrificed to produce additional units of maize.[10]

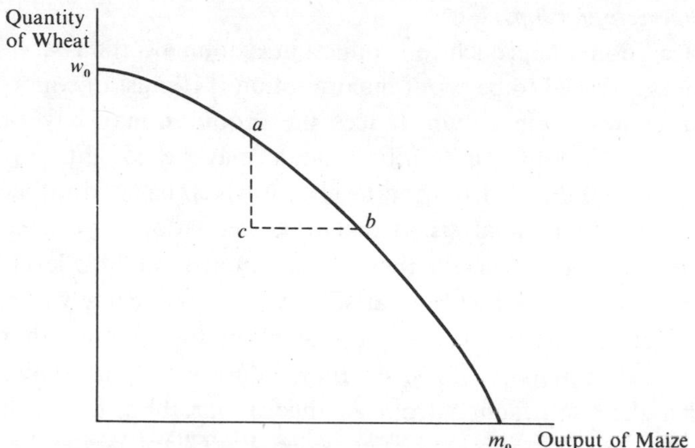

Fig. 2.6. The production-possibility curve.

Finally, it should be noted that an efficient farmer would choose to operate at some point on the production-possibility frontier. A point such as *c* in Fig. 2.6 would be considered an inefficient use of resources, since with the same level of inputs, more of at least one of the products could be forthcoming. Specifically in the *ab* segment of the curve total output of either or both products will be higher.

Opportunity costs

This is a key concept in economics which reflects the subject's central concern with choices about the allocation of scarce resources. Choosing to allocate resources in one way rules out other choices. The opportunity cost of a decision is the value of the best alternative choice which is foregone as a result of that decision. In the context of the production possibility frontier the decision to produce more maize involves switching resources from wheat production and therefore sacrificing wheat output. The value of the wheat output which could be produced with the resources switched to maize is the opportunity cost of maize production. It only makes economic sense to make the switch if the value of the extra maize exceeds opportunity cost in terms of value of lost wheat output.

In an entirely analogous way, in analysing consumers' choices about the allocation of income, purchasing more of *Y* can only mean less income available for other uses. Thus, there is an opportunity cost to the purchase of more *Y* in terms of less of other products or services.

2.3 *Economic relationships*

In the traditional approach to production economics, the goal of the entrepreneur is assumed to be profit maximisation.[11] It must of course be recognised that in certain circumstances the producer may have a different objective or indeed that multiple goals may be sought. For example one suggestion, dating from the 1950s but which has had rather limited impact on economic analysis, is that producers adopt *satisficing* rather than maximising behaviour i.e. they set minimum acceptable levels of profits and other targets and will be satisfied with any outcome which meets them. An alternative approach[12] is based on the premise that producers are indeed optimisers; however, they do not merely maximise profits but rather their satisfaction from a range of variables, of which profits may be just one. This approach is considered in Chapters 4 and 8. For most of the exposition in this chapter, the traditional approach is followed. This is because profit maximisation would seem to be a plausible objective for the producer operating in a *competitive market* and it may not entirely preclude higher level goals reflecting, for example, social and cultural desires.

It is further assumed, for the purpose of this chapter, that the individual producer is a price-taker. That is to say, in both product and input markets, the producer is unable to influence prices in any way. Again this is a reasonable assumption when the analysis is confined to competitive markets where there are many firms, none of which has sufficient market power to manipulate price.

2.3.1 *Economic optimum: the factor–product relationship*

In deciding what is the economic optimal usage of *a single variable input*, the producer requires three pieces of information (i) the marginal product of the input (MP_{x_1}), which indicates the contribution to total output which an additional unit of the input would make, (ii) the price per unit of the final product (P) and (iii) the price per unit of the variable input (p_{x_1}). The value of an additional unit of the input to the producer is the extra revenue which will be forthcoming as a result of greater input usage. This is measured by *the value of the marginal product* (VMP) i.e. $MP_{x_1} \times P$. The economic optimum,[13] yielding maximum profits, will be attained where the value of the marginal product of the variable input is equated to its price:

$$VMP_{x_1} = p_{x_1} \tag{2.5}$$

At the particular level of input usage associated with the optimal condition (equation 2.5), the producer is said to be in *equilibrium*. In equilibrium there is no incentive to alter the production plan. To demonstrate that equation 2.5 does indeed indicate the optimum position, suppose that VMP_{X_1} exceeds p_{X_1}. An additional unit of the input would then yield more to the producer in terms of extra revenue than it would cost; thus more profit would be obtained if an extra unit were employed. On the other hand, if VMP_{X_1} were less than p_{X_1}, the last unit of the input employed contributed less to revenue than it added to costs; hence less of the input should be used. The producer will only be in (profit maximising) equilibrium when equation 2.5 holds.

2.3.2. *Economic optimum: the factor–factor relationship*

To determine the appropriate level of input use when there are two variable factors of production, a producer must know the rates at which inputs are exchanged in the market (their relative prices) as well as the rates at which they can be exchanged in production (their marginal rate of substitution). To illustrate the former, we introduce the *isocost* line. This is the locus of all combinations of the two inputs which the producer can purchase with a given cost outlay.[14] Fig. 2.7 depicts an isocost line for an outlay C_0, which is simply the sum of expenditures on input X_1 (i.e. $p_{X_1}X_1$) and an input X_2 (i.e. $p_{X_2}X_2$). Hence, $C_0 = p_{X_1}X_1 + p_{X_2}X_2$. The slope of the isocost line is the ratio of input prices, $(-)p_{X_1}/p_{X_2}$. The isocost line for a larger cost outlay would be represented by a parallel line located further from the origin.

Fig. 2.7. The isocost line.

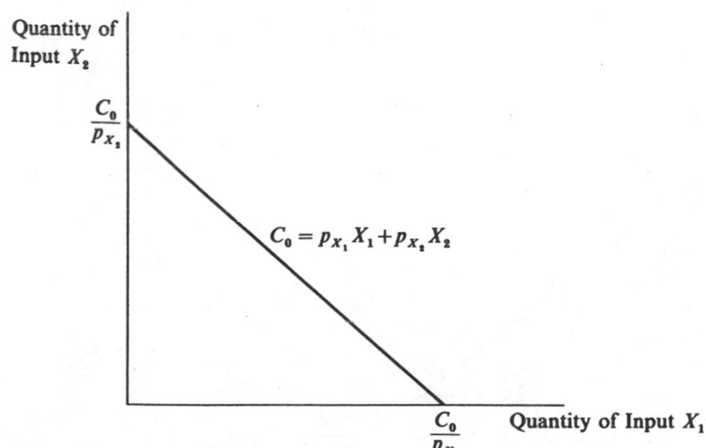

Since the producer would wish the cost outlay on variable inputs to be as small as possible, we need a rule for determining the *least cost* combination of inputs. The least cost outlay on variable inputs to produce a given output level $\bar{Q}$ is shown in Fig. 2.8 to be at the point of tangency between isocost line C_1 and the $\bar{Q}$ isoquant. Output $\bar{Q}$ could be generated by other combinations of the two inputs other than that at point A but these would be associated with higher cost outlays (represented by isocost lines such as C_2 to the right of C_1). Lower cost outlays, such as C_0, would be insufficient to generate the required level of production. Thus the optimum for any given output level is found at the point of tangency between the lowest isocost line and the appropriate isoquant. Since at this point the slope of the isoquant is equal to the slope of the isocost line, and since the slope of the isoquant is the marginal rate of substitution, the optimal condition[15] is

$$MRS \text{ of } X_1 \text{ for } X_2 = (-)\frac{p_{X_1}}{p_{X_2}} \tag{2.6}$$

The foregoing analysis provides a rule for determining the level of (minimum) costs and the combination of inputs uniquely associated with a particular level of output. This analytical process can be repeated for all possible levels of output to obtain a schedule of the minimum cost of production associated with each level of production. This schedule of minimum costs of production is the *Total Cost* (*TC*) schedule.

Given that we can now determine the least cost way of producing any stated amount of production, we can proceed to consider the problem of

Fig. 2.8. The least cost combination of inputs.

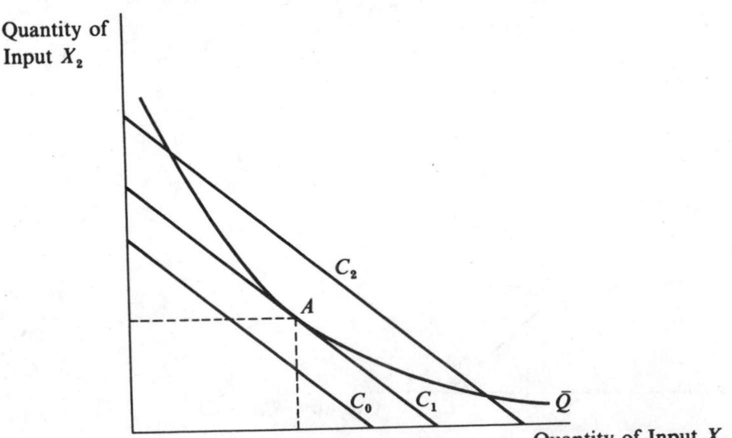

choosing the optimum level of production. In order to do this it is necessary to undertake a more detailed examination of the cost structure of a firm employing several variable inputs and some fixed factors. That is, the analysis which follows is presented in terms of the *short-run*.

Total costs (*TC*) may be divided into:

(i) *Fixed costs* (*FC*), which are associated with the fixed inputs e.g., rents or mortgage payments, depreciation on farm buildings etc., and which are independent of the level of output, and

(ii) *Variable costs* (*VC*), which arise from employing the variable factors of production such as feed, seed, fertiliser etc.

Fig. 2.9 illustrates a typical set of cost curves. Fixed cost (*FC*) is by definition constant for all levels of output. However variable costs are determined by the characteristics of the production technology. Adopting the standard assumptions about the production function that were used in Fig. 2.1, it is assumed that as output increases from a certain low level there are increasing returns so that fewer units of variable factors are

Fig. 2.9. The fixed, variable and total cost curves.

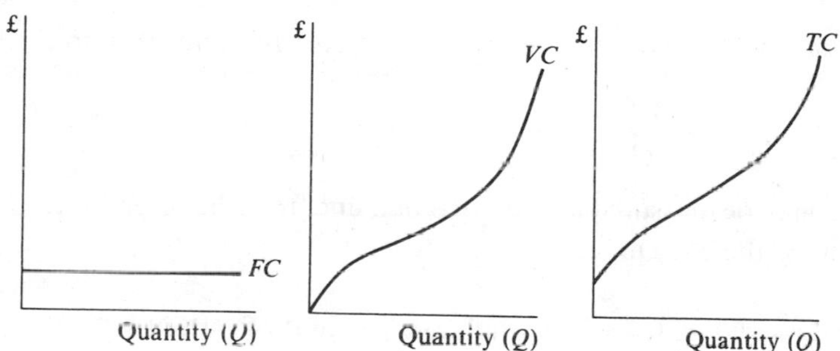

Fig. 2.10. The marginal, average variable and average total cost curves.

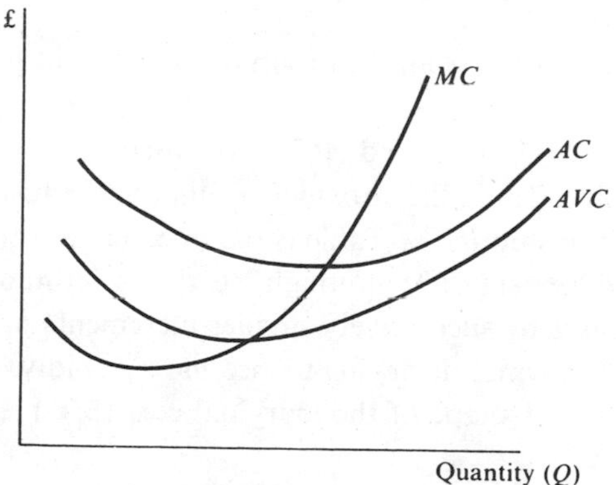

required for each extra unit of output, and the rate of increase in variable costs slows down. Once output passes a certain higher level, decreasing returns assert themselves, more units of variable inputs are needed for successive increments of output, and variable costs begin to accelerate. *Total cost* (*TC*), as shown in Fig. 2.9, is the vertical summation of the *FC* and *VC* curves.

From the total cost schedule it is possible to derive the marginal and average costs of production. These are very important concepts in the theory of the firm.

Marginal cost (*MC*) is the addition to total cost associated with the production of an additional unit of output i.e.

$$MC = \frac{\Delta TC}{\Delta Q},$$ the slope of the *TC* curve, or

$$MC = \frac{\Delta VC}{\Delta Q},$$ the slope of the *VC* curve; this is so because the change in total cost is entirely due to changes in variable cost.

Average variable cost (*AVC*) is variable cost per unit of output i.e.

$$AVC = \frac{VC}{Q}.$$

This may be measured as the slope of a line from the origin to the relevant point of the *VC* curve.

Average total cost (*AC*) is total cost per unit of output i.e.

$$AC = \frac{TC}{Q}.$$

This is given by the slope of a line from the origin to the relevant point on the *TC* curve.

Fig. 2.10 illustrates the *MC*, *AVC* and *AC* curves associated with the cost curves of Fig. 2.9, and Table 2.2 provides a numerical illustration. The most important relationship in the Table is the one between the level of output and total variable cost (*VC*); although *VC* rises continuously as output increases, it increases by successively smaller increments up to the fourth unit of output, after which it begins to rise more rapidly. This is revealed most clearly in the U-shape of the marginal cost (*MC*) schedule which reaches its minimum at the fourth unit of output; the values of the marginal cost schedule equal the *changes* in both the variable cost and total cost schedules. It can be observed that the minimum average variable cost (*AVC*) is reached at a higher output level than the minimum *MC*, and that minimum average total cost (*AC*) is reached at an even higher level of production. This corresponds to the relationships shown in Fig. 2.10, which show that *AVC* and *AC* are at their minima and rise upwards from the point where the marginal cost curve cuts them on its upward path.

Armed with an understanding of marginal cost it is now possible to proceed to an examination of the *rule for determining the optimum output* level for a firm maximising its profit from the production of an output using several inputs. It is assumed that the firm is small in relation to the whole market and that it is a 'price-taker' which can sell any amount of output at the prevailing market price. (This is an entirely appropriate assumption in relation to individual farms.) Its *total revenue* (*TR*) will increase in direct proportion to sales, and will be simply equal to output multiplied by the market price. Hence the total revenue curve will be a straight line through the origin (Fig. 2.11(*a*)). *Marginal revenue* (*MR*) is defined as the addition to total revenue due to an extra unit of output i.e.

$$MR = \frac{\Delta TR}{\Delta Q}$$

This is represented by the slope of the *TR* curve, but in this case marginal

Table 2.2. *Costs of production – a hypothetical example*

Units of output	Total variable cost (*VC*) (£)	Total fixed cost (*FC*) (£)	Total cost (*TC*) (£)	Marginal cost (*MC*) (£)	Average variable cost (*AVC*) (£)	Average fixed cost (*AFC*) (£)	Average total cost (*AC*) (£)
0	—	20	20	—	—	—	—
1	25	20	45	25	25.0	20.0	45.0
2	45	20	65	20	22.5	10.0	32.5
3	62	20	82	17	20.7	6.7	27.4
4	75	20	95	13	18.8	5.0	23.8
5	90	20	110	15	18.0	4.0	22.0
6	110	20	130	20	18.3	3.3	21.6
7	135	20	155	25	19.3	2.8	22.1
8	175	20	195	40	21.9	8.5	24.4

revenue is constant and equal to the market price, since all units of output are sold at the same price.

The firm will achieve its desired state or equilibrium when *profits* (Π), defined as *the difference between total cost and total revenue*, are maximised. In Fig. 2.11 (*a*), losses would be made at output levels lower than Q_1 and higher than Q_2, since in these ranges the total cost curve lies above the total revenue curve. The optimum level of production is given at Q^* where TR exceeds TC by the largest amount.

An equivalent way of presenting this solution is given in panel *b* of Fig. 2.11. In this figure the horizontal line is the price line. Each unit is sold at the same price, so that marginal revenue equals price, and average revenue equals price i.e. $MR = P = AR$. The marginal cost (MC) curve and

Fig. 2.11. The (short run) economic optimum.

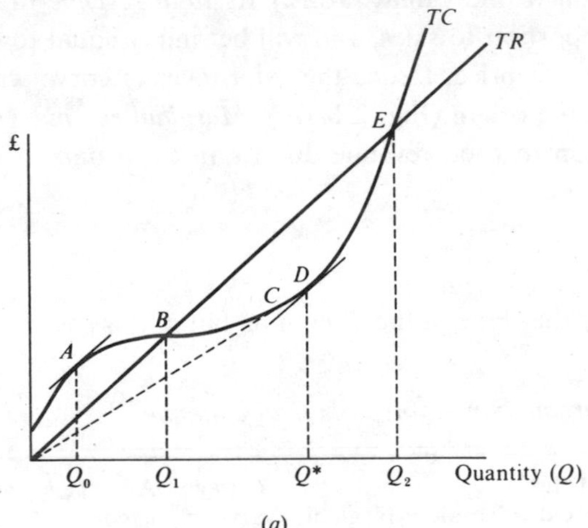

(*a*)

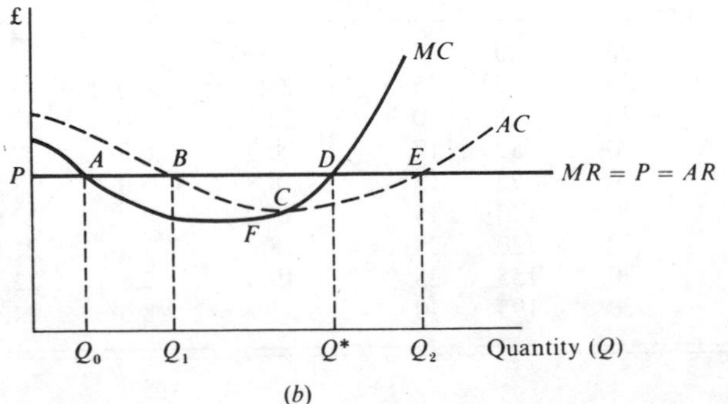

(*b*)

average total cost (AC) curve, derived from the total cost curve in the upper figure, take the usual U shape, with MC cutting AC at its minimum point. For output to be profitable, price or average revenue (AR) must exceed average cost. In other words, production must take place within the range Q_1 to Q_2. The precise profit-maximising level of output is easily found. Profits *rise* whenever the production of an extra unit of output adds more to revenue than it adds to costs i.e. $MR > MC$. On the other hand, profits *fall* when additional production adds more to costs than to revenue i.e. $MC > MR$. Therefore the profit-maximising rule is to produce to the point where marginal cost and marginal revenue are just equal. For *maximum profits*,

$$MC = MR.$$

In Fig. 2.11, this point is located at Q^* where the slope of the total cost curve (or MC) equals the slope of the total revenue curve (or MR). (A formal derivation of this condition for profit maximisation is presented below.)

Formal derivation – the profit maximising output level of the competitive firm

The producer wishes to maximise $\Pi = TR - TC$ where $TR = f_1(Q)$ and $TC = f_2(Q)$ and the output price is given. The first order condition is:

$$\frac{\partial \Pi}{\partial Q} = \frac{\partial TR}{\partial Q} - \frac{\partial TC}{\partial Q} = 0$$

i.e.

$$\frac{\partial TR}{\partial Q} = \frac{\partial TC}{\partial Q} \text{ or } MR = MC$$

The second order condition is:

$$\frac{\partial^2 \Pi}{\partial Q^2} = \frac{\partial^2 TR}{\partial Q^2} - \frac{\partial^2 TC}{\partial Q^2} < 0$$

i.e.

$$\frac{\partial^2 TR}{\partial Q^2} < \frac{\partial^2 TC}{\partial Q^2}$$

The term on the left hand side represents the slope of the MR curve (which here is zero), while the other term is the slope of the MC curve. Thus this condition states that the MC curve must be increasing and have a positive slope.

There is one important qualification to this rule. Note that in Fig. 2.11(*b*), the condition that $MC = MR$ is satisfied at two points – at output Q_0, where MC is on its downward path when it cuts the AR line, and at output Q^*, where MC is on its upward path when it cuts the AR line. But at Q_0, price ($= AR = MR$) is less than AC and so a loss is incurred. Hence in deriving the profit maximising level of output a second condition must be added, namely the *MC curve must cut the MR curve from below*.

At higher prices than that portrayed in Fig. 2.11(*b*) the MR would intersect the MC curve to the right of point D and optimal output would exceed Q^*. At lower prices the intersection would be to the left of D and the firm's optimal output would be less than Q^*. Note however that it would not be profitable for production to occur if the price were so low that it intersected with MC at a point such as F. For in such a case average revenue would be less than average total cost, and production would occur at a loss. At any price below minimum average total cost, at point C in Fig. 2.11(*b*), production would incur losses. In the short run, however, it will still be worthwhile to continue in production even if MR and AR are below average total costs, *provided* that they exceed average variable costs. For in that way a surplus is earned over recurrent variable costs which contributes to meeting the fixed costs which, by definition, cannot be avoided by ceasing production. On the basis of these simple results it is possible to define the *product supply curve* of the competitive firm as the portion of *the firm's marginal cost curve above the level of minimum average variable cost*.

For a numerical illustration of the firm's supply curve it is possible to use the hypothetical data in Table 2.2. For a small firm (farm) in competition price (P) is constant for each unit of output and is therefore equal to both average and marginal revenue (AR and MR). Whether any output is produced or not, a fixed cost of £20 is incurred. If price were only £13 it would equal the marginal cost of producing the fourth unit of output, but is less than the average variable cost. Indeed the total revenue of £52 (4×13) falls appreciably short of total variable costs (£75). The overall loss is £43 (£95 – £52). This exceeds the loss which would be made by not producing at all, since by not producing at all the loss would only be £20 (the fixed cost). Hence the profit-maximising (or loss-minimising) decision would be to cease production.

At a price of £20, the marginal cost of the sixth unit of production is met *and MR* exceeds AVC; in fact total revenue is £120, which is higher than the total variable cost of £110 but less than the total of all costs which is £130 (a loss of £10 is incurred). Thus at a price of £20 it would be profitable in the short-run to produce six units of output. At a price of £25 production, at seven units, becomes profitable with total revenue of £175 against *TC* of £155. Note that this discussion applies strictly to the short-run. In the long-run, all factors are variable and all costs must be met if the firm is to remain in production.

2.3.3 *Economic optimum: the product–product relationship*

An evaluation of the product mix that will maximise profit in the multiproduct firm requires information on (i) the marginal rate of transformation between products and (ii) product prices.

Assuming that the quantity of inputs and their prices are given, then profit maximisation is achieved by maximising total revenue. Given the prices of the products we can define an *isorevenue* line as the locus of points of various combinations of the products which yield the same revenue to the firm. For the two product case, an isorevenue line is depicted in Fig. 2.12. The slope of the line is given by the ratio of product prices (−) P_M/P_W. An isorevenue line for a higher total revenue would be given as a parallel line located further from the origin. In Fig. 2.13, a set of isorevenue lines is superimposed on the production possibility frontier and the optimum point (maximum total revenue) is given at the point of tangency between the production possibility frontier and the highest attainable isorevenue curve; in this case the point of tangency is associated with output levels Q_w'' and Q_m''. The equilibrium condition is therefore that *(MRT)* the marginal rate of transformation of maize for wheat $(\Delta Q_w/\Delta Q_m)$ is equal to the negative value of the ratio of price of maize to the price of wheat. That is

$$MRT \text{ of } M \text{ for } W, \text{ or } \frac{\Delta Q_W}{\Delta Q_M} = (-)\frac{P_M}{P_W} \tag{2.7}$$

Fig. 2.12. The isorevenue line.

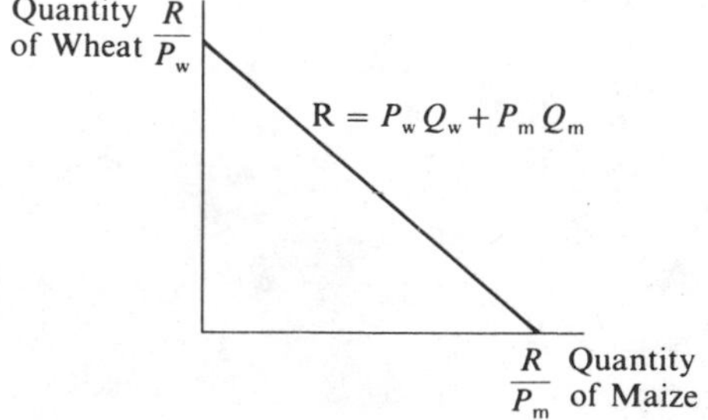

The negative sign reflects the fact that the *MRT* of two products is generally negative, since increasing output of one requires production of the other to be reduced. Application of the rule in equation (2.7) to the production frontier in the two product case, enables the profit-maximising combination of products to be determined.

2.3.4 *Economic optimum: the general case*

The preceding sections have explained and developed the rules for profit-maximisation by a firm in stages. One has examined how to choose the right combination of two variable inputs to minimise the cost of producing a given amount of output. Another has examined how to determine the optimal production level when the least cost production method has been selected. A third has explained how, if there are two products and a fixed quantity of inputs available for use, the optimal combination of outputs (and by implication, allocation of inputs to each product) can be determined. In reality, on the typical farm there are far more than two possible products and more than two factors of production. It is possible using more advanced mathematical techniques to solve jointly for the profit maximising output and input levels, plus the allocation of inputs to outputs, for such cases. The economic principles embodied within those mathematical techniques for profit maximisation are precisely those which have been presented in this chapter, and they can be appropriately described as the foundation of production economics.

Fig. 2.13. Product–product equilibrium.

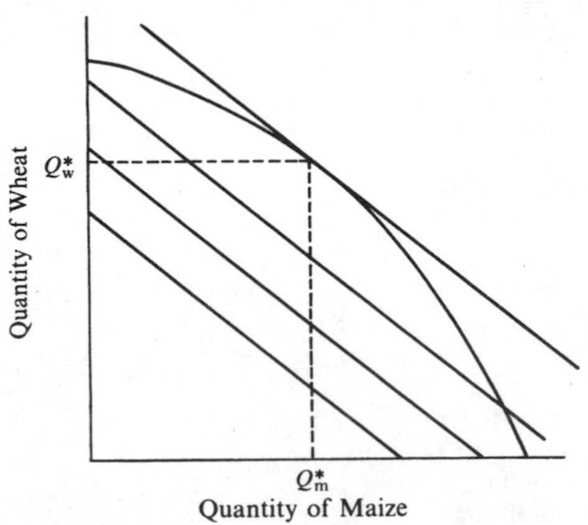

2.4 Summary points

1. The *physical relationships* in production are often expressed by a *production function* for a single product, or by a set of production functions when more than one product is produced. Three relationships are of particular interest:

   The *total product curve*, which describes the relationship between output and a single input, all other inputs held fixed. Its slope denotes the *marginal product* of the variable input.

   The *isoquant*, which depicts the combinations of two variable inputs which yield a *given* level of output. Its slope denotes the *marginal rate of substitution* of one input for the other.

   The *production possibility frontier*, which depicts the combinations of two products which can be produced with a given set of inputs. Its slope represents the *marginal rate of transformation* of one product for the other.

2. Given these physical relationships *and* the prices of inputs and outputs, a set of *economic relationships* can be established for the profit maximising producer:

   An input would be employed to the point where the *value of its marginal product* is just equal to its price.

   For a given level of output, the *least cost combination* of inputs is found where the marginal rate of substitution is equal to the (inverse) ratio of the prices of the inputs.

   For any pair of outputs, the *optimal level of production* in a multi-product firm is given where the marginal rate of transformation is equal to the (inverse) ratio of the prices of the products.

3. For the firm operating in a competitive environment, the profit maximising level of output is established where the (given) price of the product, which is equivalent to the competitive firm's *marginal revenue*, is equated to the *marginal cost* of production.

Further reading

Most agricultural economics textbooks (e.g. Epp and Malone (1981), Ritson (1977)) have sections on the economics of agricultural production, as do all general economics textbooks (e.g. Begg, Fischer and Dornbusch (1984), Call and Holahan (1983), or Lipsey (1983)). However, the books by Doll and Orazem (1984), Heathfield and Wibe (1987), Debertin (1986) and Beattie and Taylor (1985) are devoted entirely to the subject of production economics. The latter is more advanced and makes liberal use of mathematical analysis.

3

Product supply and input demand

3.1 *Introduction*

Whereas the previous chapter was concerned with the theory of supply and input demand at the level of the firm, attention now switches to supply and input demand at the *market level*. That is, we are concerned with the outcomes of the decisions of all farmers in a particular market, where the market for any commodity may be defined in relation to whole countries, regions of countries, or even at the world level. Since agricultural policy is typically made at national or regional level, and since the statistics which provide the key information about developments in the agricultural sector are usually presented for these levels, policy-related empirical research needs to focus upon market level behaviour.

Certainly, issues of market level agricultural supply are central to development strategies, and there will be a requirement that the agricultural sector should provide a growing surplus (over and above the needs of the agricultural population) of agricultural product. The reasons for this have been well documented but can be summarised as: (i) to increase food supplies and agricultural raw materials at 'low' prices, (ii) to increase the purchasing power of farmers and hence the domestic market for non-agricultural products in the rural sector, (iii) to facilitate transfers of labour and other resources from agriculture for industrial development, and (iv) to increase foreign exchange earnings from agricultural exports. The contribution which the agricultural sector can make in these areas will depend on the responsiveness of domestic producers to economic incentives and to price signals in particular. It is the purpose of this chapter to examine the economic principles which are deemed important in the analysis of product supply and input demand at the market level.

3.2 *Product supply*

As explained in Chapter 2, the supply curve of a competitive firm which maximises profit will lie along the upward-sloping portion of its marginal cost curve above its average variable cost curve in the short-run. This result rests upon certain assumptions about the production technology which have general validity. This theory concludes that as product prices rise the profit-maximising firm will increase supply. It follows therefore that an industry, such as agriculture, composed of a large number of such firms would also have an upward sloping supply curve, *since the industry supply curve will be the summation of all the individual firm curves.*

In reality, especially in the short-run, not all firms will operate at the profit-maximising level. Some may even behave in ways which to others appear to be economically irrational. But, provided that the majority of firms in an industry react to change by moving towards the theoretical optimum, the supply curve at the market level will have the upward sloping properties expected on the basis of the theory of the firm.

For the multi-product, multi-input firm and industry, the supply curve (between output quantity and its price) is just one two-dimensional relationship extracted from a complex multi-dimensional set of functional relationships between output and input use and changes in the amounts of other products. It is assumed that at the market level all these relationships in the production system will embody the basic properties implied by the theory of the firm. However, the realities of agricultural production are such that, for reasons given below, the theory of the firm has to be modified if it is to offer an adequate description of market level supply of agricultural products. Nevertheless it gives us a useful starting point.

The theory suggests that the market supply of a product will depend on the price of the commodity, the prices of other commodities which could be produced, and the prices of inputs into the production process. The relationship can be expressed in the form of a *supply function*:

$$Q_i = f(P_i, P_j, P_k, p_1, \ldots, p_n) \tag{3.1}$$

where Q_i denotes the market supply of a product i, which has P_i as its current market price. The prices of alternative products, j and k are given as P_j and P_k, and the set of (n) input prices are specified as $p_1, \ldots, p_n$.

If for the moment we assume that the prices of other products and inputs are held constant, we can trace out the relationship between the supply of commodity i and its own price, i.e. the *supply curve* or *supply schedule* (Fig. 3.1). The curve depicts how much of the commodity producers are willing to place on the market at specific market prices, other factors remaining constant. A change in own price will induce a movement *along* this curve and, since it is expected that a price increase will encourage a larger quantity of the product to be supplied, the curve slopes up from left to right. However, what is also important is by how much supply will change in response to an increase or decrease in price. A convenient measure of the responsiveness of producers to price change is termed the *elasticity of supply* or, more specifically, the *own-price elasticity of supply*. This is simply a measure which expresses the proportionate change in quantity supplied as a ratio of the proportionate change in price. The formal definition is:

$$E_i^s = \frac{\text{proportionate change in quantity supplied, } Q_i}{\text{proportionate change in own price, } P_i} =$$

$$\frac{\Delta Q_i/Q_i}{\Delta P_i/P_i} = \frac{\Delta Q_i}{\Delta P_i}\cdot\frac{P_i}{Q_i} = \frac{\partial Q_i}{\partial P_i}\cdot\frac{P_i}{Q_i},$$

where, as before, Δ denotes a small change, and ∂, the partial derivative, an infinitesimal change (see footnote 4, Chapter 2). The supply elasticity is defined for a specific point on the supply curve and so for most curves the size of the elasticity will vary along the curve. The larger the value of the elasticity, the more responsive supply is to changes in price. In particular if $E_i^s > 1$, then a 1% change in price induces more than a 1% change in supply, and supply is said to be *elastic*. If $E_i^s < 1$, the same change in price would only bring forth less than a 1% increase in quantity, and supply of the product is said to be *inelastic*.

Fig. 3.1. The supply curve.

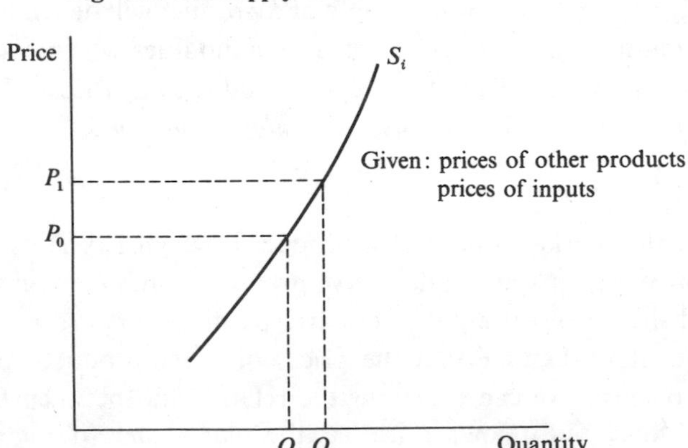

Turning now to the other parameters of the supply function, we would conclude that an increase in the price of a competing product, say P_j, will reduce the supply of product *i* at each market price. This is because the rise in price, *ceteris paribus*[1], has increased the profitability of producing product *j* relative to that of product *i*, and so the producer would be encouraged to switch resources accordingly. Diagrammatically this would be shown as a *shift* in the supply curve to the left (as from S_i^0 to S_i' in Fig. 3.2). Again knowledge of the direction of change may be insufficient for a number of analytical purposes; we would also like an estimate of the extent of the response to the change in price. A variant of the elasticity measure is frequently found useful in this regard, namely the *cross-price elasticity of supply* which is defined as:

$$E_{ij}^s = \frac{\text{proportionate change in quantity supplied, } Q_i}{\text{proportionate change in the price of another good, } P_j} = \frac{\Delta Q_i/Q_i}{\Delta P_j/P_j} = \frac{\Delta Q_i}{\Delta P_j}\cdot\frac{P_j}{Q_i} = \frac{\partial Q_i}{\partial P_j}\cdot\frac{P_j}{Q_i},$$

for an infinitesimal change. For a change in the price of a competing product, E_{ij}^s is expected to be negative, i.e. if P_j rises supply of Q_i decreases.

The supply curve will also shift in response to a change in input prices. If the price of an input, say labour, increases, *ceteris paribus*, the marginal cost of producing a given level of output will rise. In other words the cost curves of each firm and hence the supply curve, will shift upwards and to the left. A decrease in the price of a factor of production would have, of course, the opposite effect.

Fig. 3.2. Shift in the supply curve – due to an increase in the price of a competing product or in the price of an input.

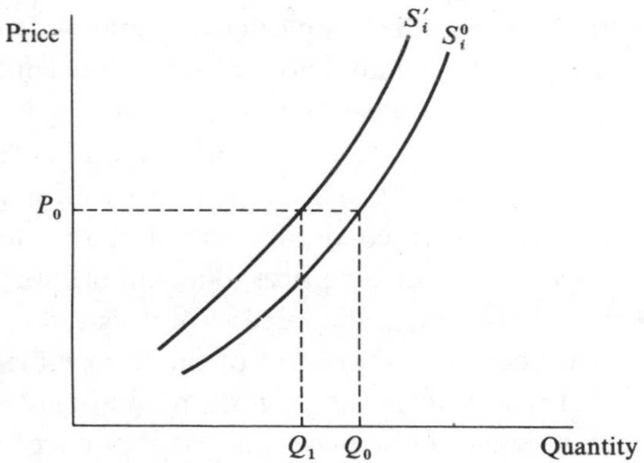

Most agricultural economists would not dispute the economic principles which underlie the supply function represented in equation 3.1. It is certainly the case that producers of, say, maize, will be concerned not only with the market price of maize but also with the prices of alternative enterprises (especially other field crops), and with the prices of inputs (fertiliser, seed, machinery, labour etc.). However, the agricultural economist would also point to a number of important omissions in the list of parameters of the supply function. First of all, it should be noted that several production activities in agriculture involve *joint products* and that the response to a change in the price of one product of a pair of joint products is quite different from that to a change in a price of a competing product. For example, sheep may be reared for mutton and wool, cattle provide beef and hides, and soyabeans yield meal and oil. An increase in the price of one joint product will cause the supply curve of the other to shift to the right; for example, the supply of mutton will be related positively both to the price of mutton and the price of wool. In the list of explanatory variables in equation 3.1 a distinction between joint and competing products should then be made.

The expression in equation 3.1 makes no explicit reference to the state of *technology* and, since a major cause of shifts in agricultural supply curves over time has been improvements in technology, this omission may be particularly serious. A fuller analysis of technological change is given in Chapter 4 and perhaps an example will suffice here. Suppose a group of farmers adopt an improved variety of fertiliser which permits a higher level of output with the same quantities of fertiliser and other inputs. Formally this could be represented as an upward shift in the production function and a downward shift in the related cost curves. Given input and product prices, the producers will find it profitable to expand output i.e. the supply curve will shift to the right.

Another source of shifts in supply which is particularly relevant to the study of agricultural markets, but which does not appear in conventional supply functions is the *natural environment*. Principally through their influence on plant growth and harvest, weather conditions, outbreaks of disease and depredations of pests will have a major bearing on market supply. For example, adverse weather conditions will shift the supply curve to the left (i.e. reduce supply at all prices), favourable weather conditions shift it to the right. However, as the vagaries of the weather and other natural phenomena are beyond the control of the farmer there is often a large discrepancy between *planned* and *realised* output, and when yields are difficult to forecast considerable uncertainty is introduced into the decision-making process. It is especially important to recognise the impact of environmental factors on agricultural supply in developing countries, since much of LDC agricultural production takes place in the Tropics and is exposed to a much more unstable environment (e.g. due to extremes in weather) than agriculture in temperate zones.

Any discussion of the forces affecting agricultural supply would be incomplete without reference to the *institutional setting* and to the role of government policy in particular. Some policy measures will have a direct impact on the supply of specific agricultural products and, wherever possible, these should be treated as explicit variables in the supply function. Examples would include production quotas, acreage allotments and prohibitions or constraints on certain input usage. In other instances, the influence of government intervention will be implicit in the product and input prices which farmers face and in the new technology provided, if this has been developed in public research institutes. Finally there will be government policies which are less commodity-specific but which nevertheless are important influences on aggregate supply. These policies would include land tenure arrangements and the public provision of credit, extension services, irrigation and rural electrification.

To summarise, a comprehensive list of factors which influence the supply of an agricultural product comprises:

the price of the product;
the prices of competing products;
the prices of joint products;
the prices of inputs;
the state of technology;
the natural environment;
the institutional setting.

By supplementing the parameters of equation 3.1 in this way, we have developed a supply function which offers a much more accurate description of production in agricultural markets. Nevertheless our model of supply is still inadequate. This is because it is *static*, by which we mean that it implies that a change in an explanatory variable will induce an instantaneous and complete response in supply: i.e. that there are no delays in adjustment. In fact, there are a number of reasons for delayed adjustment in agricultural markets and hence we must differentiate between the immediate, or short run, response and the long run response. This is the subject of the next section.

3.2.1 *The need for a dynamic specification*

Farmers make their production decisions with imperfect knowledge of the outcome of these decisions but the analysis of supply response under uncertainty cannot be readily undertaken within the framework of the static model. As we have already noted, agricultural output will be subject to a number of climatic and biological factors which, being outside the control of the farmer, may cause wide, random fluctuations in yield. But there is also uncertainty in terms of the product price which producers will receive for their output and it is this on which we focus here.[2]

For most agricultural commodities, product prices are not known with certainty at planting time or when breeding plans are made. Farmers must take these production decisions on the basis of an *expected or predicted product price* i.e. the price which, in their view, is the most likely to prevail when they come to sell their output. The precise way in which farmers formulate their expectations is by no means fully understood by economists but one hypothesis, which has been adopted widely in empirical work and which has an intuitive appeal, is that the expected price in a given production period is calculated with reference to price levels experienced in the past.

If we accept this hypothesis, the specific form of the relationship between the expected price and past prices has then to be established. A number of alternative suggestions have been forthcoming. In the simplest model farmers are assumed to take as their expected price the price received in the previous production period. This is sometimes termed the '*naive expectations*' approach since additional past price behaviour is completely ignored. Perhaps more realistically it may be supposed that the farmer takes a weighted average of prices received over several past production periods, say over the last 4 seasons. In this way the farmer is seen to recognise that prices fluctuate from period to period but that some notion of a '*normal price*' can be computed. A model of expectation formulation which is rather more complex than either of these approaches is the '*adaptive expectations*' model developed by Nerlove in the 1950s but still widely used. In his scheme farmers in each production period are seen as 'revising their notions of what is normal in proportion to the difference between what actually happened and what they previously considered as normal' (Nerlove (1958)). In other words their expected price each period is adjusted in proportion to the size of previous mistakes. The precise mathematical details of these and other models need not concern us here. The important point in the present context is that supply in a given period will be determined by the expected price of the product at planting time and this expected price in turn will be linked in some way to past product prices. As a corollary, the market price in the current production period will typically have an impact on production decisions in a number of future periods.

The need for a dynamic specification of the supply function also arises because in most cases *farmers will not be able or willing to adjust their production activities instantaneously in response to market stimuli. Firstly*, there may be a psychological resistance to change, particularly if the change involves the adoption of techniques or the production of commodities which lie outside the scope of traditional practices. Even when farmers are innovative, the process of acquiring and assessing new information has costs and takes time, perhaps several production periods, and this will give rise to delayed responses.

Secondly, *partial adjustment* to market forces may be due to institutional factors. For example, production quotas are designed to prevent farmers from taking full advantage of profitable opportunities offered by products which are already in surplus. Short run responses may also be hampered by farm tenure or other contractual arrangements, by the market infrastructure, by the availability of rural credit, and so forth.

Finally, technical characteristics of agricultural production may constrain the process of adjustment in the short run. As with industrial firms, farmers in the short run have a fixed capacity in terms of land, buildings and capital equipment and this will impede expansion in response to rising product prices. But in addition, many agricultural enterprises, particularly the production of livestock and perennial crops, are bound by biological constraints. For example, 2–3 years will lapse from the birth of a female calf to her entry into the breeding herd; it may take 3–8 years from planting cocoa trees until the first commercial harvest. Thus there may be a long delay from the time when the decision to expand productive capacity is taken and the point at which the expansion is realised. Another feature of agricultural production which hampers supply responses in the short run is crop rotation. The arable farmer, who is locked into a specific rotational pattern of production in order to reduce the incidence of pests and disease or to replenish soil nutrients, cannot immediately take advantage of market opportunities as they arise.

Our hypothesis then is that due to inertia, institutional factors or technical considerations, the full adjustment which producers would seek to make in their production activities in response to changing market conditions, will not be instantaneous but will be spread over several periods. Given a set of prices and other signals, the farmer will determine the equilibrium or long run level of output and although this desired position cannot be attained at once, he will strive towards that goal in each production period. However, because market conditions continually change, the producer must continually revise the long run position and may in fact never attain it. Consequently, farmers are reacting not just to current levels of the explanatory variables in the supply function but also to their levels in past periods; the supply function is dynamic.

BOX 3.1
Agricultural supply response in developing countries

Of the many themes in production economics perhaps the most important for agricultural economists concerned with developing countries is that of supply response. The responsiveness of farmers to economic incentives will determine to a large degree the contribution which the agricultural sector can make to economic growth, as well as the costs and benefits of government intervention in the sector. Indeed current arguments (by the IMF and the World Bank, among others) for freer agricultural markets are based in part on the premises that in many cases government policy (by creating artificially low farm prices) is biased against agriculture and that farmers will respond positively to price increases.

In the literature there has been some debate as to whether supply response in LDCs can be expected to be positive, as orthodox economic theory would suggest. Some have argued that supply response may be 'perverse' i.e. a higher price induces a lower output. In the simplest form of this argument, it is proposed that farmers in developing countries have a 'target' cash income and, if offered a higher price for their product, they can attain this income level with a reduced supply. More complex behavioural models which incorporate notions of risk and uncertainty have also been developed and again under certain theoretical conditions a 'perverse' response to price changes would be predicted (see Chapter 4). We do not have the space here[3] to elaborate on what Levi and Havinden (1982) have termed 'this rather empty controversy'. However for many policy purposes the important question is an empirical one: how do producers in the aggregate actually respond to price incentives? We therefore turn to some aspects of empirical work on supply response.

The majority of empirical studies involve the direct econometric[4] estimation of agricultural supply functions from time series (or possibly pooled cross-section and time series) data (Colman (1983)). Most of them are of a single commodity type, where, say, the output of wheat is related to the price of wheat, the price of competing products such as maize, the weather etc. (Often reliable input price data are unavailable; indeed the reliability of product price data in some developing countries may be questionable.) Given that agriculture is typified by multi-product enterprises, the partial nature of most studies is striking. It severely limits the role of economic theory in the specification of the models. This is not to say that there is no theoretical underpinning for such studies but rather that it is of

Table 3.1. *Supply elasticities*

Less than zero	
RICE	Uttar Pradesh,[a] Himachal Pradcsh,[b] Gujarat,[b] Maharashta,[b] Kerala[b]
WHEAT	Iraq[b]
MAIZE	Jordan[b]
Zero to one-third	
RICE	Assam,[b] Bihar,[a] Mysore,[b] Punjab, West Bengal,[b] Tripura,[b] Pakistan,[b] Bangladesh,[b] Thailand, West Malaysia, Japan,[b] Philippines, Egypt[b]
WHEAT	Mysore, Punjab,[b] Rajasthan,[b] West Bengal,[b] Maharashta,[b] Himachal Pradesh,[b] Pakistan,[b] Hungary, Jordan,[b] Lebanon, United States
MAIZE	Punjab, Egypt,[b] Lebanon,[b] Sudan, Philippines, United States
One-third to two-thirds	
RICE	Punjab,[a] Bihar-Orissa,[a] Peru,[b] Java, Iraq
WHEAT	Uttar Pradesh,[a] Bihar,[a] Egypt,[a] Syria, Lebanon,[a] New South Wales, U.K.,[b] France, Argentina, Chile
MAIZE	Punjab, Hungary, Sudan[a]
Two-thirds to one	
WHEAT	Gujarat,[b] Egypt,[a] New South Wales,[a] New Zealand, U.S.A.,[a] Canada[b]
More than one	
RICE	West Malaysia,[a] Iraq[a]
WHEAT	Syria,[a] New Zealand,[a] Chile[a]
MAIZE	Thailand,[b] Syria[b]

Source: Askari and Cummings (1976).
[a] Long run elasticity. [b] Short run and long run elasticity.
Unless otherwise noted, elasticities are short run. Only estimates for the Post-World War II period are reproduced here.

an *ad hoc* nature and derives largely from the fact that these studies are based on time series data in which supply response is measured at an aggregate (i.e. market) level.

Askari and Cummings (1976) provide a useful survey of a large number of empirical supply studies. An abridged version of their compilation of (own-price) supply elasticities for wheat, rice and maize is tabulated in Table 3.1. It is clear that the weight of evidence indicates that, with a few exceptions, supply response for individual agricultural products is indeed positive. The statistical analyses also suggest that supply in most cases is inelastic in the short run but more elastic in the long run, as would be expected. Some additional empirical work on supply is presented in Chapter 8, Box 8.4.

Although encouraged by the observation that producers respond positively to price incentives, several agricultural economists have expressed concern that farmers in developing countries are not given the right incentives. Schultz (1978) argued that governments in developing countries undervalue agriculture, producer prices are often kept below free market levels and 'the unrealised economic potential of agriculture in many low-income countries is large'. This is the type of argument which underpins recent concern at the World Bank (World Bank (1986)) about agricultural market distortions. For example, the work of Da Silva *et al.* (1985), although specific to the beef and dairy sectors in Brazil in the post war period, can be used here as an illustration of the possible economic costs of market distortions. The analysis is based on a dynamic econometric model of the beef and dairy markets, encompassing supply, demand, external trade and price formation. The authors conclude that without government intervention the producer prices of beef would have been on average 31% higher and of raw milk 36% higher. In turn beef supply would have increased by 7% and milk production by 17%. The net economic loss in production in both sectors amounted to 3.5 billion Cr$ or about 3% of value of production.

It should be stressed however that much empirical analysis remains to be done on this issue, particularly at the aggregate level where some research to date suggests that supply response is very inelastic (though positive) and that institutional factors and physical infrastructure may constrain agricultural production much more than poor price incentives.

3.3 *Demand for inputs*

In the process of economic development, marked changes in the relative size and interaction of the farm and non-farm sectors are to be expected. An important link between these sectors will be the market for factors of production and so, for agricultural economists, an understanding of the determinants of input usage in agriculture is essential. As we will see, the demand for inputs by farmers is a *derived* demand, that is to say it will be determined by the underlying demand for the agricultural commodity being produced and by the technical characteristics of the production function.

3.3.1 *The competitive model of input demand*

For simplicity, the analysis is confined initially to the competitive firm engaged in a production process which employs only one variable input, say fertiliser. Thus the entrepreneur must merely determine how much of this one resource to use in order to ensure maximum profits. The solution to this problem, which was stated in Chapter 2, Section 2.3.1 and which is derived more formally below, is given at the point where the value of the marginal product of fertiliser = the price of fertiliser

$$i.e.\ VMP_F = p_F$$

The value of the marginal product of fertiliser is the product of two components: the price of the final product (P) and the marginal product of fertiliser (MP_F). It represents the addition to total revenue which an additional unit of fertiliser would contribute. In other words, an extra unit of fertiliser would increase total output (by an amount indicated by MP_F) and this extra product could be sold at the current commodity price, so increasing the firm's total revenue. At the same time the extra unit of fertiliser would increase the firm's total cost by augmenting the fertiliser

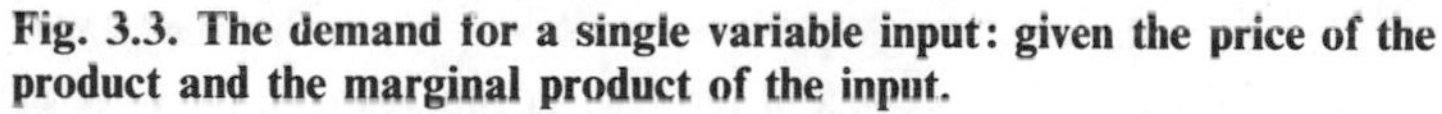
Fig. 3.3. The demand for a single variable input: given the price of the product and the marginal product of the input.

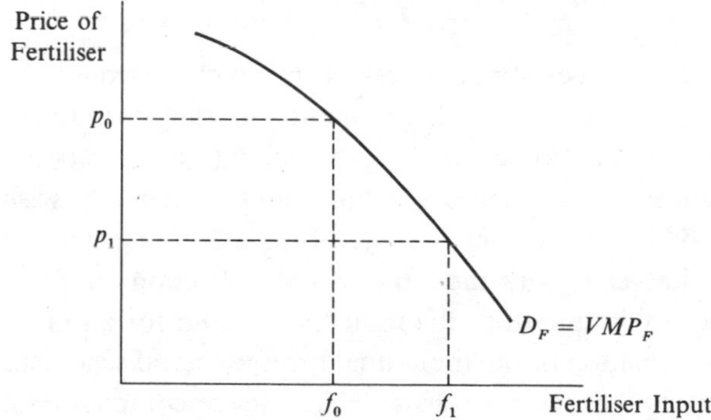

bill by the per unit price of fertiliser (p_F). The firm, being a profit maximiser, will hire a factor as long as it adds more to total revenue than to total cost, and in equilibrium the last unit of the variable input will contribute just as much to total revenue as to total cost.

Fig. 3.3 illustrates the solution. The firm's demand for fertiliser curve is simply the value of the marginal product curve, which in turn is derived by multiplying the marginal product of fertiliser at each level of input usage by the (given) product price. Given a competitive factor market, the firm can employ as much fertiliser as it wishes at the going input price, p_0, and so in accordance with our optimising rule the firm will choose to engage f_0 of fertiliser services. If the price of fertiliser were to fall to p_1, the firm would seek to expand its fertiliser input to f_1.

Formal derivation – profit-maximising input demand

The entrepreneur, it is assumed, wishes to maximise profits (Π), given the technical constraints of the production function ($Q = f(F)$), the price of the input (p_F) and the price of the final product (P). Denoting fixed costs by FC, the problem becomes:

maximise $\Pi = P \cdot Q - p_F F - FC$

subject to $Q = f(F)$

The first order condition for the optimal solution is found by setting the first derivative of profit function with respect to fertiliser equal to zero:

$$\frac{\partial \Pi}{\partial F} = P.\frac{\partial Q}{\partial F} - p_F = 0$$

or $$P\frac{\partial Q}{\partial F} = p_F$$

By definition the marginal product of fertiliser is given as $\partial Q/\partial F$ and so the first order condition implies that $P \cdot MP_F = p_F$ or, in other words, the value of the marginal product of fertiliser is equated with the price of fertiliser.

There are likely to be a number of policy settings in which we would like to go beyond the firm level in order to determine the market or industry demand for a variable input. For example, governments in developing countries frequently subsidise the usage of fertiliser and so we might wish to gauge the impact of this policy on total fertiliser use by farmers. It might at first seem that since the industry is the collection of firms producing the commodity in question, the industry demand for an input would simply be the summation of the individual firms' demand schedules for that input. Unfortunately the analysis is a little more complex than this. When the price of an input falls, all firms are encouraged to employ more of that resource and to expand output. However, as we will demonstrate in Chapter 8, the price of the final product will fall when aggregate production increases; the additional quantity of the commodity can only be sold at a lower price. This reduction in the product price in turn decreases the value of the marginal product of the input and so each firm's demand schedule for fertiliser shifts leftwards. Fig. 3.4 illustrates this point. At the initial input price, p_0, the individual firm employs f_0 of the fertiliser and when the input price falls to p_1, this firm and all other firms in the industry will seek to expand usage to f_1. The resultant increase in output by all firms will lower the market price of the product, which, as we have noted, is one of the components of the value of marginal product. In line with the decrease in *VMP*, the firm's demand curve for fertiliser shifts downwards to the left and at the new input price, each firm will employ f', not f_1, of the variable input. At the industry level, total usage at the initial fertiliser price would be F_0, being the summation over all firms of their usage levels f_0. At the lower price, p_1, industry's usage would be F', the summation of the final firm-level usage levels f'. (For comparison, Fig. 3.4 also depicts, at F_1, the industry's level of usage, if the product price had *not* changed). We conclude that the industry demand schedule for an input will be more steeply sloped (less elastic) than the summation of the individual firms' demand schedules.

To summarise, when the analysis is confined to a production process with only one variable input, the demand for the input will be determined by

the price of the input;
the price of the final product;
the marginal product of the input;

Fig. 3.4. The demand for a single variable input at the industry level: given the marginal product of the input.

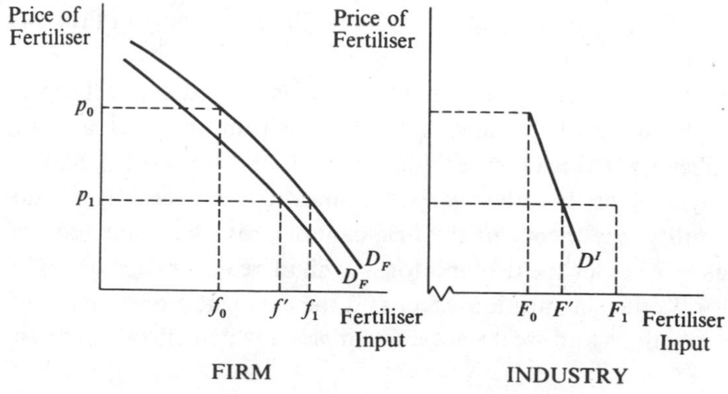

technological change, since this will change the marginal product of the input.

This list of explanatory variables must be augmented when the firm's production process involves more than one variable input. Specifically, when there are multiple variable inputs, we must add to the list:

the prices of variable inputs other than of the one being analysed;

the quantities of fixed factors.

In order to explore this a little more fully, let us assume that the firm employs two variable factors, X_1 and X_2, and so, since other factors of production are held constant, the underlying production function would take the form:

$$Q = f(X_1, X_2 \mid X_3, \ldots, X_n).$$

We may note in passing that since the levels of fixed factors determine the precise position of the total physical product curve, they also may influence the marginal products of the variable inputs.

We now consider the effects of a fall in price of input X_1, whilst the prices of X_2 and the final product remain unchanged. The response of the profit maximising firm can be divided, for analytical purposes, into two components: a *substitution effect* and an *expansion effect*. The substitution effect is due solely to the change in relative factor prices and measures the change in the least cost combination of inputs at each output level. In our example X_1 has become relatively cheaper and the firm is encouraged to substitute units of X_1 for units of X_2. The least cost combination of inputs, for a given output level, thus comprises more X_1 and less X_2. The expansion effect is the response to the overall reduction in the total cost of producing each level of output, which the fall in input price has induced. As the price of X_1 has decreased, the marginal cost of each unit of output is also reduced and to maximise profits (where marginal cost = product price), the firm will expand output and the employment of the two variable factors.

It may be concluded that the demand for X_1 is related inversely to its price i.e. as the price of X_1 falls, both the substitution effect and the expansion effect induce an increase in the demand for X_1. What will happen to the employment of the other variable input, X_2? Regrettably, at this level of generality, the theory of the firm cannot provide an unequivocal prediction as to whether the demand for X_2 will increase or decrease. This is because for X_2 the substitution effect and the expansion response work in opposite directions and we do not know *a priori* which effect will be the stronger. An accurate prediction would require knowledge about the technical conditions of production and about the elasticity of substitution in particular. What we may assert is that the greater the ease with which the inputs may be substituted, the more likely that the substitution effect on X_2 will outweigh the expansion effect and that the demand for X_2 will fall as the price of X_1 is decreased.

BOX 3.2
The demand for fertiliser: some empirical evidence

Since fertiliser can improve the fertility of the soil, increasing crop yields and allowing grassland to support more livestock, it is recognised as an important input into agricultural production both in developed and developing countries. As would be expected, it also features in the empirical work which agricultural economists undertake, and particular effort has been expended in attempts to explain fertiliser usage over time and to gauge farmers' responsiveness to price signals. Some examples of this type of analysis follow.

Hayami and Ruttan (1985, Chapter 7) try to relate fertiliser usage (total plant nutrients, $N+P_2O_5+K_2O$) per hectare to factor price ratios in the USA and Japan over the period 1880–1980. The explanatory variables comprise the prices of fertiliser and the other major inputs (land, labour and machinery), but not the price of the final product. They conclude that variations in the fertiliser–land price ratio alone explains over 90 % of the variation in fertiliser use in the USA and more than 80 % of its variation in Japan. Moreover their results suggest that there are substitution possibilities between fertiliser and labour but that the price of machinery does not significantly influence fertiliser usage in either country. Their analysis leads them to the rather surprising conclusion that 'despite enormous differences in climate, initial factor endowments, and social and economic institutions and organisation in the United States and Japan, the agricultural production function, the inducement mechanism of innovations, the response of farmers to economic opportunities have been essentially the same' (p. 187). By this they mean that farmers in both countries have demonstrated the capacity to exploit new opportunities in response to relative price changes.

A serious obstacle to the analysis of fertiliser demand in developing countries is the availability of data. Thus, for example, the set of explanatory variables used in the empirical work of the National Fertiliser Development Centre (1984) in Pakistan was to a large degree restricted to a relative price index (the price of fertiliser divided by an index of agricultural crop prices)

and a time trend. The latter was included to capture technological development and changes in environmental factors over time. Nevertheless even this partial analysis can offer a useful input into policy debates. For example, this study demonstrates that the demand for fertiliser is inelastic (perhaps of the order of −0.7) with respect to changes in the 'real' price of fertiliser. A relative price change could arise because of an upward adjustment in fertiliser prices, a downward adjustment in fertiliser subsidies or a fall in agricultural product prices due to market conditions. Furthermore the time trend (or the technological and environmental factor it represents) was judged to have much greater explanatory power than the price variable.

3.3.2 *Asset fixity in agriculture*

In the foregoing discussion of the theory of input demand it has been assumed implicitly that firms can buy or sell inputs at the same factor price. However, for some specialised, durable inputs in agricultural production, there may be a substantial divergence between their acquisition costs (purchase price to the farmer) and their salvage value (the price at which the farmer can sell the same input in the same condition at the same point in time). For example, a grain storage unit on an arable farm is an immobile resource in the sense that it cannot be moved without considerable transportation and transaction costs, it has little or no use value outside agriculture and indeed, even on the farm, it is of little use beyond the purpose for which it has been constructed. Hence the input, once installed, has a low opportunity cost.

In Fig. 3.5, the purchase price of the input is denoted as p_a and at this

Fig. 3.5. Asset fixity.

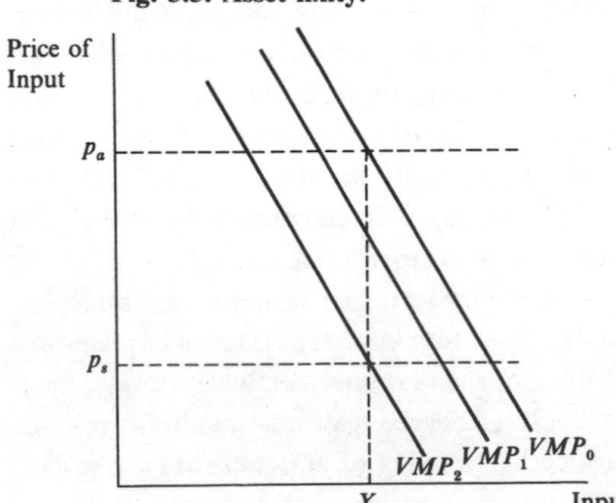

price, given the value of the marginal product of the input (VMP_0), the firm will employ X_0 of the durable asset. The salvage value of the asset is denoted as p_s. Suppose that there follows a decrease in the product price, which in turn will induce a shift, downwards and to the left, in the VMP schedule to VMP_1. Clearly the contribution of the input to the firm's revenue has fallen but it still remains above the salvage value, which is the price the producer would receive if he chooses to sell off any of the input. Even at the lower product price, there is no incentive to reduce employment of this specialised input. Only if, through further decreases in the product price, the demand curve shifts at least as far as VMP_2 (where the value of the marginal product just equals the salvage value), will the producer reduce usage of this input. The implication of this 'asset fixity' is that supply response when prices are falling may be less elastic than if prices are rising. In other words, the supply curve for some agricultural products may be asymmetric, or irreversible. Some empirical work on this subject has been undertaken by Traill, Colman and Young (1978) among others.

3.4 *Conclusions*

Agricultural economists are particularly interested in the determinants of agricultural supply, because this, together with consumer demand (the subject of Chapters 5, 6, and 7), provides the foundation for policy analysis of agricultural markets. In our treatment of supply, we have tried to emphasise the importance of product and input prices as signals directing producers' decisions about resource allocation. It has also been stressed that a dynamic approach, which recognises the time lags in agricultural supply responses, should be adopted in empirical analysis. In addition producers must take decisions in an uncertain environment in which the weather and natural hazards may undo the best laid plans. Hence some account must be taken of risk and uncertainty, issues addressed in the following chapters.

Changes in agricultural output involve changes in the demand for inputs, and many policy questions require an understanding of the determinants of input usage, as well as of product supply. An important aspect of agricultural input markets, which may be of less significance in other sectors of the economy, is asset fixity, whereby use of certain inputs does not adjust readily when prices change. In some commodity markets, asset fixity may markedly reduce the short-run responsiveness to market stimuli. It may also result in asymmetric supply functions, whereby the responsiveness of supply to upward price changes is different from that to price decreases.

The basic economic theory of supply and demand has been found to have considerable diagnostic and predictive value for agricultural markets. In order to demonstrate and underline this point empirical evidence about agricultural supply responses to price and about the demand for fertiliser have been reviewed.

3.5 *Summary points*

1. The *supply* of an agricultural product to the market will depend on the price of the product, the prices of competing products, the prices of joint products, the prices of inputs, the state of technology, the natural environment and the institutional setting.
2. The *supply curve* depicts the relationship between the quantities of a particular product which the producer is willing to supply and its price, all other factors held constant. The (own-price) *elasticity* of supply measures the responsiveness of quantity supplied to changes in the price of the product.
3. Supply of an agricultural product will not adjust instantaneously and completely in response to market stimuli. This may be because farmers have imperfect knowledge and face uncertainty particularly with regard to yields and prices, or due to producers' inertia, institutional factors and technical considerations. These may cause adjustment to be spread over several periods. A *dynamic* specification of the *supply function* is thus required.
4. The *demand for an input* will depend on the price of the input, the price of other variable inputs, the price of the product, the marginal product of the input, the quantities of fixed inputs and technological change.
5. For some specialised durable inputs in agricultural production, there may be *asset fixity* i.e. because of their low opportunity costs they are retained in production within some range of declining product price.

Further reading

A discussion of supply analysis in agricultural markets is to be found in most agricultural economics textbooks (Ritson (1977), Hill and Ingersent (1977) etc.). However Tomek and Robinson (1981) provide one of the better expositions. Colman (1983) reviews the state of the arts of estimating the quantitative supply response. Ghatak and Ingersent (1984) discuss some aspects of empirical supply analysis in developing countries.

4

Topics in production economics

4.1 *Introduction*

This chapter deals with four subject areas of importance to the analysis of production and supply. In public debates about growth and development it is common for reference to be made to (i) differences in efficiency among sectors of the economy, and to (ii) differences in efficiency in agricultural production among countries, regions, farm sizes and tenure systems. The concept of *efficiency* in economics is a complex and difficult one. Section 4.2 below presents a brief examination of the problems and the usefulness of certain measures of efficiency.

One of the principal engines of economic growth is *technological change*. The tools presented in Chapter 2 provide the basis for the explanation and definition of technological change which is set out in Section 4.3.1. Section 4.3.2 discusses the *sources of technological change*, and this is followed (in 4.3.3) by a discussion of *adoption and diffusion of agricultural technology* and its impact in the so-called Green Revolution.

Reference has already been made in Chapter 3, in the context of the need for a dynamic treatment of supply response, to the importance of *risk and uncertainty* upon farmers' decisions. Section 4.4 pursues this in slightly more detail, and indicates the implications of risk aversion in the face of uncertainty for resource allocation at the farm level and for supply response to price in general.

Fourthly Section 4.5 deals with a special topic in production (and consumption theory) which is covered by the term *duality*. The essence of this topic is that there are alternative ways of expressing the resource allocation problem for the competitive firm, which contain all the same basic technical and behavioural information. This is important at the level of empirical analysis, since it establishes the possibility of alternative approaches to the same problem. It also helps explain why, in textbooks on economics, discussion often switches rapidly from profit maximisation to cost minimisation, since these turn out to be the dual specification of each other. Duality is a fairly difficult concept, and some readers may prefer to skip this section.

4.2 *Efficiency of resource use*

A measure of producer performance in response to economic incentives is often useful for policy purposes and the concept of *economic efficiency* provides a theoretical foundation for such a measure. Using the analytical tools presented in Chapter 2, the term 'efficiency' can be defined with some precision and it is this definition which has been taken as the basis for much empirical work on the subject. Nevertheless it should be noted at the outset that the validity of the concept has been questioned by a number of authors. We will therefore try to assess its usefulness in the light of some of these criticisms.

4.2.1 *Technical, allocative and economic efficiency*

Much of the literature on efficiency is based, directly or indirectly, on the seminal work of Farrell (1957), who argued that efficiency could only meaningfully be gauged in a relative sense, as a deviation from the best practice of a representative peer group of producers. He also introduced the distinction between *technical efficiency* (where maximum

Fig. 4.1. Farrell's efficiency indices.

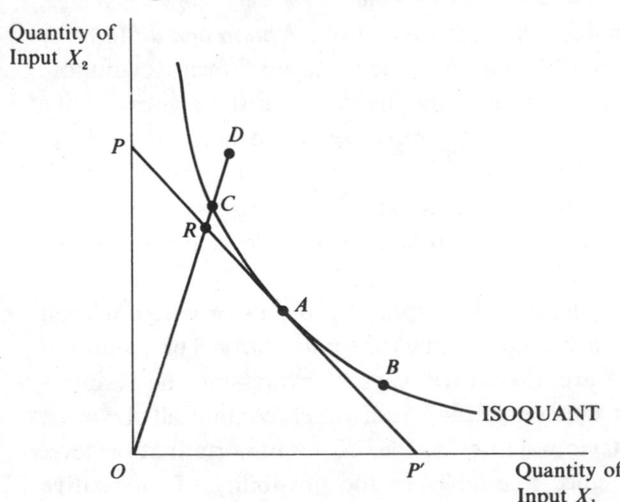

output is obtained from a given set of inputs) and *allocative efficiency* (where, given input prices, factors are used in proportions which maximise producer profits). These concepts will be explained with reference to Fig. 4.1.

The diagram shows the efficient unit insoquant for a group of farms using inputs X_1 and X_2. Farms located on this isoquant use the least amounts of these inputs to produce a unit of output. If points *A*, *B*, *C* and *D* denote farms which are producing one unit of the product, then farms *A*, *B* and C, being on the isoquant, are technically efficient but farm *D* would be judged to be technically inefficient. A measure of technical efficiency for farm *D* is given by *OC/OD*, i.e. farm *D* could reduce both inputs by a proportion *OC/OD* and still produce the same level of output. Given relative input prices, the isocost line *PP′* indicates the minimum cost of producing one unit of output and so overall economic efficiency is greatest at the point *A* on the unit isoquant. Noting that point *R* has the same level of costs as *A*, Farrell proposed that overall economic efficiency of farm *D* could be measured as *OR/OD*, with *OR/OC* representing allocative efficiency, or the divergence between the minimum cost point and the costs incurred at point *C*. The overall economic efficiency measure can be decomposed as follows:

$$OR/OD = OC/OD \times OR/OC$$

or

$$\text{economic efficiency} = \text{technical efficiency} \times \text{allocative efficiency}$$

Given these definitions, farm *A* would be economically efficient, farms *B* and *C* would be technically efficient but not allocatively efficient, and farm *D* would be neither technically nor allocatively efficient.

It should be evident that technical efficiency (maximum output from given inputs) refers only to the physical characteristics of the production process. It can therefore be taken to be a universal goal in that it is applicable in any economic system. On the other hand allocative efficiency and overall economic efficiency presume that the entrepreneurs' goal is one of profit maximisation.

BOX 4.1
Efficiency of peasant agriculture

Schultz (1964) and others have argued that, given their access to resources, peasant farmers combine inputs in a manner which yields maximum profits; peasants are 'poor but efficient'. This view has been

influential in the design of development strategies and has prompted, notably in the 1970s, a number of empirical investigations of farmers' efficiency in developing countries. For example, Lau and Yotopoulos (1971) compared efficiency on small (< 10 acres) and large farms in India in the period 1955–57. They demonstrated that small farms perform with greater economic efficiency than large farms but that the farm types are equally allocative efficient. The advantage of small farms is thus attributed to their greater technical efficiency. Sidhu (1974), again using Indian data but for a later period (Punjab, 1967/8–1970/1) drew somewhat different conclusions. His results indicate that small and large farms, as well as tractor-mechanised and non-mechanised farms, are not significantly different in terms of relative economic efficiency, allocative efficiency or technical efficiency. An explanation offered by Sidhu for the apparent divergence with the preceding analysis, is that his sample was taken at a time when agriculture in the region was being modernised (new seed varieties, fertiliser, irrigation etc.) and since larger farms had more immediate access to the modern inputs, they had the opportunity to catch up with small farms in terms of efficiency.

This type of empirical evidence, if it is accepted, suggests a picture of peasant agriculture which is much more optimistic than the typical caricature of a stagnant and unco-operative sector. At the same time it gives rise to some concern that there are substantial economic costs to the distortions of incentives (product prices and input subsidies) which at present are offered to farmers in developing countries.[1] However it must be stressed that the definition of economic efficiency is not unambiguous and that the measurement of efficiency is not a straightforward matter. Some of the conceptual and empirical problems are discussed in the next section.

4.2.2 '*The myth of efficiency*'

The controversy about the interpretation of efficiency measures concerns both the validity of the efficiency standards used and the accuracy of the empirical measures obtained. Pasour (1981) suggests that a level of performance which is achievable only under ideal conditions of perfect knowledge is not an appropriate standard against which to measure real world performance. In a similar vein he argues that performance standards derived on the assumption of profit maximisation should not be used to measure the performance of entrepreneurs whose objective functions include elements other than profit. A third area of controversy raises questions about the accuracy of empirical measures. In particular it is argued that observed inefficiency may be due solely to our inability to measure inputs accurately. For example quality differences in land and labour are often difficult to record, while the problems of measuring capital inputs and management expertise are further complications. Another pertinent argument suggests that the notion of efficiency is relevant only within the narrow confines of the perfectly competitive equilibrium and hence irrelevant to real world problems. Specifically, allocative efficiency assumes that market prices are a true measure of relative scarcity but when prices are distorted by governments or monopolies (defined in Chapter 9) or where goods remain outside the market system, the role of prices in resource allocation is greatly impaired. As a final criticism we can add the difficulty of interpreting a static efficiency measure in the dynamic setting of agricultural decision-making. Since a firm's resource allocation decisions are based on expectations over several production periods, any performance standard over a single period may be misleading. For example a farm which has installed irrigation equipment may appear to be using too much capital[2] if surveyed in a year of unusually high rainfall.

When confronted with this lengthy catalogue of criticisms, a number of authors (e.g. Rizzo (1979)) have concluded that the concept should be abandoned. At the very least great caution is urged, when reviewing empirical work on the subject. However, on a more positive note, we could accept the proposition[3] that it is valid to try to estimate producers' performance in terms of *technical* efficiency, since to a large extent the latter would avoid many of the criticisms levied upon more general efficiency concepts. In particular, measures of technical efficiency rely less heavily on the assumptions of perfect knowledge, perfectly competitive markets and the profit maximisation objective.

4.3 *Technological change*

4.3.1 *Technological change in economic modelling*

Economists usually define *technology* as a stock of available techniques or a state of knowledge concerning the relationship between inputs and a given physical output. *Technological change* is an improvement in the state of knowledge such that production possibilities are enhanced. In other words, through technological change the production function will shift over some range such that

(i) more output can be produced with the same quantity of inputs

(ii) the same output can be produced with a smaller quantity of inputs.

The impact of technological change can be illustrated with reference to the factor–product, factor–factor and product-product diagrams introduced in Section 2.2 of Chapter 2. Consider the introduction of a new wheat seed variety which increases the output response to fertiliser usage. The adoption of the better quality seed input into the production process will shift the total product curve upwards (Fig. 4.2) so that with fertiliser usage f_0, output can be increased from OA to OB. Alternatively, a given output level, say OA, can now be obtained with a reduced level of fertiliser usage (Of_1 instead of Of_0). In this factor-product case, all inputs other

Fig. 4.2. Technological change and the total product curve.

Total Product

TP_1

TP_0

B

A

O f_1 f_0 Fertiliser Usage

Fig. 4.3. Technological change and the isoquant.

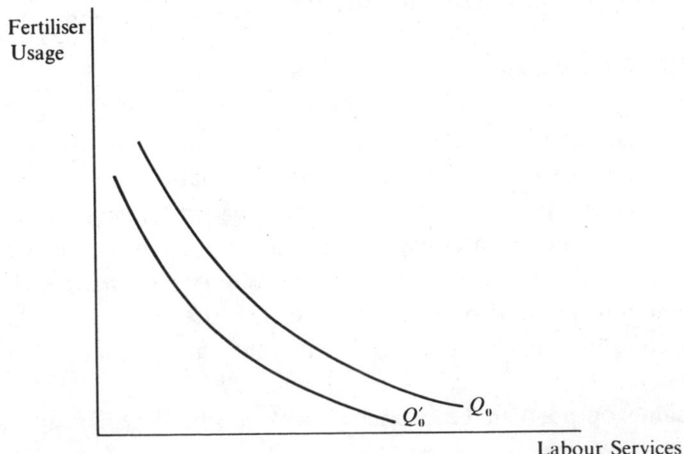

than fertiliser are held fixed. The factor–factor diagram in Fig. 4.3 allows us to illustrate the case of two variable inputs, say fertiliser and labour. In Fig. 4.3 the isoquant for output level, Q_0, depicts the various combinations of the variable inputs which yield that output level. However, under the new technology the *same* output can be obtained with less of the variable inputs i.e. the new isoquant (Q_0') for output Q_0 shifts towards the origin.

Finally, suppose the farmer produces two products, wheat and maize. The production possibilities frontier (PPF_0) in Fig. 4.4 indicates the output combinations which are available, given a set of inputs. However, since the introduction of the improved seed variety in wheat production allows more wheat to be grown with the same quantity of inputs, the frontier swivels to PPF_1. (Note that as maize inputs have not been changed

Fig. 4.4. Technological change and the production possibilities frontier.

Fig. 4.5. Neutral technological change.

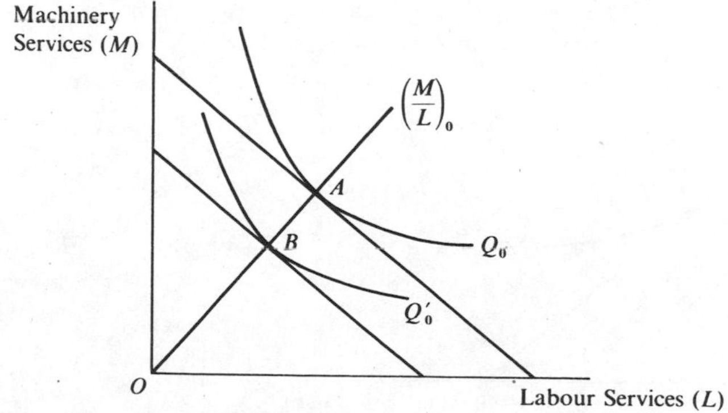

in any way, the maximum output of maize from a given set of inputs remains at m_0.)

It is often useful to distinguish types of technological change. Consider Fig. 4.5. Technological change has shifted the isoquant for a given output from Q_0 to Q'_0, in such a manner that *at constant factor prices* (of labour and machinery) both factors are saved in the same proportion as they were being used originally, and the optimal machinery to labour ratio $(M/L)_0$ remains unchanged. This type of technological change is termed *neutral*.[4]

Perhaps more frequently, technological change may be *biased*, in the sense that at constant factor prices it induces a change in optimal factor proportions. Suppose the relative marginal product of machinery services is raised by the introduction of a technologically superior tractor. If factor prices are constant, the optimal machinery–labour ratio will rise and the technological change is said to be *labour-saving*. This is illustrated in Fig. 4.6, where as the isoquant shifts, the optimal machinery–labour ratio rises from $(M/L)_0$ to $(M/L)_1$. The same level of output can now be produced by reducing labour usage more than capital usage.

Thirtle and Ruttan (1987, pp. 12–22) provide a lucid and extended explanation of neutrality and biasedness in technical change. As they note, while it makes sense to define as neutral technological change shifts which at fixed factor price ratios leave the optimal factor use ratios unchanged, this is not so at the industry level. For, whereas for the individual firm input prices are given, at the aggregate level it is more appropriate to consider factor endowments or availability as fixed; certainly that is so in the short-run. In that case a neutral technological change can be more appropriately defined as one which, with *given factor proportions*, raises the marginal product of labour in the same proportion as the marginal

Fig. 4.6. Labour-saving technological change.

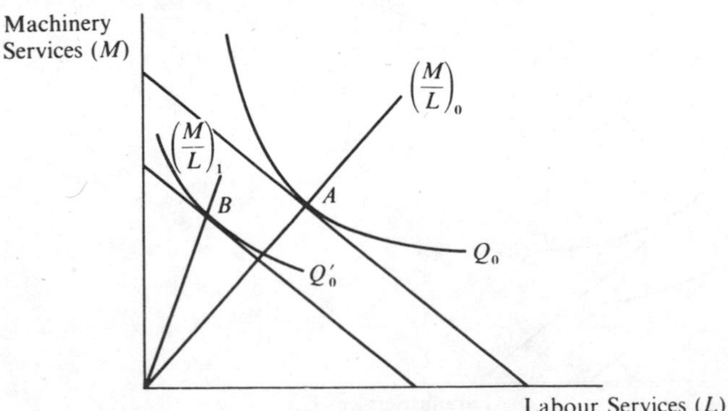

product of capital. In that case the economic interpretation of bias is 'simple and appealing. A labour-saving innovation makes labour in some sense more plentiful relative to capital than it was previously, with the result that the marginal product of labour must fall relative to capital' (Thirtle and Ruttan, 1987, p. 15).

It should be noted that in most of the economics literature, the analysis of technological change is quite narrowly focussed, since it is concerned solely with changes in the physical production process. There is little or no reference to the impact of technological change on political and social structures, on institutional and administrative systems, and on the physical infrastructure. However, as we will see below, many agricultural economists are now taking a broader perspective. It is also the case that in orthodox economic theory, technology is viewed as a factor outside the control of the entrepreneur and of the industry and so technological change is simply an *exogenous* shift in the production process. Nevertheless, in a development context in which sustained economic growth is sought, it is pertinent to ask: where is the technological change to come from?

BOX 4.2
Characteristics of technological change in the agricultural sector

Technological change has occurred in every sphere of agriculture. Much of it has been embodied in capital, i.e. in machinery, drainage, irrigation and buildings, but there have also been significant advances in the form of high yielding varieties (HYVs) of crops, improved strains of livestock, better feeds, and more effective fertilisers, pesticides and insecticides. Moreover, technological progress has been evident in cultivation and husbandry methods and in the overall managerial skills of the farmer.

Much of the technological change which has taken place in the agricultural sector has been biased, often being labour-saving (in the case of most new machinery) or land-saving (as with the HYVs and fertilisers). This does not necessarily imply that less of these factors are used. For example, with a labour saving technological change, theory suggests that the producer will employ less labour, for a given output level. However, as the marginal cost of production has fallen, the producer will wish to increase output, in order to maximise profits, and so employ more of all factors of production. There will then be a tradeoff between the initial displacement of labour due to the technological change and the increased employment of labour due to the

increase in production. In some cases, the net effect may be that more, not less, labour is employed. Nevertheless it should be noted that this type of prediction rests on the factor price ratio remaining constant, whereas in a number of developing countries, governments have chosen to subsidise the use of machinery. The reduction in the relative price of capital encourages a much greater displacement of labour and the net effect in these cases is almost certainly a reduction in labour usage. A specific case study is presented in Box 4.3.

BOX 4.3
Some consequences of farm mechanisation in Pakistan

McInerney and Donaldson (1975) analysed the major economic consequences of introducing large scale tractor technology to farms in Pakistan. Their research was based on a survey of 202 farms, just over 5% of the total number of farms which received tractors (financed by World Bank lending) in 1967–68. The economic incentives for the individual farmer to adopt the new technology were exceptionally favourable. The price of many crops had been set by the government well above world market levels, credit was made available at artificially low interest rates, and the imported tractors were free of duty and sales taxes. Of course the assessment of technological change goes beyond the calculation of the change in adopters' profits, and McInerney and Donaldson examine the wider costs and benefits to society, as well as the implications for resource use and the structure of agriculture. Here we will merely summarise their results regarding the primary concern of the farm mechanisation programme, namely the impact on farm employment.

To the extent that tractor mechanisation replaces traditional operations including those associated with the use and maintenance of animal draft power, seeding, harvesting etc., labour will be displaced. However this will be counterbalanced to some extent by the increased demand for labour services arising from the increase in cultivated land area, cropping intensity and final production. Indeed the average size of farm in the sample more than doubled (from 45 acres to 109 acres). This came about as follows: some farmers (22% of the sample) reclaimed or improved land which had been previously uncultivated, some farmers (12% of the sample) bought more cultivatable land, some (24%) rented additional cultivatable land, and the remainder (42%) reduced the amount of land which had previously been rented out to other producers and farmed this land themselves. The

absorption of land into enlarged holdings displaced tenants and owner-occupiers from the land and reduced the employment of labour (both family and hired). Thus, whereas the labour that was used *per farm* increased, the use of labour *per cultivated* acre fell by about 40%. McInerney and Donaldson calculate that between 7.5 and 11.8 full time jobs were lost for each tractor used. Even when one takes account of seasonal demands for casual labour, each tractor replaced about five jobs.

4.3.2 *Sources of technological change*

The chief sources of technological change to which a developing country might have access are

(i) 'learning by using';

(ii) private and public research and development generated within the country;

(iii) imported research and development.

Some technological change will take place on the farm or within the firm as the result of experience with a given production process. In everyday operation of the farm technical problems in production are confronted and solved. In time the producer learns how to get the most out of the inputs and the production process which has been adopted. The resultant gains in output are attributed to 'learning by using'[5] and will be a function of experience and hence time.

The second source of technological change is research and development (R & D) which may be conducted in both private and public institutions. Research may be *basic*, in which case it is undertaken with no specific commercial objective, or it may be *applied* i.e. directed to an immediate commercial end. In the *development* stage the most commercially promising research is selected and used to create new processes or products. In the industrial sector, a large number of private firms will have R & D teams; indeed private industry will be responsible for most R & D expenditure in manufacturing. In contrast, most agricultural R & D activities are undertaken by public agencies. Governments are often willing to provide the financial support for R & D because a new technology may take several years to develop, the research input may be too costly for an individual farmer to bear, and it may also be costly to disseminate information on a new process. In addition, if it proves difficult to patent or otherwise protect the researcher's interest in the new process, R & D for the private entrepreneur may not prove commercially viable. It is this latter reason which is often cited as an explanation for the observation that public agencies have been engaged on research into new breeds of livestock and new crop varieties, whereas private companies have succeeded in the development of new farm machinery and agrochemicals where patents are more easily applied.

Governments and producers in LDCs can engage in R & D in an effort to promote technological change in the agricultural sector. However it must be admitted that most of this work is conducted in the industrialised countries and many LDCs rely on the import of foreign technology. One option would be to screen foreign technology and adopt the 'best' without adaptation. The transfer of technology in this way has created some concern that the foreign technology may not always be appropriate to the needs and conditions in the recipient countries and may generate indirect costs, as well as benefits, through its impact on the social, political and physical infrastructure. An alternative, which may have fewer indirect costs, would be to select foreign technology for subsequent modification, through adaptive research, to suit local conditions.

4.3.3 *Adoption and diffusion of new technologies*

Because of the opportunities for increased output and higher income levels which technological change can offer, agricultural economists in the development field have made a particular study of the adoption and diffusion of technical innovations. *Adoption* studies relate to the use or non-use of a particular innovation by individuals (say farmers) at a point in time, or during an extended period of time. Adoption therefore presupposes that the innovation (source of technological change) exists, and studies of the adoption process analyse the reasons or determinants of whether and when adoption takes place. By convention individuals within a population are classified into (i) innovators, (ii) early adopters, (iii) the early majority, (iv) the late majority, and (v) laggards, according to the date of adoption. *Diffusion* is defined in relation to the spread of an innovation at the aggregate level viewed over time. That is, diffusion is defined as the cumulative process of adoption measured in successive time periods.

The decision of whether or not to adopt a new technology will be based on a careful evaluation of a large number of technical, economic and social factors. In this section we cannot address the full complexity of that process but we will suggest some of the elements which may influence it.

The technical attributes of a new technology may have a direct bearing on the decision making process. Specifically the more technically complex the innovation, the less attractive it may be to many farmers. Moreover, if the technology is divisible[6] (as is the case with HYVs), the farmer is able to try out the innovation on a small scale. On the other hand, if the technology is 'lumpy' (as is the case with large machinery such as tractors and harvesters), small scale trials are not possible and the farmer may be more reluctant to adopt. Moreover, the minimum scale of operation for the lumpy technology to be feasible may be too large for many farmers.

The economic potential of the new technology, in terms of yields, costs of production and profit, will also be most important. Typically, however, the economic impact of the innovation is not known with certainty. Unfamiliarity with the new technology will make the initial impact on yields and input usage uncertain. In addition the new technology may affect the extent to which the farmer is exposed to the vagaries of nature. For example, some HYVs may be more susceptible to disease than traditional varieties, whereas irrigation equipment may offset the effects of drought. Since the adoption decision must take place in an uncertain environment, the farmer's attitude to risk and in particular the degree of risk aversion must be taken into account.

As well as the technical and economic attributes of the technology, the characteristics of the farmer and the farming enterprise may influence the adoption decision. We have already noted that the farmers' attitude to risk will have a bearing on the adoption decision. Age, experience and education, the factors comprising '*human capital*', may also determine the farmer's awareness and interest in the new technology, as well as his ability to implement it. Moreover the potential adopter may be confronted with constraints in terms of purchasing power, of access to credit and information, and of poor communication links with product and input markets. With regard to the latter, the availability of complementary inputs in the quantity and at the time required may prove to be an important consideration in the adoption decision.

The diffusion process occurs over time and relies to some extent on the interaction between farmers in a given region. The process is often depicted as one of learning. Whilst a few producers will adopt the innovation rapidly, the majority will take time to become aware of the new technology and to evaluate its benefits. In this the demonstration effect of the early adopters may be important. The rate of diffusion will also depend on the extent to which the technology is location specific or is adaptable to the conditions under which most farmers operate. In addition, it is clear that the social, cultural and institutional environment will influence the speed at which the use of a new technology will spread through the farming community.[7]

BOX 4.4
The Green Revolution

The Green Revolution began in the mid 1960s with the release of new varieties of wheat from CIMMYT in Mexico and of rice from IRRI in the Philippines. When combined with correct amounts of the complementary inputs of water, fertiliser and other farm chemicals, these varieties promised yields which were higher than those from traditional varieties. In many regions of the world, the new high-yielding varieties (HYVs) (or 'modern varieties') were rapidly adopted and with quite dramatic results in some instances. India, for example, which was the world's second largest cereals importer in 1966, became self-sufficient in wheat in the late 1970s. China, Pakistan, Turkey and Bangladesh were also among those countries which recorded substantial increases in wheat production, and for developing countries as a whole wheat yields rose by 2.7% p.a. between 1961 and 1980 (World Bank (1982)). For rice, yields also rose in the same period but by only 1.6% p.a., although higher growth (more than 3% p.a.) was found in the Philippines and Indonesia which were best suited to the new varieties.

The speed of adoption, for the rice varieties, can be illustrated by the

Table 4.1. *Area planted to modern rice varieties* (thousand ha)

	Philippines	Indonesia	S. Korea	India	Pakistan	Bangladesh
1965/66	0	0	0	0	0	0
1966/67	83	0	0	888	0	0
1967/68	702	0	0	1785	4	63
1968/69	1012	198	0	2681	308	152
1969/70	1360	831	0	4253	501	264
1970/71	1565	903	0	5454	550	406
1971/72	1827	1323	3	7199	729	624
1972/73	1680	1914	186	8607	647	1065
1973/74	2177	3135	121	9718	637	1549
1974/75	2175	3387	307	10780	631	1444
1975/76	2300	n.a.	274	12742	665	1552
1976/77	2417	4049	533	13731	678	1280
1977/78	2457	4454	660	15516	852	1204
1978/79	2512	4982	929	17619	1015	1373
1979/80	2708	5366	744	—	—	1998
1980/81	2678	5416	604	—	—	2194

Source: Herdt and Capule (1983). Herdt and Capule prefer the term 'modern varieties', since new varieties may not be high yielding unless a high level of inputs is used.

change in area planted to the HYVs (Table 4.1). If these figures were translated into percentages of total rice area, we would find that the Philippines and Indonesia used HYVs on over 50% of their total rice areas by 1970 and 1976 respectively. In India, the pace of adoption has been somewhat slower, with about half of the total rice area being devoted to the HYVs by 1980. This contrasts sharply with experience in Pakistan where within five years of their introduction, the new varieties were planted in 50% of the total rice area.

Dalrymple (1986) has compiled some data on adoption rates of high yielding varieties of wheat and rice in the (non-communist) developing countries as a whole. It is estimated that by 1982–83 about 61% of the total wheat area was given over to these varieties, whilst for rice the proportion was approximately 42%. The high yielding wheat area is heavily concentrated in Asia and the high yielding rice area is almost exclusively found there.

In Table 4.2 the performance of the modern varieties of rice is compared to that of the traditional varieties. In India and Bangladesh the new varieties have produced yields two or three times higher than traditional varieties. In the Philippines and Indonesia the gains are more modest (up to 40% higher). These figures must be interpreted with some caution since, being averages, they may mask substantial regional variation within each country as well as variation between wet and dry seasons. Nevertheless when this type of data

Table 4.2. *Ratio of the yield of modern rice varieties to local rice varieties*

	Philippines		Indonesia	India	Bangladesh
	Irrigated	Rainfed			
1968/69	1.1	1.0	—	1.9	—
1969/70	1.1	1.0	—	1.8	3.2
1970/71	1.1	1.0	—	1.9	3.3
1971/72	1.2	1.1	1.4	2.3	3.1
1972/73	1.1	1.2	1.4	2.5	2.7
1973/74	1.1	1.2	1.4	2.3	2.7
1974/75	1.2	1.2	1.4	1.7	2.5
1975/76	1.2	1.1	—	2.0	2.3
1976/77	1.2	1.3	—	2.1	2.3
1977/78	1.4	1.3	—	1.8	2.0
1978/79	1.3	1.3	—	—	—

Source: Herdt and Capule (1983).

is combined with the results of farm management surveys, it is clear that the HYVs do yield more per hectare than traditional varieties, although there is some evidence that performance may fall as the proportion of the total rice area devoted to the HYVs increase (Baker and Herdt (1985)).

An attractive feature of the Green Revolution is that, in principle, the new biological technology is scale-neutral: it may be adopted by small-scale as well as large-scale farmers. However, the institutional and policy setting (especially with respect to factor markets) in which the new technology has been introduced, has often been found to be biased in favour of the large farmers. Certainly the large farmers have been the first to adopt the new varieties, although there is evidence (Feder *et al.* (1985)) that small farmers eventually catch up.

There may be other reasons why some farmers cannot gain the benefits offered by the Green Revolution: the technology may not suit their climate and soil, there may be inadequate water resources, national research institutions which could adapt the varieties to local conditions may not exist, the transport and marketing infrastructure may be deficient, and prices and other incentives may be insufficient (World Bank (1982)).

The distribution of the socio-economic benefits of new technology has been a major topic of debate in the development literature. At one extreme, there is the view that the new technology is widening the gap between rich and poor and increasing consolidation of land and economic power in the hands of the few. At the other extreme, there are those who believe that technological change is a prerequisite of development and that its contribution should be judged independently of the distributional consequences of distortions in government policies and in the institutional setting. Moreover, in the latter view, attention should also be given to the consumer gains and the multiplier (indirect) effects in the wider economy, which the introduction of the new technology generates. A guide to some of the literature in the debate is given below in the *Further Reading* section.

4.4 *Risk and uncertainty*

The model of producer behaviour which has been presented in this chapter is the standard one of profit maximization under perfect knowledge or certainty. It offers an understanding of the fundamentals of economic logic but it may prove inadequate in some real world settings and more complex models may have to be constructed. In particular, as we have noted already, farmers operate under uncertainty[8] with respect to yields and prices of inputs and final products.[9]

Much work on models of risk and uncertainty has been undertaken, particularly in the late 1960s and 1970s, but a detailed account of these models would not be practicable here. However, we can note two broad approaches which have received particular attention. In the first of these approaches, the outcome of production decisions is not measured simply in monetary terms but by the satisfaction or *utility* which the outcome generates. In an uncertain environment where there are a number of possible outcomes, each with a probability of occurrence, the producer, it is assumed, will seek to maximise *expected utility*.[10] The production decision rule will depend on the farmer's attitude to risk. Typically the farmer in developing countries is thought to be 'risk averse', which in turn implies that he is willing to forgo some income in order to avoid risk. If the product price is uncertain (i.e. price is a random variable) and the farmer is risk averse, it can be shown that a smaller level of output would be produced than under perfect certainty. In this case, the farmer does not equate marginal cost to (average) price but rather will produce at a point where marginal cost will be somewhat less than that price.

In the second approach, risk is defined as the probability that income will fall below some critical minimum or disaster level. Several authors have developed 'Safety First' models in which security or safety varies inversely with risk and in which the producer is concerned with both income and security. One such model was developed by Roy (1952) who suggested that the '*safety first principle*' should be to choose the production plan which minimises the probability that profits will fall below a specified disaster level.[11] If the disaster level is taken to be the break-even point (i.e. there is no surplus once all production costs have been met; $\Pi = 0$), and if again product price is random, then it can be shown that the farmer will choose an output level which minimises the average costs of production.

It is important to recognise that the risk models not only suggest optimal levels of output which are different from that of the certainty model but also may predict different producer responses to changes in market conditions or in the policy setting. For example, if the (average) price increases, the certainty model and the expected utility model would predict a rise in output. However, no change in production would be forthcoming if Roy's 'safety principle' were followed.[12] It could also be the case that, for the risk averse farmer operating a risky multi-product enterprise, supply response to an increase in price will be negative (Just and Zilberman (1986)). Hence, perverse supply response becomes a theoretical possibility, once uncertainty is taken into account.

4.5 *Duality*

Physical and economic relationships in production theory are not simply of theoretical interest, they are of central importance to questions of economic, social and political development. There are many spheres of decision-making where it helps to have empirical estimates of (1) elasticities of substitution between factors of production, (2) input demand elasticities to prices, (3) output response elasticities to changes in input use, and (4) elasticities of output response (supply) to prices. The statistical estimation of parameters such as these relies heavily upon the formal theory of production, and takes full advantage of the properties of *duality* which exist within the theory.

The property of duality arises from the fact that the economic decisions taken by producers (or an industry in general) entail adjusting the physical processes of production for economic ends, where the physical processes can for simplicity[13] be thought of as being represented by a production function. Thus all the economic responses reflect the underlying physical relationships and, indeed, according to the theory of profit maximisation the coefficients of supply response or input demand to price are complex functions of the physical parameters of the underlying production function.

Perhaps the simplest way of explaining the essence of duality is to return and retrace some of the ground covered in Chapter 2. There on page 21, in introducing the concepts of variable and marginal costs, we stated simply 'However, variable costs are determined by the characteristics of the production technology.' In fact the relationship is a much stronger, more precise one than this statement might suggest. This can be readily seen by returning to the physical input output data in Table 2.1 and showing that with the addition solely of information about the price of the single variable input (fertiliser) the total variable, average variable and marginal costs are precisely determined.

The first four columns of Table 4.3 repeat the fertiliser input and maize output relationships presented in Table 2.1. Given the price of fertiliser, in this case assumed to be £50 per unit, the total variable cost (column 5 of Table 4.3) is easily computed. The calculation of average variable cost and marginal cost would proceed as follows. The first unit of fertiliser, costing £50, produces an additional 0.25 tonnes of maize, so average variable cost *and* marginal cost, expressed as a rate *per tonne* of output, is £200. Adding the second unit of fertiliser adds a further 0.75 tonne of maize so that average variable cost of the first tonne of maize is £100; marginal cost falls to £66.7 per tonne of maize, and so on. Given that our example is one in which only one factor is variable, the following relationships hold:[14]

> average variable cost (*AVC*) = price of fertiliser/average product (*AP*)
>
> marginal cost (*MC*) = price of fertiliser/marginal product (*MP*)

It will be noted that the 'shapes' of the marginal cost and average variable cost curves are the mirror images of, respectively, the marginal product and average product curves depicted in Table 2.1.

The purpose of this illustration has been to show that the cost curves are in fact based upon, and embody within them, the physical relationship of the production function. Insofar as each production function has a unique total variable cost function associated with it (for any given set of input prices) that cost function is said to be a *dual* of the production function. It is, with the input prices combined into it, an alternative way of expressing the production function. This is a very important property for empirical analysis by those who wish to measure at an aggregate level the sort of relationships referred to in the opening paragraph of this section.

Table 4.3. *Re-examination of the basis of cost curves*

Units of fertiliser input	Maize output (tonnes)	Average product of fertiliser (*AP*)	Marginal product of fertiliser (*MP*)	Total variable cost (*TVC*)	Average variable cost (*AVC*)	Marginal cost[a] (*MC*)
0	0	—	—	0	—	—
1	0.25	0.25	0.25	50	200	200
2	1.0	0.5	0.75	100	100	66.7
3	1.8	0.6	0.8	150	83.3	62.5
4	2.8	0.7	1.0	200	71.4	50.0
5	3.5	0.7	0.7	250	71.4	71.4
6	3.7	0.62	0.2	300	81.1	250.0
7	3.8	0.54	0.1	350	92.1	500.0
8	3.6	0.45	−0.2	400	111.1	−250.0[b]

[a] The marginal cost of output, expressed here as a rate per tonne, is calculated with reference to additional units of *input*. In Table 2.2 no reference was made to input quantities; costs were presented for each successive unit of output – implicitly associated with them were increases in input quantities.
[b] Marginal cost becomes negative since costs have increased but output has declined.

For instance if the appropriate data are available it would be possible to estimate a production function directly. But often the correct data are unobtainable and it would be easier (subject to the assumption that firms in the industry are cost-minimisers) to estimate the dual cost function in which costs of production are expressed as a function of input prices and the observed level of production. Provided that the data are generated by a process of cost minimisation the parameters of the production function could be obtained by mathematical transformation of the estimated cost function.

Formally the cost function, defined as the minimum cost required to produce a specified level of output, given input prices, is written as:

$$\tilde{C} = \tilde{C}\,(p_1, \ldots, p_n, \overline{Q}) \tag{4.1}$$

It can be shown that by differentiation, we can derive input demand functions which have as determinants input prices and the level of output.[15]

As we have demonstrated, the producer problem can be depicted as one of maximising profits, given product and input prices, and subject to the constraints of the production function. Once this problem is solved, we can derive the product supply function and input demand equations. In duality theory, however, we can make use of the *indirect profit function*, which is defined as the maximum profit associated with a given set of product and input prices. It may be written formally as:

$$\tilde{\Pi} = \tilde{\Pi}\,(P, p_1, \ldots, p_n) \tag{4.2}$$

This function, like the product supply and input demand functions discussed earlier, depends on the product and factor prices. Again it can be shown that by differentiating, we can derive the supply and input demand equations.[16] Thus, *if* we were given a mathematical specification of equation 4.2, it would be a simple matter to obtain the input demand and product supply equations and this can be a useful short cut. Further, note that as well as the equivalence between the production function and cost function already mentioned, there is an equivalence between the production function and the profit function. The dual functions all contain the same information.

The usefulness of these duality results in empirical work has been demonstrated by a number of studies. Examples of the use of profit functions in the analysis of input demand at the farm level are provided by Sidhu and Baanante (1981) for the Indian Punjab, Pitt (1983), for Java, and Haughton (1986) for West Malaysia. On the other hand, Henry

(1985) chose to estimate a cost function in his study of the Guyana rice industry.

4.6 *Conclusions*

In the development literature there has been much debate on the efficiency of peasant agriculture. In this chapter we have presented the economic principles underlying the concept of efficiency but we have argued that the term must be used with some caution. To be more specific, of the two components of economic efficiency, much of the controversy centres on allocative efficiency. The use of technical efficiency, which relies less heavily on assumptions of producer objectives, perfect knowledge and competitive markets, is not so problematic.

One of the main tasks of development policy is the promotion of technological change in the agricultural sector and so a substantial portion of this chapter has concerned the economic analysis of technical change. Whilst an understanding of these principles is essential for the agricultural economist working in the development area, there are other issues which we have barely touched upon. In particular the distribution of the benefits of technological change may be biased towards specific agro-climatic regions and particular groups within the agricultural sector. What we would stress however is that many of the problems of distribution arise not so much because of the nature of technology or the economic forces which it sets in motion, but rather because of distortions created by the country's social and political infrastructure, which after all is not immutable.

4.7 *Summary points*

1. *Economic efficiency* can be decomposed into *technical efficiency* (where maximum output is obtained from a given set of inputs) and *allocative efficiency* (where, given input prices, factors are used in proportions which maximise producer profits).
2. The relevance of the concept of efficiency (and of allocative efficiency in particular) has been questioned, principally in those cases where prices are distorted, and producers have imperfect knowledge and may pursue goals other than profit maximisation.
3. *Technological change* is an improvement in the state of knowledge such that production possibilities are enhanced. Technological change may be *biased* and in particular may be *labour-saving*. The chief sources of technological change are 'learning

by using', private and public research and development, and imported research and development.

4. The decision of whether or not to *adopt* a new technology will depend on its technical attributes and economic potential, the characteristics of the farmer (in terms of age, education and experience) and whether there are constraints on purchasing power, access to credit and information or poor communication links with product and input markets.
5. The *diffusion* of a new technology over time or across a given population of farmers will depend on social, cultural and institutional factors, as well as on whether the technology is only usable in particular agro-climatic conditions.
6. Farmers make their production decisions with imperfect knowledge of the outcome of these decisions. Specifically they operate under *uncertainty* regarding yields and prices. The analysis of markets with risk and uncertainty calls for more complex models and these may yield very different results from models assuming perfect information.
7. By making use of *duality* theory the producer's problem of finding the profit maximising level of output can be represented in a number of equivalent ways. Duality theorems demonstrate an equivalence between the *production function and the cost function* and between the *production function and the profit function*.

Further reading

Many of the issues concerning technological change in agriculture in developing countries are reviewed in Hazell and Anderson (1986). Of particular note is their discussion of the impact of the Green Revolution on income distribution, which contrasts the earlier, pessimistic evaluation (e.g. Griffin (1979)) with more recent, and more optimistic, evidence (e.g. Pinstrup-Anderson (1982)). Eicher and Staatz (1985) present a number of interesting papers on issues concerning agricultural growth. Feder *et al.* (1985) provide a useful survey of the literature on adoption of agricultural innovations. Thirtle and Ruttan (1987) review the literature on the impact of economic forces on the generation and diffusion of technical change.

In this chapter we have not considered the origins of technology or, more precisely, the determinants of the type of research which is undertaken. One view, put forward by Hayami and Ruttan (1985) and quite pervasive in the development economics literature, is that new technologies reflect the relative scarcity of factors in agriculture and that research in both private and public agencies responds to long term trends in relative factor prices.

We have also omitted any discussion of *appropriate technology* for developing countries. Two polar views in the debate are those of Schumacher (1974), that 'small is beautiful', and of Emmanuel (1982) that 'appropriate technology is underdeveloped technology'. Stewart (1978) discusses the characteristics of appropriate technology and considers the difficulties of getting such a technology developed and used. A persuasive approach, suggested by McInerney (1978), is to focus less on the characteristics of particular pieces of 'hardware' and more on the full effects (including the indirect impact on the broader economic, social, political and environmental infrastructure) of introducing any technological package.

For those wishing to pursue the discussion of duality in production economics Beattie and Taylor (1985) and Debertin (1986) are useful references. Heathfield and Wibe (1987) introduce major recent developments in the economics of production and cost functions.

5

Theory of consumer behaviour

5.1 *Introduction*

The purpose of all agricultural production is the satisfaction of consumer wants. In this chapter we will present an analytical framework with which consumer behaviour can be studied. At the outset we must distinguish between human requirements in physiological or nutritional terms and demand for agricultural products which is expressed in economic terms. The study of the former, while useful as a means of identifying instances of malnutrition or other forms of deprivation, does not offer any information on how consumption patterns alter as consumers' economic circumstances change. The analysis of a number of important policy questions requires an understanding of consumer demand as expressed in the marketplace.

For example, the policy analyst might require information on the following:

In the course of economic development with average incomes rising, which sectors in the economy will prosper and which will decline in importance? Within the agricultural sector, which producers will enjoy an increasing demand for their products and which producers will face a stagnant or declining market?

How would the pattern of consumption change, if the distribution of income were to change? Will an increased rate of urbanisation have any effect on consumption?

If the price of a particular food product is changed, say by imposing a sales tax or a subsidy, how will consumers respond? What will be the effect on consumption of that product, the consumption of other foods, the government exchequer etc.?

A basis for theoretical and empirical work on these types of questions is provided by the traditional or neoclassical model of consumer behaviour and it is with this approach that this chapter is concerned. In the traditional model, the consumer, it is hypothesised, has some sense of preference among different products and he or she will attempt to get the most satisfaction out of consumption allowed by a limited budget. The decision-making unit is taken to be the individual consumer, although the analysis could apply equally to the household, provided the one who controls the purse-strings also acts to maximise the welfare of the whole household. In presenting the model, extensive use is made of indifference curves. This piece of apparatus is not strictly necessary to derive the main conclusions of demand theory but it is nevertheless adopted here for two reasons. In the first place, indifference curves, although fundamentally rather abstract, are extremely useful analytical devices in a number of settings and since we will wish to use them later in this book, it is convenient to introduce them at this point. The second reason is that the neoclassical demand model specified in this form is completely symmetric with the production model of Chapter 2, where isoquants in production take the place of indifference curves in consumption. In this way the elegance of the neoclassical approach is made the more apparent.

5.2 *The basic relationships*

A consumer's demand for a commodity is the amount of it which the consumer is willing and able to buy, under given conditions, per unit of time, in a specified market, and at specified prices. It should be stressed at the outset that *demand is not the same as desire or need.* The economic analysis of demand is concerned with actual market behaviour. Willingness to purchase the commodity is clearly a necessary condition but it is not enough: the potential consumer must also have the ability to purchase the good.[1] As already noted, this distinction is particularly important when the analysis concerns the demand for food and the design of food policy.

Traditional economic theory suggests that, given the consumer's tastes and preferences, the demand for a commodity will be determined by:

the price of the product;
the prices of other products;
the consumer's income.

It is hypothesised that the consumer gains *satisfaction*, *welfare*, or *utility* from the consumption of goods and in deciding how much of each good to purchase, he or she will try to obtain the greatest possible satisfaction. The choice, however, is constrained by the consumer's *purchasing power* or income, and will be influenced by *the prices of the goods available*. The theory recognises that consumer behaviour will depend to some degree on individual preferences, which may be linked to the age, sex, education, religion, social class, location or other characteristics of the consumer. However, the theory does not attempt to explain the formation of tastes (this is left to the behavioural scientists) but rather it asserts that at a given point in time, a consumer's tastes and preferences can be taken as given.

Based on these assumptions about the consumer, the theory presented in Section 5.3 will be used in Section 5.4, to derive the following three basic relationships:

The demand function. The relationship between the quantities of a good (say Q_1) and the economic factors which influence the consumer's choice can be conveniently summarised in the *demand function*:

$$Q_1 = f(P_1, P_2, \ldots, P_n, M) \tag{5.1}$$

where Q_1 is the quantity of the good purchased in a given time period, $P_1, \ldots, P_n$ are the prices of the (n) consumer goods in the market and M denotes the consumer's income. This relationship, which will be derived formally below, is specified given the consumer's tastes.

In the analysis of applied economics problems it is useful to present graphically elements of this demand relationship. Two devices are often employed: the *demand curve* and the *Engel curve*.

The demand curve. The demand curve, or demand schedule, is the representation of the quantities of the commodity which the consumer is willing and able to purchase at every possible price over the relevant range, all other factors being held constant. A typical demand curve is presented in Fig. 5.1. It is downward sloping indicating an inverse relationship between price and quantity, i.e. the lower the price, the more Q_1 the consumer will buy. A change in (own) price would induce a movement *along* the demand curve. As all other factors are held constant, the demand curve can be represented mathematically as:

$$Q_1 = f(P_1 \mid P_2, \ldots, P_n, M)$$

Note that if there is a change in income or in a price other than P_1, the whole demand curve will *shift*. Shifts in the demand curve are considered in Chapter 6.

The Engel curve. The Engel curve depicts the relationship between the quantity of a good purchased and consumer income, all other factors held constant. If, as income rises, the consumer chooses to buy more of a particular commodity, the commodity is termed a *normal good* (Fig. 5.2(*a*)). On the other hand, if less of a good is purchased as income rises, the commodity is termed an *inferior good* (Fig. 5.2(*b*)). Some foods (perhaps wheat and rice) which may be normal goods at low income levels may become inferior goods at high income levels. Thus at higher incomes beef, poultry, fish and dairy products might be examples of normal goods, whereas staples such as millet, sorghum, root crops and beans might be inferior goods.

Fig. 5.1. The demand curve.

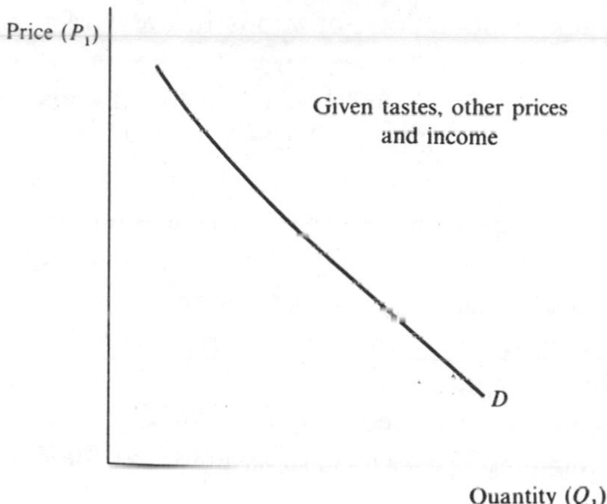

Fig. 5.2. The Engel curve.

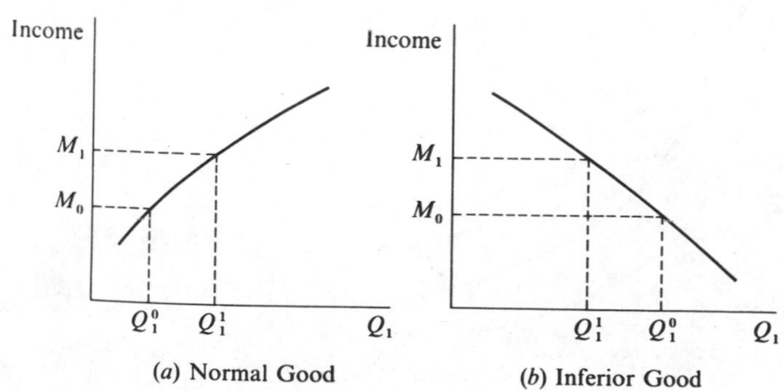

The Engel curve is the graphical representation of the following form of the demand function:

$$Q_1 = f(M \mid P_1, P_2, \ldots, P_n)$$

5.3 *The analysis of consumer choice*

As noted above, it is hypothesised that the consumer seeks to maximise the satisfaction derived from the consumption of goods and services. The precise relationship between the consumers' satisfaction and consumption need not be specified. Consumer theory only requires that a number of general propositions about the nature of consumer preferences should hold. These are:

The consumer can compare any two combinations (or bundles) of goods and decide whether one bundle is preferred to the other or that he or she is indifferent between them, i.e. the consumer can rank combinations of goods in order of preference.

The consumer is consistent in his or her choices. In particular, if bundle A is preferred to bundle B and bundle B is preferred to a third bundle, C, then the consumer will prefer bundle A to bundle C. This is known as the *transitivity* assumption.

The consumer prefers more of a good to less of it. If bundle A contains more of one good and no less of the other goods than bundle B, then A will always be preferred to B. This is the *non-satiation* assumption.

Consumer preferences can be illustrated graphically using a device known as an *indifference map* (Fig. 5.3). Here we assume that there are

Fig. 5.3. The indifference map.

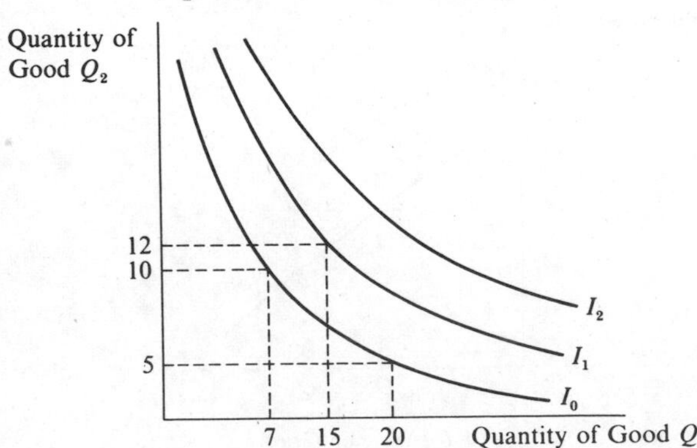

only two goods, Q_1 and Q_2. For example, Q_1 might be 'food' and Q_2 might represent the aggregate quantity of all other goods. Each *indifference curve* (I_0, I_1, I_2) identifies the various combinations of Q_1 and Q_2 which yield the *same* level of satisfaction. Hence five units of Q_2 with 20 units of Q_1 is as satisfactory to the consumer as 10 units of Q_2 and 7 units of Q_1 (both points lie on the same curve I_0). The combination of 12 units of Q_2 and 15 units of Q_1 is preferred and hence is associated with a higher indifference curve (I_1). The assumptions of non-satiation and transitivity imply that no two indifference curves can intersect.

The indifference curve is assumed to be smooth, downward sloping and convex to the origin.[2] Its particular shape reflects a *diminishing marginal rate of substitution* between the two goods. If the quantity of Q_2 is successively reduced by equal amounts, increasing quantities of Q_1 are required to leave the consumer indifferent to the change. The marginal rate of substitution (*MRS*) is the term given to the slope of the indifference curve: the slope becomes less steep as the quantity of the commodity measured on the horizontal axis (Q_1) increases.

$$\text{Slope of the indifference curve} = \frac{\Delta Q_2}{\Delta Q_1} = MRS \text{ of } Q_1 \text{ for } Q_2$$

At any given time, the consumer has a fixed money income which will act as a constraint on consumption behaviour. Given consumer income (M_0) and commodity prices (P_1 and P_2), the limits to choice can be represented by a *budget line* (Fig. 5.4). If the consumer spends all available

Fig. 5.4. The budget line.

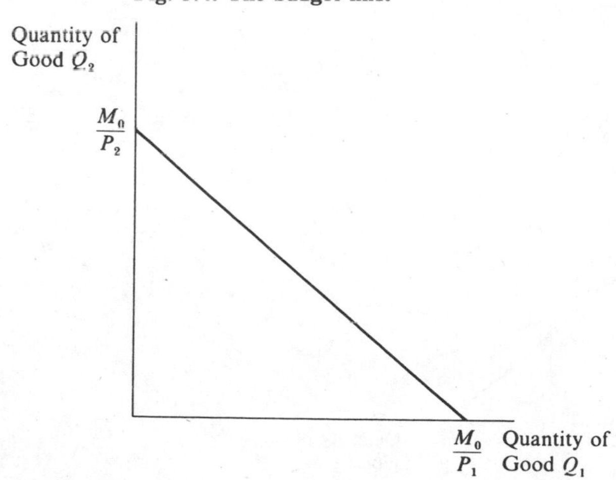

income on Q_1, then at most M_0/P_1 units of Q_1 could be obtained. On the other hand, if all income is spent on Q_2, M_0/P_2 units of that good could be purchased. Alternatively some combination of the two goods could be chosen. *The budget line depicts the budget constraint or the set of maximum feasible consumption choices, given the levels of income and prices.*[3] Its slope[4] is given as the ratio of the two product prices, P_1/P_2. A consumer with a higher income would have a greater choice available. The budget line would be further out from the origin but, since the consumer faces the same relative prices, it would have the same slope.

The consumer will wish to select the consumption pattern out of all those available which will yield the highest possible level of satisfaction. In terms of Fig. 5.5, this will be the combination of Q_1 and Q_2 associated with the highest attainable indifference curve. *The point of tangency between this highest attainable indifference curve and the budget line defines the optimal consumption pattern,* Q_1^* *and* Q_2^*. Hence consumer equilibrium[5] is found at the point where the slope of the indifference curve is the same as that of the budget line i.e.

$$MRS \text{ of } Q_1 \text{ for } Q_2 = (-)\frac{P_1}{P_2} \tag{5.2}$$

This equilibrium condition applies to all consumers, irrespective of the position of their indifference curves. Each consumer, in seeking maximum satisfaction from consumption will equate his/her marginal rate of substitution with the ratio of commodity prices. But all consumers in a given market face the same relative prices and so, at equilibrium, all

Fig. 5.5. The consumer equilibrium.

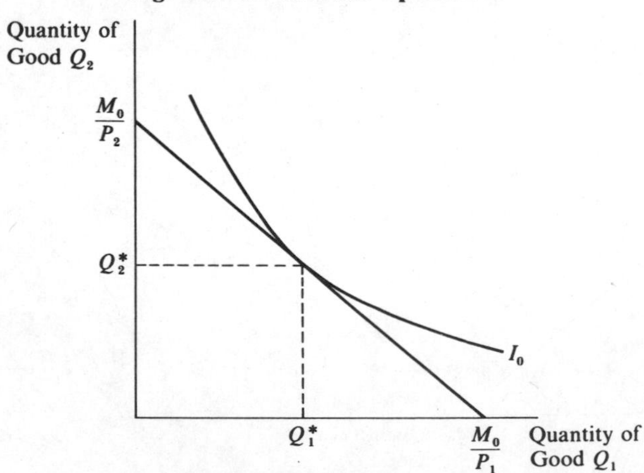

consumers have the same rate of commodity substitution. Relative prices therefore provide a direct measure of the rate at which consumers substitute one good for another.

BOX 5.1
The form of the budget constraint

The budget line in Fig. 5.4 defines the consumer's range of choices, given fixed income and commodity prices.[6] Consumer choice will be further constrained however, if there are some basic survival needs which must be met. This complication is illustrated in Fig. 5.6, in which minimum required quantities of food and shelter are denoted by Q_1^{min} and Q_2^{min} respectively. Since these needs must be met, the 'free' choice of a consumer with budget line AB would be restricted to the area *EFG*. Clearly the lower the consumer's income, the more the basic survival requirements will constrain choice. If income were so low that only the minimum quantities could be purchased (the budget line *CD* passes through point *E*), then the consumer has no choice whatsoever.

In the analysis in this chapter we will assume that the budget constraint which delineates the consumer's set of consumption choices is linear. However there may be instances in which this assumption is inappropriate. One such case might be the barter economy in which goods are traded directly for other goods. The costs of undertaking transactions and of obtaining information on trading opportunities may be high in such a system. In particular it may be a difficult and time-consuming task to discover who is willing to trade and at what rates of exchange. Consider Fig. 5.7 in which a consumer's initial endowment of two goods, food and clothing, is

Fig. 5.6. Basic survival needs.

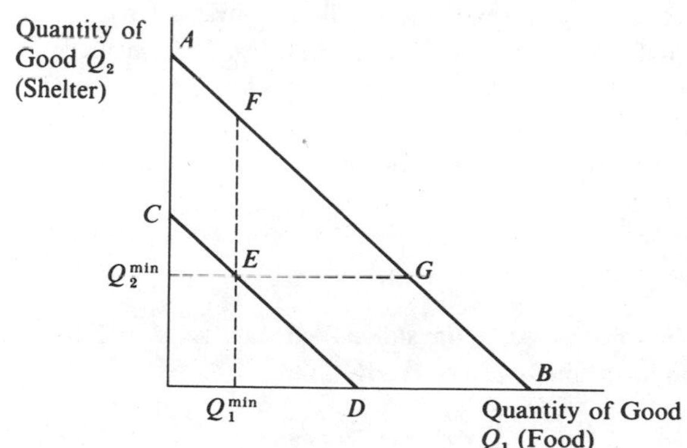

Fig. 5.7. The barter market.

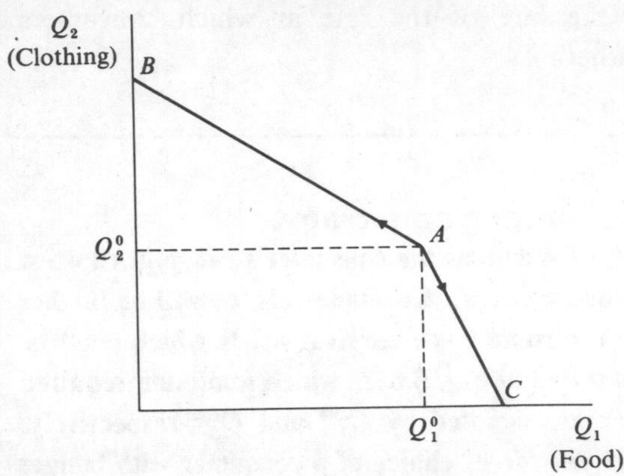

represented by point A. Because of information costs the rate of exchange at which the consumer could trade food for clothing (along AB) is likely to differ from the rate at which clothing could be traded for food (along AC). In this case, the 'price' of food (in terms of clothing) is lower when the consumer 'sells' food (i.e. gives up some food for extra clothing) than when clothing is sold for additional units of food. This type of non-linear constraint is unlikely to occur in a fully monetised, competitive economy.

Formal derivation – the utility maximising equilibrium

It is postulated that for each consumer there exists a *utility function* of the general form

$$U = U(Q_1, \ldots, Q_n)$$

where $Q_1, \ldots, Q_n$ are the quantities of the (n) goods consumed by him or her and U denotes the total utility or satisfaction attained as a result. The precise nature of this functional relationship will be governed by the particular tastes and preferences of the individual consumer. The consumer has a given money income (M) and faces given market prices $P_1, \ldots, P_n$ at which the commodities may be purchased.

Formally the consumer problem may be stated as

$$\text{maximise } U = U(Q_1, \ldots, Q_n)$$

$$\text{subject to } P_1Q_1 + P_2Q_2 + \ldots + P_nQ_n = M$$

This is a problem in constrained optimisation and can be solved by the 'Lagrangian multipliers' method. We specify

$$L = U(Q_1, \ldots, Q_n) + \lambda(M - P_1Q_1 - P_2Q_2 - \ldots - P_nQ_n)$$

It can be shown that maximisation of L implies maximisation of the utility function. The first order conditions for the maximum are obtained by differentiating L with respect to $Q_1, \dots, Q_n$ and λ, and by equating each term to zero.

$$\frac{\partial L}{\partial Q_i} = \frac{\partial U}{\partial Q_i} - \lambda P_i = 0 \quad i = 1, \dots, n$$

$$\frac{\partial L}{\partial \lambda} = M - P_1 Q_1 - \dots - P_n Q_n = 0$$

We will not present the second order conditions but merely assert that these conditions will be fulfilled if the indifference curves are convex to the origin.

Returning to the first order conditions, we have $(n+1)$ equations in $(n+1)$ unknowns $(Q_1, \dots, Q_n, \lambda)$. Thus, in principle, we can solve the system of equations and specifically the solution will yield the (utility-maximising) demand functions (c.f. equation 5.1 which is written for $i = 1$):

$$Q_i = f_i(P_1, \dots, P_n, M) \quad i = 1, \dots, n \tag{5.3}$$

It should be stressed that, according to the traditional theory of demand, the consumer's demand for a given product will depend on the prices of *all* goods in the market, as well as consumer income.

In addition, we should note that $\partial U/\partial Q_i$ is the marginal utility of good i and so the first order conditions also inform us that (by taking the ratio of any two of the first n equations),

$$\frac{MU_i}{MU_j} = \frac{P_i}{P_j} \tag{5.4}$$

It can be shown (Koutsoyiannis (1979, Ch. 21)) that the ratio of marginal utilities is equivalent to the slope of the indifference curve, which in turn describes the marginal rate of substitution. Hence equations 5.4 and 5.2 denote the same equilibrium condition.

5.4 *Variations in the consumer's equilibrium*

We will now proceed to analyse the effect of price and income changes by examining how they change equilibrium consumption via different types of shift in the budget constraint.

If consumer income increases, with product prices remaining the same, there will be a parallel shift in the budget line to the right. The increased purchasing power permits more of both goods to be purchased. A new equilibrium will be found at the point of tangency between the budget line and a (higher) indifference curve. The locus of such equilibria as income changes is termed the *income-consumption line* (ICL). One such locus is depicted in Fig. 5.8(*a*). We cannot make a general prediction as to how consumption of the commodities will change: the response to the income change will depend on whether the good in question is a normal or an inferior one. In Fig. 5.8(*a*), both goods are normal and so their consumption increases as income rises. In Fig. 5.8(*b*), good Q_2 is again normal but Q_1 is inferior; with the increase in income, consumption of Q_1 falls.

By tracing out the relationship between consumption of a particular good and income (i.e. the combinations of Q_1^0 *and* M_0, Q_1' and M_1, etc.), we derive the Engel curves of Fig. 5.2.

Variations in the consumer optimum which are due to changes in price may be analysed with the aid of the *price-consumption line*. If the price of a commodity (say Q_1) falls, *ceteris paribus* the budget line swivels in the manner shown in Fig. 5.9(*a*). The maximum amount of Q_2 which can be bought has not changed but the budget constraint now cuts the Q_1 axis at a higher level, since, with the same income, more of this good can now be obtained. For each price of Q_1 there is a preferred consumer equilibrium and the locus of these points generates the price-consumption line (*PCL*) in Fig. 5.9(*b*). In this figure, as the price of Q_1 falls, the consumption of both goods increases i.e. the goods are *complements*. We might have this type of price-consumption line if, for example, Q_1 and Q_2 were coffee and sugar respectively. Hence as the price of coffee falls, the demand for coffee increases and this in turn induces an increase in sugar consumption. Alternatively, the goods being analysed might be *substitutes*, yielding a

Fig. 5.8. The income–consumption line.

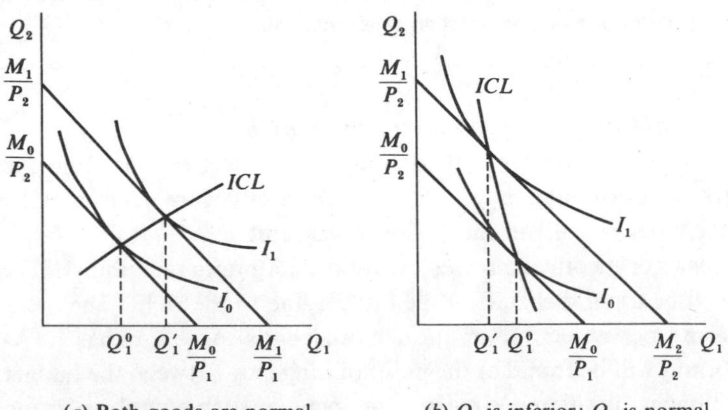

(*a*) Both goods are normal

(*b*) Q_1 is inferior; Q_2 is normal

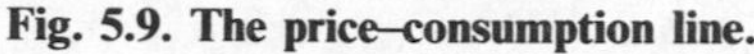

Fig. 5.9. The price–consumption line.

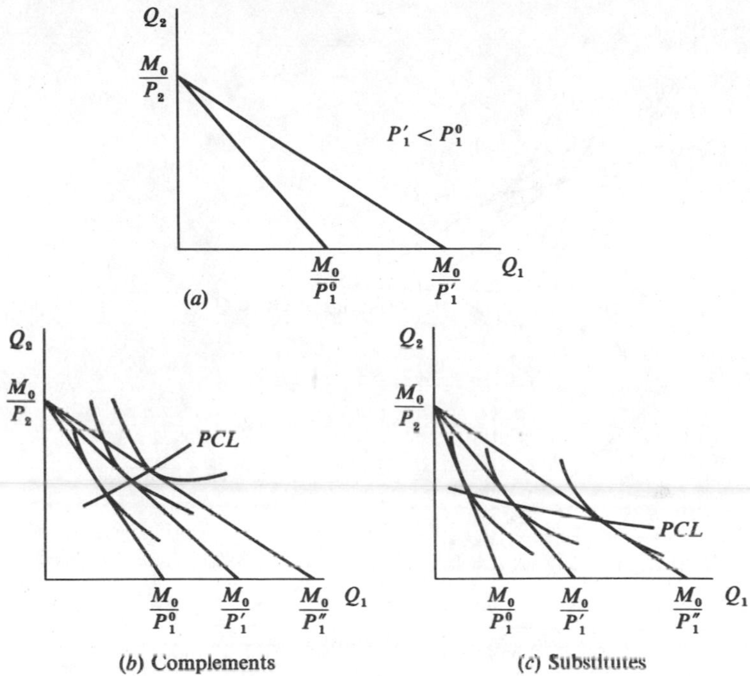

price consumption line of the form in Fig. 5.9(*c*). In this case, as the consumption of Q_1 (say, coffee) increases in response to the fall in its price, the consumption of Q_2 (say, tea) decreases.

As the price of Q_1 falls (from P_1^0 to P_1' to P_1''), *ceteris paribus*, the associated quantities (Q_1^0, Q_1' and Q_1'') can be read off the price–consumption line. These combinations can be plotted, thus generating the *demand curve* for good Q_1. This is illustrated in Fig. 5.10.

BOX 5.2
Food subsidies

Indifference curve analysis can be used to explore the effects of alternative government policies on the consumer. Suppose the government is considering the adoption of a programme to increase the welfare of some needy section of the community and that this might take the form of a price subsidy on bread.

Denote the consumption of bread by Q_1 and that of all other goods by Q_2. The initial equilibrium of a consumer representative of the target

Fig. 5.10. Derivation of the demand curve.

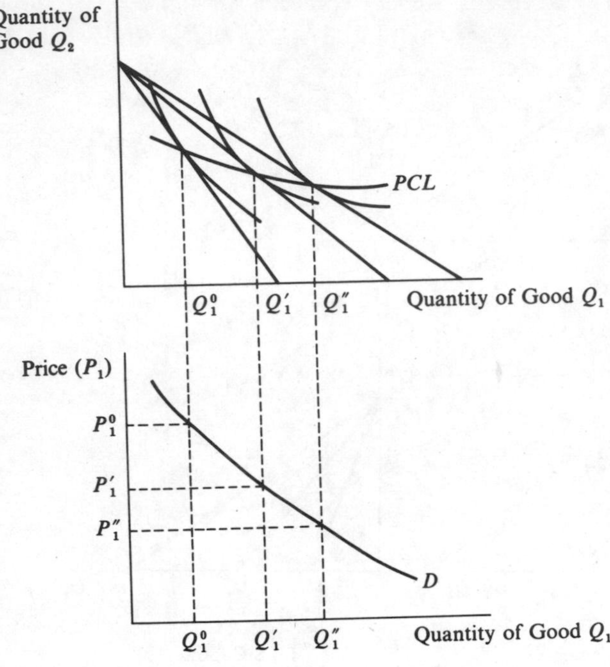

Fig. 5.11. Food subsidy.

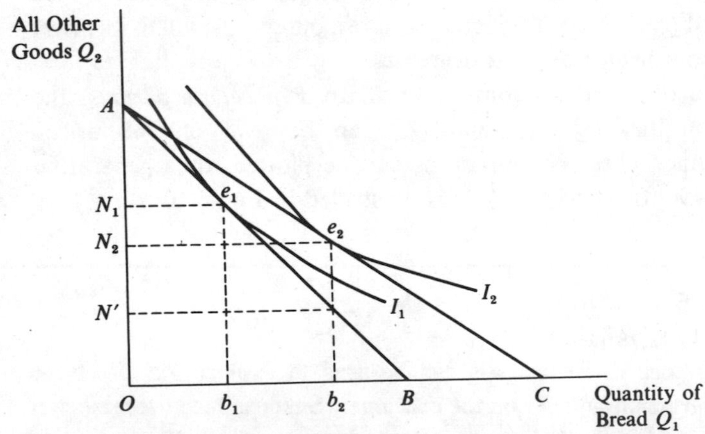

group, given the budget line AB, is illustrated in Fig. 5.11 as point e_1. In the absence of government intervention, the consumer chooses Ob_1 units of bread and ON_1 units of all other goods.

Under the food subsidy programme, the consumer is able to purchase

bread at a lower price, indicated by the new budget line AC. (We assume that consumers outside the target group are unaffected by this policy and so continue to buy the goods at the original prices.) At the subsidised price, the consumer attains a higher level of satisfaction of welfare (I_2) consuming more bread (Ob_2) and less of other goods (ON_2). This level of bread consumption costs AN_2 in terms of foregone consumption of all other goods. That is to say, since the consumer can at most purchase OA of other goods then if ON_2 units are chosen, AN_2 units have been given up. However, in the absence of the policy, the same quantity of bread would have cost the consumer AN' (i.e. at the old prices, the consumer could only obtain Ob_2 units of bread by giving up AN' units of other goods). The difference, ($AN' - AN_2$) or N_2N', must be paid to the bread producers by the government. It thus represents the cost to the taxpayer of the food subsidy programme. This analysis is taken a little further in Box. 5.3.

5.5 *Income and substitution effects*

The demand curve indicates the change in consumption, as the consumer moves from one equilibrium to another, in response to a price change, *ceteris paribus*. For some analytical purposes it is useful to decompose this overall change or *total effect* into two separate elements. In the first place, there is a change in relative price i.e. a change in the terms at which one product can be exchanged for another. The change in relative price will induce a *substitution effect*. In addition, when a product price changes, with money income and all other prices held constant, the *real* purchasing power or *real* income of the consumer also changes. In other words, the market opportunities open to the consumer will alter. Specifically, if a product price falls, real income (and with it, the level of satisfaction) rises, and *vice versa*. The change in real income induces an *income effect* on quantity demanded.[7]

Let us define these terms rather more precisely. The *total effect* of a price change is the total change in quantity demanded as the consumer moves from one equilibrium to another; it can be measured from the demand curve. The total effect of a price change can be divided into two components: (1) the *income effect*, which is the change in quantity demanded resulting from a change in *real income*, all prices and money income held constant, and (2) the *substitution effect*, which is the change in quantity demanded resulting exclusively from a change in *relative price*, after compensating the consumer for the change in real income.

Fig. 5.12 illustrates how the decomposition of the total effect for a good

Q_1 can be analysed when its price changes. For a number of analytical purposes it is useful to treat Q_2 as 'all other commodities'. If commodity Q_1 accounts for only a small proportion of the consumer budget, expenditure on Q_2 will be approximately equal to money income. The initial equilibrium of the consumer is denoted by point e_0, where Q_1^0 of good Q_1 is consumed. With a *fall* in the price of Q_1, the budget line swivels to the right and a new equilibrium is established at e_1, with a higher consumption level of Q_1'. The change in Q_1 consumption, $(Q_1' - Q_1^0)$, defines the *total effect*.

In this example, the consumer's real income has risen, as indicated by the movement to the higher indifference curve (I_1). In order to gauge the effect of this change, we must 'adjust' income to keep the consumer's real purchasing power as before. This (hypothetical) adjustment is termed *compensating variation* and is shown graphically by a parallel shift in the new budget line (represented by the dashed line) until it is tangential to the original indifference curve (I_0). At this point (e') the consumer faces the new relative price but is at the same level of satisfaction as before the price change occurred.

The *substitution effect* (*SE*) is measured as the change in consumption as the consumer moves along the original indifference curve from e^0 to e' i.e. $(Q_1'' - Q_1^0)$. It is the result of the change in relative price, with real income constant. Here, since Q_1 is now relatively cheaper than Q_2, the substitution effect induces a higher level of Q_1 consumption. Indeed the substitution effect is always *negative* i.e. as price falls, the substitution effect will always increase consumption.

Fig. 5.12. Income and substitution effects.

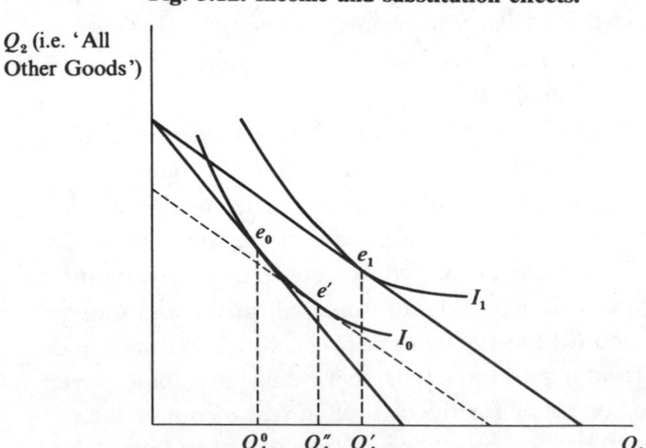

The income effect (*IE*) is measured by the change in consumption due exclusively to the change in real income. In Fig. 5.12, arising from the movement e' to e_1, this change in consumption is $(Q_1' - Q_1'')$. In our example, real income rises, as a result of the price change, and the income effect induces an increase in consumption. Thus Q_1 is a *normal good* (as defined in Section 5.2). In Fig. 5.12, the substitution effect and the income both indicate a higher level of consumption in response to the fall in price.

If Q_1 were an *inferior good* (as defined in Section 5.2), the income effect and the substitution effect would work in opposite directions. This is illustrated in Fig. 5.13, where, again for a price fall, the substitution effect increases the quantity demanded $(Q_1'' - Q_1^0)$ but, in response to the rise in real income, the consumer reduces consumption of the inferior good $(Q_1' - Q_1'')$. Nevertheless in this case the substitution effect outweighs the income effect so that the overall change (the total effect) as a result of the price fall, is an increase in quantity demanded.[8]

As noted above, the demand curve incorporates both the substitution effect and the income effect of price changes. However, a special type of demand curve, called the *compensated demand curve*, can be constructed. This curve measures the substitution effect only and is drawn for a constant level of *real* income. It is a useful device in some applications of welfare economics and so will be discussed in more detail in Chapter 10.

Fig. 5.13. Income and substitution effects – inferior good.

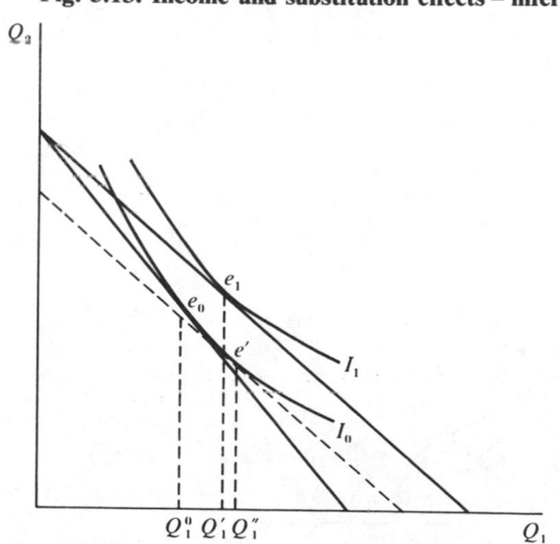

BOX 5.3
Income supplements vs. food subsidies

An alternative policy to the food subsidy programme of Box 5.2 might be a direct income supplement to consumers in the target group. For purposes of exposition, let us assume that bread (Q_1) does not account for a large proportion of the consumer budget, in which case Q_2, 'all other goods', will provide an approximation of money income.

Before government intervention, the typical consumer in the target group would be at equilibrium at e_1, in Fig. 5.14. The higher level of satisfaction or welfare (I_2) which was attained by introducing a subsidy could be reached by augmenting consumer income by *AD*, the income supplement being represented by a parallel shift in the budget line to *DE*. At the new equilibrium, e_3, the consumer buys more bread (Ob_3), as well as a greater quantity of other goods (ON_3). The cost of the programme to the government (or rather the taxpayers) would be *AD*.

Let us now compare the two programmes by superimposing the food subsidy diagram (Fig. 5.11) upon Fig. 5.14 to produce Fig. 5.15. In this example, the consumer purchases more bread under the food subsidy policy than under the income supplement programme. This may be an important consideration if the government is concerned to increase the level of nutrition in the target group or if there is surplus production to be disposed of. How do the costs of the programmes compare? As noted above, the cost of the food subsidy programme is N_2N'. On the other hand, the income supplement programme costs the taxpayer less i.e. $AD = FG$ is less than N_2N'. So if

Fig. 5.14. Income supplement.

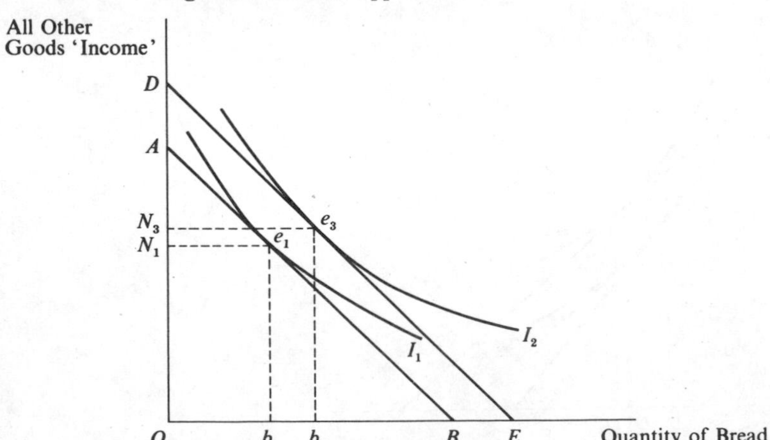

budget considerations are uppermost, the income supplement would be preferred.

5.6 *Summary points*

1. In the same way that production theory begins with the individual firm, *demand theory takes the individual consumer* as the decision-making unit and establishes a number of propositions about how the individual responds to changes in market conditions.
2. While it is recognised that *tastes and preferences* are important determinants of consumer behaviour, the theory is not concerned with the formation of tastes. At a given point in time, *tastes are taken as given.*
3. Given the consumer's tastes and preferences, the demand for a commodity will be determined by the price of the product, the prices of other products and the consumer's income.
4. Tastes and preferences reflect, among other things, the need for basic necessities. Demand theory relates to the economic behaviour of consumers attempting to satisfy their needs and wants with limited incomes. Given income and market forces *what some consumers are able to purchase may be insufficient for their needs.*
5. The *demand curve* depicts the relationship between quantities

Fig. 5.15. Food subsidy vs. income supplement.

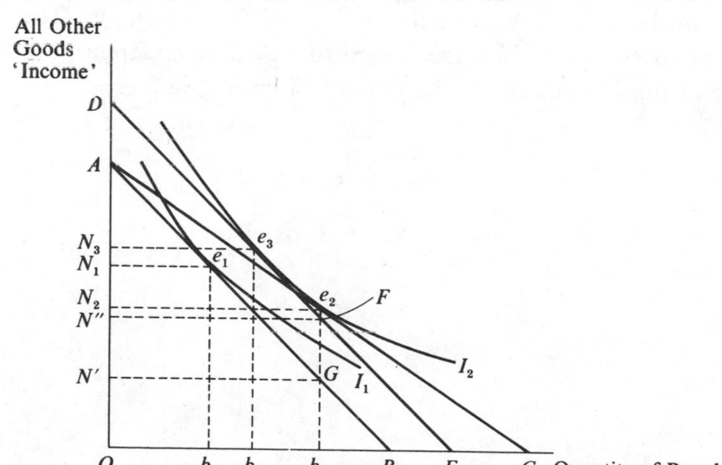

which the consumer is willing to purchase and the product's price, all other factors held constant. The *Engel curve* plots the relationship between quantities which the consumer is willing to buy and the consumer's income, all other factors held constant.

6. The consumer's equilibrium, or point of maximum satisfaction, is established where the *marginal rate of substitution* between two goods in consumption is equated to the (inverse) ratio of their prices. Hence relative prices provide a direct measure of the rate at which consumers substitute one product for another.
7. For some analytical purposes it is useful to decompose the effect of a price change on consumption into two separate elements: the *substitution effect* which is induced solely by the change in relative prices (with real income held constant) and the *income effect* which is created by the change in *real* income.

Further reading

Most standard economics textbooks will cover many of the aspects of demand theory covered in this chapter e.g. Samuelson and Nordhaus (1984, Chapter 19), Begg, Fischer and Dornbusch (1984, Chapters 4 and 5), and Call and Holahan (1983, Chapter 3). Good introductions to the traditional theory can also be found in Laidler (1981) and Green (1976).

For specific treatment of demand for agricultural products, the reader is referred to Ritson (1977) and Tomek and Robinson (1981).

As noted in the introduction to this chapter, the main theoretical conclusions can be derived without the use of indifference curves. The alternative approach is based on the notion of 'revealed preference'. A brief outline of this hypothesis can be found in Lipsey (1983).

6

Economics of market demand

6.1 *Introduction*

The traditional theory of demand, outlined in the preceding chapter, is based on an analysis of the individual consumer. However in applied economics we are rarely concerned with the actions of the individual; rather for many analytical purposes we are interested in *market demand* i.e. the aggregate demand of a number of individuals in a specified market.[1] Certainly the typical producer will wish to focus on the actions of consumers as a group, the total demand for the product, rather than the purchases of any single consumer.

6.2 *Basic demand relationships*

6.2.1 *The market demand curve*

The market demand curve may be simply constructed by horizontally summing every individual demand curve in the market. As we have noted, the demand curve for the individual consumer is drawn given the particular level of income of that consumer. The position of the market demand curve will therefore depend both on the number of

Fig. 6.1. The market demand curve.

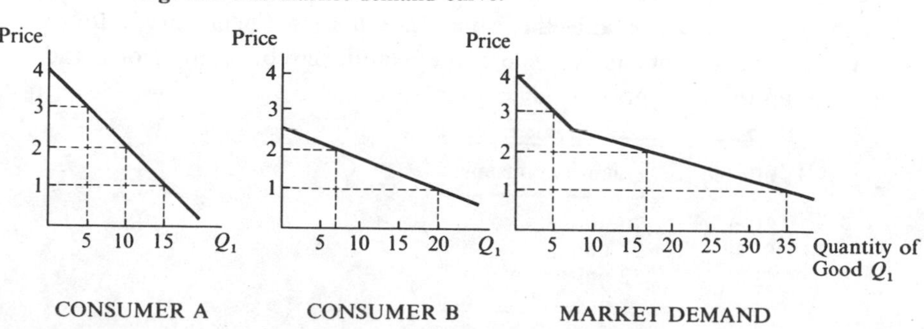

individuals included in the summation (i.e. the market population) and on the level of income which each consumer receives (i.e. the distribution of income). Fig. 6.1 illustrates the derivation of a market demand curve for a market in which there are only two consumers (*A* and *B*). At a price of £3, market demand for good Q_1 is 5 units (i.e. the 5 units purchased by *A*). At the lower price of £2, market demand increases to 17 units (10 units from *A* plus 7 units from *B*). At £1, *A* consumes 15 units and *B* 20 units, giving a market demand of 35 units.

6.2.2 *The market demand function*

The market demand function for Q_1 may then be specified as:

$$Q_1 = f(P_1, \ldots, P_n, M, POP, ID)$$

But since Q_1 is just one product in the full set of *n* products in the market, it is convenient to write a general demand function:

$$Q_i = f_i(P_1, \ldots, P_n, M, POP, ID) \quad i = 1, \ldots, n \tag{6.1}$$

where Q_i denotes the total demand for the *i*th product, *M* is defined as per caput income, *POP* is the market population and *ID* is an index of income distribution. As before, $P_1, \ldots, P_n$ denote the per unit prices of all the market goods. To demonstrate the properties of the demand function, it was useful in the preceding chapter to vary one parameter while maintaining the *ceteris paribus* assumption (i.e. holding all other parameters constant). It would however be unrealistic to follow that approach in the analysis of the variable, *POP*. If there is a change in population, it is likely to affect per caput income (viz. population growth without an equivalent increase in total income will lower per caput income). Moreover population changes may be expected to affect income distribution and possibly even tastes (as the age and sex distribution of the population will also alter).

As an illustration of the importance of the distribution of income, consider the following simple example, in which there are two consumers with the same tastes and the same (non-linear) Engel curves for a particular good. For each consumer the relationship between income and consumption of the good is given as:

Income	Quantity consumed
£100	20 units
£150	28 units
£200	32 units

If aggregate income were £300 and this was divided equally between the two consumers, market demand for the product would be 56 units. If, on the other hand, one consumer received £100, while the other got £200, aggregate consumption would be lower, at 52 units.

In this example, the consumers respond by the same degree to market stimuli. However, with respect to the demand for many food products, there is empirical evidence that low income consumers are more responsive to changes in income than are high income consumers. In other words, income elasticities of demand (defined below) are larger for low income groups than for high income groups. This in turn implies that, in a period of income growth, a shift in the structure of the income distribution, with larger income increases for the low income groups than for the high income groups, would generally lead to greater increases in the demand for foodstuffs than would be the case if income distribution remained unchanged.

BOX 6.1
Income distribution and the demand for mutton

Whereas there has been a great deal of quantitative research on the relationship between income and consumption, there has been much less attention given to the effect on demand of changes in the pattern of income distribution. This neglect is particularly worrisome when the analysis concerns developing countries experiencing a rapid rise in per caput income. However it is not altogether surprising. One of the most serious limitations to a full consideration of income distribution effects is the paucity of reliable statistical information regarding the distribution of disposable income and the pattern of consumption in relation to different income levels.

As an example of the type of analysis which has been undertaken, we present some of the results from Saleh and Sisler (1977). They developed a method of measuring the impact of changes in income distribution on the consumption of mutton in urban Iran. Iran in the ten years prior to their analysis experienced a rapid growth in per caput income (Gross National Product rose at an annual rate of 9.3%, while population grew at 3% p.a.).

The Lorenz coefficient (*L*), can be used as a measure of the extent of income inequality in the population. This index ranges in value between 0 and 1: as the income distribution approaches equality, the coefficient approaches zero and as income inequality increases, it approaches one.[2] The following table illustrates the manner in which changes in the Lorenz coefficient and per caput income (or rather total expenditure in this case) affect the demand

for mutton. Reading down any column shows that for a given income distribution consumption of mutton increases with per caput total expenditure. For a given level of per caput total expenditure reading across a row in the table reveals that consumption of mutton falls as income inequality increases (i.e. as the Lorenz coefficient rises from 0.34 to 0.39). For example, at a total expenditure level of 28400 rials, consumption falls by about 4% (279922 tons to 268529 tons) as income inequality increases and the Lorenz coefficient increases from 0.34 to 0.39. Saleh and Sisler estimate that an increase in per caput income of about 10% would be required in order to offset the impact of this change in income distribution.

Average per caput total expenditure (rials)	Lorenz coefficient		
	0.34	0.364	0.39
25700	262569	256610	251176
28400	279922	273963	268529
31200	296398	290264	284830

6.2.3 *Shifts in the market demand curve*

As we have noted, the *market demand curve* depicts the relationship between consumption of a particular good and its own price, *all other determinants of demand being held constant.* In mathematical notation, the market demand curve for good Q_1 can be represented as:

$$Q_1 = f_1(P_1 \mid P_2, \ldots, P_n, M, POP, ID)$$

A change in the product's price will induce a movement *along* the market demand curve. A *shift* in the curve, however, will occur if one or more of the other determinants of the demand function changes.

In Fig. 6.2 the market demand curve for a particular good, say butter, is given by D_0. At a price P_0, Q_0 of butter would be consumed. A rightward shift in the demand curve to D_1 would induce a higher level of consumption (Q') at P_0. This shift could be caused, for example, by

An increase in per caput income, assuming butter is a normal good

An increase in the price of a substitute, say margarine. As the price of margarine rises, consumers reduce their consumption of margarine and increase their purchases of (relatively less expensive) butter

A decrease in the price of a complement. If butter is used as a spread for bread then as the bread price falls, consumers are induced to buy more bread and with it, more butter.

6.3 *Elasticities of demand*

So far the analysis has been concerned only with the *direction* of changes in demand induced by changes in either a price or income. However, it is also important to determine *how much* the amount demanded will change in response to a change in one of its determinants. As in Chapter 3 (Section 3.2), it is convenient in this context to choose, as a measure of the responsiveness to market stimuli, an index which will be independent of the measurement units of the respective variables. This measure is termed an *elasticity* and in demand analysis it can be expressed for any explanatory variable which can cause demand to change. The most commonly used elasticities are the own-price elasticity, the cross-price elasticities and the income elasticity. In each case, the measure will be defined as the ratio of the proportionate change in the quantity demand for a particular good to the proportionate change in a specified determinant of demand.

Fig. 6.2. Shift in the demand curve.

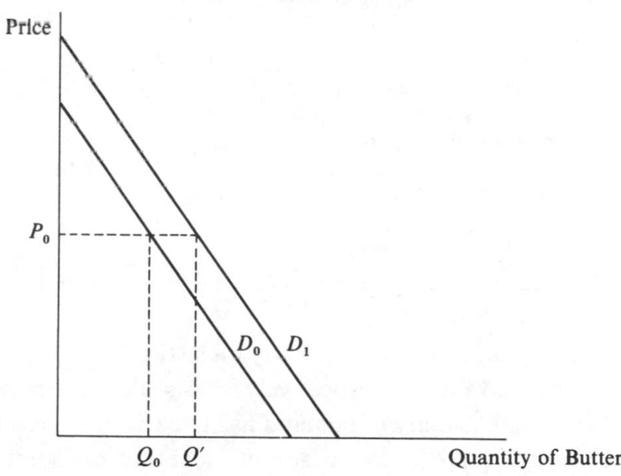

6.3.1 *The own-price elasticity of demand*

The own-price elasticity of demand measures the sensitivity of demand of a good (Q_i) to changes in its price (P_i), *ceteris paribus*. Specifically, it is defined as

$$\varepsilon_{ii} = \frac{\text{proportionate change in the quantity demanded } (Q_i)}{\text{proportionate change in the price of product } i}$$

$$= \frac{\Delta Q_i/Q_i}{\Delta P_i/P_i} = \frac{\Delta Q_i}{\Delta P_i} \cdot \frac{P_i}{Q_i}$$

$$= \frac{\partial Q_i}{\partial P_i} \cdot \frac{P_i}{Q_i}, \text{ for an infinitesimal change.} \qquad (6.2)$$

The own-price elasticity will be non-positive (the inverse relationship between quantity demanded and price has already been established) but the negative sign is by convention often omitted when elasticities are presented in books and journals. Its numerical value will vary from zero to infinity. Elasticity will be zero if quantity demanded does not change at all when the product price changes. The larger the elasticity, the larger the percentage change in quantity for a given percentage change in price. Below we classify and interpret types of price elasticity.

Value of Elasticity	Interpretation	Terminology
$\varepsilon_{ii} = 0$	Quantity demanded does not change as price changes	Perfectly inelastic
$0 > \varepsilon_{ii} > (-)1$	Quantity changes by a smaller percentage than price	Inelastic
$\varepsilon_{ii} = (-)1$	Quantity changes by the same percentage as price	Unitary elastic
$(-)1 > \varepsilon_{ii} > (-)\infty$	Quantity changes by a larger percentage than price	Elastic
$\varepsilon_{ii} = (-)\infty$	Consumers will purchase all they can at a particular price but none of the product at a higher price	Perfectly elastic

Panels *a*, *b* and *c* of Fig. 6.3 illustrate perfectly inelastic, unitary elastic and perfectly elastic demand curves respectively. It should be stressed, however, that the own-price elasticity of demand has two components: the reciprocal of the slope ($\Delta Q_i/\Delta P_i$), and a specific location or point of evaluation on the curve (P_i/Q_i). For most demand curves therefore, the value of the elasticity will depend on which point on the curve is being considered. This is best illustrated by reference to a linear demand curve (Fig. 6.4). The curve has the same slope at each point i.e. $\Delta Q/\Delta P$ is a constant. In the range A to B, quantity is relatively small and price is relatively high. On the other hand, between B and C, quantity is relatively large and price is relatively low. Thus, referring back to the formula 6.2, it is evident that the elasticity in the range A to B will be greater than in the range B to C.[3]

The price elasticity of demand not only provides a measure of the response in terms of quantity consumed when the product price changes; it can also be a guide to the resultant change in total amount spent by consumers (i.e. the total revenue to the sellers). As noted in Chapter 2, total revenue is defined simply as price times total quantity purchased. If

Fig. 6.3. Price elasticities of demand.

Price D Quantity

Price D Quantity

Price D Quantity

(*a*) Perfectly Inelastic (*b*) Unitary Elastic (*c*) Perfectly Elastic

Fig. 6.4. Linear demand curve.

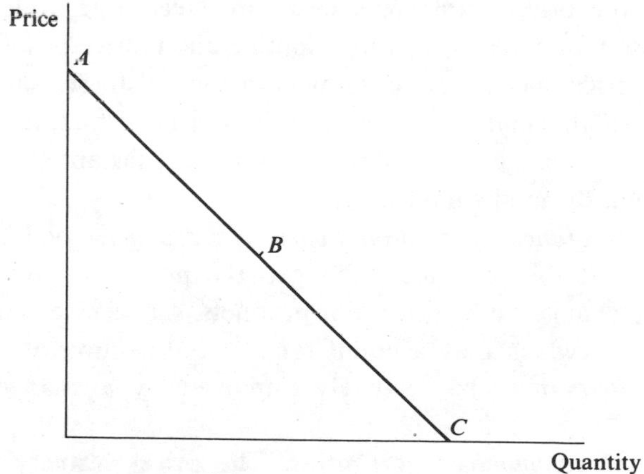

the price of the product falls, there will be an increase in quantity sold: what happens to total revenue depends on the extent of the increased sales relative to the price cut. If demand is inelastic, a change in price causes a less than proportionate change in quantity consumed; from this it follows that total revenue will fall when price is reduced, and will rise when price is raised. If, on the other hand, demand is elastic, a change in price induces a more than proportionate change in quantity demanded: in this case total revenue rises when price is reduced, and falls when price is increased. It should be clear that the price elasticity of demand will be a parameter of particular interest to producers, and particularly to those producers who have sufficient market power to influence product price.[4]

Given the importance of the price elasticity of demand, it is pertinent to note some of the factors which may affect its numerical value:

(i) *The availability of substitutes.* The demand for a commodity is more elastic if there are close substitutes for it. A small rise in price will have a relatively large effect on consumption, as consumers switch to other commodities which are fairly similar but have not changed in price. For example, the demand for beef might be price elastic if there are a number of meat products (mutton, pork, poultry) which are viewed as adequate substitutes. Consumer preferences will determine to a large degree which products are considered to be 'fairly similar' but, regrettably, traditional economic theory gives no guidance on the matter. The importance of preferences in this context is perhaps most clearly demonstrated where there are religious strictures on the consumption of certain types of food products.

(ii) *The number of uses to which a commodity can be put.*[5] A commodity with several uses will be relatively more elastic because of the range of markets in which the price change will exert an effect. For example, electricity can be used for cooking, heating, lighting and motive-power. A small reduction in price may attract customers in each of these markets and the impact on total demand may be quite large. In contrast, tea has only one use – as a beverage – and it may require a substantial price change to affect total demand significantly.

(iii) *The proportion of income spent on a particular product.* The higher the product's share of the consumer's budget, the more sensitive the consumer will be to changes in its price. For products, such as seasonings (e.g. salt and pepper), which may account for a trivial portion of total expenditure, consumers may be relatively unmoved by a change in price.

(iv) *The degree of commodity aggregation.* The price elasticity will depend to a large extent on how widely or narrowly a commodity is defined. The demand for beef is expected to be more price elastic than the demand for all meat, which in turn may be more price elastic than the demand for all food. Commodity aggregation reduces the number of substitutes and increases the budget share.

We conclude our discussion of own price elasticities of demand by giving some empirical examples. Firstly, Da Silva (1984) reports the following estimates of own-price elasticities for livestock products in Brazil in the period 1947–79:

Beef −0.22;
Liquid milk (urban areas) −0.14;
Dairy products −0.16.

The demand for each of these products is found to be price inelastic. In Brazil, middle and high income groups (together less than 40% of the population) account for about 90% of the consumption of beef, milk and dairy products, and so their average share in the consumer budget is much less than would be the case if the low income group had a greater weight in consumption. Moreover, liquid milk and dairy products (an aggregate commodity) have few substitutes and only poultry was found to be a significant substitute for beef. Hence we might conclude that in this context low price elasticities are acceptable.

Table 6.1. *Own price elasticities for selected products: Great Britain*

	Own price elasticity
Carcase Meat	−1.49
Beef and Veal	−2.13
Mutton and Lamb	−1.61
Pork	−2.12
Fish	−0.71
Milk and Cream	−0.38
Eggs	−0.26
Sugar and Preserves	−0.42
Potatoes	−0.18
Other Fresh Vegetables	−0.68
Fresh Fruit	−0.30
Oranges	−0.89
Apples	−0.28
Pears	−1.41
Fats	−0.14
Butter	−0.17
Margarine	−0.56

A more detailed analysis has been undertaken by the U.K. Ministry of Agriculture, Fisheries and Food (MAFF (1985)) and although a developed country example, it serves to illustrate the importance of the availability of substitutes, budget shares and commodity aggregation (Table 6.1) Some products (e.g. milk, eggs, sugar, potatoes) are price inelastic because they lack close substitutes and, taken separately, do not account for a large proportion of the food budget. On the other hand, the individual meats are price elastic, since, in the British context, there are ample substitution possibilities with other meats and their budget share is relatively large. It is also evident that where commodity groups have been broken down into individual product categories (i.e. carcase meat, fresh fruit and fats), that the demand for the aggregate is less price elastic than the demand for each of its components.

6.3.2 *Cross-price elasticity of demand*

A cross-price elasticity of demand is a measure of how the quantity purchased of one commodity (Q_i) responds to changes in the price of another commodity (P_j), *ceteris paribus*. More precisely,

$$\varepsilon_{ij} = \frac{\text{proportionate change in the quantity demanded of good } i}{\text{proportionate change in the price of good } j}$$

$$= \frac{\Delta Q_i}{\Delta P_j} \cdot \frac{P_j}{Q_i} = \frac{\partial Q_i}{\partial P_j} \cdot \frac{P_j}{Q_i} \qquad (6.3)$$

The sign of cross-elasticity is negative if goods i and j are complements and positive if i and j are substitutes. For example, the cross-price elasticity of beef with respect to the price of mutton would be positive; as beef and mutton are substitutes a rise in the price of mutton is likely to cause some switching from mutton to beef. The cross-price elasticity of sugar with respect to the price of coffee might be negative; if sugar and coffee are complementary goods a rise in the price of coffee reduces coffee consumption together with consumption of the complementary product, sugar.

In classifying goods in this way, we are focussing on the change in quantity demanded resulting from a price change *without* compensating for the change in the level of real income. In other words, we are using the *total effect* of a price change as a basis for classifying goods into substitutes and complements. From an empirical standpoint, this is often the only feasible way to proceed. However, we should note that it is possible that two goods which are substitutes in terms of the *substitution effect* may have a negative cross-price elasticity if the *income effect* is sufficiently strong (refer to Section 5.5 for an explanation of these effects).

If the price of good *j* rises, consumers are induced to buy more of the substitute, good *i*. But the increase in price also reduces real income (a fixed money income can then buy less than before the price rise), thus prompting a reduction in consumption of both goods. This income effect may outweigh the substitution effect, resulting in an overall fall in the demand for Q_i and hence a negative cross-price elasticity.

Returning to the study of the demand for livestock products in Brazil (Da Silva (1984)), a low, positive (0.09) cross-price elasticity for beef with respect to poultry was computed. In other words, poultry is a ('gross') substitute for beef: if the price of poultry rose by 5% the quantity of beef consumed per caput would rise but only by 0.45%.

Again the work of MAFF (1985) provides us with a more detailed illustration:

	Elasticity with respect to the price of		
	Beef and veal	Mutton and lamb	Pork
Beef and Veal	−2.13	0.21	0.03
Mutton and Lamb	0.50	−1.61	0.13
Pork	0.08	0.15	−2.12

Source: MAFF (1985). The estimates have been generated for Great Britain 1976–83.

In this table, the diagonal elements are own-price elasticities, with cross-price elasticities being recorded in the off-diagonal elements. All cross-price elasticities are positive, indicating that within this meat group, each product acts as a (gross) substitute for the other two. For example a 5% rise in the price of beef will increase the demand for mutton and lamb (by 2.5%) and pork (by 0.4%). Note also that the cross-price elasticity of demand for, say, beef with respect to mutton is not of the same magnitude as the cross-price elasticity of demand for mutton with respect to the beef price: cross-price elasticities are *not* symmetric.

6.3.3 *The income elasticity of demand*

In analogous fashion, a measure of the responsiveness of demand to a change in per caput income, *ceteris paribus*, is defined as:

$$\eta_i = \frac{\text{Proportionate change in quantity demanded } (Q_i)}{\text{Proportionate change in income } (M)}$$

$$= \frac{\Delta Q_i/Q_i}{\Delta M/M} = \frac{\partial Q_i}{\partial M}\cdot\frac{M}{Q_i} \qquad (6.4)$$

Again the elasticity has two components: the reciprocal of the slope of the Engel curve (as in Fig. 5.2) and the point on the curve at which the elasticity is to be computed. The numerical value of the income elasticity will thus vary at different points on the Engel curve.

Sometimes the income elasticity is computed in terms of consumer expenditure on the product rather than quantity demanded. Hence,

$$\eta_i = \frac{\partial E_i}{\partial M} \cdot \frac{M}{E_i} \quad \text{where } E_i = P_i Q_i \text{ denotes consumer expenditure}$$

on good *i*. If the commodity is a homogeneous one, in the sense that there are no significant differences in quality, then the two versions of the income elasticity will be identical. However, it may be the case that there are marked quality differences and these are reflected in higher per unit prices for the product. For example, as the consumer's income increases, he or she may buy more meat but also choose more expensive cuts. The income elasticity specified in expenditure terms will then be higher than the income elasticity of the quantity consumed.[6]

The income elasticity will be positive for normal goods since, by definition, demand rises with increases in income in these cases. Since the Engel curve for an inferior good has a negative slope, its income elasticity will be negative. As we have noted already, some staple food products may be inferior goods, but for most foods income elasticities are positive, although less than unity. Indeed Engel, a German statistician after whom the Engel curve is named, argued that an increase in income is associated with a less than proportionate increase in food expenditure, that is, the demand for food is income inelastic. This proposition, known as *Engel's Law*, has been empirically verified on many occasions. Although individual low-income consumers might have an income elasticity for food of greater than unity, for the average consumer in society food is income inelastic. This observation has important implications for the agricultural sector, since in the course of economic development, with per caput incomes rising, the demand for food will grow less rapidly than that for other products.

There is also empirical evidence that income elasticities of individual food products decline as incomes increase. Higher income consumers will have smaller income elasticities for foodstuffs than lower income consumers.[7] Thus with economic growth, the market demand for food products will become less income elastic.

BOX 6.2
Income elasticities of demand for food in relation to economic growth

For a selection of countries, income elasticities of demand for the major food products are presented in Table 6.2 below. A number of broad conclusions can be drawn from these empirical estimates:

For all regions (with the exception of rural Egypt), the demand for 'total food' is income inelastic i.e. Engel's Law is verified.

For each food product and for total food, the income elasticity is lower in the developed countries (UK and USA) than the developing countries. This is particularly striking for some commodities: sugar, meat, vegetables, milk, eggs and fats. Indeed a number of these appear as inferior goods (negative income elasticities) in the UK and the USA.

In each of the developing countries, income elasticities vary markedly across the range of products. In some countries, the demand for meat, fruit, vegetables, milk and eggs is found to be income *elastic*, and in all cases the demand for these products is more elastic than that for cereals.

There is a significant difference between urban income elasticities of demand and rural income elasticities. In Egypt and India, rural income elasticities (with one exception) are larger than urban income elasticities. In Indonesia, urban income elasticities are higher for vegetables, fruit, fish and total food.

These results have a number of implications for development planning. These empirical estimates confirm that, as already noted, income elasticities for food decline as income grows in the course of economic growth and the proportion of total expenditure on food will decrease. Hence the focus of economic activity will shift away from the agricultural sector. For Egypt and India, in our example, an increasing degree of urbanisation would have the same effect. Furthermore, the empirical results for individual food products imply that as income grows, the pattern of production within the agricultural sector will have to change. As expenditure on some products (namely livestock products, fruit and vegetables) increases more rapidly than on staple foods (e.g. cereals), increased specialisation in livestock and horticultural production will be required.

Table 6.2. *Income elasticities of demand for agricultural products in selected countries*

	Egypt 1974/75		India 1973/74		Indonesia (Java) 1978		Colombia 1972	Mexico 1977	UK 1980	USA 1972/73
	Rural	Urban	Rural	Urban	Rural	Urban				
Cereals	0.15	0.61	0.21	0.48	0.15	0.23	0.58	−0.16	0.01	0.08
Sugar	0.75	1.26	0.66	1.33	n.a.	n.a.	n.a.	0.02	−0.26	0.16
Vegetables	0.52	1.33	0.83	0.78	0.67	0.66	0.76	0.42	0.12	−0.05
Fruit	0.94	2.09	1.39	1.48	1.66	0.86	0.79	1.21	0.49	n.a.
Meat	0.98	1.74	0.97	1.14	0.98	1.29	0.81	1.02	0.10	0.34
Fish	0.76	1.50			1.17	1.01	n.a.	0.99	−0.01	n.a.
Eggs	1.07	2.01			1.08	1.92	n.a.	0.57	−0.09	−0.54
Milk	n.a.	n.a.	1.06	1.59			0.83	0.57	0.06	0.18
Fats and Oils	0.84	1.48	0.70	0.99	n.a	n.a.	n.a.	0.17	−0.03	−0.32
Total Food	0.75	1.28	0.79	0.82	0.74	0.72	0.64	0.09	0.62	

Source: F.A.O. (1983).

6.4 *Properties of demand functions*

In this section we will present, without formal derivation,[8] the properties of demand functions which are implied by the theory. The purpose is twofold. Firstly, it can be shown that by imposing the full weight of consumer theory we can reduce the computational burden in empirical analysis. This will prove particularly helpful when a full set of commodities (i.e. 'complete demand systems') is being analysed. Secondly it is also important to establish the relationships among price and income elasticities. The theoretical framework can offer some insights useful for policy analysis, even if only a limited amount of empirical evidence is to hand.

We will discuss these properties under three headings: the homogeneity condition, the Slutsky Equation and Slutsky Symmetry conditions, and Engel aggregation.

6.4.1 *Homogeneity condition*

From the analysis of the consumer problem (Chapter 5) it can be deduced that, if all prices and income are increased by the same proportion, demand for a given product will remain unchanged. In economic terminology, there is no 'money illusion'; consumers are assumed to evaluate their income in real terms, and to recognise that a doubling of all prices cancels out exactly a doubling of money income, leaving purchasing power unchanged. From this proposition, the following condition can be derived:

$$\varepsilon_{i1}+\varepsilon_{i2}+\ldots+\varepsilon_{ii}+\ldots+\varepsilon_{in}+\eta_i = 0 \quad i = 1,\ldots,n \tag{6.5}$$

This states that, for a given product (i), the own-price elasticity, all cross-price elasticities and the income elasticity must sum to zero. We would expect that the sum of cross-price elasticities would be positive (since substitution among goods is more common than complementarity) and so the own-price elasticity would be larger in absolute terms than the income elasticity (for a normal good). Thus, an estimate of an income elasticity would give us a lower limit to the own-price elasticity for that product. Suppose, for example, that for a particular developing country we have estimated, from household survey data, that the income elasticity for rice is 0.8 but, because of the absence of reliable time series data, we are unable to estimate price elasticities. From equation 6.5 we can establish that the own-price elasticity of rice must be at least (−)0.8.

From an empirical standpoint, when dealing with n commodities there are $(n+1)$ elasticities to be estimated for each product (n price elasticities and 1 income elasticity). However, by applying equation 6.5, we are saved the trouble of estimating 1 elasticity for each product. This is because, given estimates of n elasticities for a particular good, the remaining elasticity can be derived from the equation.

6.4.2 *The Slutsky equation and Slutsky symmetry*

Demand theory suggests that an understanding of consumer responses to price changes will be important in the analysis of commodity markets. In particular we have noted that the effect of a price change can be decomposed into a price substitution effect and an income effect. The decomposition is sometimes written in the form of the *Slutsky Equation*, as follows:

$$\varepsilon_{ij} = E_{ij} - \eta_i w_j \tag{6.6}$$

where ε_{ij} is the cross-price elasticity of demand, η_i is the income elasticity of good i, w_j is the budget share of good j, and E_{ij} denotes the price substitution effect expressed as an elasticity. The budget share j is defined simply as the amount of expenditure on good j divided by total expenditure (i.e. the budget). Thus in equation 6.6 it can be seen that the smaller the budget share of good j, the smaller the contribution of the income effect to the cross-price elasticity.

As already noted, there is ample empirical evidence to suggest that income elasticities vary with income class. Specifically, the income elasticity for food will in general be much higher in low income households than in high income households. Moreover, the budget share of a given food will also vary by income class. Again, low income households spend a larger proportion of their income on food than high income families. These observations, when combined with the Slutsky Equation, suggest that price elasticities will depend to some extent on income level. Timmer *et al.* (1983) go further, arguing that the substitution elasticity for food products will be larger (in absolute terms) in low income households than in high income ones. This reinforces the point that price elasticities will vary with income class. For example, they estimate, using the Slutsky Equation and some observed 'empirical regularities' that the own-price elasticity (that is to say, where $i = j$ in the formula) for rice might be -0.99 for low income classes and -0.1 for high income classes. Hence low income consumers are likely to be much more responsive to changes in food prices in terms of quantities consumed than other consumers.

Slutsky symmetry concerns the proposition that the substitution effect

(s_{ij}) on the quantity demand of good i in response to a change in the price of good j is the same as the substitution effect (s_{ji}) on good j of a change in price of good i. In other words, the substitution effects are symmetric ($s_{ij} = s_{ji}$). This is *not* to say that the cross-price elasticities of the two products will be symmetric (indeed we have noted in Section 6.3.2 that they will usually not be). However the symmetry condition can be used to derive the following relationship between cross-price elasticities:

$$\varepsilon_{ij} = \frac{w_j}{w_i}\varepsilon_{ji} + w_j(\eta_j - \eta_i) \quad i \neq j \tag{6.7}$$

where w_i is the budget share of good i or expenditure on i as a proportion of total expenditure.

If the income elasticities of the two goods are of similar magnitude, then

$$\varepsilon_{ij} \approx \frac{w_j}{w_i}\varepsilon_{ji}$$

where $\approx$ denotes 'approximately equal to'. Thus, although cross-price elasticities are not symmetric, they are closely related. This condition can be useful in reducing the number of parameters to be estimated in empirical analysis. For, if income elasticities and ε_{ij} are known, ε_{ji} can be derived. Again this saving in computation can be important in demand analysis in which a larger number of commodities are examined.

6.4.3 *Engel aggregation*

An obvious restriction which follows from the budget constraint is that the sum of expenditure on individual items must equal total expenditure or income. A second restriction, following from the budget constraint, therefore constrains income elasticities:

$$w_1\eta_1 + w_2\eta_2 + \ldots + w_n\eta_n = 1 \tag{6.8}$$

This states that the weighted sum of income elasticities of all goods in the consumer's budget is one. The weights are the budget shares of the respective goods. The condition does not imply that all income elasticities must be small, since the weights, by definition, are fractions.

For the full set of commodities, there are n income elasticities but having estimated $(n-1)$ of these, the remaining elasticity may be obtained using equation 6.8. Again, a restriction implied by demand theory can be used to ease the computational burden in empirical analysis.

6.5 *Dynamics in demand analysis*

The theory of demand described above assumes instantaneous adjustments to price and income changes. The importance of the time dimension was noted in our analysis of supply in Chapter 3. It is certainly the case that in the real world consumers may often react with some delay to market stimuli, and adjustment to a new equilibrium position may be spread over several time periods. This implies that we must distinguish between the immediate or short-run response and the full adjustment or long-run response. Consider Fig. 6.5. Initially the consumer is at equilibrium, consuming Q_0 of the product whose price is P_0. Suppose the price then falls to P_1. The consumer would then wish to consume Q_1 but, for reasons to be discussed below, can only increase consumption to Q' initially. In the next period, the consumer can move a bit closer to the preferred or long-run consumption level (i.e. to Q''), in the following period to Q''' and so on. Where there are lags in adjustment we would expect the response to a price or income change to be larger in the long-run (when all adjustments have been made) than in the short-run. For example, Da Silva (1984) estimated that, in Brazil, the long-run price and income elasticities for beef and dairy products were approximately twice the size of their short-run counterparts.

Lags in adjustment may arise (i) where there is price or income uncertainty, (ii) where there is habit formation, (iii) where the product is a durable good and (iv) where there are institutional constraints.

In an uncertain environment, current consumption will depend in part on expectations of future prices and future purchasing power. For example, if a price fall is expected at a later date, the consumer may choose

Fig. 6.5. Partial adjustment to long run equilibrium.

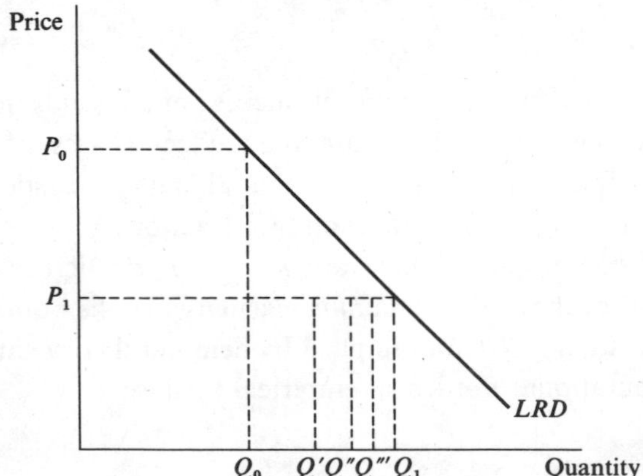

to defer purchase; if the price is expected to rise, purchase plans may be brought forward. As in the analysis of supply (Section 3.3) it may be hypothesised that the expected value of a particular variable (here price or income) will be determined with reference to past levels of that variable. Thus current purchases will depend on current and past levels of prices and income. The corollary of this is that a change in price or income in the current period will influence consumer behaviour for several periods in the future. These considerations are likely to be particularly relevant in the analysis of consumer products which take a large share of the consumer's total budget e.g. houses, motor cars etc., but they may not be significant in the analysis of demand for individual food products.

Marshall (1927) was among the first to recognise the limitations of static demand assumptions. He noted that adaptation to a change in price is gradual and that (1927, p. 807) '...habits which have once grown up around the use of a commodity while its price is low are not quickly abandoned when its price rises again'. More recently the influence of habit formation on demand has been stressed by Scitovsky (1976, 1978). Terming the phenomenon 'addiction-asymmetry', he argued that, although it would be undoubtedly a feature of the consumption of products such as drugs, cigarettes and alcohol, for which both a physiological and psychological dependency may arise, such behaviour might be 'pretty nearly universal'. A consumer may become attached to any aspect of a higher standard of living once he has experienced it. Scitovsky's analysis implies not only that there is a lag in the adjustment to a price or income change but that the demand curve is kinked (Fig. 6.6).

Fig. 6.6. Asymmetric demand curve.

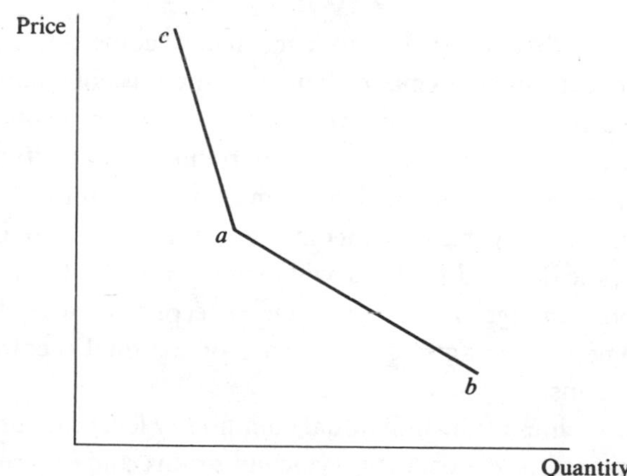

A consumer, at point *a*, would move down the arm *ab* if the price of the product falls but up the more inelastic segment *ac* if the price rises. Although there have been many studies of the demand for food products which incorporate lags to take account of consumer inertia, there have been few attempts to date to introduce asymmetry or irreversibility into the demand functions.[9]

The durability of some goods is another source of delays in consumer response. Consider the consumer who purchases a house but soon thereafter gains a salary increase. According to the static demand function for houses, he should spend more on that item but it is more likely that he will choose to remain 'below' the new equilibrium position for some time. This source of adjustment lags is usually ignored in the analysis of food products. However, with the use of refrigerators and freezers, many food products are storable and may be treated, for some analytical purposes, as durable goods.

Finally adjustment lags in consumer response may be due to constraints imposed by the institutional environment. These constraints can take many forms. For example, for some products, such as housing, there will be a delay between the decision to purchase and acquisition, because of the time required to fulfil a number of legal and fiscal requirements. In other cases, the purchase of the good in a given period may depend on the availability and terms of credit. Indeed the availability of the good itself on the market may be regulated by the government (for example, by means of import controls); the waiting lists which are thus created are further evidence that the assumption of instantaneous adjustment may be inappropriate in some cases.

6.6 *Conclusions*

In the traditional theory prices and consumer income are the main determinants of consumer demand. In the analysis of many development issues, the income elasticity, by which consumer responsiveness to an income change is measured, is a particularly important parameter. Firstly, by Engel's Law, which seems to have universal validity, we can predict that as per caput incomes grow in the course of economic development, the demand for food will increase but less than in proportion to the income change. Hence the focus of economic activity will shift away from agriculture; agriculture's share of national income will decline in relative terms.

A study of income elasticities at the individual commodity level can also be instructive. Some agricultural products, typically grains and starchy roots, have low, perhaps negative income elasticities. Other food products such as meat and livestock products are more income elastic. A given increase in income will thus change the pattern of consumption; the demand for these food products with high income elasticities will rise relative to that for other products in the food budget. These changes will in turn signal shifts in resource usage within the agricultural sector.

Another useful observation concerning income elasticities is that low income households tend to have larger income elasticities for food products than high income families. The income distribution at a point in time will then be a significant determinant of food consumption patterns. Moreover, in the course of economic growth, the income distribution will change and the precise way in which this occurs will have implications for food consumption levels in the various income strata as well as for the agricultural sector itself.

Some knowledge of price elasticities is also an essential input to many policy analyses. The theory suggests that the demand for food in the aggregate and for some individual food products will be price inelastic. As we will see in the next chapter, price fluctuations will be more pronounced in agricultural markets in which demand is inelastic. On the other hand, the demand for some products (e.g. those with close substitutes) may be price elastic and some empirical analyses suggest that the demand for food products is more price elastic in low than in high income households. Since governments frequently choose to regulate market prices (e.g. by import tariffs, sales taxes, and subsidies), a measure of the consumer responsiveness is needed in order to predict the resultant changes in consumption and exchequer costs or revenues.

The forcgoing suggests that there is a primary need for quantitative information on the sign and magnitude of these consumption parameters. Indeed, for those countries which rely heavily on exports of agricultural products, the need is not so much for information on the domestic markets but on the structure of demand in the destination markets, and these may well be in the developed countries.

It has been argued that the traditional approach to demand analysis can offer some useful insights. However we have also noted that some aspects of real world markets lie outside its scope. In particular the static theory will be found wanting in these problem areas where there are lags in consumer response, possibly arising from habit formation or institutional constraints. In these cases more complex dynamic models need to be specified. Other reformulations of demand theory are considered in the next chapter.

6.7 *Summary points*

1. *Market demand* is the aggregate demand of a number of individuals in a specified market. In addition to product prices and (per caput) income, market demand will depend on population (i.e. the number of consumers in the market) and income distribution.
2. A number of *demand elasticities* are distinguished: the own-price elasticity (with a negative sign), cross-price elasticities (negative for complementary goods, positive for substitutes), and income elasticities (positive for normal goods, negative for inferior goods).
3. Theory suggests that demand functions should exhibit certain *properties* (Engel Aggregation, Slutsky Symmetry and Homogeneity). These properties are useful both because they establish the interrelationships among price and income elasticities and because they reduce the number of demand parameters to be estimated in empirical analysis.
4. A *dynamic* specification of the demand function may be required if (i) consumers face uncertainty regarding future price or income levels, (ii) habits develop around the consumption of the product, (iii) the product is a durable one, or (iv) there are institutional constraints to instantaneous adjustments.
5. The demand curve may be *asymmetric*. In particular, when there is habit formation, consumers' response to an upward price movement may be more inelastic than to a downward price movement.

Further reading

Tomek and Robinson (1981) present a useful treatment of many of the aspects of the demand for agricultural products which we have covered in this chapter.

Phlips (1983), Deaton and Muellbauer (1980), and Thomas (1987) cover much more advanced material and provide detailed discussion of empirical issues. Partly because of the paucity of reliable data series over time in many developing countries, much empirical work makes use of household budget surveys. Thomas (1972) provides one of the best reviews of statistical analysis based on this type of cross-sectional data.

Timmer *et al.* (1983) offer a comprehensive analysis of food policy issues in developing countries, which makes explicit use of the traditional tools of consumer theory as presented in this chapter.

7

Developments in demand theory

7.1 *Introduction*

This chapter, the last of the three devoted to demand analysis, examines areas of demand theory where advances have been made in recent years. Firstly, two reformulations of demand theory are presented. Both provide important insights into the analysis of some spheres of economic activity in which the traditional theory has had little to offer. These include advertising, product differentiation, and production and consumption activities for which there is no formal market. Elements of the 'new' theories have been adopted in the study of agricultural households in developing countries and so will be encountered again in Chapter 8. Secondly, the concept of duality can be applied to demand theory in an analogous fashion to its application in supply analysis (Chapter 4). Again we will find that there may be analytical and empirical advantages from exploiting dual relationships.

7.2 *'New' theories of demand*

The 'new' theories of demand which we wish to introduce here were developed by Lancaster and Becker in the 1960s. They are 'new' in the sense that they are major reformulations of demand theory but some of the premises on which they are based have been suggested in much earlier works in the economics literature. As will become clear the two approaches do have some common features. We begin with Lancaster's model.

7.2.1 *Lancaster's model of consumer demand*

A number of topics cannot be analysed easily within the framework of traditional demand theory. These include advertising effects on demand, product differentiation and the demand for new or 'improved' products. Lancaster has suggested an alternative model of consumer behaviour which may prove a more useful basis for analysis in these subject areas.

In his model, the consumer is not interested in market goods as such but rather in their characteristics or attributes. For example, the characteristics of a food product would include the nutrients: calories, protein, vitamins and so forth; a motor car would have a certain engine capacity, miles per gallon, number of seats etc. The consumer gets satisfaction from consumption of the characteristics which in turn are derived from the market goods. The relationship between consumer satisfaction (or utility) and the consumption of characteristics is defined by the utility function:

$$U = U(Z_1, \ldots, Z_m)$$

where Z_i denotes the total amount of characteristic i consumed. (Recall that the utility function in the traditional theory is specified in terms of the quantities of goods consumed.) Each characteristic, it is assumed, is quantifiable and can be objectively measured. The total amount of the ith characteristic possessed by a set of market goods is the sum of the amounts of the characteristic possessed by each good separately:

$$Z_i = b_{i1}Q_1 + b_{i2}Q_2 + \ldots + b_{in}Q_n = \sum_{j=1}^{n} b_{ij}Q_j \quad i = 1, \ldots, m$$

where b_{ij} is the quantity of the ith characteristic possessed by a unit amount of the jth good. For example, suppose Z_1 denotes the characteristic 'calories' and that a pint of milk contains 320 calories and a loaf of bread 1200 calories. Then the total calories consumed from milk and bread would be

$$Z_1 = 320Q_M + 1200Q_B$$

where Q_M denotes pints of milk and Q_B denotes loaves of bread. The consumer faces a conventional budget constraint, limiting total expenditure on market goods:

$$P_1Q_1 + \ldots + P_nQ_n = M$$

or

$$\sum_{j=1}^{n} P_jQ_j = M$$

Formally the consumer problem is specified as maximise

$$U = U(Z_1, \ldots, Z_m) \tag{7.1}$$

subject to

$$Z_i = \sum_{j=1}^{n} b_{ij} Q_j \tag{7.2}$$

and

$$\sum_{j=1}^{n} P_j Q_j = M \tag{7.3}$$

Given prices and the level of income, the maximum amount of each characteristic which a good can provide can be determined, and consumers with the same income will face the same range of choices in terms of characteristics. The consumer problem will then be to find the goods or combinations of goods which are efficient in the provision of characteristics and which yield the maximum level of utility. It is assumed that consumers will differ in terms of their tastes and preferences regarding the characteristics, *not* in their perceptions of the efficient set of choices.[1]

To illustrate the nature of consumer equilibrium in Lancaster's model, let us assume that there are two food products (Q_1, Q_2), each possessing two characteristics, say nutrients (Z_1, Z_2). The product Q_1 provides the nutrients in the proportion OM, while Q_2 offers them in the proportion ON in Fig. 7.1. Note that in this figure the axes are measured in units of the characteristics. Given the prices of the market goods and given a level of consumer income, the maximum amounts of the characteristics which can be obtained from Q_1 are denoted by Z_1' and Z_2', and from Q_2 by Z_1'' and Z_2''. However, combinations of the two food products can also be purchased and so the efficient set of consumer choice is indicated by the line MN. Consumers, since they maximise satisfaction, will be in

Fig. 7.1. Consumer equilibrium in Lancaster's model.

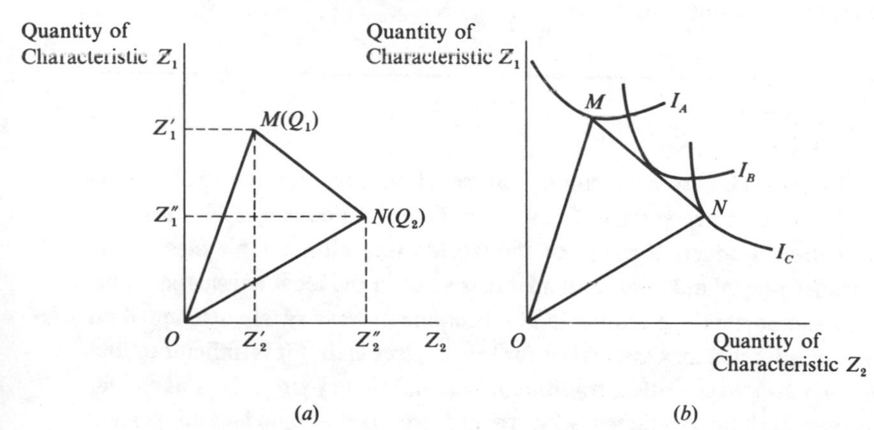

equilibrium somewhere along this line. The precise position of an individual consumer's equilibrium will depend on his or her indifference map. Fig. 7.1 (*b*) presents three possible solutions. Consumer *A* chooses to purchase only product Q_1, consumer *B* buys a combination of the two food products, and consumer *C* purchases only Q_2.

Lancaster's theory can be useful in a number of areas in which the traditional theory is barren. Firstly, the theory suggests that goods which provide the same characteristics will be closely related in consumption (and in particular will have larger cross-price elasticities). Thus the demands for beef and chicken will be more closely related than the demands for beef and, say, newspapers. Although this may seem intuitively obvious, it is not a conclusion which can be drawn from traditional theory. Traditional theory has nothing to say about which products are close substitutes.

Secondly, the theory helps us to understand two pervasive phenomena of everyday life: product differentiation and advertising. Since consumers will have different tastes regarding the attributes of market goods, it may pay firms, or indeed the same firm, to produce an array of brands of the product, each having slightly different characteristics. Nor is this solely a feature of markets in manufactured goods. The variety of retail food products is also evidence of product differentiation. Even for relatively unprocessed food products such as fruit and vegetables, growers continually search for new varieties, not in order to obtain higher yields (although in some cases this may be a prime concern) but to alter the characteristics of the product in terms of colour, taste, texture etc. Advertising, on the other hand, can be used as a means of persuading consumers to purchase one brand rather than another, thus altering the consumer's preference map.

BOX 7.1
Advertising

Advertising is a common feature of modern society. The multinational corporations, such as Coca Cola, General Foods and Nestles, will promote their products throughout the world using all available media; the small trader may simply place an advertisement in the local newspaper. But, despite its importance in economic life, economists have rarely attempted an analysis of advertising. One reason for this neglect is that it is difficult to find a role for advertising within traditional demand theory since, it is assumed, consumers have given tastes with regard to market goods and perfect

knowledge of prices and income. If consumers have imperfect knowledge of market opportunities, *informative advertising* (i.e. about where goods can be bought and at what prices) can be incorporated into the model. However, much of modern advertising is not of this type.

Lancaster's model of demand does offer a basis for the analysis of advertising. Firstly, tastes are not assumed to be given and so it may be possible for an individual producer to manipulate consumer preferences to his advantage. Consider Fig. 7.2, which again illustrates a market where two food products (Q_1 and Q_2) provide two characteristics, (Z_1 and Z_2), but in different proportions. For given prices and income the efficient set of consumer choices is given as *MN*. Some consumers, such as the one illustrated with indifference curve I_0, may obtain greatest satisfaction by purchasing a combination of both market goods i.e. equilibrium is initially at point *E* where I_0 is tangential to *MN*. The producer of good Q_2, however, may be able by some advertising ploy to alter consumer preferences in such a way that more of Q_2 is bought. In the figure, the indifference curve associated with the highest level of satisfaction, following a successful advertising campaign, becomes I_1 and in the new equilibrium the consumer only purchases Q_2.

Lancaster's model can also be used to illustrate the gains which may be obtained, at least in the short term, by deceptive advertising. In Fig. 7.3, for given prices and income, the maximum amounts of the characteristics which can be obtained from Q_1 and Q_2 are defined by points *M* and *N* respectively. The efficient set of choices would therefore lie somewhere along *MN* and we depict a consumer who with indifference curve I_0 would choose to buy a

Fig. 7.2. Advertising and the consumer's indifference map.

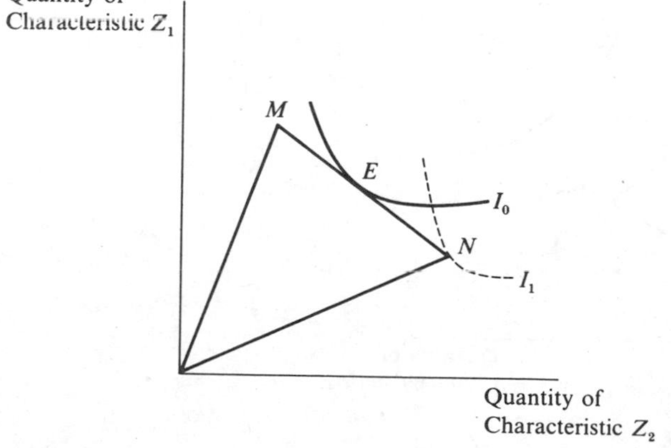

combination of both market goods. However, the producer of Q_2, by making false claims for the product, could lead the consumer to believe that Q_2 could yield N' of the characteristics. The consumer may as a consequence purchase Q_2 only, as shown in the figure. Of course the consumer cannot in fact reach this higher indifference curve (choice is indeed limited to MN) but this will be discovered only after the good has been bought. Clearly a deceptive advertising campaign would only be undertaken if the producer were not relying on the same consumers purchasing the good again at a later date.

Finally, Lancaster's model may provide a basis for the analysis of the demand for new products or of quality changes in existing products. Consumer behaviour with regard to existing goods can be used to gauge the demand for the characteristics which the new or improved product possesses, albeit to a different degree.

Some drawbacks of the model concern its empirical application. It is important to identify and measure all relevant characteristics. For a food product, appearance, colour, taste and size, as well as nutrient content, may determine the level of purchases but some of these attributes may be difficult to quantify. In addition, most applications will require some assumption as to the distribution of preferences in the market and it is unlikely that the analyst will have much information on which to base this choice.

Fig. 7.3. Deceptive advertising.

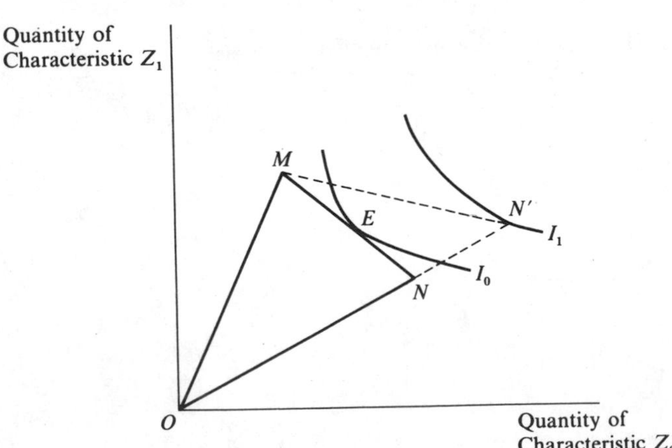

7.2.2 *Becker's model of consumer demand*

Like Lancaster, Becker tries to reformulate the theory of demand in such a way that the economist's ability to analyse real world problems is enhanced. There are some similarities between the two 'new' approaches but also significant differences. In particular Becker takes as the decision-making unit the household rather than the individual consumer and focuses on the allocation of household time. This is an important departure because many household activities do not pass through any marketplace and so are not amenable to traditional economic analysis. Becker's model on the other hand may provide insights into problems in which non-market time is a major element. In this section we will outline the Becker model but, given the importance of non-market activities in agricultural households in developing countries, we will wish to return to his model in the next chapter.

Becker argues, as Lancaster does, that the consumer is not interested in market goods as such but in another set of entities from which utility is directly obtained. However, in Becker's model, these entities are not the measurable characteristics of goods but rather 'basic commodities', such as 'nourishment', 'comfort', and 'entertainment', which are produced by the consumer through the productive activity of combining purchased market goods with the household's own time. All market goods and household time are inputs into a household production function for each basic commodity:

$$Z_i = f(Q_1, \ldots, Q_n, t_1, \ldots, t_n) \quad i = 1, \ldots, m \tag{7.4}$$

where Z_i denotes the quantity of basic commodity i, t_j is the amount of household's time to be combined with market good j. The production relations are specified for a given state of household technology. For example, the consumer purchases a food item, say beef, and by combining it with household time (in cooking) and given the nature of the household technology (namely, the kitchen equipment), produces 'nourishment'. The basic commodities are sometimes termed 'Z-goods'.

In a given period, the consumer has a finite amount of time available, which may be spent in the labour market and in household production:

$$T = t_w + \sum_{j=1}^{n} t_j \tag{7.5}$$

where T denotes total available time, t_w is the time spent in the labour market and t_j is the time spent on good j. The consumer also faces a budget constraint:

$$M = \sum_{j=1}^{n} P_j Q_j \tag{7.6}$$

The consumer problem is then to maximise the utility function

$$U = U(Z_1, \ldots, Z_m)$$

subject to the constraints[2] of the production functions 7.4, time 7.5 and the consumer's budget 7.6.

Becker's model contains elements of traditional demand theory and production economics; the consumer seeks to maximise utility and minimise the cost of household production. The consumer will respond to changes in the prices of market goods, income, the opportunity cost of time (i.e. the wage rate), as well as to changes in the productivity of goods and time in the production process.

The demand for a market good is a derived demand, analogous to the derived demand by a firm for a factor of production. For example, if there is a fall in the price of beef, a market good used in the production of nourishment, the consumer will use relatively more beef in the production of nourishment and produce more nourishment (as this basic commodity uses the relatively cheaper market good more intensively than other commodities). The full extent of the change in the demand for beef will depend on the elasticities of substitution in production and consumption.

Becker's model, in stressing the importance of the allocation of time in consumer or household decision-making, has opened up a host of problems to economic analysis. These include the study of

(i) activities which involve the use of non-market time (e.g. recreation, commuting, home crafts);
(ii) the supply of labour;
(iii) investment in human capital (which affects the productivity of the consumer's time); and
(iv) fertility (or the demand for children);
(v) nutritional status.

A number of these topics are important in the analysis of agricultural households in developing countries and Becker's model may be adapted in order to analyse farm-level decision making in the LDCs. We take up this point again in the next chapter.

7.3 *Duality in demand analysis*

The theoretical developments of equivalent (dual) structures, described in Chapter 4 Section 4.5, are equally applicable in the analysis of demand. Indeed each of the dual functions in production has its counterpart in consumption. We will use this section to briefly introduce some of the major interrelationships which can be derived.

The consumer problem has been depicted as one of choosing quantities of goods, $Q_1, \ldots, Q_n$, so as to *maximise* satisfaction or *utility subject to a budget constraint* that total expenditure should not exceed available income (M). The solution yields a set of demand functions of the form $Q_i = f(P_1, \ldots, P_n, M)$, and, implicitly, a maximum utility level, say U^*. However, the problem can be reformulated as one of choosing quantities so as to *minimise the total expenditure* to achieve a *given utility level* (this is directly analogous to the firm choosing input levels so as to minimise the cost of producing a given level of output (Chapter 4)). If the given utility level in the latter problem is set equal to U^*, then the solution will yield the *same* set of quantities as in the original problem and the minimum total expenditure, M^*, will be equal to the given M in the original problem. Formally the cost minimisation problem can be written as:

minimise

$$M = \sum_{i=1}^{n} P_i Q_i \tag{7.7}$$

subject to

$$U(Q_1, \ldots, Q_n) = U^* \tag{7.8}$$

The solution yields cost minimising quantities of goods, $Q_1, \ldots, Q_n$, which depend on prices and on the level of utility, U^*, *not* prices and income, *viz.*

$$Q_i = h_i(P_1, \ldots, P_n, U^*) \quad i = 1, \ldots, n$$

These are, in fact, *compensated demand functions* since they indicate how quantity demanded will change in response to changes in price, with utility constant (diagrammatically, we would keep the consumer on the same indifference curve).[3] By substituting the optimal cost minimising quantities back into the objective function (7.7), we obtain a *cost function* or *expenditure function*:

$$M = \Sigma P_i Q_i = \Sigma P_i h_i(P_1, \ldots, P_n, U^*) = C(P_1, \ldots, P_n, U^*) \tag{7.9}$$

Equation 7.9 yields the minimum cost of obtaining the utility level U^* at given prices, $P_1, \ldots, P_n$ (this is directly analogous to the firm's cost function which expresses minimum cost of producing a given output for given input prices). Further, by differentiation of a specific cost function, the compensated demand functions can be obtained.[4]

It is important to note that whereas the utility function is measured in arbitrary units of consumer satisfaction, the cost function is measured on a monetary scale. This property has made its use particularly attractive (since data on monetary values are available, whereas those on satisfaction are not) in several analytical areas, including some welfare economics applications such as the measurement of cost of living indices and household welfare comparisons. Moreover, the cost function has been at the core of much recent empirical work on consumer demand. For example, in deriving their *Almost Ideal Demand System* (AIDS), Deaton and Muellbauer begin by specifying a flexible functional form for a cost function.[5]

By returning to the original, utility-maximisation, problem, another set of dual relationships can be obtained. There the set of demand functions which yield maximum utility are specified in terms of prices and income (or total expenditure). By substituting these optimal quantities back into the objective function (i.e. the utility function, $U = U(Q_1, \ldots, Q_n)$), we obtain what is termed an *indirect utility function* which expresses utility as a function of prices (rather than quantities) and income:

$$U^* = U^*(P_1, \ldots, P_n, M) \tag{7.10}$$

This represents the *highest* utility which can be obtained with alternative (given) prices and income. If on the other hand, we begin with a specific indirect utility function, the demand functions can be retrieved simply by differentiation.[6] This clearly offers a useful short cut in analytical work. In addition the indirect utility function provides an alternative starting point for empirical studies.[7]

Finally, it should be noted that the indirect utility function and the cost function are intimately related. Indeed, and this is the essential dualistic property, they are alternative ways of writing the same information. By rearranging or 'inverting' one, we can obtain the other.

$$U^* = U^*(P_1, \ldots, P_n, M) \leftrightarrow M = C(P_1, \ldots, P_n, U^*)$$

7.4 *Conclusions*

The major portion of this chapter has been devoted to two significant reformulations of the traditional demand theory. The first, due to Lancaster, emphasises the importance of the characteristics of market goods and proves to be particularly useful in analyses where the consumer would be expected to pay particular attention to the attributes of products. Hence Lancaster's model of consumer behaviour is well suited to the analysis of the demand for durable goods, such as housing, and of topics in marketing research, such as advertising, new products, product differentiation and product quality.

The second reformulation of demand theory outlined here was suggested by Becker. He has developed a theory of household production, which is an integration of the theory of the consumer with that of the firm. Since his model places emphasis on activities within the household and on the allocation of household time, in particular, it offers a useful basis for the analysis of transactions which do not pass through the marketplace. In many developing countries agricultural households allocate a large portion of time to water-carrying, fuel gathering, handicrafts and food production for home use, all activities for which no formal market exists. Hence, the Becker model should offer some insights in the study of these households, as we will see in the next chapter. In addition the model can be, and has been, used as the framework for the study of household decision-making regarding nutrition, health status, education and the number of children in the household.

The final topic of this chapter was the extension of duality theory to demand analysis. The approach is directly analogous to that in production economics. A considerable advantage of adopting one of the alternative routes, suggested by duality theory, in tackling a given consumer problem is that of analytical convenience. To give just two examples, a demand function can be derived by differentiation rather than by solving a complete maximisation or minimisation problem; and a set of estimating equations with desirable properties can be generated from a cost function or indirect utility function, without reference to the underlying utility function.

7.5 *Summary points*

1. Two 'new' theories of demand have been presented. Although they are still based on the hypothesis that the consumer (or household) maximises utility or satisfaction, that satisfaction is not obtained *directly* from market goods. Both approaches attempt to provide insights in areas where the traditional theory is relatively barren.
2. In the *Lancaster model*, the consumer is interested in the characteristics or attributes of products. Uses for this model have

been found in the analysis of demand for durable goods and of topics in marketing research (advertising, product differentiation, product quality, new products).

3. In the *Becker* model, which treats the household as the decision-making unit, satisfaction is derived from another set of entities (such as 'nourishment') which are produced in the household with a combination of market goods and time. The model can be seen as a synthesis of production theory and consumer theory. It has proved to be most useful in the analysis of problems in which time and non-market activities are especially important e.g. labour supply, fertility, human capital and so forth.
4. Duality theory can be applied to the analysis of demand in a directly analogous fashion to its application in production economics. In demand theory, the key relationships are the *utility function*, the *indirect utility function* and the *cost function*.

Further reading

Lancaster (1971) provides the most comprehensive statement of his model, although good introductions to his approach can be found in Green (1976, Chapter 10) and Laidler (1981, Chapter 8).

Perhaps the best summary of the Becker model and its applications is to be found in Michael and Becker (1973). Household production theory is presented and extended in Deaton and Muellbauer (1980, Chapter 10). Additional references on this topic will be suggested in the next chapter.

Thomas (1987, Chapter 2) and Deaton and Muellbauer (1980, Chapter 2) both offer accessible treatments on duality in demand analysis.

8

Equilibrium and exchange

8.1 *Introduction*

Having presented the main elements of production theory and the theory of consumer behaviour, we are now in a position to bring together these two segments of the market in order to analyse the determination of market prices and quantities exchanged. The principles discussed in this chapter are important for a number of reasons. Firstly, the interactions of supply and demand forces are the cornerstone of the neoclassical approach to economic analysis. Secondly, in some quarters (e.g. the World Bank and IMF) more emphasis is being placed on the role of the marketplace in the allocation of resources in the agricultural and other sectors of the developing economy. Finally, a number of concerns of development economists centre on the functioning of agricultural commodity markets. Specifically, it is noted that prices of some agricultural products are highly variable in the short run and that this price instability may discourage investment and may induce income instability for producers. Moreover, over the longer term, agricultural prices may decline relative to other product prices.

A large portion of this chapter will be concerned with the theoretical analysis of competitive markets. (Some features of imperfect markets and some more practical aspects of agricultural markets are considered in the next chapter.) We begin by defining the concept of market *equilibrium* which is determined at a market price at which the desires of consumers and those of producers are equally balanced. Much of economic analysis of markets focuses on market equilibrium or changes in market equilibrium. However we feel it should be indicated at the outset that there may be problems concerning the existence of equilibrium, its uniqueness and its stability. It may also be the case that some markets are out of equilibrium for protracted periods and so we may be confronted with *disequilibrium*.

Even if the market functions well the government may decide for some reason that the market (equilibrium) price is too high or too low. Although government intervention will be more fully discussed in Chapter 12, it is convenient to introduce some aspects of market regulation at this juncture.

Economic conditions are forever changing and the static model of supply and demand is of limited usefulness in these circumstances. We therefore conclude our discussion of product markets by presenting the two main approaches to the analysis of market change. In the analysis of *comparative statics*, we compare market equilibrium under one set of economic conditions with equilibrium when one or more economic parameters are altered. In the study of *dynamics*, we are more concerned with how the market behaves once it is shocked from its equilibrium position; it is the mechanism by which we return to an equilibrium (if indeed the system does return to an equilibrium) which is of interest in this case.

Comparative statics and dynamics can prove to be powerful tools in the study of commodity markets (and indeed factor markets) of developing countries at the national and international levels. At these levels the dichotomy of producers and consumers is a useful device. On the other hand, if we are dealing with more micro-level problems of the agricultural sector, consumers and producers cannot be so readily distinguished. Specifically, in the *agricultural household*, production and consumption activities take place within the same economic unit. Typically some portion of farm output will be sold in the market and some will be consumed within the household. An additional complication is that there will also be some activities which never pass through the marketplace. The agricultural household does not therefore fit neatly within any of the economic models considered thus far but rather requires special attention. We conclude this chapter by considering ways in which agricultural household decision-making can be analysed. Essentially we present a synthesis of elements of the consumer and producer theories developed in Chapters 2 and 7.

8.2 *The definition of equilibrium*

Equilibrium is a property of interactions of agents within an economic system. As Hirshleifer (1976, p. 19) states, 'a system is in equilibrium when the forces acting upon it are so balanced that there is no net tendency to change'. Much of this chapter will be concerned with equilibrium in competitive product and factor markets. In these markets equilibrium is achieved when a price is established at which the quantities offered for sale exactly equal the quantities demanded by purchasers; at this price there is no tendency for price or quantity to change.

The determination of an equilibrium price is illustrated in Fig. 8.1, in which the demand and supply curves in a competitive product market are presented. It will be recalled that the market demand curve is the sum of the demand curves of individual consumers, and that the market supply curve is the sum of the supply (marginal cost) curves of firms in the industry. There is only one price (P^*) that will satisfy buyers and sellers simultaneously. At this price, which is determined by the intersection of the two curves, the amount supplied just equals the amount demanded (Q^*). How is the equilibrium price brought about? If the market price were *lower* than P^*, say P_0, consumers would wish to purchase more than sellers would wish to supply: at P_0, there is *excess demand* of $(Q_0^d - Q_0^s)$. Some consumers are willing to pay a much higher price than P_0 for the quantity Q_0^s and so competition among consumers will bid up the price of the good. At the same time excess demand will put pressure on producers to increase supplies but they will only be willing to do so at higher prices. Hence at prices below P^*, there will be upward pressure on price. Conversely, if the price were set *above* P^*, say at P_1, there will be more of the commodity offered on the market than consumers wish to purchase at that price. Hence at P_1, there is *excess supply* of $(Q_1^s - Q_1^d)$ and competition among sellers will tend to force the price downwards. Only at the price–quantity combination (P^*, Q^*) will the wishes of consumers and

Fig. 8.1. The determination of the equilibrium price.

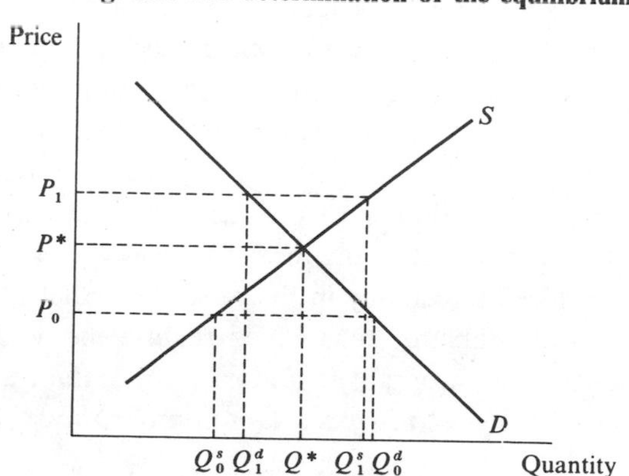

producers be in balance and there will be no tendency for further change.

It is the interactions of consumers and producers in the marketplace which determines the market price and quantities exchanged. Indeed this interaction is central to the neoclassical approach to the analysis of many economic problems: the solution rests on 'supply and demand'.

Formally, a competitive market can be represented as follows:

$$QD_t = f(P_t, M_t) \tag{8.1}$$

$$QS_t = f(P_t, W_t) \tag{8.2}$$

$$QD_t = QS_t \tag{8.3}$$

Equations 8.1 and 8.2 are typical demand and supply functions, in which M_t and W_t denote two *exogenous* or *independent* variables, say income and weather respectively; for simplicity, other exogenous variables are omitted here. The subscript t indicates that the variables are observed at a particular time period, t. Equation 8.3 is the market clearing identity, which states that for equilibrium at time t, quantity demanded and quantity supplied must be equal. In this system of three equations, there are three *dependent* variables – demand, supply and price – and by solving the three equations, market price and quantity exchanged (i.e. quantity demanded and quantity supplied) are determined simultaneously. Hence this type of model is often termed a *simultaneous* system.

8.2.1 *Partial vs. general equilibrium*

For most of the analysis in this book we adopt a *partial equilibrium* approach. As the term implies, partial equilibrium analysis concerns the study of a restricted subset of the economic system – a set of consumers and producers of a particular product or of closely related products – in isolation from the conditions prevailing in the rest of the economy. A fundamental characteristic of the partial equilibrium approach is the determination of price and quantity in a market using demand and supply curves constructed on the *ceteris paribus* assumption. Indeed it turns out that in a large number of problem areas the links between a given sector of the economy and the rest of the system can be ignored without a significant loss of accuracy in the model's predictions. However, there are also certain problem areas which require the whole economic system to be modelled if acceptable standards of accuracy are to be maintained. In such cases, *a general equilibrium* approach must be adopted.

The general equilibrium approach recognises the interdependence among all sectors in the economic system: the markets of all commodities and all factors of production are interrelated and the prices in all markets are determined simultaneously. Fig. 8.2 illustrates a simple two-sector economy. The government sector and the foreign sector are excluded. In addition, the production of intermediate goods[1] (i.e. those outputs of some firms which are used as inputs by other firms) is ignored. We consider only a consumer sector comprising households, and a production sector comprising firms. Consumers' incomes derive from expenditure by producers on factor services (particularly labour) supplied by consumers. These incomes are spent by households in the acquisition of commodities produced by firms. The expenditures of households become the receipts of firms, which they in turn pay households for their factor services. Hence a 'circular flow' of income and expenditure, between households and firms, is established. This sequence of income and expenditure, which are measured in monetary units, is sometimes called the *monetary flow*. On the other hand, the *real flow* is the exchange of physical commodities, produced and offered by firms, for factor services offered by households.

One might ask: where would agriculture fit in this framework? A commercial farm which sells all its produce in the marketplace could be treated simply as a firm. However, many farms in the developing countries are not of this type but rather are 'agricultural households' which produce some output for commercial sale and retain some for home consumption. The agricultural household is a combined production and consumption

Fig. 8.2. The circular flows in a simple economy.

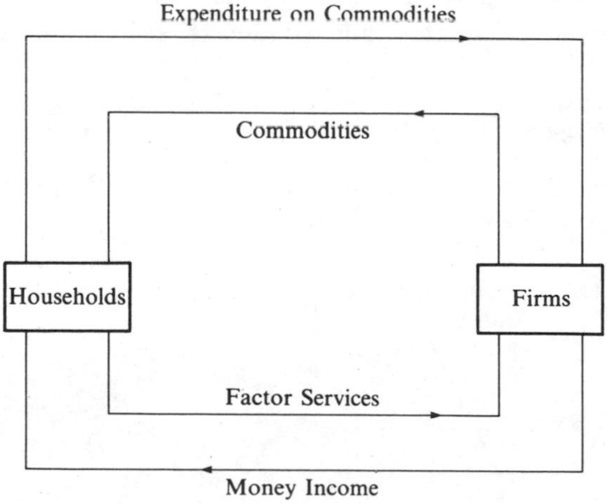

Expenditure on Commodities
Commodities
Households
Firms
Factor Services
Money Income

unit. At the other extreme there is the subsistence farm which produces exclusively for home consumption, with no marketed surplus. Neither the subsistence farm nor the agricultural household fit neatly into the two-sector model of Fig. 8.2. Nevertheless the simple framework is a useful means of introducing the concept of general equilibrium. It hardly needs stating that general equilibrium models designed to analyse real world problems will be considerably more complex.

The choice between partial and general equilibrium approaches is made on pragmatic grounds, by judging which works better in producing accurate predictions. Partial equilibrium analysis permits more precise modelling of a specific market than would be feasible if the entire economic system in which the market is embedded were studied. On the other hand, since linkages with other markets are ignored, inevitably some inaccuracies are introduced. Clearly the case for using partial equilibrium analysis is strongest when only weak linkages with other sectors exist.

8.2.2 *Existence, uniqueness and stability of an equilibrium*

Whether a partial equilibrium approach or a general equilibrium approach is adopted, three questions arise:

Does an equilibrium exist?
If it exists, is the equilibrium solution unique?
If it exists, is the equilibrium solution stable?

These issues can be illustrated with the use of the demand and supply curves of partial equilibrium analysis. In Section 8.1, we depicted a typical market in which a single equilibrium point (P^*, Q^*) was determined and this equilibrium solution was stable i.e. if a price other than P^* were set, the action of consumers and producers would return the market to equilibrium. However, consumers' and producers' behaviour may not

Fig. 8.3. No equilibrium exists.

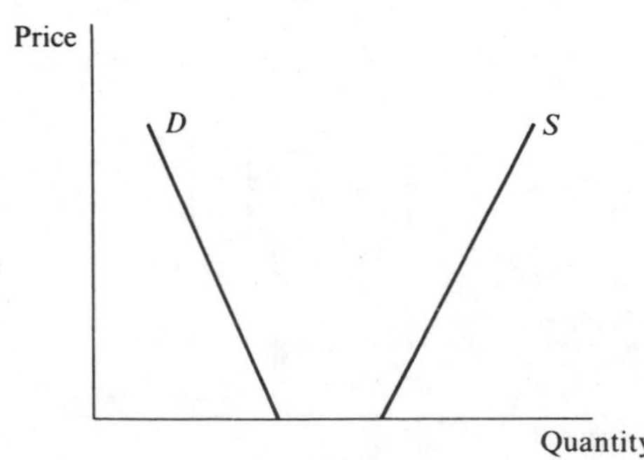

always ensure that this is the case. Consider Fig. 8.3. Here the demand and supply curves are of the usual form (i.e. the demand schedule is negatively sloped and the supply schedule has a positive slope) but they do not intersect. At every (positive) price, there is excess supply and no equilibrium exists. In Fig. 8.4(*a*), we depict an example of multiple equilibria. Contrary to the 'law of demand' which states that the quantity demanded decreases as price rises, the demand curve in this case is positively sloped in the low price range. This backward-bending demand curve intersects the supply curve at two points: P_1^* and P_2^*. Another example of multiple equilibria, with a backward-bending supply curve, is illustrated in Fig. 8.4(*b*). This form of supply curve has been found to be relevant in the analysis of some problems in fisheries economics and in labour economics.[2]

Finally, the equilibrium solution will be unstable if, after some shock, market forces induce movement further away from the equilibrium point. Fig. 8.5 depicts this case, in which both consumers and producers behave in a 'perverse' manner (contrary to that normally assumed). At a price higher than P^*, there will be excess demand which will drive the market price up further, at a price below P^*, excess supply will drive the price lower. Returning to Fig. 8.4(*a*), we can note that the equilibrium at P_1^* is stable but that the equilibrium at P_2^* is not. It would be rare indeed to observe a market in unstable equilibrium, since the slightest disturbance would prompt movement away from such an equilibrium. For this reason, economists choose to focus attention principally upon stable equilibria.

For the most part it will be assumed that we are dealing with the 'typical' market in which a unique, stable equilibrium exists. The purpose

Fig. 8.4. Multiple equilibria.

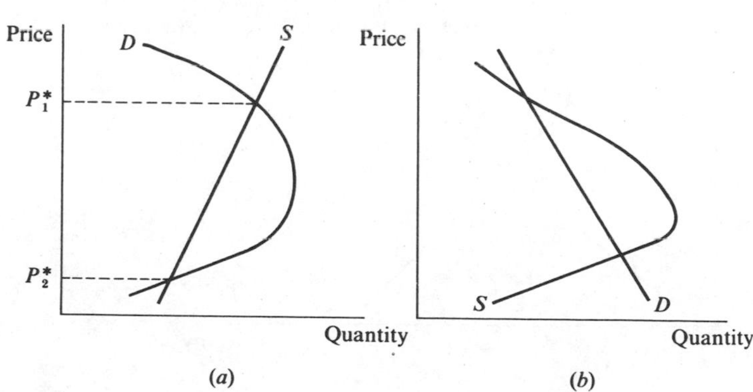

of this section has been to suggest that this assumption may not always be appropriate.

8.2.3 *Disequilibrium*

We turn now to a brief discussion of market disequilibrium. Here we posit that a market equilibrium exists but that in a given period, market transactions are not conducted at the market clearing price. In our terminology, disequilibrium simply means 'not in equilibrium'. Some authors however define disequilibrium as a situation in which the competitive market equilibrium is not attained, perhaps because of government intervention (see Section 8.2.4 below) or because there are monopoly elements in the market (see Chapter 9). Since in these cases an equilibrium may be established (albeit not the competitive equilibrium), we would not consider them to be examples of disequilibrium.

Disequilibrium may occur simply because the determining conditions are ever-changing and although corrective forces are tending to bring the market to equilibrium, price may often be far from its equilibrium level. Disequilibrium may be less likely in the many agricultural commodity markets in which, as we will see in Section 8.3, stocks or inventories adjust to facilitate market clearing. However, where there are long production cycles, full stock adjustment may be difficult and, moreover, some agricultural products are highly perishable and cannot be stored, at least without some loss in quality. In addition, disequilibrium can arise in any market in which the economic agents have incomplete information about the nature of the demand and supply schedules.

Fig. 8.5. Unstable equilibrium.

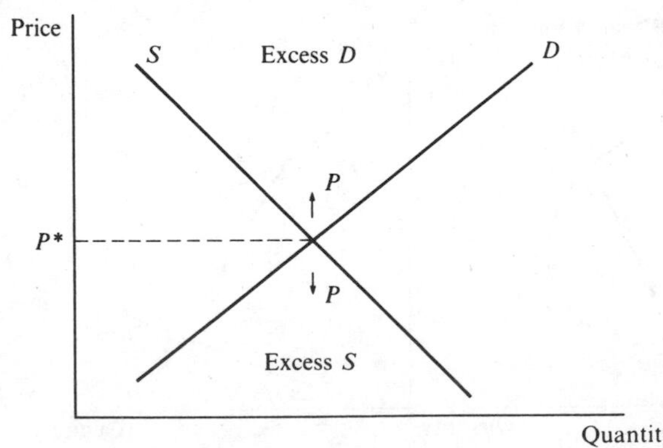

Fig. 8.6. Disequilibrium.

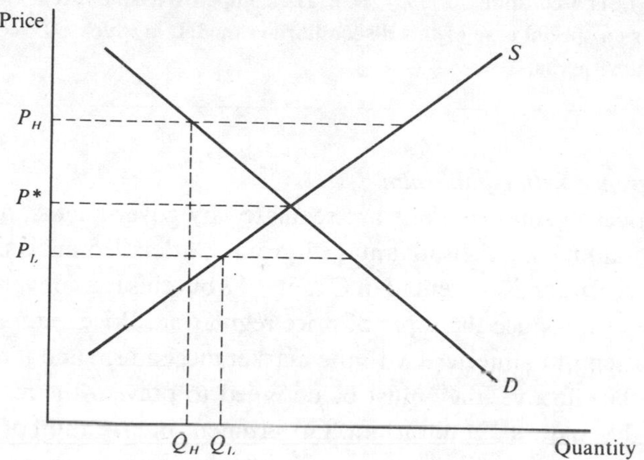

An important feature of disequilibrium is that prices which are either too high or too low relative to equilibrium levels, tend to *reduce quantities exchanged* in markets. This point can be illustrated with the aid of Fig. 8.6. The market price P_H is too high to equate demand and supply. Indeed at this price, there is excess supply, but only Q_H will be purchased and there will be some unsatisfied suppliers unable to find customers. On the other hand, the price P_L is too low to clear the market. There is excess demand (or unsatisfied consumers) at this price, since only Q_L will be supplied to the market. Hence, at a price which diverges from its equilibrium level, the *lesser* of the supply and demand quantities will be exchanged.

Formal model of disequilibrium

A formal model which permits disequilibrium has been developed by Quandt (1978). The key equations can be specified as follows:

$$QD_t = f(P_t, M_t) \tag{8.4}$$

$$QS_t = f(P_t, W_t) \tag{8.5}$$

$$Q_t = \min(QD_t, QS_t) \tag{8.6}$$

$$\mathrm{d}P_t = \lambda(QD_t - QS_t) \tag{8.7}$$

Equations 8.4 and 8.5 are simple demand and supply functions, as before. Equation 8.6 states that the quantity exchanged in the market (Q_t) is the lesser of the two quantities, QD_t and QS_t. Finally, (equation 8.7) price

adjusts over time in accordance with the degree of excess demand in the market (λ is a constant: $0 < \lambda < \infty$). The competitive equilibrium can be viewed as a special case of this disequilibrium model, in which $QD_t = QS_t$ for all time periods.

8.2.4 *Interference with equilibrium*

The prices in some markets are regulated by governments, often with the aim of aiding some disadvantaged group. A detailed analysis of government intervention is presented in Chapter 12 but this is a convenient point at which to introduce the topic of price regulation. Price regulation is a deliberate attempt to interfere with the market mechanism and if price controls are to be effective, they must be designed to prevent the market from reaching the 'natural' equilibrium. Government intervention of this type takes two forms: *price ceilings* and *price floors*.

Price ceilings are often introduced when the equilibrium market price is considered so high that, if it prevailed, some groups within society would be severely disadvantaged. Fig. 8.7 illustrates some of the consequences of this form of price regulation.[3] The market is initially in equilibrium at the price-quantity combination (P_0, Q_0). However, following an increase in demand (to D_1), the government announces that P_0 is to be the maximum price at which the commodity is to be sold. Thus, instead of the market adjusting to the new equilibrium (P_1, Q_1), output remains at Q_0 and there is unsatisfied demand ($Q' - Q_0$). Since price is not allowed to discharge the function of allocating supplies to potential consumers, other methods of

Fig. 8.7. A price ceiling.

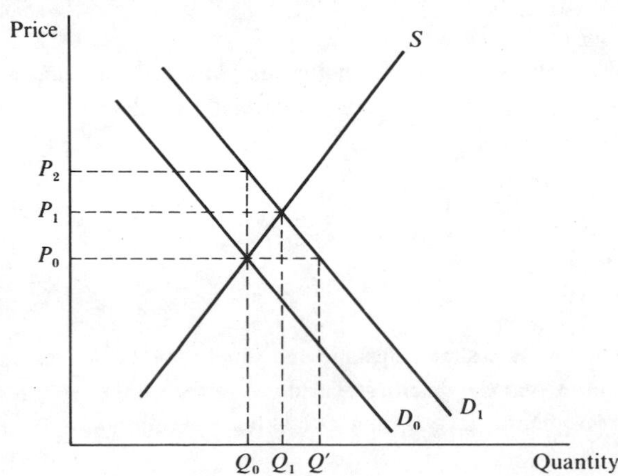

matching supply and demand are required. These may include the issue of ration cards or coupons and the establishment of priorities by type of customer. However, these attempts to 'manage' the shortage may not be wholly successful.

Although the official price may remain at P_0, the 'real' price is likely to rise towards P_2, the price which consumers are willing to pay for the quantity, Q_0. This may occur because consumers either choose to queue for the good and hence incur an opportunity cost of waiting time in obtaining the good, or offer some side-payment to the seller. In addition, since producers cannot raise the price openly, they may resort to the subterfuge of reducing the quality of the product. There is also the possibility that so called *black markets*, in which the regulated product is traded (illegally) at a price higher than P_0, will be created. Although such markets may perform the useful function of satisfying market demand, they tend to work counter to whatever objectives the government had for introducing price controls.

Finally, we should note some reactions to the imposition of the price control which may exacerbate the shortage. A common consumer response to shortage is hoarding i.e. in an attempt to reduce the risk of not obtaining future supplies, domestic stocks are built up. However, the greater the proportion of current supply which is hoarded, the less is available for current consumption. Furthermore, with the imposition of a price ceiling, producers may direct some of their output to uncontrolled markets (e.g. foreign markets) which hitherto were unattractive, or they may switch resources to the production of unregulated products. Each of these responses aggravates the shortage.

Price controls and rationing of basic foodstuffs and other primary products have been adopted as the means of market regulation in a number of centrally planned economies, but in market economies these instruments have been used only in periods of crisis such as wartime and the oil crisis of the mid 1970s. Other examples of the use of price ceilings include the general price 'freezes' imposed in many countries during periods of rapid inflation, rent control in housing markets and the regulation of interest rates and foreign exchange rates in financial markets.

Price ceilings are set in markets where the equilibrium price is considered 'too high'. Conversely, governments may introduce *price floors* where the equilibrium price is deemed to be 'too low'. Returning to Fig. 8.6, P_H might be set as the lowest price at which the product (or factor service) can be bought. However, at this price, there is excess supply and the quantity exchanged in the market is lower than the equilibrium amount. To ensure that P_H remains the effective price in the market, the government may act as a 'buyer of last resort', taking any surplus supplies offered at that price. In this case there is no incentive for suppliers to try to circumvent the regulated price: the black market problem is however replaced by the problem of disposal of government stocks of the supported commodity.

An important example of the use of price floors is provided by the intervention support policy in agricultural product markets in the European Community (E.C.). The protectionist nature of the Common Agricultural Policy (CAP) has been the cause of much concern among developing countries which wish to promote their exports of primary products. Some of the main elements of the E.C.'s price support policy are sketched out in Box 8.1. Price floors have also been set in a number of labour markets, including agricultural labour markets. The implications of minimum wage legislation are discussed in the next chapter.

BOX 8.1
Price support under the Common Agricultural Policy (CAP)

One of the principal methods by which the CAP raises farm prices above free market equilibrium levels is intervention support. For several agricultural products, the floor of the domestic market is established by setting an *intervention price* at which the E.C. intervention agencies are obliged to purchase any quantity offered (subject to certain quality standards). When in the early 1960s, the CAP was drafted, the original six member states were net importers of most agricultural products and the intervention system was intended primarily to fulfil a buffer stock role of price stabilisation i.e. *seasonal* surpluses could be stored and released in subsequent periods of supply deficits (Hill (1984)). In addition to intervention support, the domestic market is protected from cheaper imports from Third Countries (non-member states) by a *threshold price*, or minimum import price, above the intervention price. To raise the import price to this threshold level, an import tax or *variable levy* is imposed.

The full complexity of the price support scheme cannot be captured in a simple diagram, but Fig. 8.8 may illustrate some possible consequences of the policy. The Community demand and supply curves for the product are depicted by D_h and S_h respectively. It is assumed that the Community can buy any amount of product on the world market without affecting the

world supply price (P_w). Thus, in the absence of price regulation, the equilibrium market price would be established at P_w, at which Community demand of Q_1 comprises Q_0 from domestic producers and $(Q_1 - Q_0)$ from Third Countries. Suppose it is then decided to support the domestic market at a higher level, P_I, by means of intervention purchases. Clearly this floor price would collapse, if imports were permitted at P_w and so a variable import levy of at least $(P_I - P_w)$ must also be imposed. At P_I, Community consumers wish to purchase Q_2 only, whereas domestic producers are willing to supply Q_3. The excess supply $(Q_3 - Q_2)$ at the floor price is bought in by the intervention agencies and stored. Ignoring storage and handling costs, the exchequer cost of intervention support is $P_I(Q_3 - Q_2)$. As an alternative to storage, the surplus can be sold outside the Community but only at or below the world price, P_w. Thus in order to export the surplus a subsidy or *export refund* of $(P_I - P_w)$ per unit must be paid to the exporter. In this case the cost to the exchequer will be $(P_I - P_w)(Q_3 - Q_2)$.

Although the initial intention may have been to use intervention buying as a means of managing seasonal surpluses, the production of chronic surpluses has been a major feature of the CAP to date. Overproduction has arisen because price policy has been used primarily as a method of maintaining farm incomes and the administered price regime has been relatively inflexible in the face of rapid expansion of production (due mainly to technological progress) and slow growth in demand. The list of surplus products seems ever growing but the problem has been most obvious for dairy products, cereals,

Fig. 8.8. Intervention support under the C.A.P.

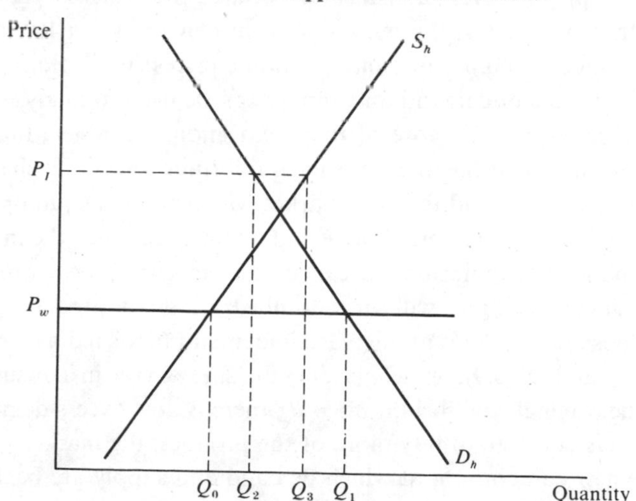

beef, sugar and wine. As the burden of maintaining huge stocks of these products becomes increasingly intolerable, some means of disposal must be found. The main methods which have been tried have been: (i) to increase domestic utilisation, e.g. by subsidising the use of the surplus product as livestock feed,[4] (ii) to provide food aid to developing countries and (iii) to subsidise exports, by granting export refunds, as we have already noted. The latter course has been the cause of much concern in Third Countries, since subsidised E.C. exports have undercut other exporters in the world market. In addition, the high level of protection has severely restricted access by Third Countries to the Community's market. Moreover, it has insulated the Community from the effects of internal and external fluctuations in supply and demand, and so increased the volatility of the world market (Johnson (1979)).

8.3 *Equilibrium in product markets*

In this section we will present a fuller discussion of price determination in competitive markets, giving particular attention to changes in equilibrium over time. Specifically, we wish to consider (i) the effects of exogenous disturbances on equilibrium values of price and quantity, and (ii) the adjustment process, when there are time lags in the response of economic agents to market stimuli.

8.3.1 *Comparative statics*

Equilibrium in Section 8.2 was determined by the intersection of demand and supply curves constructed under the *ceteris paribus* assumption. In other words, the curves were drawn for *given* levels of other product prices, income, population, input prices, technology etc. However, the concepts of demand and supply can be used to analyse the effects of a change in one or more of these exogenous variables. In this analysis, it is assumed that the market is in equilibrium before the change in the exogenous variable and that the market will also be in equilibrium after the change. The comparison of price and quantity between the initial equilibrium and final equilibrium is called the *method of comparative statics*. Some simple examples will serve to illustrate the approach.

Firstly, suppose that there is an increase in demand (depicted as a shift from D_0 to D_1 in Fig. 8.9), which is due to, say, a rise in consumer income.[5] At the original equilibrium price P_0, there is now excess demand and as consumers compete to buy more of the product, the market price is bid up. The new equilibrium, at which demand and supply are back in balance, is at the price-quantity combination (P_1, Q_1) i.e. at a higher price and larger quantity than prevailed before the income change. For a given shift in demand, the price change will be greater (and the change in quantity smaller), the more inelastic is the supply curve. Hence in Fig. 8.10, a rightward shift in the demand schedule (D_0 to D_1) induces a larger increase in price when the supply curve is perfectly inelastic (S_0) than when it is more elastic (S_1).

As we noted in Chapter 3, producers cannot instantaneously make the full adjustment to changes in market conditions. Three interrelated situations can be identified:

Fig. 8.9. Comparative statics: increase in demand.

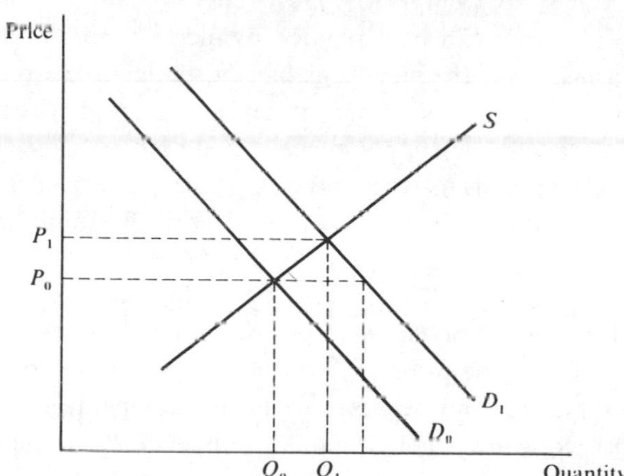

Fig. 8.10. Comparative statics with different elasticities of supply.

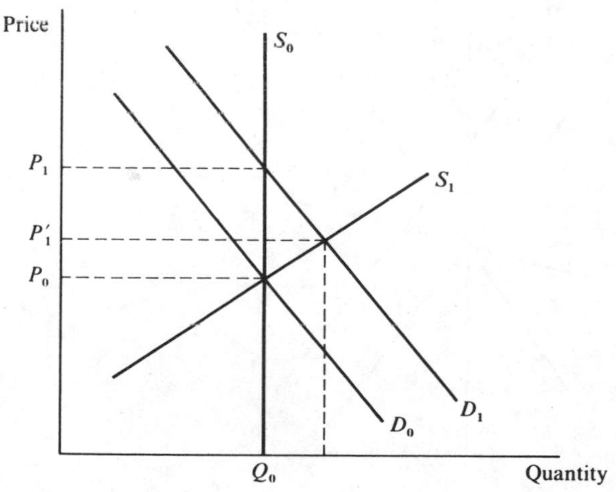

(i) The *very short run*, in which supplies are given and no change in production is possible. This might be particularly relevant for perishable products which at time of harvest must be placed on the market regardless of price. In this case the supply curve (S_{VSR} in Fig. 8.11) is perfectly inelastic.

(ii) The *short run*, in which producers can alter the levels of variable factors of production and hence move along their current marginal cost curves. The short run supply curve (S_{SR}) is more elastic.

(iii) The *long run*, in which producers can vary the usage of all inputs, and producers and resources can enter or leave the industry. The long run supply curve (S_{LR}) will be still more elastic. In particular, if output can be expanded by increasing the number of firms/farms and if the new firms have a similar cost structure to the old, then increases in output can be achieved without a large price rise and the supply curve is quite flat.

For a given, permanent shift in demand (D_0 to D_1 in Fig. 8.9) the subsequent increase in price will be smaller the greater the flexibility which producers have in decision-making i.e. the longer the 'run'.

In our second example (Fig. 8.12), the disturbance to equilibrium is due to a rightward shift in the supply curve (S_0 to S_1), which in turn may be generated by, say, a fall in the price of a variable input. At the original equilibrium price (P_0), there is now excess supply, and competition among sellers drives the price down to the new equilibrium level, P_1: an increase

Fig. 8.11. Comparative statics: different lengths of run in supply.

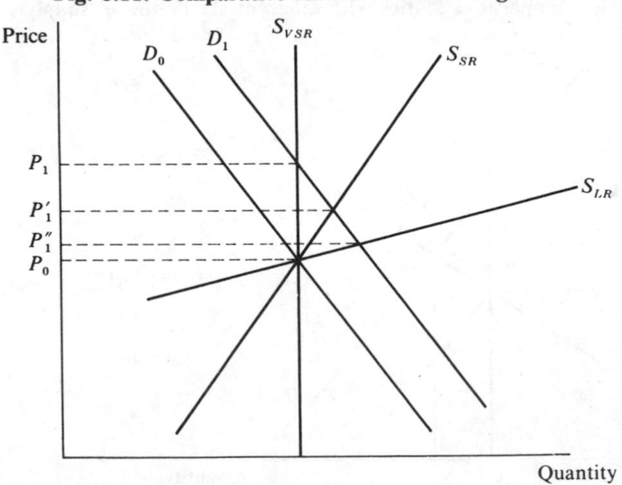

in supply has thus lowered the equilibrium price but increased the equilibrium quantity exchanged. The extent of these changes will depend on the elasticity of the demand curve. For a given shift in supply, the price change will be greater (and the change in quantity smaller) the lower the elasticity of demand. Fig. 8.13 illustrates this point: with a perfectly inelastic demand curve (D_0), the shift in the supply curve induces a price decrease to P_1 but with a more elastic demand curve, price would fall only to P'_1.

In order to illustrate the usefulness of comparative statics Boxes 8.2 and 8.3 provide simple applications of the way in which comparative statics can be used (a) to explain policies which reduce instability in agricultural commodity prices, and (b) to explain long-term trends in commodity prices.

Fig. 8.12. Comparative statics: increase in supply.

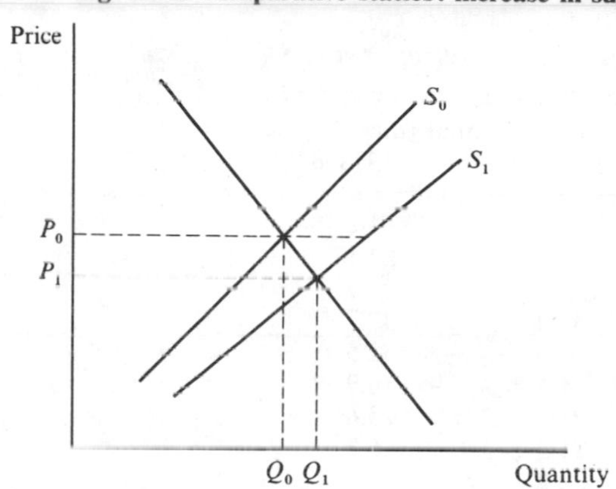

Fig. 8.13. Comparative statics with different elasticities of demand.

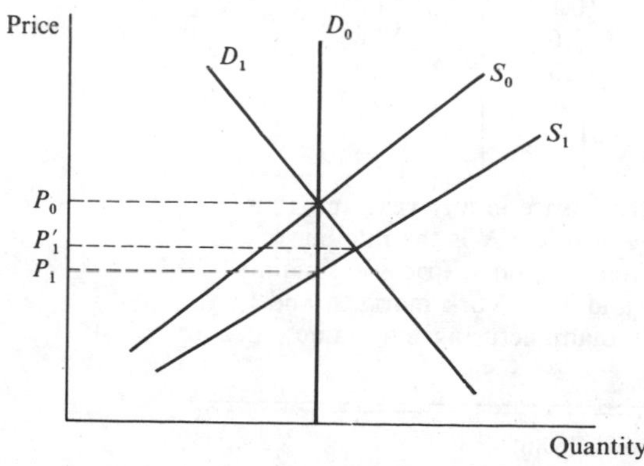

BOX 8.2
Instability of agricultural product prices and the buffer stock scheme

In the short term, prices of agricultural commodities tend to fluctuate more than the prices of non-farm products. Agricultural supply, which for most crops is seasonal, is affected in a random manner by environmental factors such as weather, pests and diseases. Moreover, as we have observed (Table 6.1), demand for most agricultural products is relatively unresponsive to price changes. As comparative statics analysis would suggest, the interaction of variable supply with inelastic demand generates large price and revenue fluctuations.[6]

A number of studies have tried to estimate the extent of instability in agricultural markets. Scandizzo and Diakosavvas (1987) review the main conceptual and empirical problems encountered in such analyses. They

Table 8.1 *Price instability indices, 1964–84*

Commodity	International price 1964–84	1978–84
Sugar	90.8	51.5
Cocoa	37.3	34.1
Rice	33.0	21.9
Coffee	32.0	37.7
Palm Kernels	27.5	32.5
Wheat	24.3	16.9
Tea	21.7	23.6
Jute	21.2	26.8
Soybeans	20.8	9.9
Beef	16.7	11.3
Corn	16.6	15.6
Rubber	16.1	14.0
Sorghum	15.6	13.6
Cotton	14.3	10.7

Note: Index $= \frac{1}{N}\Sigma\left[\frac{P_i - \bar{P}_i}{\bar{P}_i}\right]^2$

where P_i is the actual price in any year and $\bar{P}_i$ is the exponential trend price; N is the number of years of observations on prices. Prices are mainly from the London and New York markets, and they are deflated by the manufacturing unit value index (1984 = 100).

Source: World Bank (1986).

suggest that a reasonable definition of instability was proposed by Coppock (1977), viz.: 'Instability should not be understood to mean any deviation from a fixed level. It means *excessive* departure from some *normal* level.' Since for many economic variables there is a time trend, trend values of the variable could be taken as the 'normal' level, and deviations from the trend as a measure of instability. This is essentially the approach in World Bank (1986), whose results, reproduced in Table 8.1, offer some indication of the extent of recent price instability in world commodity markets. The indices measure the average deviation from the price trend in a given year. For example, in the 1974–84 period, the price of sugar in a given year would 'typically' be 51.5% above or below the trend value for that year. Price variability in these agricultural markets is of a much higher order than would be found in the markets for manufactured goods.

Governments in developing countries frequently take measures aimed at price stabilisation and indeed there have been efforts, mainly directed through UNCTAD, to promote stabilisation schemes for internationally traded primary commodities. A popular stabilisation device is that of *buffer stocks*, by which reserve stocks are built up to raise market price in periods of abundant supply and released to lower prices in periods of deficient supply. The mechanism is illustrated in Fig. 8.14. In this example, supply (in the very short run) is represented by S_1 in a low production year and by S_2 in a high production year. It is assumed that producers do not store any of the output. Thus in a 'bad' harvest year, Q_1 of the product will come on the market and will sell at a price P_1; in a 'good' year, the larger harvest of Q_2 will sell at P_2. It is further assumed that each output level has an equal chance of

Fig. 8.14. A buffer stock scheme.

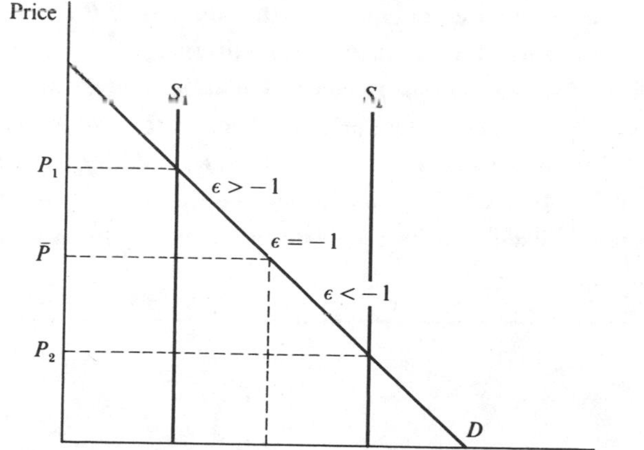

occurring. Without government intervention, the market price will fluctuate between P_1 and P_2. However, a government agency, say a marketing board, could withdraw $(Q_2 - \bar{Q})$ from the market in a 'good' year and put this amount into storage. This action has the effect of reducing supply in the market to $\bar{Q}$ (the mean of Q_1 and Q_2) and hence raises price to $\bar{P}$. In the low production year, the agency can release $(\bar{Q} - Q_1)$ from storage, thus augmenting market supply and lowering price from P_1 to $\bar{P}$. By use of buffer-stocks, market price has been stabilised at $\bar{P}$ (the mean of P_1 to P_2). This example has been constructed in such a way that the regulated quantity $(\bar{Q})$ is associated with the unitary elastic point of the linear demand curve (at which total revenue is maximised) and hence producers' revenues are higher under the stabilisation programme: total receipts are larger at $\bar{Q}$ than at either Q_1 or Q_2. (Note that in the range of output $\bar{Q}$ to Q_2 demand is inelastic (and marginal revenue negative) and so, as we noted in Chapter 6, an increase in price will raise total revenue. Conversely, in the output range Q_1 to $\bar{Q}$, demand is elastic and a decrease in price will increase total revenue.) Furthermore, stocks will be 'self-liquidating' over time, since there will be the same number of 'good' and 'bad' harvests.

It must be stressed that the foregoing example of the buffer-stock scheme relies on a number of simplifying assumptions and it may be a poor representation of the operation of buffer stocks in practice. In particular, we have assumed implicitly that the agency knows the precise nature of the demand curve and the probabilities of supply fluctuations, and that the costs of handling and storage are negligible. Furthermore, the effects of price stabilisation on producers and consumers depend on the form of the demand and supply functions, on the source of instability and on the reactions of producers to the stabilisation policy. The full complexity of the analysis cannot be discussed here[7] but we should make the point that the benefits which price stabilisation offers the producer can be overstated. Contrary to our example, producers' returns can be reduced by a buffer stock scheme, if demand for the product is elastic at low prices but inelastic at high prices. Moreover, price stability is not synonymous with income stability. It can be demonstrated that if the demand elasticity (in absolute terms) exceeds 0.5, income will be less stable under a price stabilisation scheme than under free market conditions.[8]

BOX 8.3
The long term trend in agricultural product prices

Another instance in which comparative statics might provide some insights is in the analysis of long term trends in agricultural product prices. In planning food policies in the longer run, it may be useful to consider the impact of actual or potential structural changes in demand and supply, ignoring year to year fluctuations.

The demand for many agricultural products may grow slowly over time, at least in the markets of the developed countries. This is because, in these markets, population growth is slow and although per caput income may be rising, the income elasticities of demand for most agricultural products are low. Indeed, as we noted in Chapter 6, the income elasticities for these products may decline with economic growth. Hence agricultural producers in developed countries or in developing countries which export to developed countries' markets do not enjoy the benefits which rapid growth in demand for their output might bring. Additional problems may be encountered in some markets. For example, some primary commodities such as wool, rubber and jute, may face increasing competition from synthetic products and the demand for some foodstuffs may be subject to adverse changes in consumer tastes.[9] Finally, the growth in demand for a given product may be influenced by the policy environment i.e. access to markets will be determined by the degree of protectionism.

The main determinant of shifts in agricultural product supply over time is likely to be the rate of technological change. As we have observed, technological progress has been marked in all spheres of agriculture and, given the competitive nature of the sector, the adoption and diffusion of new techniques has been rapid in developed countries and also in some developing countries. When the growth in demand is outstripped by the growth in supply, a downward trend in prices will be generated (Fig. 8.15). (Again note that the fall in the equilibrium price over time will be more pronounced, the less price elastic is the demand curve.)

It is often argued that the demand trend depicted in Fig. 8.15 is 'typical' of agricultural product markets. However, it should be noted that if the growth in demand is more rapid than the growth in supply, the trend in agricultural product price would be reversed. Under what circumstances might this occur? Since in the LDCs population growth is more rapid and income elasticities for agricultural products are higher than in the developed countries, the growth in demand can be substantial *if* per caput incomes rise.

Certainly in the future the markets of the developing countries may become increasingly important for the producers of some agricultural products. Indeed there is now growing interest in the prospects for increased trade among the developing countries (sometimes termed 'South–South' trade) and far greater economic co-operation among LDCs. On the supply side, the growth in production may abate as fewer new areas are brought into cultivation (i.e. land supply becomes fixed) and as environmental constraints, a consequence of modern farming methods, are encountered.

The foregoing should be read as an illustration of the use of comparative static analysis rather than as a comprehensive guide to the factors influencing the long term trend in agricultural prices. There are several alternative hypotheses which we have not presented (a useful summary of this literature may be found in Scandizzo and Diakosavvas (1987)). Whether a downward trend in agricultural prices has been observed in the past is an empirical question but the statistical analysis[10] is also bound by a number of conceptual and methodological limitations. If a generalisation were to be made (always a precarious undertaking), it would be that a downward trend has been found for some commodities and for some LDCs in specific sub-periods.

8.3.2 *Dynamics*

In the analysis of comparative statics we study changes in equilibria, but we are not explicitly concerned with how the market moves from one equilibrium to another or with how long the process might take.

Fig. 8.15. Long term trend in price.

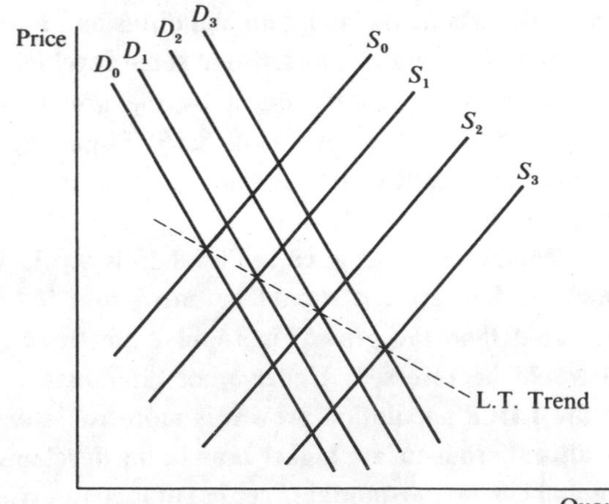

In contrast, dynamic models involve time in an integral way and focus explicitly on the time-path of economic variables.

Returning to Fig. 8.9, suppose that the shift in demand occurs in a particular time period, $t+1$, and that until that time the market was at equilibrium, with market price at P_0. Unless price and quantity adjusts instantaneously to the new equilibrium (P_1, Q_1), the actual time-path of adjustment needs to be considered. A possible time-path for price is shown in Fig. 8.16. Although we specify discrete time periods ($t+1$, $t+2$, etc.) in this figure, it is assumed that price moves through time in a smooth and continuous fashion. In this example, with damped oscillations, price moves towards P_1, the new 'stationary' value, but note that the process takes several time periods and that initially price diverges markedly from P_1. This suggests that comparative statics analysis may be misleading if the movement from one equilibrium to another is slow. Moreover, the knowledge that an equilibrium is stable (recall Section 8.2.2) is of little value if it takes many years to attain equilibrium.

In the specification of the price adjustment mechanism in dynamic models, a common approach is to assume that price variation over time depends on the degree of excess demand in the market.[11] In a simple form, the rate of change in price is assumed to be proportional to the level of excess demand.[12]

When a product can be stored, market clearing is facilitated not only by adjustments in price but also by *changes in the level of stocks or inventories*. This role of storage is particularly important in many agricultural product markets, since it permits supply, which becomes

Fig. 8.16. A time-path for market price.

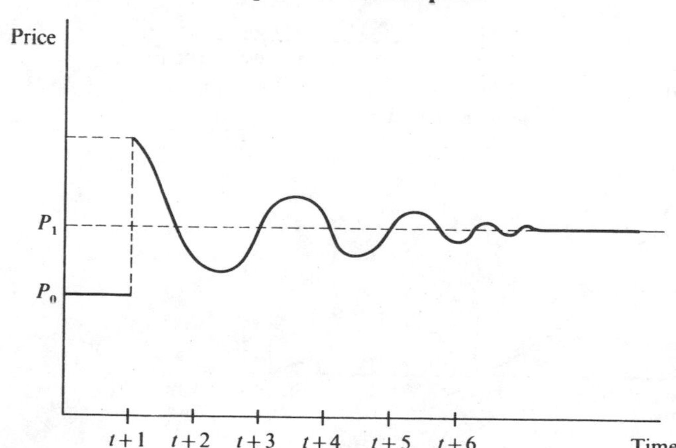

available at a specific point in the year, to be matched to a more regular pattern of demand. For example, wheat may be harvested over a period of, say, two months, but it is consumed throughout the year; wheat stocks may ensure an orderly pattern of price movements within the season.

Small scale farmers in developing countries may not have storage facilities and so must sell all their output at harvest when prices are relatively low. Those farmers with storage facilities do not operate with this disadvantage. For this group the storage decision will depend on the current market price, the expected future price and the cost of storage. The latter will include the costs of handling, depreciation on the storage facilities, losses due to product deterioration, the opportunity cost of the financial investment tied up in the stored product, and so forth. In essence, the price must rise throughout the year to cover these storage costs. A 'typical' seasonal price pattern, for a crop which is harvested once a year, is illustrated in Fig. 8.17(*a*). The market price is low in the harvest quarter (since supply is large relative to demand) and rises, as a function of the cost of storage, to a peak prior to the next harvest. As the market anticipates the increased quantity and lower prices which the new harvest will bring, price tends to fall quite rapidly in the month or so before the harvest begins. In the course of the harvest year, the change in price

Fig. 8.17. 'Typical' seasonal patterns.

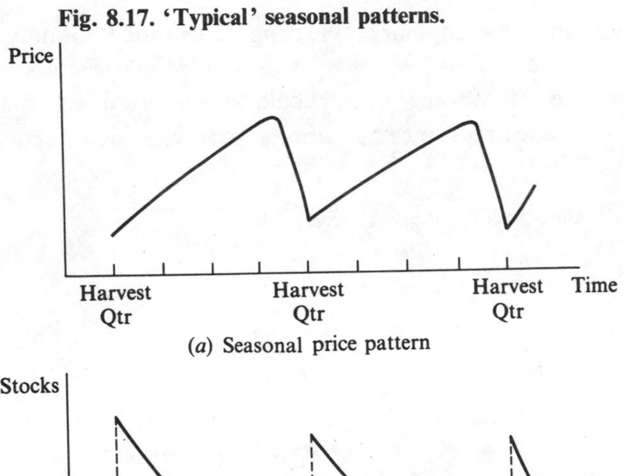

(*a*) Seasonal price pattern

(*b*) Seasonal stocks pattern

should be sufficient to induce steady release of the product from storage. Producers' stocks would also exhibit a seasonal pattern (Fig. 8.17(*b*)) in which inventories would be highest at harvest but would be depleted during the crop year.[13]

A formal dynamic model

A simple dynamic model, with inventories, could be specified as follows:

$$QD_t = f(P_t, M_t) \tag{8.8}$$

$$QS_t = f(P_t, W_t) \tag{8.9}$$

$$P_t = f(\Delta I_t, Z_t) \tag{8.10}$$

$$\Delta I_t = I_t - I_{t-1} = QS_t - QD_t \tag{8.11}$$

As before, we have a demand equation (8.8) and a supply equation (8.9). Each is a function of price in a given time period (P_t). In addition, demand will depend on the level of an exogenous variable, say income, (M_t), whilst supply will vary with the level of, say, weather (W_t). We then specify an explicit price adjustment mechanism (8.10), namely that price is a function of the *change* in inventories (denoted by ΔI_t) and some exogenous factor (Z_t). In this type of model, the market clearing identity takes the form of equation 8.11. This equation simply states that any slack in the market (i.e. demand and supply need not be equal) will be taken up by a change in stock levels, which in turn is defined as the difference between inventories at time *t* and inventories in the previous period ($t-1$).

The cobweb model A dynamic model which has received particular attention by agricultural economists, is the *cobweb model*. In some agricultural product markets, the time paths of prices and output appear to exhibit regular fluctuations, or cycles. For example, in some countries cycles of about 3 years for pigs and 3–5 years for potatoes have been observed. Since the cobweb model provides an explanation for certain types of cyclical behaviour, it has been used as the basis of theoretical and empirical analysis of several product markets. A simple form of the model is presented here.

The dynamics in the model derive from the particular specification of the supply relations. It is assumed that production plans are based on current price and that there is a one period time lag in production response. Hence the expected price (P_t^*) for output sold in period *t* is equal to the actual price in the previous period (i.e. $P_t^* = P_{t-1}$). Since it is also assumed that production plans are fully realised, there is a lag between price changes and adjustments in supply (i.e. *short run* supply is a function of lagged price). However, in the *very short run*, supply is assumed to be perfectly inelastic: production forthcoming at harvest is sold in the market irrespective of price. In a competitive market, the market clearing price in a given period is then determined by the demand for the (given) output.

The type of cyclical behaviour which the cobweb model can generate is illustrated in Fig. 8.18(*a*). Suppose that in the initial period price is set at P_0. On the assumption that this price will prevail, producers supply Q_1 in the subsequent period. This quantity however sells at P_1, the market clearing price determined by the intersection of the demand curve and the very short run supply at Q_1. Producers now base their production plans on P_1, and in the next period, supply Q_2. This output in turn determines a higher price, P_2, and so the process continues, assuming there is no exogenous disturbances. The time path of the market price is depicted in Fig. 8.18(*b*). (As we are observing price only at a series of discrete time periods (1, 2, 3, etc.) the time path is disjoint.) It is clear that in this case the process will converge to the equilibrium price P^*; this type of time path is described as *damped oscillatory*.

However, the cobweb model can encompass two other types of cyclical process. In Fig. 8.19, an *explosive oscillatory* time path is created and in Fig. 8.20, the cycle is continuous, with *undamped oscillations*. The type of cycle which is created will depend on the precise form of the demand and supply relations. Specifically, for linear demand and supply curves, the following characteristics will be exhibited:

Fig. 8.18. Damped oscillations.

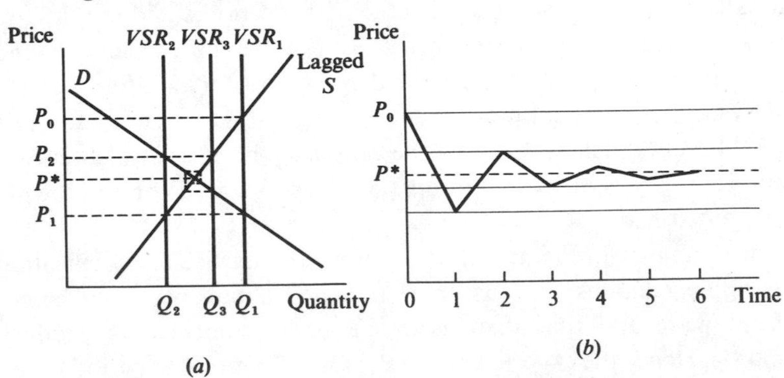

(i) If the absolute slope of the demand curve is less than that of the supply curve, a disturbance will lead to oscillations in price and quantity which are damped and which converge to equilibrium.

(ii) If the absolute slope of the demand curve is greater than that of the supply curve, a disturbance will set in motion oscillations in price and quantity which are divergent or explosive and which lead the market away from equilibrium.

(iii) If the absolute slopes of the demand and supply curves are equal, the oscillations will be of constant magnitude about the equilibrium.

Fig. 8.19. Explosive oscillations.

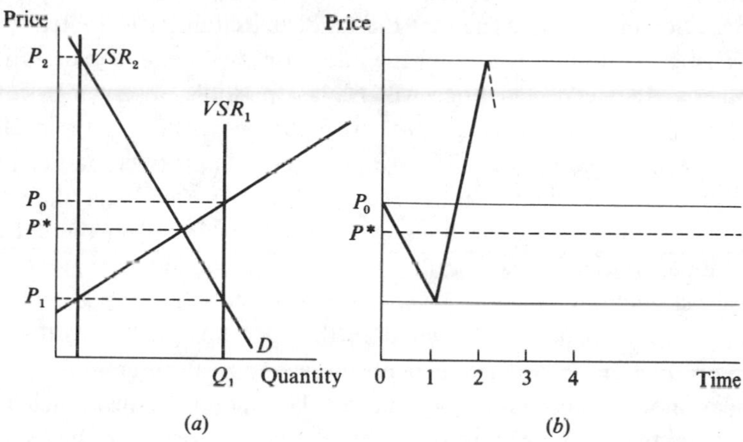

Fig. 8.20. Undamped oscillations.

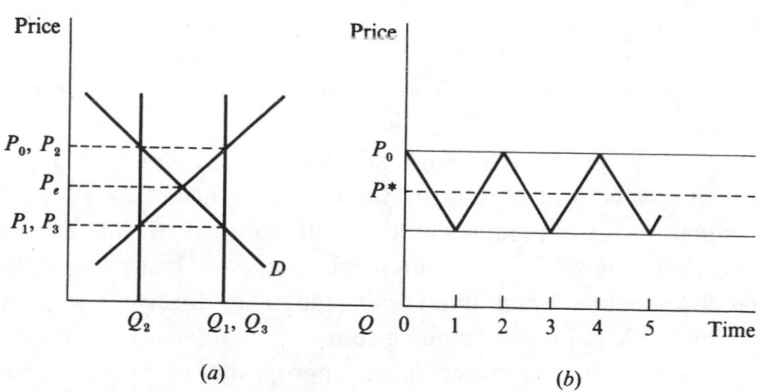

The version of the cobweb model presented here can be represented by three equations, a supply function, a demand function and a market-clearing identity:

$$QS_t = f(P_{t-1}) \quad (8.12)$$

$$QD_t = f(P_t) \quad (8.13)$$

$$QD_t = QS_t \quad (8.14)$$

To emphasise that the market clearing price is determined by demand, equation 8.13 is often inverted: $P_t = f^{-1}(QD_t)$.

By explicitly introducing dynamics, the cobweb model offers a better representation of those markets in which price and quantity cycles are observed. However, it must be stressed that the form of the model presented above is too elementary to provide the basis for a comprehensive analysis. Some authors argue that the model's usefulness is limited by its 'unrealistic' assumptions and by the adoption of the naive expectations hypothesis (that expected price will be last period's observed price) in particular.[14] Whereas this assumption might be justified if the cyclical behaviour predicted by the model were observed in product markets, this is not the case. Price and quantity cycles, when they are observed, appear to be continuous, but continuous cycles are only found in the cobweb model under rather special conditions. Moreover the model suggests that the cycle should have a length of twice the production lag but several 'real world' cycles appear to be longer than this, perhaps four times the time lag in production. In order to explain these empirical observations, more complex models have been constructed. The modifications which have been suggested include the introduction of 'shift factors' into the demand and supply functions, of 'partial adjustment' of producers to price changes, and of an expectations hypothesis with more behavioural content.

8.4 *Production and consumption activities within the agricultural household*

In the analysis of demand and supply, two separate sets of economic agents, consumers and producers, are defined. This is a useful approach in the study of product markets at the national and international levels. However, development economists are also interested in the analysis of the agricultural household, the main form of economic organisation in the poorest developing countries, and here the dichotomy between consumers and producers is less appropriate. In the agricultural household, production and consumption activities take place within the same economic unit. Some farm output is produced for sale and some is used for home consumption. Some inputs, such as fertiliser, are brought in, and other inputs, e.g. family labour, are supplied by the household. The analysis of the agricultural household thus requires a synthesis of consumer theory and the theory of production economics. An additional complication is that much household activity never passes through the marketplace.

8.4.1 *The theory of the agricultural household*

Current approaches to modelling the agricultural household are based on the work of a number of economists in the 1960s (e.g. Mellor (1963), Nakajima (1970), Sen (1966)), although a similar analysis had been suggested much earlier, in the 1920s, by Chayanov. Singh *et al.* (1986a) have recently provided an overview of agricultural household models, together with a number of empirical case studies.

A simple representation of the production activities of the agricultural household is given in Fig. 8.21. Here, one variable input, labour, with a total time availability of OL_t is applied to a fixed land area. It is assumed that time is divided between two activities: labour and leisure. It is further assumed that the price of the product is set by the market and so given to the household. The production response curve, OP, depicts the relationship between the value of farm output (or income) and labour usage. Its slope indicates the marginal productivity of the variable input, labour. Hence in Fig. 8.21, diminishing returns to labour are assumed. As a

Fig. 8.21. Production response curve.

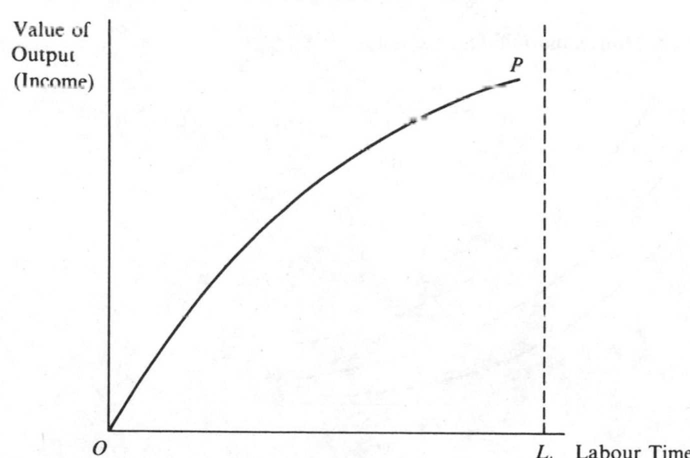

consumer unit, the household obtains utility from the income generated by farm production and from leisure; the indifference map for the household is depicted in Fig. 8.22. The utility obtained from any amount of income is offset by the loss of utility from leisure foregone in production activities as well as by the disutility generated by the drudgery of farm work. The slope of a given indifference curve measures that amount of income which is needed just to compensate the household for a small increase in household labour utilised. The slope represents the valuation of a marginal unit of household labour utilised and so is termed the 'marginal valuation of household labour'. There may however be some minimum, or subsistence, level of family income, which may be determined by both social and physiological factors. At this point (*OM*) the indifference curves are horizontal, indicating that no amount of leisure can compensate for income levels below the subsistence level.

The household will seek to choose the combination of output and leisure which will maximise utility, given the constraints imposed by the production response curve. The solution to this problem is sometimes termed the 'subjective equilibrium', because it is determined by the indifference map specific to the agricultural household. The equilibrium conditions will depend on whether the farm household has any opportunity to hire outside labour or to sell its own labour services off the farm. We will deal in turn with case (a) where there is no labour market, and (b) where such a market exists.

(a) *The agricultural household without access to a labour market* The equilibrium solution in this case can be illustrated by transposing the

Fig. 8.22. Household indifference map.

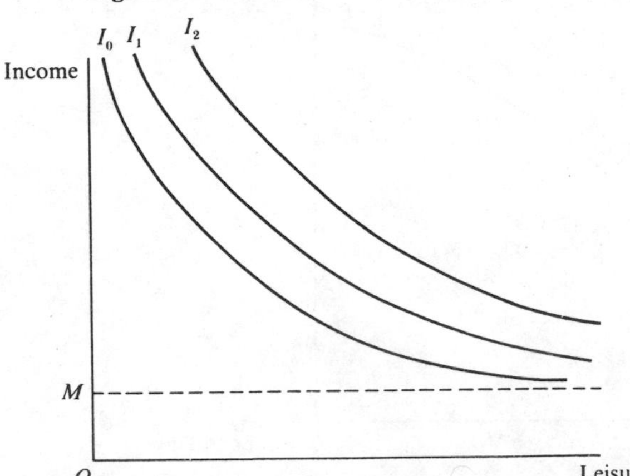

indifference map of Fig. 8.22 and putting it and the production response curve on the same diagram (Fig. 8.23(*a*)). In this figure the horizontal axis when read from left to right measures the labour usage from total available time L_t, and when read from right to left measures the leisure time taken from L_t. The equilibrium solution is located at the highest utility level attainable within the confines of OP. This optimum is found at the point of tangency (E), where OL_f family labour is used in production and L_fL_t or (OL_t-OL_f) time is spent at leisure. At this point the marginal valuation of household labour is equated to the value of the marginal product of labour. The solution in terms of the marginal relationships is illustrated in Fig. 8.23(*b*). Through any point of the

Fig. 8.23. (*a*) Agricultural household without a labour market.
(*b*) Agricultural household without a labour market: marginal relationships.

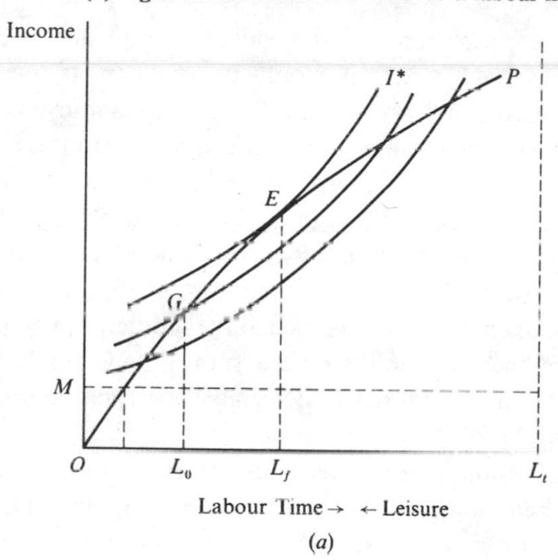

(*a*)

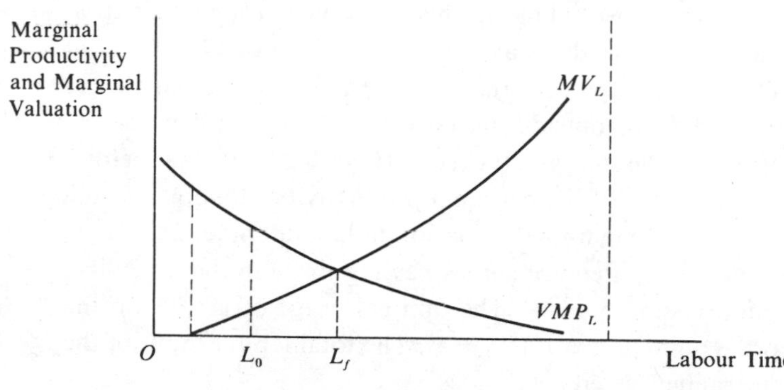

(*b*)

production response curve OP there will pass an indifference curve. The 'marginal valuation of labour' curve, MV_L, indicates the slope of the indifference curve at that point. (A minor complication is that until the value of output reaches the minimum subsistence level (OM), the marginal valuation of labour is zero.) The slope of the OP curve measures the marginal productivity of labour, or more accurately, the value of the marginal productivity of labour; it is depicted as VMP_L in Fig. 8.23(*b*). At the point G on the production response curve, the value of the marginal product of labour (or slope of OP) exceeds the marginal valuation of labour (or slope of the indifference curve passing through G). This suggests that more labour than OL_0 should be utilised in production. The optimal solution is given at the intersection of VMP_L and MV_L, which in turn coincides with the tangency point, E, in the upper diagram.

(b) *The agricultural household with access to a labour market* In this case it is assumed that the household is able not only to work on its own holding but to hire additional labour or to sell some of its own labour time off the farm, at a competitively determined wage rate. The wage rate, w, is the slope of the 'wage line' WW' in Figs. 8.24 and 8.25. The amount of labour used on the farm (OL_f) is determined (as in the case of the profit maximising firm of Chapter 2) by the equality of its value of marginal product with the wage rate (i.e. $VMP_L = w$). It is important to note that this production decision is taken without reference to the indifference map and thus is independent of the household's labour supply decision. The indifference map is still of course required to determine the total labour time expanded by the household.

In Fig. 8.24(*a*), the household's subjective equilibrium implies that OL_e of labour will be forthcoming and L_eL_t will be taken as leisure. The total labour input is determined at the tangency of the household indifference curve with the wage line. At this point the marginal valuation of household labour equals the wage rate.[15] Of the household's total labour input (OL_e), OL_f is spent working on the family farm and L_fL_e is spent in wage employment outside the farm. This solution can also be depicted in terms of the marginal curves (Fig. 8.24(*b*)). As before, VMP_L represents the value of the marginal productivity of labour, or the slope of OP. However, the marginal valuation of labour curve, MV_L, now represents the slope of indifference curves passing through the wage line, not the production response curve. The optimal usage of labour on the farm is given at the point where $VMP_L = w$. The total labour input of the household is determined where $MV_L = w$.

In Fig. 8.25, the household will choose to hire labour services from outside the family. Of the farm labour input OL_f, the household itself provides OL'_e, with the remainder L'_eL_f being found in the labour market. Again the subjective equilibrium is found where the marginal valuation of labour (or slope of the indifference curve) is equal to the wage rate (or slope of the wage line). The difference between Fig. 8.24 and Fig. 8.25 is whether point H lies to the left or right of point E, the marginal conditions for the optimal solution are the same in both diagrams.

Singh *et al.* (1986a) present a 'basic model'[16] which captures the salient features of agricultural household decision-making and which has many

Fig. 8.24. (*a*) Agricultural household selling labour. (*b*) Agricultural household selling labour: marginal relationships.

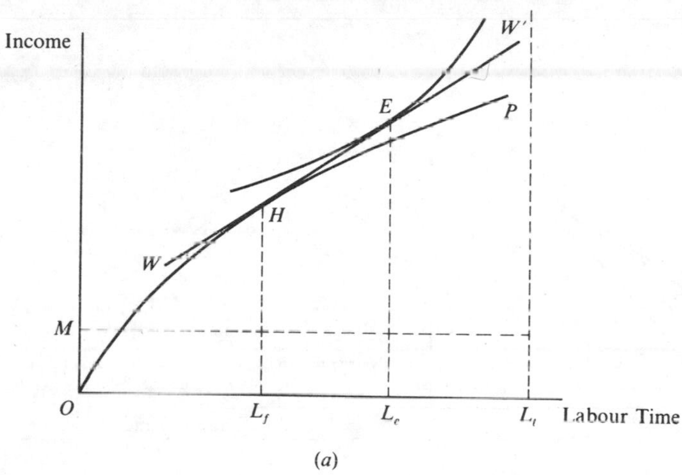

(*a*)

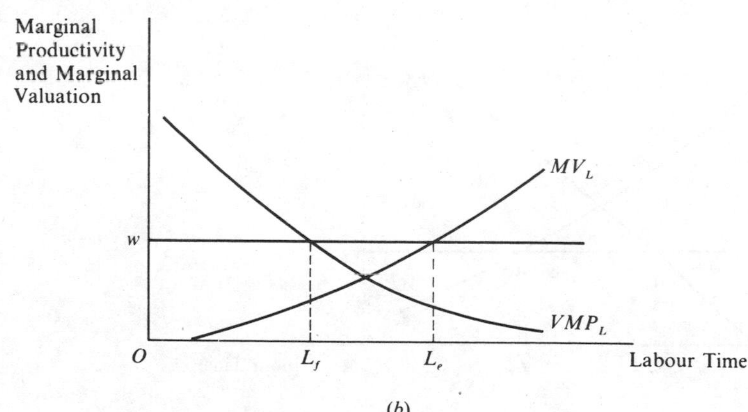

(*b*)

similarities with the foregoing analysis. In their model, the agricultural household has a fixed land resource and uses a single variable input, labour. In addition the household is assumed to be a price-taker, receiving a fixed price for its output and buying or selling labour at a fixed wage. An important feature of the model is its recursive character. By this we mean that the production decisions of the household are independent of its consumption and labour supply decisions. However the production decisions determine profits, a component of household income, which in turn influences consumption and labour supply choices. This one-way relationship is known as the 'profit effect'. It is worth noting at the outset

Fig. 8.25. (*a*) **Agricultural household hiring labour.** (*b*) **Agricultural household hiring labour: marginal relationships.**

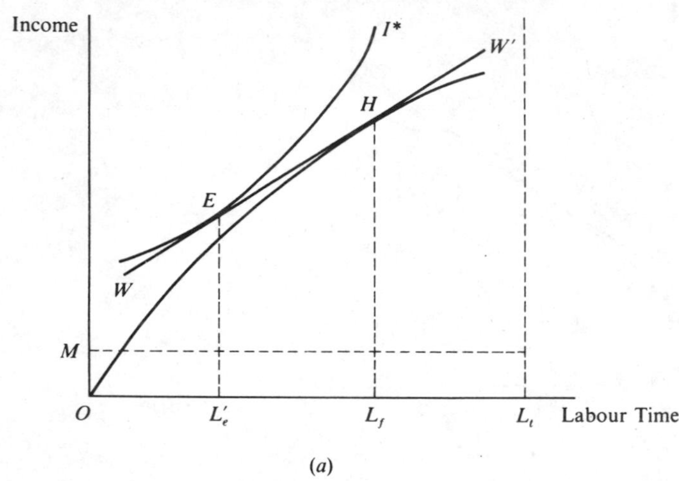

(*a*)

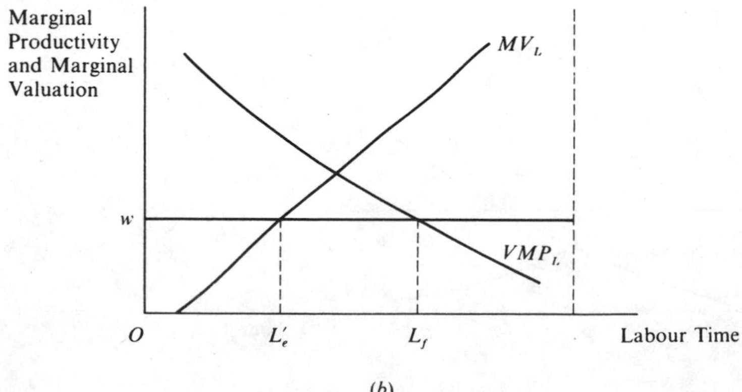

(*b*)

that if the profit effect is unimportant in a particular empirical setting, an integrated household model of the type we are about to present would not be required. We elaborate on this point later.

It is assumed that the household wishes to maximise the satisfaction arising from consumption of its agricultural output (Q_a), of a purchased market good (Q_m) and of leisure (Q_r). The utility function would then take the form:

$$U = U(Q_a, Q_m, Q_r) \tag{8.15}$$

The household faces, however, a budget constraint, a time constraint and a production constraint. Firstly, the budget constraint can be written as:

$$P_m Q_m = P_a(Q - Q_a) - w(L - F) \tag{8.16}$$

where P_m and P_a are the prices of the market good and the agricultural product respectively, w is the wage rate, Q is total farm output, L is the total labour input and F is the family labour input. The term $(Q - Q_a)$ denotes the household's *marketed surplus* and will be non-negative, the term $(L - F)$ will be positive if labour is hired, and negative if the household supplies labour off-farm. The constraint simply states that expenditure on the market good must equal net cash income.

The time constraint is written as

$$Q_r + F = T \tag{8.17}$$

where T is the total amount of household time which is available for allocation to work or leisure (having deducted the time spent in meeting the basic requirements for human maintenance such as sleeping, eating, fuel gathering etc.). This constraint states that the allocation of time to leisure, farm production and off-farm employment cannot exceed the total time which the household has at its disposal. Finally, the production function imposes a constraint on farm production:

$$Q = f(L \mid A) \tag{8.18}$$

where A is the household's (fixed) land resource.

The constraints (8.16, 8.17 and 8.18) can be collapsed into a single constraint which is analogous to Becker's full income constraint (Section 7.4):

$$P_m Q_m + P_a Q_a + wQ_r = wT + \Pi \tag{8.19}$$

where $\Pi = [P_a f(L \mid A) - wL]$, a measure of farm profits. The right-hand side of this equation represents the value of full income, which has two components, farm profits and the value of the household's total stock of time (wT). On the left-hand side we have household 'expenditure' on the market good, on home consumption of farm output and on leisure. The household will thus seek to maximise the utility function, 8.15, subject to the full income constraint, 8.19.

In this constrained maximisation problem, the household chooses the consumption levels of farm output, the market good and leisure, and the level of total labour usage in agricultural production. However, with respect to the latter decision, the first order condition is simply

$$P_a \frac{\partial Q}{\partial L} = w$$

i.e. the value of the marginal product of labour is equated to the wage rate. This optimal condition is independent of the levels of the other choice variables; the demand for labour on the farm will depend only on the price of the final product, the wage rate, the technical parameters of the production function and the level of the fixed input, land. The optimal usage of labour yields maximum farm profits and hence determines the maximum level of full income. It then only remains to find the optimal levels of the other choice variable, given this budget constraint. The first order conditions in this case are analogous to those of the utility maximisation problem of Section 5.2 of Chapter 5 and yield demand functions of the standard form, for the three consumption items – the agricultural output (Q_a), the purchased market good (Q_m) and leisure (Q_r):

$$Q_a = f_a(P_a, P_m, w, Y^*) \qquad (8.20)$$

$$Q_r = f_r(P_a, P_m, w, Y^*) \qquad (8.21)$$

$$Q_m = f_m(P_a, P_m, w, Y^*) \qquad (8.22)$$

where Y^* is the value of full income associated with profit-maximisation, and where w, the wage rate, is also the price of leisure. The 'profit effect', noted above, is transmitted through the variable Y^*. In particular, if there is a change in the price of the agricultural product, this will lead to adjustments in labour usage on the farm and to a change in farm profits. The latter, since farm profit is a component of household income, will in turn induce changes in the level of consumption of home produce, the purchased market good and leisure (and hence the household's own labour supply).

The distinguishing feature of the agricultural household model is the inclusion of the profit effect. If the profit effect is unimportant, then there is little need for an integrated model of this type. The profit effect will be weak if (a) profits are only a small proportion of the household's full income, (b) profits are relatively insensitive to changes in product prices or (c) consumption of a particular commodity of interest is unresponsive to changes in full income. It is then an empirical question whether for a given sample of agricultural households the profit effect is in fact negligible, and hence whether an integrated agricultural household model is required. We present some empirical results in Box 8.4.

BOX 8.4
Agricultural household models: some empirical evidence

Singh *et al.* (1986a) present some empirical results from a number of studies in which the approach broadly accords with the basic model presented above. Their table of selected elasticities is reproduced here. In each case, attention focuses on a single product or on aggregate farm output, treated as a single product. The first two columns of this table present the elasticities of demand for the home produced output and for the purchased market good, as the price of the agricultural product changes. The elasticity of supply of the product to the market is given in the third column and the elasticity of the household's supply of labour (the converse of the consumption of leisure) is presented in the final column.

Response to changes in the price of the agricultural commodity

Country	Agricultural commodity	Consumption of the agricultural good	Consumption of the market purchased good	Marketed surplus	Labour supply
Taiwan	Farm Output	0.22	1.18	1.03	−1.54
Malaysia	Rice	0.38	1.94	0.66	−0.57
Korea, Rep.	Rice	0.01	0.81	1.40	−0.13
Japan	Farm Output	−0.35	0.61	2.97	−1.01
Thailand	Farm Output	−0.37	0.51	8.10	−0.62
Sierra Leone	Rice	−0.66	0.14	0.71	−0.09
Northern Nigeria	Sorghum	0.19	0.57	0.20	−0.06

The results suggest that as the agricultural product price rises, the household increases its marketed surplus. Recall that in Chapter 3 we noted

that there has been some discussion as to whether supply response in developing countries is positive, as economic theory suggests; these results at least indicate that it is, although the degree of responsiveness varies markedly across the studies. In each case, the total output response to an increase in the agricultural product price is strong enough to outweigh any increase in home consumption of the product. These empirical studies also record positive cross-price elasticities of demand for the market-purchased good and negative labour supply elasticities. The latter suggests that labour supply (leisure) decisions are affected by the profit effect and that leisure is a normal good.

The most striking feature of this table, however, is that four of the seven studies report a positive own-price elasticity of demand for the agricultural good. To see how these apparently perverse results can arise, consider Fig. 8.26 in which the household demand for the agricultural good, rice is depicted as D_0. According to traditional demand theory, an increase in the price of rice (to P_1) would reduce consumption from Q_0 to Q_1. However, the agricultural household produces, as well as consumes, the farm product and the increase in price raises farm profit and hence household (full) income. This (positive) profits effect, depicted as a shift in the demand curve to D_1 in Fig. 8.26, can be strong enough to outweigh the usual (negative) consumer response.[17] Thus, in the figure below, consumption (Q') at the new price level is greater than at the original price.

Fig. 8.26. The profit effect of a price rise on household consumption.

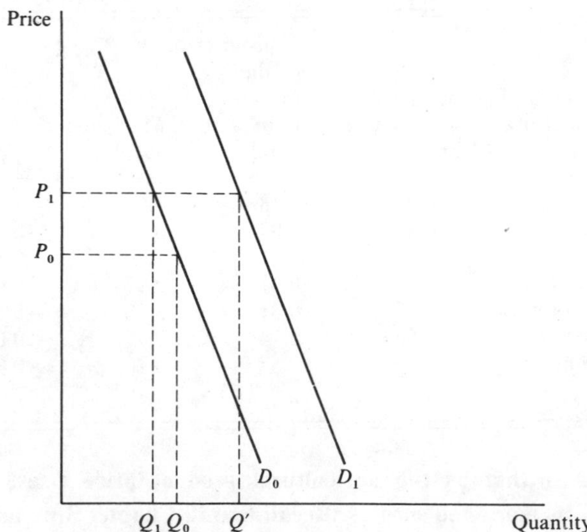

8.4.2 *The Z-goods model of the agricultural household*

The foregoing model of the agricultural household represents the activities of commercial or semi-commercial farmers who consume part of their output and sell the rest. However, in some regions, e.g. Southern Africa (Low (1986)) the production of many farms never enters the market. It might then be more appropriate to conduct an analysis of these households using a model which places greater emphasis on non-market activities. Becker's household production function approach, introduced in Section 7.4 of Chapter 7, seems particularly well suited for the task and it is therefore rather surprising that although it has been frequently used in the study of the allocation of non-market time in developed countries, there are few examples of its application in the developing countries.

The main features of the Becker model are again:

(i) The household seeks to maximise utility which is derived not from market goods, but from basic commodities or 'Z-goods'. The Z-goods may be defined as any non-traded output of the household. In the present context, they might include food processing, home maintenance (fuel gathering, water carrying, handicrafts etc.), the number and quality of children.

(ii) The Z-goods are produced by the household using as inputs the household's time and purchased market goods. The production relationship is defined by a conventional production function.

(iii) The household faces a budget constraint, whereby expenditure on market goods cannot exceed money income, and a time constraint, whereby work time, together with time spent in household production activities cannot exceed the household's total allocation of time.

It can be shown that equilibrium of the household is given where the marginal rate of substitution between any pair of Z-goods in consumption equals the ratio of their marginal costs in production. Marginal cost of production of Z-good, Z_i, will be a function of the prices of market goods and time and of the productivity of each in producing Z_i.

The solution of the constrained maximisation problem yields the optimal amount of home work time and wage work time which the household should allocate. Leisure is often not given explicit treatment. In contrast, the foregoing model of the agricultural household distinguished between labour (either farm work or wage work) and leisure. However, the differences between the two models are not so great and arise more from the emphasis placed on particular economic variables rather than from the philosophy implicit in the research methodology. Both are exercises in constrained utility maximisation in which the allocation of household time is of central importance. The differences lie in terms of the definition of the parameters of the utility function and in the specification of the constraints.

8.5 *Conclusions*

In this chapter we have brought together two branches of traditional economic theory: the theory of production (in the form of the supply curve) and the theory of consumer behaviour (in terms of the demand curve). In most economic analyses explicit consideration must be given to the relationships of supply and demand since it is their interaction in the market place which determines the market price and quantities exchanged. Although much of this chapter (and indeed of subsequent chapters) focuses on equilibrium and changes in equilibrium, we have suggested that equilibrium conditions need not always prevail. We have also tried to indicate some of the consequences when governments attempt to prevent the market equilibrium from prevailing.

The study of product markets in developed and developing countries is an important pursuit of agricultural economists. Many of the interesting problems to be analysed will involve changes in the determining variables of demand and supply. Economic growth will shift the product demand curve, technological change will shift the supply curve and so forth. Static theory however would provide few insights into the effects of these changes and alternatives must be sought. A simple and often useful approach is to consider the comparative statics of market changes. In those cases where we are concerned with the path of adjustment when the market is shocked out of equilibrium, a more complex dynamic analysis may be attempted.

The common form of economic organisation in the agricultural sector of LDCs is the agricultural household which combines the functions of consumption and production. Hence when we wish to study the behaviour of the agricultural household, the conventional dichotomy of economic agents into consumers and producers is no longer appropriate. In the agricultural household model to which we have given most attention in this chapter, the interdependence of consumption and production activities is introduced through a 'profit effect'. The latter results from the increase in income which arises from higher crop prices. If the profit effect is negligible, the agricultural household model will not offer much more than the conventional approach. It should be stressed that the relevance of this model is not confined to LDC farmers. It is also applicable to family farms in industrial countries, and to self-employing firms generally.

We have now introduced most of the conventional analytical tools which agricultural economists use. We are now in a position to consider more specific aspects of agricultural markets.

8.6 *Summary points*

1. A market is in *equilibrium* when the quantity offered for sale at the ruling price exactly matches the quantity demanded at that price. There may however be situations in which an equilibrium does not exist, where there is more than one equilibrium or where the equilibrium is unstable.
2. *General equilibrium* analysis concerns the study of the whole economic system, with the interdependence among all sectors of the economy being handled explicitly. In *partial equilibrium* analysis attention focuses on a restricted subset of the economic system – typically a set of consumers and producers of a particular product – in isolation from the rest of the economy.
3. When a market is out of equilibrium (i.e. in *disequilibrium*), the lesser of the supply and demand quantities will be exchanged.
4. When the equilibrium price is deemed to be too high, the government may impose a *price ceiling*. The 'real' price may however rise above this ceiling, as black markets develop, product quality is reduced, side payments are elicited etc. When the equilibrium price is considered to be too low, a *price floor* may be established and the government may undertake to be 'buyer of last resort' at that price. The main problem with this form of market regulation is the disposal of government stocks.
5. In *comparative statics* analysis, market equilibrium under one set of economic conditions is compared with equilibrium when one or more economic parameters are altered. The outcome in terms of price and quantity changes will largely depend on the elasticities of demand and supply. The study of *dynamics* attention focuses on the time path of adjustment once the market is shocked out of equilibrium. The *cobweb model* has been used to depict the dynamics of some agricultural product markets. When a product is storable, market clearing is facilitated not only by changes in price but also by changes in the level of stocks.

6. In the *agricultural household*, consumption and production activities take place within the same economic unit. In the simple version of the model considered here, the total use of labour on the farm (and hence the level of output) is determined by equating the value of the marginal product of labour to its price (the wage rate). As a separate decision, the amount of the household's own labour input is found by equating its marginal valuation of labour to the wage rate. The consumption and production activities are interlinked through the *profit effect* i.e. the effect on the household's income of a change in the profitability of the production enterprise.

Further reading

All standard textbooks in microeconomics have a section on equilibrium in competitive markets. Few however discuss the problems encountered when equilibrium conditions do not hold. Two exceptions worth noting here are Hirshleifer (1976) and Koutsoyiannis (1979).

For those readers interested in empirical analysis, Labys (1973) discusses approaches to the quantification of price and storage relationships and an example of the econometric analysis of disequilibrium in agricultural markets is provided by Ziemer and White (1982).

A most useful, though quite advanced, treatment of price instability in commodity markets is given in Newbery and Stiglitz (1981). As noted in the text, Scandizzo and Diakosavvas (1987) review the main theoretical and empirical arguments concerning long term agricultural price movements, as well as offering substantial empirical work of their own.

Readers wishing to pursue the brief discussion of the C.A.P. and the LDCs should find Matthews (1986) very pertinent. A general (and gentle) introduction to the workings of the C.A.P. is given by Hill (1984).

With respect to agricultural household models, Levi and Havinden (1982) provide a short introduction to the analysis of equilibrium in the farm-household. A review article of these types of model has also recently been published (see Singh *et al.* (1986(*b*))).

9

Analysis of agricultural markets

9.1 *Introduction*

Markets exist to facilitate the transfer of ownership of goods from one owner to another. *Each time* ownership of something changes hands, whether it be a goat or a bicycle, a price is determined. This is truc whether the exchange of ownership takes place in a barter economy or using money as the medium of exchange. If in a particular barter transaction ten chickens are exchanged for a goat then the price of the goat is ten chickens and that of one chicken is one-tenth of a goat. Clearly it is impossible to trade in tenths of a goat, so that if the person originally owning the chickens had had only five he would have been unable to conclude a barter exchange with the goat owner unless the latter could have been persuaded to accept the much lower price of five chickens per goat. Putting together barter deals is a cumbersome way of achieving transfers of ownership. It is far easier to arrange this in a money economy, where chickens and goats can both be sold for units of currency. In this way the goat owner may be able to buy the chickens without having to sell his goat to the chickens' owner. He can sell his goat at a money price equal to that of ten chickens, and then spend half of the notes or coins he receives on buying the five chickens on offer.

In the previous chapter exploring the nature of market equilibrium, the equilibrium price was presented as that which enabled the last marginal unit supplied to the market to be sold to a willing consumer for money. At a higher price less would be demanded even though producers would find it profitable to sell more, while at a lower price consumers would like to purchase more but producers would only find it profitable to supply less. The equilibrium solutions examined in Chapter 8 were all derived for markets which were assumed to be subject to *perfect* or *pure competition* (many buyers and sellers). In practice, however, not all markets are competitive. Some may be *oligopolistic* (few sellers) and in others competition may be typified as approximating *monopoly* (one seller) or *monopsony* (one buyer). Oligopoly is not common in agricultural product markets although it may occur in markets for modern industrially produced inputs. It will not therefore be discussed in this chapter. Monopoly and monopsony are however important features of agricultural product markets due to the creation of state trading organisations, often called marketing boards. The first half of the chapter is therefore devoted to a comparison of market equilibrium in conditions of monopoly and monopsony with that which would occur where there are many buyers and sellers.

Exchanges of ownership do take place directly between producers (farmers) and food consumers. This is particularly the case in less-developed countries where it is not uncommon for members of producers' families to transport surplus produce to a nearby market for direct sale to the final consumer; but in industrialised countries the proportion of output sold in this way is very small and the bulk of produce is sold off the farm to wholesale merchants, special state commodity trading organisations, or directly to large food processing firms. In these markets much farm produce is transformed (e.g. from wheat to cakes and biscuits), often using industrial food processing techniques, before being sold through supermarkets or restaurants to final consumers. In these circumstances the immediate demand for farm produce arises not from households but from a variety of firms and state organisations *and* it is shops, restaurants and supermarkets which supply food to households not farmers. These structural characteristics of food and agricultural markets are of considerable importance and Sections 9.3–9.5 of this chapter are devoted to a brief consideration of the interaction of supply, demand and price formation at identifiable stages (i.e. ownership exchange levels) in the distribution chain running from the farm to food consumption by individuals and households.

9.2 *Degrees of market competition*

9.2.1 *Many buyers and sellers*

In examining how markets achieve or move towards equilibrium it was argued, in the last chapter, that it is produced by the competitive interaction of many buyers and sellers each acting to maximise their satisfaction (utility) and profits respectively. For economists a special form of this, which is sometimes called *perfect competition*, is commonly used as a paradigm or standard of market behaviour. This is because, as we shall see in the next chapter, perfect competition (or the slightly weaker form *pure competition*) is assumed to result in price–quantity equilibria which are *economically efficient* in a special sense.

A *perfectly competitive market* for a good or commodity is one defined to have the following set of properties:

1. Firms are independent profit maximisers, and consumers are utility maximisers with independent tastes.
2. There are many sellers (firms) and buyers (consumers), none of whom has a large enough market share for their decisions to affect market prices. Sellers and buyers are price takers.
3. All firms have identical technology, production functions and management ability.
4. The product is homogeneous so that consumers are indifferent between the produce of alternative suppliers.
5. Factors of production are freely mobile in the economy, so that there are no barriers to firms wishing to enter or leave the market.
6. Seller and buyers have perfect knowledge and foresight about market conditions, and adjust their decisions accordingly.

For many analytical purposes these are an unnecessarily restrictive set of conditions and it is sufficient for markets to be efficient that *pure competition* should exist in which properties 3 and 6 above are relaxed. Very often, to avoid the overtones of superiority associated with the words 'perfect' and 'pure', economists use the term *atomistic competition* to describe markets in which many buyers and sellers compete in pursuit of their own personal advantage.

Because price and quantity (equilibrium) determination in competitive markets has already been examined in Section 8.2 of the previous chapter it will not be repeated here. It is however worth recalling that a competitive equilibrium exists where the market demand curve for the product concerned intersects with its market supply curve. (The former is the sum of the demand curves of all consumers for the product, and the latter the sum of the upward sloping portions of the marginal cost curves of all the competitive firms producing the product.) In such an equilibrium competitive firms equate the market price (their marginal revenue) with their marginal cost of production.

9.2.2 *Monopoly*

The market structure which is the polar opposite of perfect competition is termed *monopoly*. Its distinctive feature is that there is a *single supplier* of the product but, in addition, it requires (i) that there should be barriers to entry of new suppliers and (ii) that there are no close substitutes for the product. If these two conditions were not met, monopoly would be a short-lived phenomenon.

The monopolist, as the only seller of the product, faces the market demand schedule, which in general is expected to be downward sloping. The reader will recall that, in contrast, the competitive firm has a horizontal demand curve for its product, since it can sell any quantity at the (given) market price. Moreover, the total revenue curve for the monopolist is not a straight line as in Fig. 2.11(*a*) (Chapter 2). The monopolist's total revenue function can have a variety of shapes,

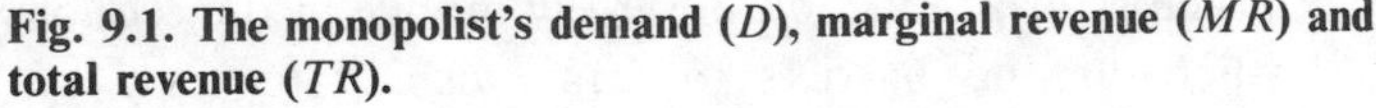

Fig. 9.1. The monopolist's demand (*D*), marginal revenue (*MR*) and total revenue (*TR*).

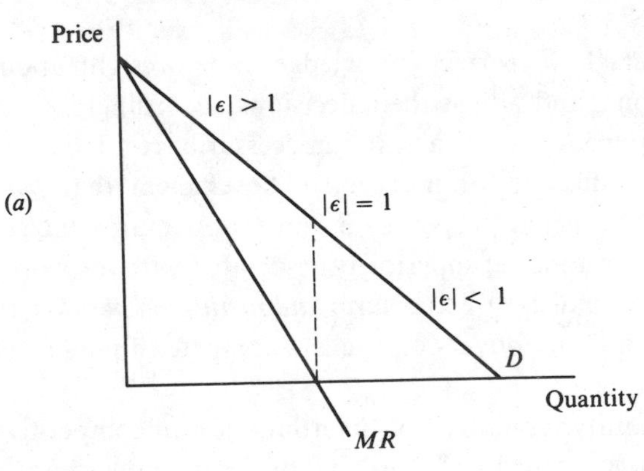

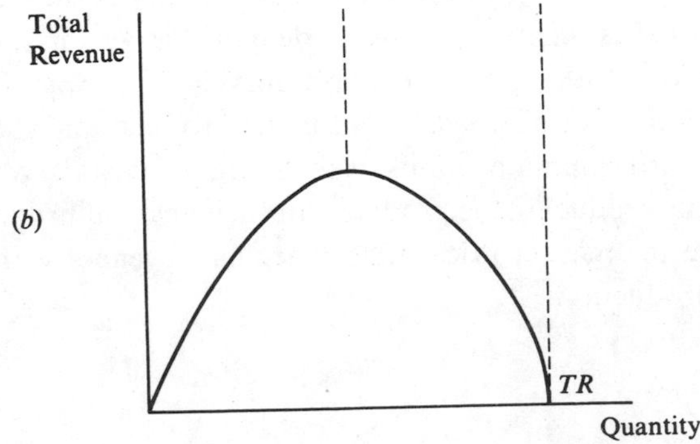

depending on the precise nature of the demand curve. If, for simplicity, we assume that the downward-sloping demand schedule is linear, the total revenue curve takes the form shown in Fig. 9.1. In the elastic portion of the demand curve, total expenditure by consumers (and hence total revenue for the producer) increases as price falls; in the inelastic section total revenue decreases as price falls. At the midpoint of the linear demand curve, demand is *unitary elastic* (that is the price elasticity of demand = 1) and, as we shall see, total revenue is at a maximum.

It is usual to assume that the monopolist's marginal cost function is equivalent to the supply curve of the competitive industry. That is, for purposes of comparing competitive equilibrium to that under monopoly, the monopolist is treated as if it had taken over all the competitive firms in the industry and was operating with their collective cost structure. The monopolist is also assumed to seek to maximise profits. The output level which maximises profits, is found at Q_0 in Fig. 9.2 where the difference between total revenue (TR) and total cost (TC) is greatest. At this level of output, the slopes of the curves are equal, implying that marginal cost (MC) equals marginal revenue (MR). This will be recognised as the same condition for profit maximisation as was established in the analysis of the competitive firm. However, for the competitive firm, price (or average revenue, AR) and marginal revenue are identical; for the monopolist, the MR curve lies below the AR curve and price (P) is greater than MR. An additional feature of the solution is that as long as total costs rise with output, the profit maximisation point will be located on the rising portion of the total revenue curve, that is, where demand for the product is *elastic*. We shall elaborate these points below.

Fig. 9.2. The monopolist's profit maximising output.

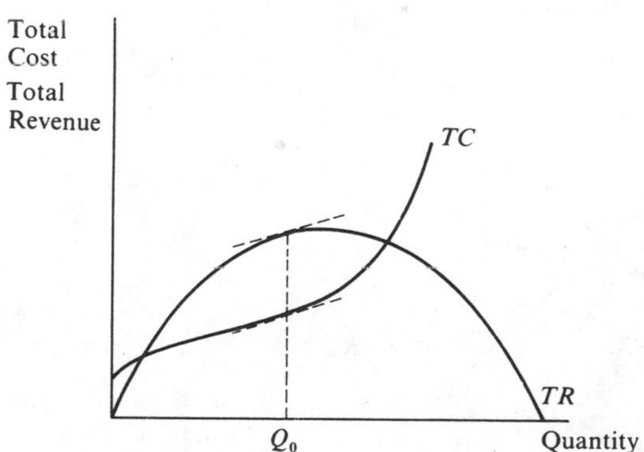

The relationship between marginal revenue and price is given as:[1]

$$MR = P\left(1 + \frac{1}{\varepsilon}\right) \tag{9.1}$$

where ε denotes the price elasticity of demand. Since ε has a negative sign, equation 9.1 implies that $P > MR$, except in the special case of perfectly elastic demand,[2] and the more inelastic the demand curve, the greater the difference between price and marginal revenue. Furthermore, note that marginal revenue is positive where demand is elastic ($|\varepsilon| > 1$), negative where demand is inelastic ($|\varepsilon| < 1$), and zero where demand is unitary elastic ($|\varepsilon| = 1$). These relationships are illustrated, with the aid of a linear demand curve in Fig. 9.1.

By superimposing (in Fig. 9.3) 'typical' U-shaped cost curves on to the demand (average revenue) and marginal revenue curves, an alternative illustration of the (short run) monopolist's profit maximisation solution can be derived and this can be compared to equilibrium in a competitive market. At Q_0, *marginal costs and marginal revenue are equal*. The price charged is P_0, the price associated with Q_0 on the demand curve (that is Q_0 is determined by the intersection of the marginal revenue and marginal cost curves of the monopolist). P_0 equals average revenue ($AR(Q_0)$) and since this clearly exceeds the average cost of producing Q_0, $AC(Q_0)$, the monopolist earns *supernormal profits* shown by the shaded area as equal to $AR(Q_0) - AC(Q_0)$ *times* the number of units produced, Q_0. This

Fig. 9.3. Equilibrium for the monopolist.

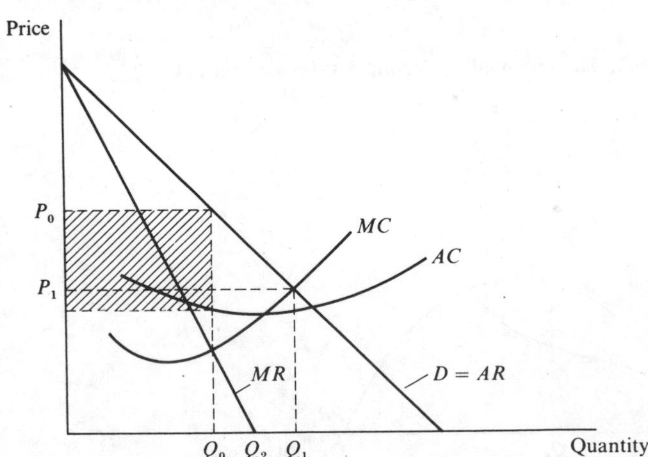

equilibrium can be directly compared to that of a competitive industry which would occur where *marginal cost and average revenue are equal*; at price P_1 and quantity Q_1. It can therefore be seen in the context of this comparison that monopolisation of a competitive industry would result in lower output, higher prices to consumers, and supernormal profits to the monopolist. While it is not reasonable to assume that any firm would suddenly wish to take over a myriad of small firms and turn a competitive industry into a monopoly, this comparison provides a simple explanation of why society usually arms itself with powers to control monopoly and to prevent firms exploiting monopoly power to drive up prices and obtain excessive profits. It should also be stressed that the monopolist does not have control over *both* price and output. The monopolist can decide upon a particular level of production but the market will determine the price at which this volume can be sold. Alternatively, if the monopolist sets a particular price, the market demand curve will determine how much can be sold.

Note that the monopolist operates in the elastic segment of the market demand curve. Even if costs of production were zero, it would not be optimal to produce more than Q_2, because beyond that point (in the inelastic portion of the demand curve), marginal revenue is negative.[3]

Whereas it is a simple matter to predict the monopolist's supply decision for a given demand curve and given cost function, it is not possible to establish a unique relationship between price and quantity supplied. In particular, the marginal cost curve is *not* the monopolist's supply curve. With a given *MC* curve, various quantities may be supplied at any one price, depending on the specific demand relationship (and the corresponding marginal revenue curve).

Formal derivation – monopolist's profit maximising equilibrium

Profits $\Pi = TR - TC$,

where TR **denotes total revenue and** TC **total cost. Both will depend on the level of output. The first order condition for profit maximisation is found where** $\mathrm{d}\Pi/\mathrm{d}Q = 0$**, namely**

$$\frac{\mathrm{d}\Pi}{\mathrm{d}Q} = \frac{\mathrm{d}TR}{\mathrm{d}Q} - \frac{\mathrm{d}TC}{\mathrm{d}Q} = 0$$

or where

$$\frac{\mathrm{d}TR}{\mathrm{d}Q} = \frac{\mathrm{d}TC}{\mathrm{d}Q} \text{ i.e. } MR = MC$$

In words, profit maximisation requires that marginal revenue = marginal cost. Note however that under monopoly, $MR \neq P$ but rather

$$MR = P + Q\frac{\partial P}{\partial Q}.$$

See footnote 1 of this chapter for the derivation.

Input demand The monopolist's demand for a variable input can be derived quite readily, since the principles which we discussed in the context of the competitive firm (Section 2.3.1) apply equally here. The monopolist, like the competitive firm, will employ additional units of an input as long as the increase in input use adds more to total revenue than to total cost.

As was noted in Section 2.3.1, for the competitive firm the contribution to total revenue which is made by an additional unit of a variable input is termed the value of the marginal product (*VMP*) of that input. For a variable input, labour, *VMP* is calculated as the marginal product of labour (the extra output arising from the expansion in employment) *times* the (constant) price of the product (since each additional unit of output can be sold at the prevailing market price). Hence, in obvious notation, $VMP_L = MP_L \cdot P_Q$. However, for the monopolist, price declines with output and the change in total revenue due to a change in output is given by marginal revenue, not price. If then the monopolist employs an additional unit of labour the resultant change in total revenue is given as the marginal product of labour *times* marginal revenue. This is termed the *marginal revenue product* (*MRP*) of the variable i.e., for the labour input, $MRP_L = MP_L \cdot MR$. It has already been demonstrated that for a monopolist, marginal revenue is less than product price. Hence the marginal revenue product of a factor to a monopolist is below the value of its marginal product. The two magnitudes are depicted in Fig. 9.4.

If the market for the variable input is a competitive one, the monopolist can purchase any amount of the factor at the prevailing wage rate. The supply of labour to the monopolist is then perfectly elastic, as shown by S_L, at wage rate w_0, in Fig. 9.4. The monopolist will be in equilibrium at the point where the marginal revenue product of labour and the marginal cost of labour are equal i.e. where $MRP_L = w_0$. If both the monopolist's product demand curve and production function are the same as those in a competitive industry, we can conclude that employment under a monopoly would be less than in a competitive industry (i.e. $L_m < L_c$) since the competitive industry equilibrium will be where $VMP_L = w_0$. This is the

Fig. 9.4. Relationship between marginal revenue product (*MRP*) and value of marginal product (*VMP*).

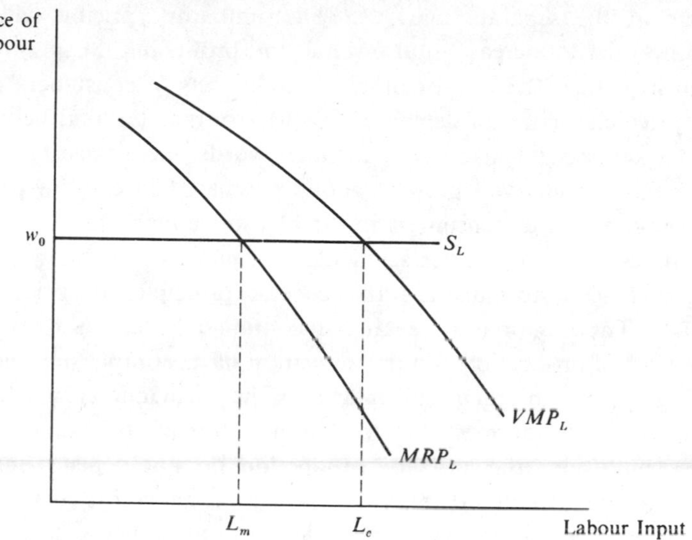

corollary of the proposition that the monopolist would produce less of the product than would a competitive industry.

Formal derivation – monopolist's equilibrium input demand

Assume that output is a function of a single variable factor i.e. $Q = f(L)$. The monopolist will then wish to employ this input in such a way as to maximise profits.

$$\Pi = TR - TC = P \cdot Q - (wL + F)$$

where L = units of labour employed, F = fixed costs, and w denotes the (given) wage rate. The first order condition for profit maximisation is:

$$\frac{\partial \Pi}{\partial L} = P\frac{\partial Q}{\partial L} + Q\frac{\partial P}{\partial Q}\frac{\partial Q}{\partial L} - w = 0$$

Rearranging, $\left(P + Q\dfrac{\partial P}{\partial Q}\right)\dfrac{\partial Q}{\partial L} = w.$

We have shown that $(P + Q\ (\partial P/\partial Q))$ is the expression for marginal revenue and $(\partial Q/\partial L)$ is the marginal product of labour. Thus, the equilibrium condition is that labour should be used up to the point where $MR.MP_L = w$ or where the marginal revenue product = the (given) wage rate.

Price discrimination Under certain circumstances, the monopolist may be able to segment the product market and charge different prices to consumers in the separate markets.[4] Discriminatory pricing will be practised in order to increase total revenue and profits but it can only be successful if (i) there are two or more separable sets of consumers with different price elasticities of demand, *and* (ii) arbitrage (selling) between the sub-markets cannot take place. In other words, there must be some form of barrier which will prevent goods purchased in the low-priced market being re-sold to consumers in the high-price market.

The simplest form of market segmentation, namely that of two sub-markets, will serve to illustrate the general principles of price discrimination. The monopolist, seeking maximum profits, has to decide upon the level of production and the allocation of this output (and hence the selling price) in each sub-market. The demand curves (and corresponding marginal revenue curves) in the sub-markets have different elasticities but, since the costs of production do not depend on the destination of the product, there is a common marginal cost curve.

Suppose that the allocation of a given level of output between the two sub-markets is such that MR_1 (the marginal revenue in sub-market 1) is higher than MR_2 (the marginal revenue in the other sub-market). By shifting a unit of output from sub-market 2 to sub-market 1, total revenue would increase. Indeed it will be profitable to reallocate output as long as the marginal revenues differ in the two sub-markets. An equilibrium condition must then be that $MR_1 = MR_2$. In deciding how much output to produce, the monopolist will take account of marginal costs as well as the marginal revenue in each market. The optimal level of output is that at which the additional cost of producing the last unit of the product just equals the marginal revenue from sales. Combining these conditions, the optimal strategy for the monopolist is given as:

$$MC = MR_1 = MR_2.$$

Fig. 9.5 illustrates this solution. Here the demand curve in sub-market 1 is less elastic than that of sub-market 2. The curve ΣMR is constructed as the *horizontal* sum of MR_1 and MR_2. The intersection of this curve with marginal cost (MC) establishes the optimal level of output (Q^*). This output is then distributed between the two sub-markets such that Q_1 is sold at price P_1 in sub-market 1 and Q_2 at price P_2 in sub-market 2, ($Q_1 + Q_2 = Q^*$). Note that these prices equalise marginal revenue (at MR^*) and that the higher price is charged in the sub-market with the less elastic demand. The latter point can be demonstrated by recalling the

Fig. 9.5. Price discrimination by a monopolist.

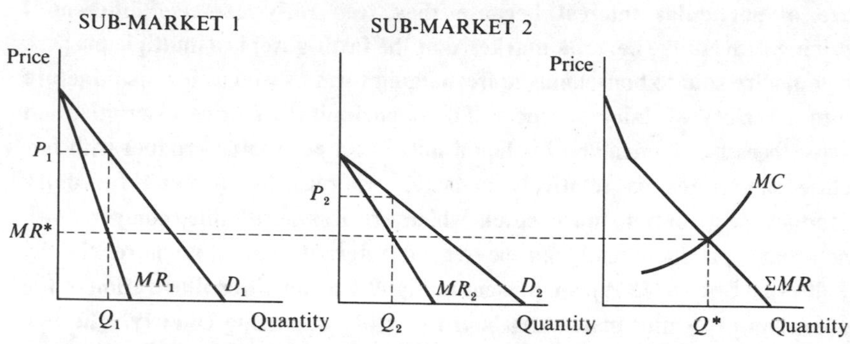

relationship between price and marginal revenue expressed in equation 9.1. Since in equilibrium, $MR_1 = MR_2$, then

$$P_1\left(1+\frac{1}{\varepsilon_1}\right) = P_2\left(1+\frac{1}{\varepsilon_2}\right)$$

where ε_1 and ε_2 are the price elasticities in the two sub-markets. It follows that if $|\varepsilon_1| < |\varepsilon_2|$, then $P_1 > P_2$. For example if $\varepsilon_1 = -2$ and $\varepsilon_2 = -4$, then $P_1 = \frac{3}{2}P_2$. This formula also makes it clear that if the elasticities in the two sub-markets are identical, there is no scope for price discrimination (i.e. $P_1 = P_2$ in this case).

BOX 9.1
Marketing boards and price discrimination

Governments sometimes sanction the formation of agricultural producers' groups or organisations whose activities sometimes resemble the behaviour in the model of monopoly presented above. The main examples are the marketing boards, or marketing orders, which are found in both developed and developing countries. In fact there are considerable variations in the objectives, powers and activities of marketing boards[5] and it may be rather foolhardy to generalise about their operations. Our discussion here will therefore be confined to the type of board[6] which is established to promote the interests of producers and which, by controlling supply of the product, endeavours to exert some monopoly power in the market place. It should be emphasised, however, that the board may still face competition from the producers of close substitutes and unless it can differentiate its product, e.g. by building up a strong brand image,[7] its market power may be very limited.

A number of countries have milk and dairy marketing boards and these are of particular interest because they frequently exercise differential pricing. Raw milk (i.e. milk marketed at the farm-gate) is a multiple purpose commodity sold to households in fresh liquid form as well as for manufacture into a variety of dairy products. The opportunity for price discrimination arises because the demand for liquid milk, as a perishable product with few close substitutes, is relatively inelastic, whereas the demand for dairy products (e.g. butter and cheese), which are less perishable, compete with non-dairy products and can be traded internationally, is more elastic. Following Sadan (1979), we present in Fig. 9.6 a simplified illustration of the operation of a milk marketing board in a net importing country. The two markets for raw milk (liquid milk and manufactured milk) are represented in the same diagram. The demand for liquid milk is depicted as D_1; for simplicity, the demand for dairy products is assumed to be perfectly elastic (D_2). The theory of price discrimination presented above would suggest that the board, having sole control over raw milk supply, would sell a total quantity of Q_T and allocate Q_1 of this to the liquid milk market (at the price P_1) and the remainder to the dairy product manufacturers at P_2.

There is however the matter of revenue or profit distribution to milk producers, and this introduces an additional complication into the analysis. A common practice is to adopt a *pool pricing* arrangement by which an equalised or blend price is paid to all producers. Pool pricing however is inconsistent with the optimal solution which we have derived. Because the equalised price will be a weighted average of the liquid milk price and the

Fig. 9.6. Price discrimination by a milk marketing board.

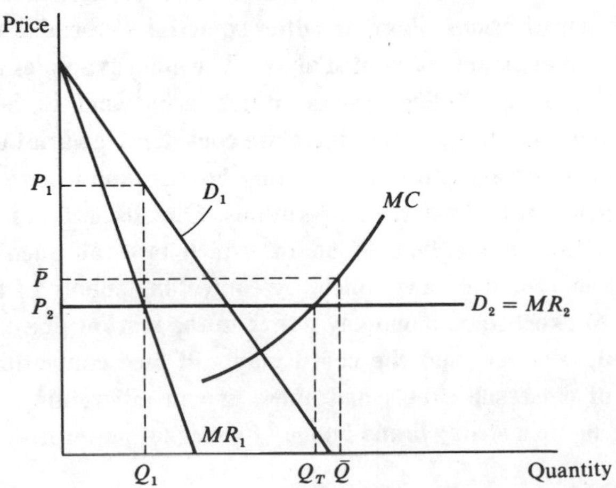

manufactured milk price, it is necessarily higher than the latter and so will encourage overproduction. Returning to Fig. 9.6, the equalised price is given by $\bar{P}$ (where $\bar{P} > P_2$) and would be calculated as

$$\bar{P} = P_1\frac{Q_1}{\bar{Q}} + P_2\left(1 - \frac{Q_1}{\bar{Q}}\right)$$

Overproduction of $\bar{Q} - Q_T$ results. The welfare implications of the practice of pool pricing have been discussed extensively in the literature.[8]

Regulation of monopoly Unrestricted monopoly is relatively rare. In most countries, there are legal barriers to the formation of monopolies and those monopolies which do exist (e.g. railways, gas, electricity, telephones) are usually either under government ownership or regulated by governments. Here we will analyse the effects of two forms of regulation, price control and taxation, on the monopolist's price and output decisions.

A common form of government regulation is the introduction of *price ceilings* in monopolists' product markets. The maximum price at which the product may sell, will be set below the profit-maximising price, P_0 in Fig. 9.7. A price ceiling with particular appeal is that represented by P_c, since it would encourage marginal cost pricing.[9] The demand curve

Fig. 9.7. Price ceiling.

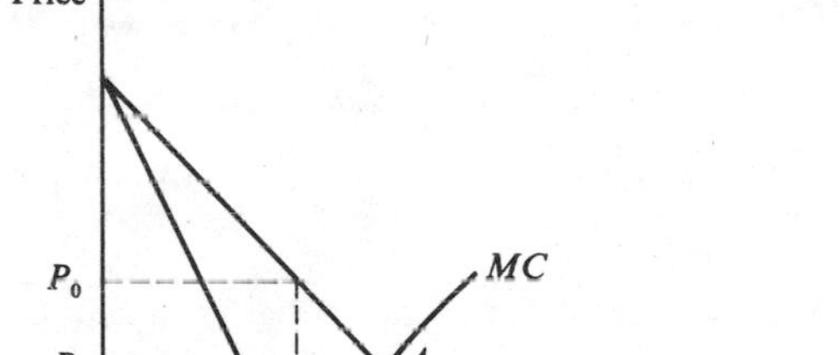

facing the monopolist then becomes kinked, i.e. P_cAD, since the section of the original curve above A has been eliminated by the price ceiling imposed. The marginal revenue curve, on the other hand, becomes discontinuous, consisting of the segments P_cA and BMR. In order to maximise profits under these conditions, the monopolist will produce Q_c at P_c. It will be noted that the imposition of a price ceiling in a monopolist's market increases the quantity sold (from Q_0 to Q_c). (This is in marked contrast to the conclusions in Section 8.1.4, in which a price ceiling in a competitive market reduced the quantity consumed). Indeed the choice of P_c as the price ceiling causes the monopolist's equilibrium output to increase to that which would be produced by a competitive industry, and it would reduce supernormal profits.

An alternative way of regulating monopoly is to impose a *lump sum tax* on the monopolist's supernormal profits. Since the effect of this policy is simply to shift a given sum from the producer to the government exchequer, it has no impact on the price or output of the firm. As the tax is analytically equivalent to an increase in the firm's fixed costs, it can be depicted as a shift in the average cost curve (AC_0 to AC_1 in Fig. 9.8). Of the original profits, P_0FGH, the government now extracts $GHIJ$. If the government were intent on achieving marginal cost pricing, the lump sum tax could be combined with a per unit *subsidy* on output. Referring again to Fig. 9.7, we could compute a subsidy per unit produced in such a way

Fig. 9.8. Lump sum tax.

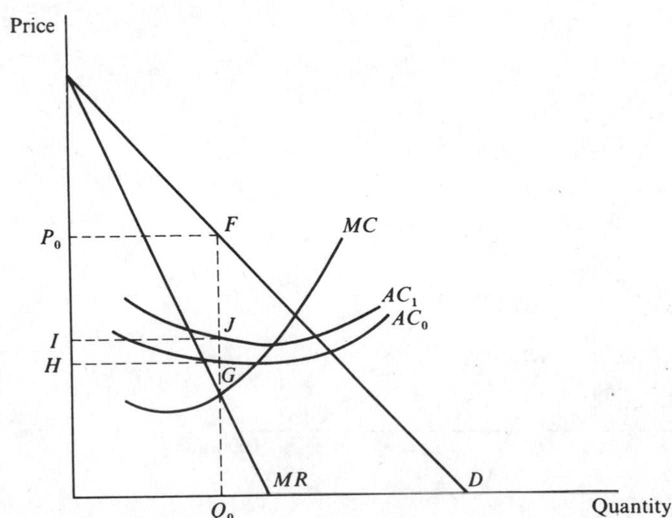

as to lower the marginal cost curve until it intersects the marginal revenue curve at *B*. This would induce the monopolist to produce Q_c at a price P_M. At the same time, the government might impose a lump sum tax, equal to the subsidy but payable regardless of output. In this way, the monopolist would be prevented from benefiting at the taxpayers' expense.

The principal drawback of all these measures is that the regulating authority is required to have complete information about the structure of demand and costs of production.

9.2.3 *Monopsony*

In the previous section we analysed the position of the single seller or monopolist in the product market. This is a form of economic organisation in which the producer is a price-maker rather than a price-taker. We now consider the exercise of monopoly power in the factor market. Specifically, we will examine the *single buyer* of a factor or the *monopsonist*,[10] who will be able to determine the price of an input. In the analysis of the agricultural sector this model of economic behaviour may be relevant in a number of instances. As we have noted farm products are inputs into the food processing, packing and distribution sectors and it may be the case that in a particular region there is only one processor (say, a meat packer) with whom all local beef producers must trade. Alternatively, a marketing board may have the sole title to purchase and distribute a given agricultural product. Another example might be a large landowner who is the only employer of hired labour in a local region.

The purchaser of an input, it is assumed, is faced with an upward sloping supply curve for that input. That is to say, additional units of the factor will be forthcoming only at a higher per unit input price. The monopsonist, being the sole buyer of input, must distinguish between the average factor cost (i.e. the per unit price of the factor) and the marginal factor cost (*MFC*) of obtaining the input. The latter is the additional expense incurred in purchasing an incremental unit of the factor. The monopsonist will weigh the marginal expense of the additional input against its marginal benefit to the firm, which, as we have seen, is indicated by the marginal revenue product of the input. By the usual reasoning, the optimal condition for the monopsonist will be to employ the input up to the point where the marginal revenue product and the marginal factor cost are equal i.e.

$$MFC = MRP$$

This solution is depicted in Fig. 9.9, where the supply of labour is given by S_L and the marginal revenue product of labour[11] as MRP_L. The supply curve represents the average factor cost of employing the variable input; the marginal factor cost curve (*MFC*) lies above it. Following the optimality rule, the monopsonist would employ L_0 of the input and this amount of the factor would be obtainable at a wage w_0. Note that the factor is paid less than its marginal revenue product. For comparison in a competitive industry equilibrium employment would be at L_1 with a wage rate of w_1, that is at the point where the supply curve of labour intersects the demand curve for it. Thus monopsonists have the power to reduce labour employment and wages.

It may be instructive to compare the combined effects of monopoly and monopsony with perfect competition in both the product and factor markets. Consider Fig. 9.10. In a competitive industry, L_1 units of labour would be employed at w_1; this solution is found by equating the demand for labour (*VMP*) with its supply (S_L). On the other hand, the monopolist in the product market is concerned with the marginal revenue product (*MRP*) of the input, not *VMP*, and if the firm is also a monopsonist in the labour market, *MRP* will be equated with marginal factor cost (*MFC*), not average factor cost. Thus the combination of monopoly and monopsony results in a lower level of employment (L_0) and a lower wage rate (w_0) than under perfect competition, and also than under monopoly alone or monopsony alone.

Fig. 9.9. Monopsony in the factor market.

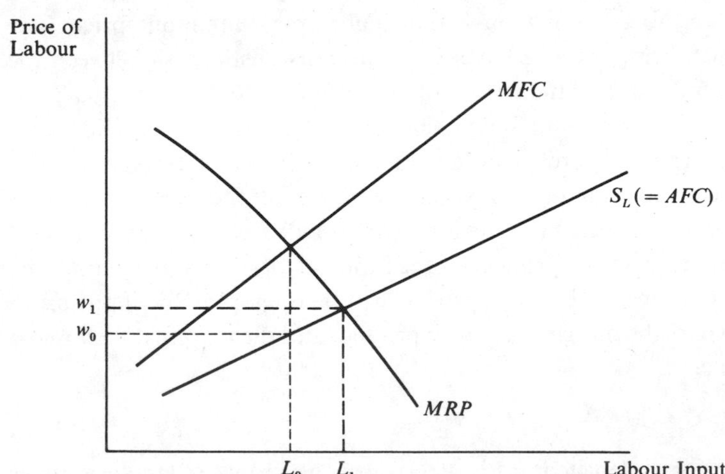

Fig. 9.10. Monopoly/Monopsonist vs. competition.

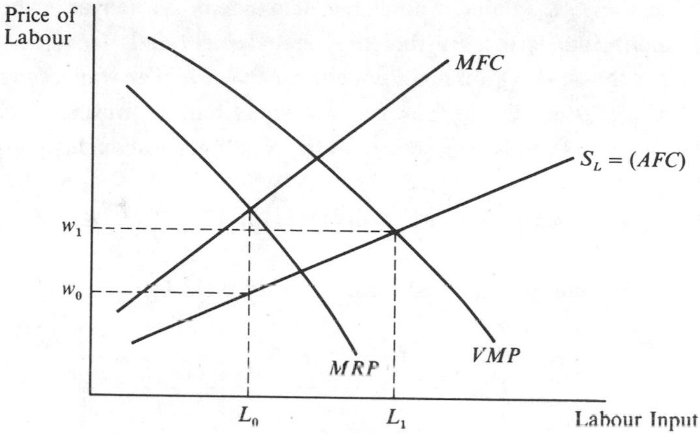

BOX 9.2
Monopsony and agricultural labour markets

Monopsony power in agricultural labour markets can arise where, within a locality, there is a high concentration of landownership and little or no opportunity for employment outside agriculture. As Griffin argues, in his description of the agricultural sector of less-developed countries, 'an unequal distribution of landownership, a defective tenure system, and privileged access to the capital market may combine to give landowners monopsony power over labour and where this occurs the result will be lower wages and less employment than would otherwise be the case' (Griffin (1979), p. 31). Whether these conditions are commonly observed in developing countries and whether monopsony powers are widely exercised are empirical questions which will not be explored here.[12] What can be noted, however, is that the free market operation of agricultural labour markets is often restricted by policy; wage rates are frequently regulated either by minimum wage legislation or by 'social' convention. We wish to focus on the regulation of labour markets here, not only because it is quite widespread, but because its impact with regard to employment depends critically on the structure of the factor market.

A competitive labour market is illustrated in Fig. 9.11. The competitive equilibrium would be found at a wage rate w_0, at which L_0 units of labour would be employed. If a minimum wage rate $\bar{w}$ is imposed, the labour supply curve becomes $\bar{w}$ *ES*; that is since no labour can be engaged at a wage below $\bar{w}$, the supply curve is horizontal at this minimum wage. As a consequence,

an unemployment gap will be created; at $\bar{w}$, L_2 units of labour would seek employment but only L_1 units would be demanded. Moreover, when compared to equilibrium levels, we find that employment falls from L_0 to L_1. Thus although those who gain employment receive a higher wage, fewer workers are engaged than in the absence of regulation. However, if the labour market exhibits monopsony, an entirely different conclusion is reached.[13]

Monopsony in the labour market is depicted in Fig. 9.12. Again the

Fig. 9.11. Minimum wage legislation: competitive market.

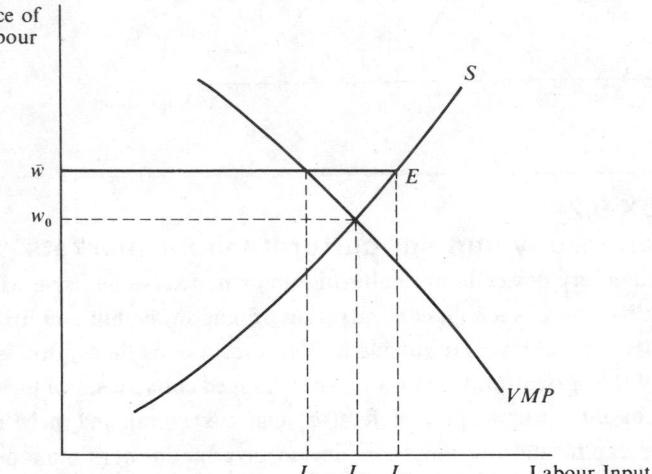

Fig. 9.12. Minimum wage legislation: monopsony.

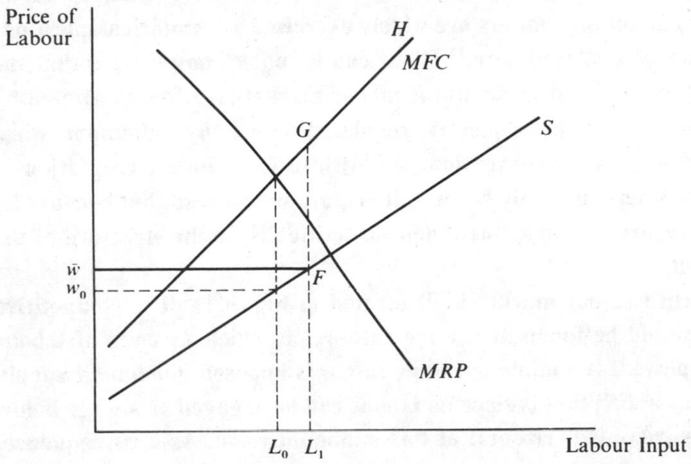

monopsonist, equating marginal factor cost with marginal revenue product, employs L_0 at a wage w_0. As before, the introduction of a minimum wage, $\bar{w}$, alters the shape of the supply curve (to $\bar{w}FS$) since no labour will be forthcoming at less than the statutory minimum rate. The marginal factor cost curve also changes[14] (to $\bar{w}FGH$), and applying our optimality rule, we find that the monopsonist will respond to the introduction of the minimum wage by *increasing* employment to L_1, each unit of labour being paid $\bar{w}$.

Our analysis therefore suggests that, although minimum wage legislation can have adverse employment effects in competitive labour markets, it can generate higher wages and greater employment opportunities where monopsony exists.

BOX 9.3
Monopsony and marketing boards

Some marketing boards have been established in response to monopsonistic practices in agricultural product markets. Producers of some farm products may find that they are at the mercy of a single buyer (or a group of buyers acting in concert). Certainly there is a high degree of concentration among buyers in a number of markets. For example, in West Africa in the 1940s (prior to the formation of the export produce marketing boards), three or four firms dominated the export trade in cocoa, palm oil and groundnuts, with one firm alone taking almost 40% of Ghana's cocoa exports.[15] Even though concentration is not a sufficient condition for us to presume predatory behaviour, farmers associate it with low farm gate prices. Whether monopsonistic exploitation is real or perceived, a number of marketing boards have been created in order to improve farm incomes by conferring on farmers countervailing power.[16] It is hoped that thereby producers can become 'masters of their own markets'.

However, whereas some marketing boards have been set up in order to counter monopsony in the food industry, those marketing boards which have exclusive licence to purchase a product from farmers and sell it on to processors and wholesalers are themselves able to act as monopsonists. A number of export marketing boards fall into this latter category.[17] Since each of these marketing boards is the sole buyer of a specific crop, it can establish the price which farmers receive and this price can be set below the marginal valuation placed on the product by the board. In this way a surplus can be extracted from the agricultural sector and it is this fiscal role of marketing boards which has attracted the interest of some governments in

developing countries. Indeed a number of marketing boards have been established primarily as government agencies to act as instruments of government financial policy. It should be noted that these boards probably do not seek to actually maximise profits, but simply use their monopsony power to push down the price at which they purchase products.

The importance of the fiscal role is illustrated by the performance of the West African marketing boards. As Blandford (1979) has argued, the use of the West African boards as a fiscal device was not the original purpose of their creation but in many cases it rapidly became one of their chief functions. In the early years of their operation (in the late 1940s), only about 2% of the boards' total sales value accrued to the government but by the fifth year, this had risen to 28.5% for the Ghana Cocoa Marketing Board (GCMB), to 20% for the Nigerian Cocoa Marketing Board, and to some 12% for the Gambia Produce Marketing Board for groundnuts (GPMB). Throughout the 1950s and 1960s, the tax burden, as a proportion of sales value, remained high for the GCMB (over 33% on average) and the Western State Marketing Board (over 18%), although the GPMB maintained a much lower rate of taxation (under 7%). These revenues made a substantial contribution to the respective government exchequers. For example, in the period 1967/68–1971/72, between 23 and 36% of Ghana's government revenue was obtained from the GCMB.

Levi and Havinden (1982) also emphasise the fiscal role of some export marketing boards. Specifically, they analyse the operation of the Sierra Leone Produce Marketing Board for palm kernels. Their results, generated by a simple static supply model, suggest that if producers had been given the board's surplus and export duty in the period 1962/72, the producer price would have been about 30% higher than the actual price received and supply would have been almost 18% higher than actual production over that period. In the same period, the board recorded an average annual surplus of almost 1 million (constant 1961) Leones but the average loss in producer income amounted to 1.8 million Leones.[18]

9.3 *Structure and functions of agricultural markets*

The focus of this section is upon markets for farm products, but the discussion is equally applicable to the markets for the inputs which farmers buy.

If the series of changes of ownership and economic processes by which products are transferred from the primary producer (the farmer) to the final consumer are thought of as marketing chains then it is apparent that there are many alternative *marketing chains*. This is well exemplified by the chains identified by Timmer *et al.* (1983) which are presented in Box 9.4. Such chains may be described in *institutional* terms according to the categories of business of those who take over ownership of the product at some point in the marketing chain, or they may be described *functionally* in terms of the *value-adding activities* performed in the marketing chain. (Timmer *et al.* in fact combine both institutional and functional elements into their description of alternative chains).

9.3.1 *Market institutions*

A very general institutional description of a food marketing chain might be that it involves five groups of economic agents, and that (following Hill and Ingersent 1977, p. 132) a 'shape' to their activities may be assumed which is based upon the number of agents in each class.

Producers — Country Dealers — Wholesalers/Processors — Retailers — Consumers

---

BOX 9.4
Agricultural marketing chains

Timmer *et al.* (1983, pp. 166, 167) present five alternative marketing chains which may simultaneously operate in agricultural output markets. The symbols *T*, *S* and *P* are used to denote the various marketing services which may be provided by one of the two parties to any exchange in ownership. Thus in the simplest chain (1) either the farmer or the consumer may undertake the costs of transport (*T*), storage (*S*), or processing (*P*). The five (slightly adapted) alternatives are:

1. **Farmers, *S*, *P*, *T* rural consumer.**
2. **Farmer *S*, *P*, *T* rural retailer *T* rural consumer.**
3. **Farmer *S*, *T* resident processor or assembler *P*, *S*, *T* rural retailer *T* rural consumer.**
4. **Farmer *S*, *T* resident processor or assembler *P*, *S*, *T* non-resident wholesaler *S*, *T* urban consumer.**
5. **Farmer *S*, *T* non-resident wholesaler *P*, *S*, *T* urban wholesaler, retailer, or consumer.**

In this simplified description many (hundreds of thousands of) producers sell their produce to a much smaller number of *country dealers* (*or merchants*) who perform the vital function of concentrating large numbers of small sales into large lots for sale to the *wholesaling and processing sector*. While the number of firms in the latter sector may be very much smaller than the number of producers, it will generally be large enough to permit the wholesale market to be described as competitive, especially as barriers to entry of new firms may not be high. At the right-hand end, the distribution chain widens out again as produce passes into *retailing* outlets which in turn sell to the millions of consumers and consuming households.

In several respects this stylised description is oversimple. There are many specialised types of firm within the wholesaling/processing sector which can only loosely be described by either of those two terms; there are small grain mills in LDCs which grind the grain of farmers and consumers without ever taking ownership of it – they provide a special service; there are companies owning grain or meat storage facilities the operations of which cannot be described aptly as either wholesaling or processing. Furthermore there are companies which are *vertically integrated* to perform several stages of the chain. In sugar production companies operating refineries often also operate the sugar plantations and own or organise transport and storage operations up to the point of sale to retailers. That is the stages from primary production, assembly, processing through to wholesaling may all be integrated under one management. There may of course always be a number of such integrated operations competing with one another as well as competition from an unintegrated, more atomistic sector.

For the purposes to be pursued here it is however convenient to set aside the qualifications which have just been stated and to accept the diagrammatic presentation of the marketing chain as involving five classes of owner and four transfers of ownership in the marketing chain; while recognising that in specific cases there may be more or less transfers than this. On the principle that all changes of ownership entails fixing a price, there will therefore be a hierarchy of prices one for each level of transfer. Sales of produce from farmers to country dealers take place at what may be called the *producer or farm-gate price*. Sales from dealers to wholesalers involve what can be termed a *wholesale price*. Because frequently the amount of processing undertaken in the wholesaling/processing sector is large, commodity descriptions which apply to sales from merchants to processors are not applicable to sales to retailers. Wheat moves into the processing sector but emerges as bread, flour and in many other forms; beef carcasses are transferred into it only to emerge in tins, pies or frozen forms. Thus sales from processors/wholesalers to retailers can also be described as occurring at *wholesale prices*, but (except in the cases of fruits and vegetables which frequently pass to consumers without any processing) with these prices relating to processed products rather than the primary products produced on farms. *Retail prices* are those which apply to the final transfer of ownership from retailers to consumers.

9.3.2 *Market functions*

Many functional aspects of the marketing chain are readily apparent from the institutional description above. The institutions perform a variety of different functions including *assembly*, *transport*, *storage*, *processing*, *financing*, *distribution* and *grading*. This is a short list which embraces activities involved in exporting and importing produce as well as in intranational marketing. All these functions share two prime characteristics: (1) that they add value to the product, and (2) that they require a variety of inputs to perform, and so incur costs. Provided that the value-added (return for the product minus the cost of all inputs) in each function is positive, firms or individual entrepreneurs (including farmers themselves) will find it profitable to compete to supply the service entailed.

In rural areas consumers' demand for additional services may be low and much of the market may be restricted to trade in the primary products. Urban consumers however will have to pay for transport and storage costs (unless they are prepared to travel to the rural areas to buy produce directly from producers) and their generally higher incomes may (and does) generate more demand for processed forms of product embodying higher levels of service. Such processed forms often involve combining primary product with tin cans, chemicals, and packaging materials as well as with the less tangibly obvious inputs required to make the products available on market stalls or shop shelves. Put simply, urban consumers are likely to have a higher demand for value-added services than rural consumers (the majority of whom may be farmers in LDCs), and to be prepared to pay for specialised firms to supply these.

As incomes generally rise the demand for services grows as consumers require improvements in convenience and quality in the food products they purchase. Consequently the tendency is for a progressively increasing proportion of the price consumers pay for food to reflect the service component, and for the relative return to the primary product to decline. This is an issue taken up more fully in Section 9.5 below, but for the moment suffice it to say that there is a tendency for *marketing margins* to increase with economic growth. In asserting this the relevant marketing margin is *the difference between the retail price of a product and the price received by farmers for its agricultural product content*; this is known as the *retail-farmgate margin*. Marketing margins may, however, be studied between any of the market levels at which prices are commonly determined. Thus attention might be focussed upon the *retail-wholesale margin* or upon the *wholesale-farmgate margin*.

Whichever margin is under scrutiny it may be said to reflect the value-added by some part of the marketing chain. Certainly it reflects the perception of value-added by those consumers who have demonstrated a willingness to pay the price for it. In a very general sense consumers are prepared to pay for the *utilities* created by the marketing system, and it is common in the literature to refer to the marketing system as creating *time*, *space* and *form* utilities. This is a useful way of summarising the contributions of the marketing system, and from the preceding discussion each of these three utilities should be self-explanatory. What they are intended to signify is that the marketing system operates to transport produce to where consumers wish to take delivery of it, at times they find convenient and in the forms desired.

9.4 *Simultaneous equilibrium at two market levels*

In this section, as in Tomek and Robinson (1981, Ch. 6), the analysis of margins is confined to a consideration of two levels of exchange of ownership only. One of these is at the farm-gate to country dealer exchange and involves formation of a farm-gate or producer price. The other will be described as the exchange involving the retail price, but could equally well be thought of as applying to some intermediate exchange involving the wholesaling sector.

Demand at the retail level can be thought of as involving two separate components (1) demand for the basic farm product, and (2) demand for a package of services. This being so the demand for basic produce can be described as a *derived demand*; it derives from the *primary demand* at the retail level for combinations of foodstuff and services. The derived demand curve is obtained by subtracting the value of the demand for services at each point on the primary demand curve. This relationship is shown in Fig. 9.13 for the case where the demand for services per unit of consumption is constant at all retail prices so that the two curves are parallel.

While the diagram only portrays the derived demand for the basic farm product, readers will realise that there is also a *derived demand curve for the services combined with the food*, which in this case is perfectly elastic at a price equal to the constant vertical difference between the primary and derived demand curves. This price reflects the value of services combined with the basic food product and is therefore equal to the value of the retail to farm-gate margin.[19]

In the context of this analysis, farm-gate level supply of the basic commodity can be thought of as *primary supply* of the product. There will also be a supply function for the services which consumers wish to purchase. When this supply function is combined with the primary supply function of the product what may be termed the *derived supply* curve is obtained. As shown in Fig. 9.13 the derived and primary supply curves are shown as being parallel implying that there is a perfectly elastic supply curve for marketing services at a price equal to the difference between the retail and farm-gate prices at equilibrium. Again this is an assumption which may need to be altered to fit specific cases.

Given these supply and demand concepts, Fig. 9.13 illustrates a situation of simultaneous equilibrium at both the retail and farm-gate levels of the market. This equilibrium is such that the retail and farm-gate markets both clear the same quantity of basic produce q_e. At the farm-gate level the primary supply and derived demand curves intersect at this quantity at a market clearing price of P_f. At the retail level the primary demand and derived supply curves also meet at a quantity equivalent to q_e but with the retail price at the higher level P_r to reflect equilibrium in the supply and demand for the marketing services combined with the basic agricultural product.

Fig. 9.13. Primary and derived functions and marketing margins.

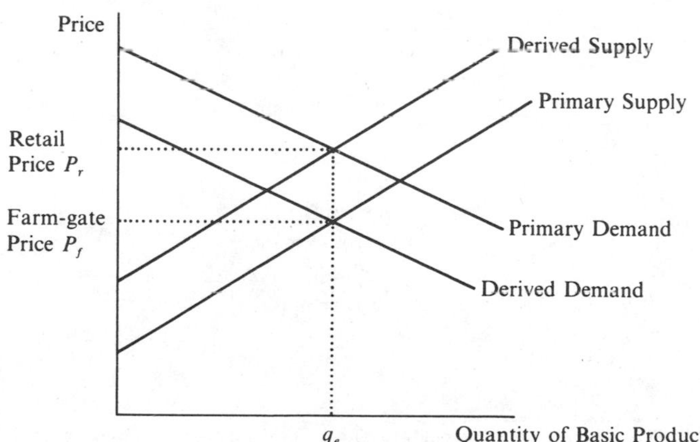

Clearly this is a useful abstract presentation of the realities of markets since the volume of produce (in processed form) sold in the retail market does have to be matched by the sale and purchase of the corresponding quantity of basic agricultural raw material at lower market levels. It also underlines the need to recognise the complementarity which exists between the markets for basic foodstuffs and for marketing and processing services. Marketing margins reflect the economics of supply and demand for such services, and it is important to acknowledge that such margins reflect the provision of 'marketing utilities' to consumers and that they are not excess profits to 'middlemen' in the marketing chain.

If the analysis in Fig. 9.13 is so important why, as throughout the rest of this book and most others, is supply-demand analysis presented without any explicit recognition of marketing margins, and as if farmers sold produce directly to consumers? If the demand for services is approximately perfectly price elastic at any point in time, as assumed in Fig. 9.13, then it will be true that shifts in the primary supply or primary demand curves will cause equilibrium prices to change by equal amounts at all levels of the market. To see this consider the effect of an upward shift in the primary demand curve in Fig. 9.14. Because by assumption the shift entails no shift in the demand for services the derived demand for basic product must shift upward identically with primary demand. And since both demand curves have identical slopes, as do the two supply curves the increase in retail price from P_r to P_r' must be the same as that in the farm-gate price from P_f to P_f'. This being so, if margins are basically fixed in the short-run, analysis which takes no explicit account of them will be capable

Fig. 9.14. The effect of a shift in derived demand for basic product.

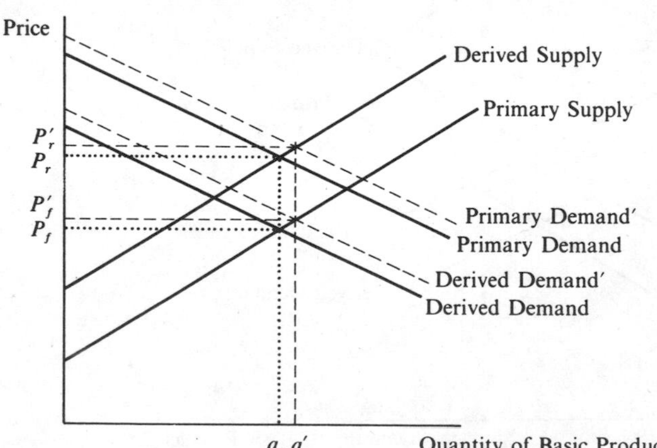

of revealing the essential effects of shifts in supply and demand upon both consumers and producers. Certainly it will provide correct estimates of changes in all relevant quantities, prices, revenue and expenditures.

9.5 *Marketing margins and farm prices*

It is not unusual to encounter the view that the farmer's share of the retail price of food products is too small, and that retail-farm-gate margins are excessive and include elements of excess profit. In many instances this charge has been judged to be unsupported since a careful analysis of the profits of 'middlemen' and processing firms shows them to be commensurate with the business risks involved. Frequently farm-retail margins are high because the transport system to major urban retail markets is inefficient and costly. This is undoubtedly a factor behind the large difference between the *retail-farmgate margins* for rice in African and Asian countries noted in Table 9.1. Population densities in Africa are recorded as substantially less than in Asia, hence road networks are not as intensive, transport services are less frequent and more costly, and average haulage distances are greater. It is therefore probable that the differences in the marketing margins of the three groups of countries shown are primarily due to genuine differences in the cost of delivering

Table 9.1. *Comparison of real farm and retail market prices for rice, 1969–83*

	Africa	Asia	Latin America
Open market retail prices			
Farm Price as Percentage of Retail Price:	52	79	64
Average Prices in constant PPP Dollars:			
retail price	826	562	563
farm price	391	453	345
Marketing Margin	435	109	218
Number of Countries	9	6	6

Notes: 1. Retail prices and marketing margins are in constant purchasing power parity dollars per metric ton. Farm prices are for the paddy equivalent to a metric ton of rice, assuming a milling rate of 65%.
2. All figures are simple averages of individual country data. The percentage figures are the simple average of individual country percentages.
3. Approximately 12–13 years of data were available per country.
Source: FAO (1985).

rice to retail markets rather than to innate inefficiency and excess profits by the agents involved in the distribution chain.

What is certain however is that producers as well as consumers are likely to benefit from any improvements in the transport and marketing system which reduce distribution costs. This is easily seen using Fig. 9.15. With a high cost of supplying marketing services at P_M the *derived supply curve* at the retail level is formed by the vertical addition of P_M to the *primary* (or farm level) *supply curve*. The intersection of the derived supply and *primary* (retail level) *demand curve* produces an equilibrium retail price P_R. This implies that the farm-gate price at equilibrium will be P_F which equals $P_R - P_M$. If the building of a new metalled highway to replace an old dirt road resulted in a fall in the marketing costs to P'_M the derived supply curve would shift downwards, and would intersect with the primary demand curve to give an equilibrium retail price at P'_R. Thus the retail price would fall and the market would be expanded with demand rising from *a* to *b*. But the farm-gate price would also rise from P_F to P'_F; such a rise being necessary to induce the increase in output from *a* to *b*. In other words the benefit of the reduction in marketing costs is shared between producers and consumers, with the relative shares depending on the slopes of the supply and demand curves – readers can experiment themselves with the effects of changing the slopes of the functions. This underlines the importance to producers of having an efficient marketing system.

It is a message which is repeated in slightly different form in Chapter 11 in examining the economics of trade. There it is shown that high transport

Fig. 9.15. Effects of reducing marketing costs.

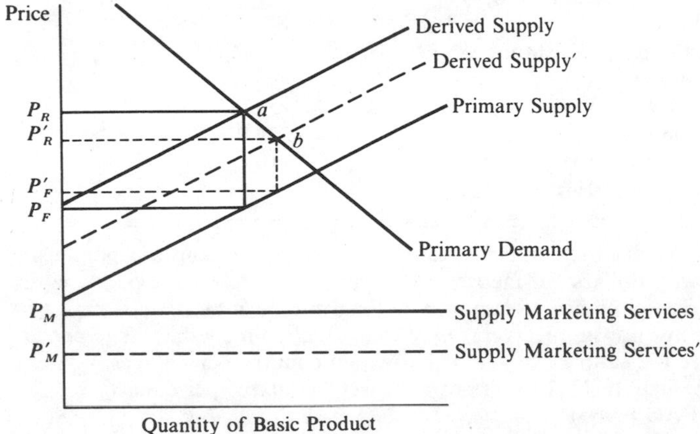

costs can prevent some producers from competing in markets and can isolate them from trade. Low international transport and handling costs are seen to be a key to the expansion of trade and to permitting LDC producers to participate beneficially in world markets.

It is important, however, not to use this argument about the desirability of more efficient low cost marketing, processing and distribution as a source of confusion and concern over the tendency of marketing margins to grow as a result of increased demand for new marketing services as incomes grow. Peas may be bought in the pod or in frozen, shelled form in sealed packages. Purchasers of frozen peas are buying a lot of additional processing and marketing services and consequently pay for a much higher retail-farmgate margin than do buyers of peas in pods, which require little more than collection and transportation before presentation in retail markets. As consumers 'trade up' from peas in the pod to the frozen form the average marketing margin for all peas will rise. This should be recognised for what it is, namely the result of a changing pattern of consumption between what are for consumers two separate products, but ones which are (in this hypothetical case) treated as one for the purposes of data collection. What is important in terms of marketing efficiency is what happens to the separate marketing margins for the two types of peas. If the margins fall for a constant quality product, marketing efficiency is increasing.

9.6 *Conclusions*

This chapter has reviewed the economics of some key aspects of processes of price determination in agricultural output and input markets. Exhaustive coverage of this fascinating subject has not been possible, but the intention has been to show that in economic analysis it is important to recognise the influence which institutional structure has upon price formation and resource allocation. The behaviour of markets with many buyers and sellers (perfect competition) was contrasted with what may happen when there is only one seller (monopoly) or one buyer (monopsony). In the second half of the chapter attention was switched to consideration of the marketing chains which exist for agricultural products, and to the fact there are complex structures of vertically linked markets. In these chains each stage adds value to the produce of the stage immediately below it. Retailers add value to the product delivered by the wholesale sector, wholesalers add value to the output of the processing sector, and so on down to the farm where farmers add value to the inputs they buy. As has been seen in a simple way, the prices farmers receive and the quantities they can sell are very much dependent upon the performance of firms above them in the marketing chain. Hence the institutional structure of such chains has to be considered in economic analysis of agricultural markets.

9.7 *Summary points*

1. Each time *ownership* of a product changes a *price* is determined.
2. *Perfectly competitive markets* are ones in which (among other conditions) the many buyers and sellers are too numerous for any individual to affect market price. *Perfect competition* is used in microeconomics as a paradigm, or standard, of market behaviour. *Pure or atomistic competition* are terms to describe markets with the main features of perfect competition.
3. *Monopoly* exists where there is a single supplier in a market, and *monopsony* where there is a sole buyer. *Oligopoly* is where there are only several suppliers, each able to influence price and *oligopsony* where there are only several buyers.
4. According to theory, *prices and profits* can be expected to be higher if there is *monopoly or monopsony* than if there is *perfect or atomistic competition*, and the quantity traded will be lower.
5. *Price discrimination* is where a different price for the same product is charged in different markets.
6. Products reach final consumers through a marketing chain in which a succession of firms transform basic products and add value to them. A *marketing margin* exists as the price difference of the product between any two stages in the marketing chain *e.g.* the retail-farm-gate margin or the retail-wholesale margin.
7. The demand for agricultural products as they leave the farm (i.e. at the farm-gate) is a *derived demand*, which is dependent upon (derives from) demand for food products at the retail level.

Further reading

For more extensive comparisons of market equilibrium under perfect competition and monopoly any basic microeconomic textbook can be consulted. Among those recommended are: Chapter 8 of Begg, Fischer and Dornbusch (1984), Chapter 23 of Samuelson and Nordhaus (12th Edn, 1984) and Chapters 19, 20 and 22 of Lipsey (6th Edn, 1984).

There is no standard solution to the problem of profit-maximising equilibrium for an oligopolistic market with few sellers, which is why the topic has not been covered here. Readers interested in the theory of oligopoly are recommended to consult Chapter 21 of Lipsey (1984), Chapter 5 of Begg *et al.* (1984) or Chapter 24 of Samuelson and Nordhaus (1985).

There are comparatively few up-to-date books which provide a comprehensive treatment of price determination in agricultural markets, plus a full economic analysis of such markets. One such is the Second edition (1981) of Tomek and Robinson. Chapters 3 and 4 of Timmer *et al.* (1983) deals with these issues specifically for less-developed countries. Also the book *Marketing Agricultural Products* by Kohls and Uhl now in its fifth edition (1980) provides a good comprehensive introduction to all aspects of markets and marketing.

10

Welfare economics

10.1 *Introduction*

Economic policy causes changes in the level and structure of economic activity. Policy intervention (such as to impose foreign exchange rationing, or to provide investment grants) is undertaken because it is judged by the relevant political authorities to produce an outcome which is superior to the alternative without the intervention. Conceivably that superiority may be judged by non-economic criteria (such as electoral success), but an inevitable question is whether it is superior in economic terms. *Welfare economics* is the body of economic theory which has addressed this question by trying to establish criteria for economic superiority and also operational procedures to permit one outcome to be compared to another.

The starting point for this theoretical analysis is the concept of '*Pareto optimality*' named after the Italian-born economist Vilfredo Pareto.[1] Pareto stated what with hindsight seems an obvious and wholly acceptable criterion namely that *one state of the economy would be classed as superior to another if moving to it makes at least one individual better off without making anybody else worse off*. However this is in fact a weak criterion, since it does not allow comparison of the normally observed situation in which improving the lot of one or more people usually involves loss to at least one other person. (How economists address this issue of how to balance some peoples' losses against others' gains is dealt with in Section 10.4). But despite being a weak criterion, Pareto efficiency has a crucial significance in economic theory since any *general equilibrium* in a *competitive economic system* would possess the necessary properties for Pareto optimality and as observed in Chapter 9 competitive equilibrium is the standard against which alternatives are usually compared. Thus

Section 10.2 explores the relationship between Pareto efficiency and the equilibrium conditions which would exist in perfectly competitive markets.

An important conclusion which emerges from the analysis is that even if a general competitive equilibrium existed, although it would be Pareto optimal, it is not possible to state that it would be a socially optimal outcome. This is because, as discussed below, the equilibrium income distribution which accompanies the equilibrium allocation of goods and services may not be judged to be socially optimal; certainly there will always be those who consider themselves underpaid and others to be overpaid. If the competitive income distribution were generally judged to be socially unfair there would be grounds for rejecting the existing competitive equilibrium and opting for a policy intervention to achieve income redistribution. Income redistribution is achieved by taxing some members of society in order to subsidise others. As will be shown (in both this chapter and Chapter 12) departures from competitive equilibrium for whatever reason, including the application of taxes and subsidies, lead theoretically to a loss of economic efficiency. Hence there is a policy trade-off between economic efficiency and greater equity of income.

Apart from equity considerations there may be other grounds for policy intervention. Markets may not be atomistically competitive but may be influenced by monopoly power; markets may be judged not to possess adequate foresight to achieve what would be in the longer run interests of society. These and other reasons for intervening in markets are reviewed briefly in Section 10.3. But whatever the justification given for policy intervention, how are we to judge whether that intervention improves social welfare when there are both losers and gainers? An answer to this is provided by the *compensation principle* discussed in Section 10.4 below. This compensation principle is of particular importance in agricultural policy analysis since it is widely applied in determining the net social costs of policy. The way it is applied is explored fully in the final Chapter (12), in which the social costs and benefits of a number of different policies are analysed. In that analysis the welfare benefits to consumers and producers are measured by changes in what are defined as *consumer and producer surplus* respectively. These are key concepts in policy welfare analysis, and section 10.5 is devoted to an explanation of them.

Policy intervention in the economy may arise for many reasons, as for example to change the distribution of income, but also (as reviewed in section 10.3) because of the existence of some condition, such as monopoly, which violates the norms of perfect competition and prevents the attainment of Pareto optimality. While social welfare might be improved by policy action in such circumstances, *the theory of the second best* underlines the difficulty of devising general rules for selecting appropriate policies in what is in reality the prevailing real world situation of imperfect markets. This important matter of the theory of the second best is taken up in Section 10.6.

10.2 *Competitive markets and Pareto optimality*

For economists, the welfare implications of the equilibrium conditions achieved in competitive markets represent a very important 'benchmark' from which to evaluate market intervention policies designed to adjust equilibrium. The nature of this benchmark is succinctly summarised by Just, Hueth and Schmitz (1982, pp. 25–6) in the following excerpt:

> The important relationship between competitive equilibria and Pareto optimality is that, *when a competitive equilibrium exists, it attains Pareto optimality*. This result, formerly known as the first optimality theorem, is sometimes referred to as the theorem of Adam Smith. In the *Wealth of Nations*, published in 1776, Smith argued that consumers acting selfishly to maximise utility and producers concerned only with profits attain a 'best possible state of affairs' for society, given its limited resources, without necessarily intending to do so. Although more than one best (Pareto-efficient) state of affairs generally exists, Smith was essentially correct.

To explain this statement, including the important caveat in the last sentence, it is necessary to state the general conditions required for an economy-wide equilibrium to be a Pareto optimal state, to evaluate the extent to which the equilibrium of a competitive market fulfils them, and then to consider why there are many Pareto-optimal states.

There are three first-order criteria which have to be met before a market equilibrium can be adjudged to be Pareto optimal. These are:

1. *The exchange efficiency criterion* – according to this criterion the market allocation of a given bundle of products between consumers should be such that it is not possible to redistribute them so that the utility (welfare) of any individual is increased without decreasing the utility of others.
2. *The production efficiency criterion* – this requires that the allocation of factors of production between products is such that it is not possible to reallocate them so that the output of any

product is increased without reducing output of some other product.

3. *The top level criterion (as it is called by Ng (1983, p. 36)) or output efficiency criterion (Ritson 1977, p. 232)* – this requires that the combination of products actually produced (and made available for allocation under criterion 1) should be such that there is no alternative combination which will allow the utility (welfare) of any individual to be increased without decreasing the utility of others.

To what extent do the equilibria in competitive markets fulfil these three conditions?

10.2.1 *The exchange efficiency criterion*

It has already been shown in Chapter 5 that, for any consumer, a condition for a utility-maximising equilibrium is that the marginal rate of substitution between any pair of commodities consumed equals their price ratio.[2] Furthermore, it was shown (in Fig 5.5) that such an equilibrium can be graphically represented as the point of tangency between the *budget line* (which has a slope equal to the relative price of the two products) and the *highest achievable indifference curve*. In a competitive market, since consumers are price takers and face identical pairs of relative prices, the equilibrium for all consumers must be one in which their marginal rates of substitution for each pair of products are identical.

In a two-consumer, two-commodity example it can be demonstrated (using an Edgeworth-box consumption diagram) that for any fixed combination of total available products A and B, *allocations between consumers which satisfy the conditions for competitive equilibrium also satisfy the exchange efficiency criterion for Pareto optimality.*

To construct the appropriate Edgeworth consumption box consider first the indifference maps (showing commodity combinations of equal utility) of consumers M and N for products A and B. These are shown as Fig. 10.1 (*a*) and 10.1(*b*) with product axes of equal length; that is $O_NA = O_MA$ and $O_NB = O_MB$ to signify that there is a fixed bundle of the two products to be shared between the two consumers.

If Fig. 10.1 (*b*) is rotated through 180° and placed on top of Fig. 10.1 (*a*) the Edgeworth-box consumption diagram shown as Fig. 10.2 is obtained. As a result any point inside or on the boundary of the box represents a complete allocation of the available amounts of A and B between the two consumers. At the top right-hand corner N receives all of both products and M nothing. At the top left hand corner N receives all of A and M obtains all the available B. (Readers should check for themselves that at any interior points such as x and y products A and B are fully allocated, but in such a way that both M and N receive some of each product.

In Fig. 10.2 the points of tangency between the indifference curves of the two consumers are mapped out as the so-called *contract curve*, $O_N O_M$ which shows all the points at which consumers' marginal rates of substitution are the same. Thus all points on the contract curve are potential competitive equilibria, but there is insufficient information within the analysis so far to tell us exactly where the unique equilibrium point will be on the contract curve. To determine that, it will be necessary to consider the interaction between demand, supply and price formation, which we will do when we consider the top-level criterion.

An important property of the contract curve derives from the fact that *any point not on the contract curve is Pareto inefficient in the sense that there must exist a point on the curve which is Pareto-superior to it*. To see this,

Fig. 10.1. Elements of the Edgeworth box diagram.

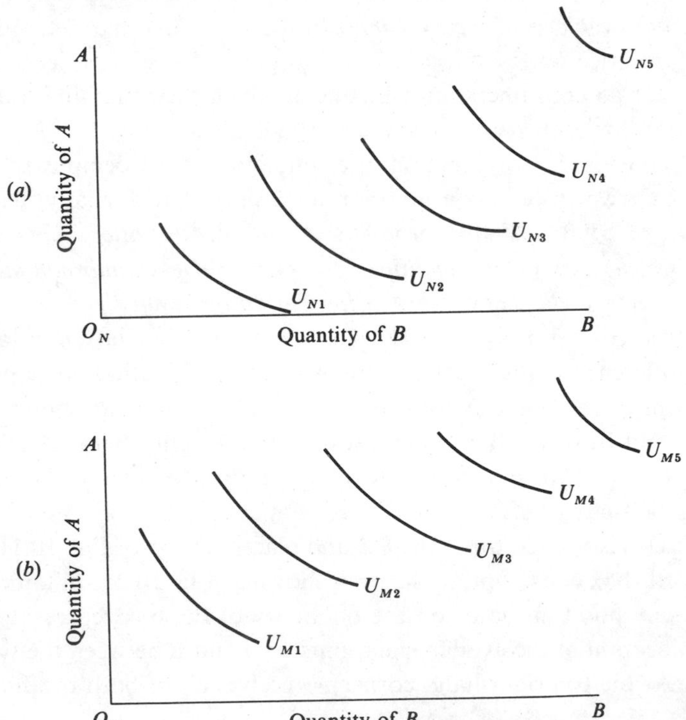

consider the two points x and y in Fig. 10.2. At x consumer M receives O_Ma of A and O_Mb of B with the remainder of both products allocated to N; N achieves the level of utility represented by indifference curve U_{N4} while M obtains a lower level of satisfaction than U_{M1} (since x lies closer to O_M than does U_{M1}). If M were to sell bb' of B to consumer N in exchange for aa' of A – *i.e.* if the allocation of products shifts to x from y – then M will increase his utility to U_{M1} without any loss of welfare to N who remains on indifference curve U_{N4}.

By moving from x to y consumer M can compensate N for the loss of aa' of product A, by offering him bb' of B, and improve his own well-being in the process. Thus y is Pareto-superior to x (which does not fulfil the exchange efficiency criterion), and because it is a preferred outcome it might be expected that competitive market forces will tend to bring about outcomes (on the contract curve) such as y rather than x.

Fig. 10.2. Exchange efficiency and the contract curve.

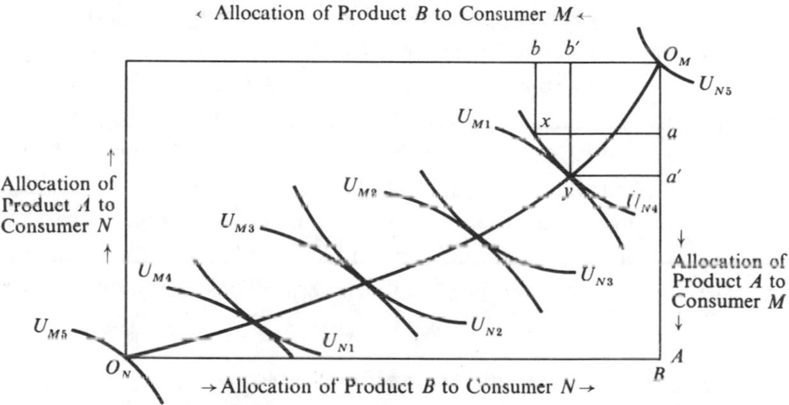

10.2.2 *The production efficiency criterion*

As was demonstrated in Chapter 2, one of the conditions for the optimal allocation of any pair of inputs to production is that their marginal rates of substitution along the relevant product isoquant be equal to the inverse of their relative price (see Fig. 2.8 and equation 2.6). Since in a competitive market the relative prices of inputs are the same for all firms it follows that, *at equilibrium in such a market, the marginal rate of substitution between any pair of inputs must be the same for all products and firms*. For the case in which fixed quantities of two inputs are allocated to the production of two products such potential equilibrium points can be explained using another Edgeworth box diagram.

In Fig. 10.3 isoquants (refer back to Fig. 2.4) replace the indifference curves of Fig. 10.2, and the axes relate to the allocation of the two inputs *X* and *Y* to the production of *A* and *B*. Thus the length of the horizontal axis reflects the amount of input *Y* available and the height of the vertical axis shows the quantity of input *X* to be distributed. The *contract curve* traced out by the points of tangency of the isoquants for product *A* and product *B* show the output combinations which fulfil the competitive equilibrium condition stated above. Thus, at *j* the level of output of *A* is given by isoquant I_{A3} and that of *B* by isoquant I_{B3}. Again it should be noted that point *j* is Pareto-superior to any point such as *k* which lies off the contract curve. At *k* output of *A* is at the level I_{A3} but that of *B* falls below I_{B3}. By switching *bb′* of input *X* from *B* to the production of *A* and switching *a′a* of input *Y* from *A* to *B* the output combination *j* can be reached; this entails holding output of *A* at I_{A3} but increasing that of *B* to I_{B3}. Thus, more *B* is obtained for no loss of *A*, which makes point *j* Pareto-superior to *k*.

Put in another way, point *j* indicates that if output of *A* at level I_{A3} is required the highest attainable level of *B* is I_{B3}; any other allocation of resources other than *j* along I_{A3} will produce less *B* than I_{B3}. Competitive markets with the properties previously defined, in which firms strive to maximise their profits, would be expected to allocate resources from points such as *k* to others such as *j* lying on the contract curve.

The combinations of output along the contract curve in Fig. 6.3 can be redrawn to indicate the maximum amount of product B which can be achieved for any given output of *A*, and vice-versa. These are shown as the

Fig. 10.3. Production efficiency and the contract curve.

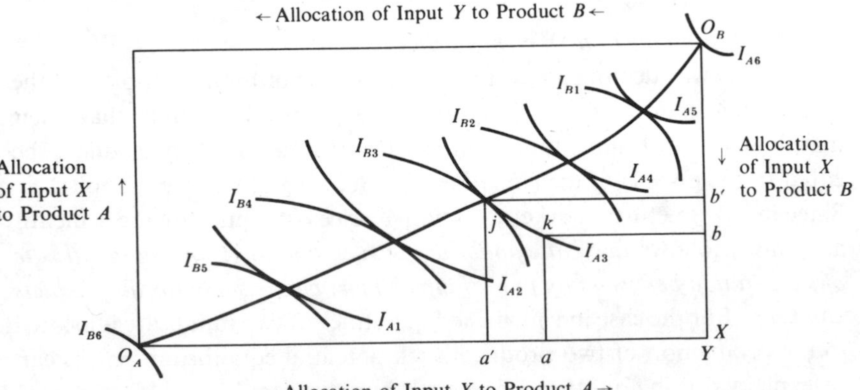

production possibility curve, $A_{max}B_{max}$, portrayed in Fig. 10.4 (and defined in Chapter 2 in relation to Fig. 2.6).

10.2.3 *The top level criterion*

In our two-input, two-product, two-consumer model the equilibrium requirement for Pareto optimality requires that the production and exchange efficiency conditions hold simultaneously. This will occur (*a*) when product prices are determined by competitive forces such that their ratio equals (i) the marginal rate of substitution of products for both consumers, and (ii) the inverse of the marginal rate of transformation of products, and (*b*) when production is on the production possibility frontier.

An output combination, and its distribution, which fulfils the above criteria simultaneously is that shown as O_M in Fig. 10.4. This point represents an output level *A* of product *A* and *B* of product *B*. The slope of the production possibility frontier at *OM* is tangential to the relative product price line P_B/P_A denoting that the marginal rate of product transformation is the inverse of the price ratio as is required for competitive equilibrium. Output combination *AB* is then shown as being allocated (using an Edgeworth-box diagram identical in structure to that in Fig. 10.2) between the two consumers at a point *z* on the consumption contract curve, where *z* is a point such that the marginal rate of

Fig. 10.4. The top-level criterion for Pareto-optimality.

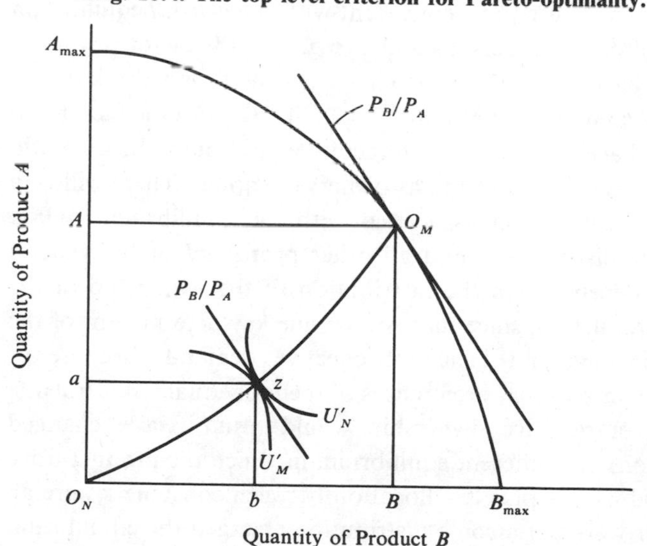

substitution of B for A by both consumers also equals the price ratio P_B/P_A; this fulfils the exchange efficiency criterion. At z, O_na of the total A produced goes to consumer N and aA to consumer M; O_nb of the B produced goes to consumer A and bB to consumer B.

What has been stated using Fig. 10.4 is that in certain well-defined theoretical conditions, competitive markets will generate equilibrium prices which enable simultaneous fulfilment of the production and exchange efficiency conditions for Pareto-optimality (in which no-one can be made better-off without someone else being made worse off). This is a strong statement of considerable importance insofar as it provides a basis for arguing that *competitive markets are efficient*. It is, moreover, a result which does not depend upon restricting analysis to the $2 \times 2 \times 2$ case, but extends to situations of many products, inputs and consumers. It is the analytical basis of intellectual support for policies of non-intervention in markets and for private entrepreneurship and competition in all areas of economic activity. At the same time, however, it is important to recognise that this does *not mean* that the outcomes of competitive markets are those which maximise the welfare of society, *or* that the sort of competition which is observed in reality is of a type which necessarily leads to Pareto optimality. These are issues taken up in the next section.

10.3 *Reasons for policy intervention in markets*

The Pareto-optimal solution identified in Fig. 10.4 was for a particular set of conditions, not all of which were made fully explicit. For the equilibrium in the figure to be consistent with the *general* equilibrium for an economy of only two persons and two goods, the factor payments to those persons have to result in incomes consistent with the levels of expenditure involved in the solution at point Z. Thus, both the factor and product markets have to be in simultaneous equilibrium. Income will accrue to individuals as workers and as owners of capital. There will be a particular income distribution associated with the equilibrium in Fig. 10.4. That income distribution, and all other properties of the general equilibrium, will depend upon the distribution of the ownership of the fixed factors of production, since that will be one key determinant of the distribution of income and hence of effective demand. Because of differences in the consumption preferences of the individuals concerned, a different pattern of resource ownership would result (via a changed income distribution) in a different equilibrium in which the product price ratio and the product mix plus its allocation between consumers were all different. In other words, if income distribution changed the equilibrium in Fig. 10.4 would be associated with some point other than O_M on the production possibility frontier. This other equilibrium would also fulfil all three conditions for Pareto-optimality. Thus, there are an infinite number of possible Pareto-optimal equilibria, one for each possible distribution of factor ownership and income. But which of the many possible distributions is to be preferred in the real economy of many competing interests, in order to *maximise social welfare*? In the absence of any observable *social welfare function* (an equivalent at the whole of society level of the individual's utility function), there is no objective way of determining the socially optimal allocation of resources. This is an issue resolved through the political process of each country. Where it is judged that a greater measure of equality in income and consumption is desirable than that generated by market forces a large number of policies of market intervention may be pursued by the State. The list of possible interventions is enormous but includes subsidised food, subsidised housing, subsidised agricultural inputs, progressive income taxation, and wealth taxes. Note, however, that subsidies involve consumers of products and inputs paying less than their seller's receive. As Ritson states (1977, p. 246):

> a government policy which results in the owner of a factor receiving a different sum from the price paid for the resource by the producer, or a consumer paying a different price for a product than that received by the producer, means the non-fulfilment of the Pareto conditions. *Such a departure from the Pareto conditions may be termed a loss in economic efficiency.*

Thus the income distribution gains achieved by such policies have to be weighed against losses in economic efficiency. Such trade-offs are entirely acceptable, but the economists' role is to point out that they exist and to try and quantify them as far as is possible.

Justification for political intervention in markets also arises because markets often do not exhibit the ideal characteristics of pure competition. There may be industries with only a few producers (*oligopoly*) or even only one producer (a *monopoly*), which are able to restrict output and push up prices and profits; this represents a loss of Paretian efficiency. Alternatively, there may be systematic deficiencies in the market knowledge of important groups of producers or consumers which lead to market inefficiency and instability. Certainly perfect foresight does not exist, and it may be judged that, in the face of price instability and uncertainty, socially desirable decisions may not be taken without the active intervention of the state. (In particular, infant industries in LDCs may need special measures of state support if they are to succeed and grow into mature viable ones). Questions which always have to be posed when this justification for policy intervention is advanced are 'does government have better forecasting ability than the private sector' and 'is the government a good judge of when to cease a particular type of intervention?' In addition, in these circumstances, there is the question of what form of policy would be optimal. This turns out to be difficult in general to determine, something revealed by the theory of the second best reviewed in Section 10.6 below.

State intervention in markets is also common in connection with so-called *public goods* and in cases where private economic activity generates significant *external costs* which are not automatically borne by the producer or consumer of the product. Public goods are ones which if made available at all are then available to everyone. National defence, or quarantine restrictions to control the importation of animal and plant diseases are both types of public good. In neither case could individuals purchase their own protection from these very different forms of attack from abroad, but its provision by the State out of taxes may be presumed to benefit all members of society.

In agriculture, short-term competitive pressures may lead farmers to adopt cropping practices which lead to soil erosion on their own holdings or those of others; widespread use of inorganic fertilizer, insecticides and herbicides may have harmful effects on ground and surface water supplies, causing eutrophication or even outright poisoning of the water; intensive poultry and pig units may produce smells which are offensive to those living close by and may reduce their 'quality of life'. These effects of agriculture are *external* in the sense that there is no automatic market mechanism which imposes their equivalent money value as a cost on the entrepreneur who is responsible for producing them. They are external to the accounting system of private costs and benefits generated by the market system. In the absence of legislation to prevent entrepreneurs creating external costs, there are *social costs* to be counted against the net private benefits created by particular forms of enterprise and exchange. Such costs can be *internalised* to the producer through legislation forcing him to invest in measures to control social costs and to stop polluting waterways or the air. In these ways producers are forced to bear the full social costs of production and pass them on to the consumers of his product. Private and social costs and benefits are thus brought into line. As a corollary, note that the higher production costs may be expected to lead to lower output and to a reallocation of resources.

In other cases, where *external benefits* arise which cannot be appropriated by producers through the market, governments may intervene to subsidise production. In such cases public equity ideally would require that the taxes to pay for such subsidies should be imposed on those who obtain the external benefit; in this way again the benefits would be internalised.

10.4 *Welfare criteria for policy choice*

Economists have invested considerable intellectual effort to establish criteria which will permit selection of a 'socially best' policy from among a set of alternatives. The Pareto-principle, while valuable from the standpoint of establishing the efficiency of competitive equilibria, is clearly not an adequate or operational criterion. It is not adequate because, as has already been indicated, there is an infinity of Pareto-optimal competitive equilibria corresponding to the infinity of possible income distributions. It is not operational because there is no way of checking that the effect of any particular policy change is such that some people are made better off and none are made worse off (this is so because changes in individuals' welfare are subjective and cannot be readily measured). Nevertheless, in the real world it is generally the case that economic policy changes cause some individuals to lose as well as others to gain. This is something that will become abundantly clear when agricultural policy measures are analysed in Chapter 12, but a couple of simple examples here will suffice to emphasise the point; if a government decides to ban imports because they are undercutting local producers, the local producers gain but foreign ones lose; where governments manage to impose price ceilings on foodstuffs, farmers lose because prices are reduced but consumers gain.

To overcome these problems the *compensation principle* was developed out of the work of Kaldor (1939). According to the *Kaldor compensation test*, state X is preferred to state Y if the gains of the gainers are more than sufficient to permit the losers (from a shift from Y to X) to be fully compensated. (For a diagrammatic illustration of this see Box 10.1). Note that in applying this principle it is not necessary that the losers should actually be compensated, only that they *could* be. Hicks (1940) extended the compensation test by suggesting that a state X should only be judged socially superior to Y if the 'losers could not profitably bribe the gainers to oppose the shift from Y to X.'

These compensation tests have been shown to have weaknesses, in that in certain theoretically defined circumstances they may simultaneously establish X to be superior to Y *and* Y to be superior to X.[3] Thus the compensation tests might be unable to achieve a ranking of alternatives. In practice, however, the Kaldor compensation test is widely applied to policy analysis. Certainly agricultural policy analysis of the type presented in Chapter 12, Section 12.2, is designed to be applied in conjunction with the test 'can the gainers compensate the losers?' This is so in the sense that the analyst strives to measure the benefits and costs which would accrue to different sectors (e.g. domestic consumers and producers, foreign consumers and producers, taxpayers) and to present these to policy makers and interested parties to enable them to form judgements about the balance of benefits and costs from a particular policy change. It is not the economists' job to make this judgement for society (although of course he/she will have an individual opinion); it is ultimately the politician's job.

The economists' job in policy analysis is to identify and measure the costs and benefits which arise from policy changes and it is to questions of measuring *changes in consumer and producer welfare* that we now turn in the next section of this chapter.

BOX 10.1
The compensation principle

Comparison of alternative bundles of goods using the compensation principle can be readily applied to alternative consumption points in the Edgeworth box diagram presented as Fig. 10.5. According to previous analysis (in Fig. 10.2), point *y* has been shown to be Pareto-superior to *x*, since a shift from *x* to *y* would increase consumer *M*'s utility while maintaining *N*'s constant. Similarly *w* is Pareto-superior to *x* since that

Fig. 10.5. Illustration of the compensation principle.

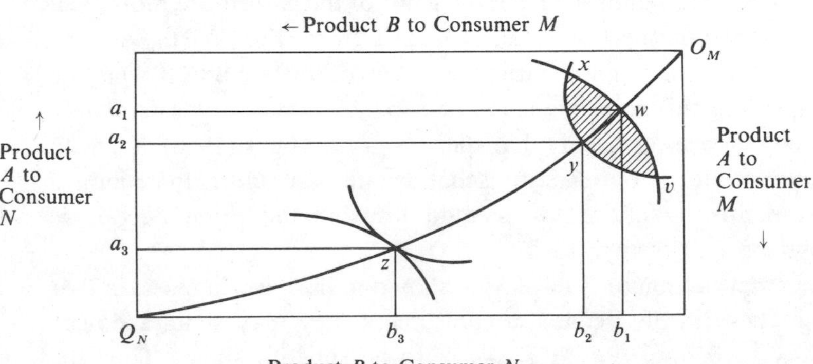

enables *N*'s utility to increase while *M*'s remains constant. In fact all points in the shaded area yield greater welfare than *x* (or *v*), although there is always a Pareto-optimal point lying between *w* and *y* on the contract curve which is preferred to other points in the area. There is no need to invoke the compensation principle to demonstrate this since no one has lost anything from the changes examined.

However, compare the welfare implications of moving from *x* to *z*. From *N*'s point of view the move from *x* to *z* is equivalent to *losses* of $a_2 - a_3$ of product *A* and $b_2 - b_3$ of product *b*; this is so because in terms of utility *y* is as good as *x* to consumer *N*. However from M's standpoint the move from *x* to *z* is equivalent to *gains of* $a_1 - a_3$ of product *A* and $b_1 - b_3$ of product *B*; since bundle *w* conveys as much utility to *M* as *x* does. Thus *M*'s gains exceed *N*'s losses in commodity terms, and *M could compensate N* fully for *N*'s losses and still obtain higher consumption and satisfaction. That is *M* could give back to *N* $a_2 - a_3$ of *A* and $b_2 - b_3$ of *B*, and would still be better off by amounts $a_1 - a_2$ and $b_1 - b_2$.

10.5 *Consumer and producer surplus*

Changes in *consumer surplus* and *producer surplus* are extensively used monetary value measures of the welfare benefits or costs arising from changes in agricultural policy. There has been considerable debate about the theoretical justification for employing them[4] but the prevailing view is that in most situations they are acceptable approximations of the underlying welfare values which theory might advocate.

Consumer surplus It will be recalled from Chapter 5 (Fig. 5.12) that the effect of an own-price change upon the demand for a good could be divided into an income and a substitution effect. Following Hicks (1941 and 1943) the income effect can be used as a basis for a money income measure of the welfare gain or loss from a price change, under conditions where the marginal utility of income remains constant. It can further be shown that the measure of consumer surplus, which was first proposed by the French engineer Dupuit in 1844 and later brought more fully into the discipline of economics by Marshall (1930), is in some conditions identical to Hicks' *compensating variation* measure of the income effect. To see this consider Fig. 10.6.

In Fig. 10.6(*a*) a consumer is assumed to possess an amount of money income, M_0, which may be spent either on good *A* or retained for expenditure on other goods. At price P_0 of good *A* the consumer would maximise utility/welfare at point *a* by purchasing Q^0 of *A* and retaining M'_0 of income for other uses. If the price were to fall to P_1 utility would be maximised at point *b* by purchasing Q^1 of *A* and retaining M''_0 of income. Thus at P_0 demand would be for Q^0 and at P_1 for Q^1. These points therefore lie on the consumer's ordinary demand curve which is plotted in Fig. 10.6(*b*) as the line passing through *a* and *b*.

If we now try to identify the income and substitution effects of the price change, there are two alternative ways that theoretically might be pursued. The first asks the question 'how much income could be given up at the new lower price P_1 and still leave the consumer as well off (i.e. on indifference curve I_0) as before the price fall? This is obtained by finding a point of tangency, *c*, between indifference curve I_0 and a budget line of the same slope as M_0P_1. *Comparison of points c* and *b* indicates that $M_0 - M_1$ of income could be given up at the new price P_1 and leave the consumer with the same utility as before the price fall. In that sense

Fig. 10.6. Compensating and equivalent variation.

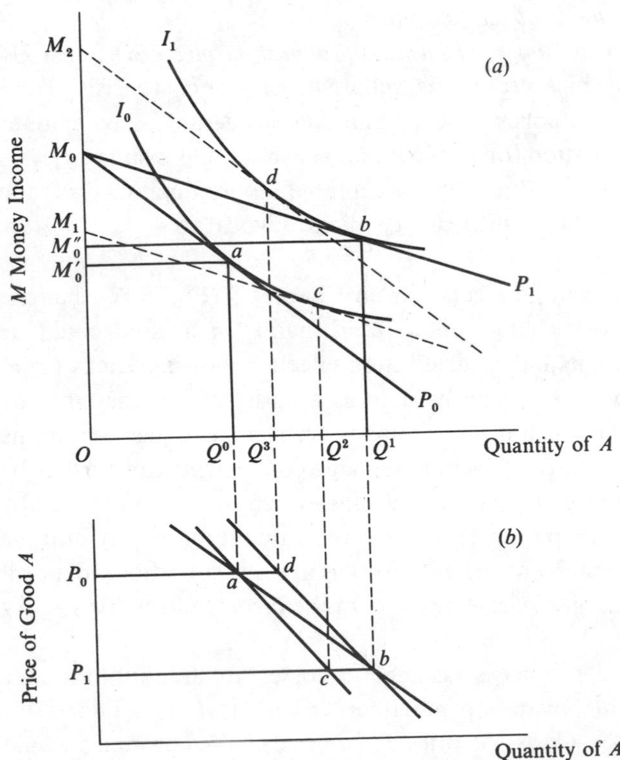

$M_0 - M_1$ can be accepted as a money measure of the benefit (extra welfare) to the consumer of the price fall; alternatively it can be interpreted as the maximum amount the consumer would be *able or (possibly) willing to pay* to bring about the price change *or to compensate losers* for it. Following Hicks (1941), this amount is also known as the *compensating variation.*

The substitution effect of the price fall identified using the method of compensating variation is shown in Fig. 10.6(*a*) as a move from *a* to *c*; these points lie on the *compensated demand curve* (for indifference level I_0) plotted through points *a* and *c* in Fig. 10.6(*b*). It can be shown[5] that P_0acP_1, the area which lies below this compensated demand curve and between the two price lines has a monetary value identical to the compensating variation $M_0 - M_1$.

The second alternative for isolating the income and substitution effects is to ask the question 'by how much would income have to rise at the original price P_0 for the consumer to be as well off as he would be if price fell to P_1?' This is obtained by finding the point of tangency, *d*, between the indifference curve I_1 and a budget line of slope M_0P_0. This is the method of *equivalent variation* and it reveals, in this case, that the effect of a price fall is equivalent to increasing consumer's income by $M_2 - M_0$. Using this method the substitution effect is the move from *d* to *b*. Plotting these points in Fig. 10.6*b* gives a compensated demand curve evaluated for utility level I_1. Again the area P_0dbP_1 lying below this curve and between the price lines has a monetary value equal to the equivalent variation $M_2 - M_0$.

It is apparent from Fig. 10.6(*b*) that, for a normal good such as *A*, the ordinary demand curve passing through *a* and *b* lies between the two alternative compensated demand curves, and that the area P_0abP_1 is a close approximation to the values of both compensating variation and equivalent variation. Indeed, *note* that if there is no income effect the ordinary and compensated demand curves coincide. In that case the area under the ordinary demand curve is an exact measure of both compensating and equivalent variation. In more general applications where the income effect is small the monetary value of the area P_0abP_1 *which is the Marshallian consumer surplus* will be a close and acceptable approximation to the Hicksian measures of the consumer welfare effects of a price change.

Marshall himself (1930, p. 124) defined consumer surplus to be the 'excess of the price which he (the consumer) would be willing to pay for the thing rather than go without it, over that which he actually does pay'. To visualise this concept of the surplus which a consumer obtains from buying a product at the going (marginal) market price consider the shaded area *abP* under the demand curve and above the price line *P* in Fig. 10.7. The unit of consumption at Q_1 would be purchased at the market clearing price *P*, but the demand curve signifies that the consumer would have been prepared to pay a price *r* for that unit. In that sense the consumer would have been willing to pay *rP* more than he had to to obtain that item and may be judged to have gained a surplus of that amount. Similarly at point Q_2 the consumer's surplus per unit of product is *sP*. The summation of such surpluses for each unit purchased yields a total consumer surplus for the Q_3 units purchased equivalent to the monetary value of the shaded triangle *abP*.

Strictly speaking certain precise conditions need to be fulfilled in order for the sum of the 'triangles' under individuals' demand curves to equal the 'triangle' under the market demand curve. Generally economists are prepared to accept consumer surplus measured as the triangle under market demand curve on the grounds that any 'aggregation error' is small in relation to the errors which arise in actual measurement. This is also true in the case of producer surplus which is explained below in relation to the firm's marginal cost curve, but is applied in Chapter 12 in relation to the market supply curve.

Producer surplus As a counterpart to the concept that consumers may gain a surplus from transactions, economists have explored the notion that producers may also gain in some way. Questions about the form and interpretation of any such gain, and of how it should be measured are

Fig. 10.7. Consumer surplus.

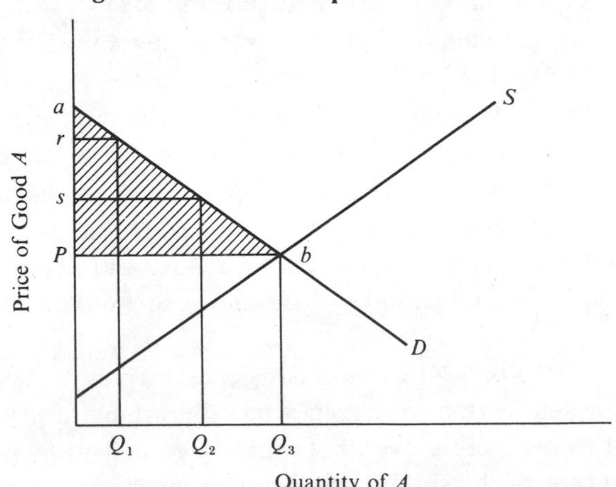

more problematic than those which have arisen with consumer surplus. As Currie *et al.* (1971, p. 754) stated:

> Whereas on the demand side consumers may be considered as a relatively homogeneous group, the situation on the supply side is complicated by the existence of diverse groups of sellers. There are, for example, sellers of final products (that is, firms) and sellers of services of land, entrepreneurial ability, labour and capital. All of these may receive surpluses of some sort. One source of confusion over the concept of producer surplus is to whom the term 'producers' refers. There are two possible interpretations which have not been carefully distinguished in the literature. The first interpretation is that the term refers solely to the owners of firms. The second is that it refers to the owners of factors of production.

The full complexities of the debate can be short circuited if we base our analysis on the competitive firm and industry in which firms own all the fixed factors of production and where the variable factors are in perfectly elastic supply at a given price for the period of the analysis.[6] If we further restrict the problem to analysing the producer welfare effects of changes in output or variable input prices (to reflect the policy analysis in Chapter 12) then a simple Marshallian approach can be adopted towards measurement.

The simple approach can be readily examined by considering, as in Fig. 10.8, the effect of a price increase from P_0 to P_1 on a competitive firm with a supply curve equal to its short-run marginal cost curve. The price increase causes equilibrium output to increase from Q_0 to Q_1. The extra total revenue generated equals $P_1Q_1 - P_0Q_0$, that is by the difference in area of the two rectangles $OP_1bQ_1 - OP_0aQ_0$. Since, however, by definition the area below the supply curve represents the *direct* (*variable*) *costs* of production, Q_0abQ_1 of the extra revenue has to cover the direct costs of increasing output which leaves P_0abP_1 as the *producer surplus*.

If, as discussed in the case of consumer surplus, it is assumed that the surpluses of individual producers can be added up, then *the change in producer surplus can be measured* (by extension from Fig. 10.8 to the market level supply curve) *as the area above the supply curve and between the price lines.*

What though is the economic interpretation and rationale for producer surplus measured in this way? The theory of firms in a competitive market is that at equilibrium in the long-run each firm operates at minimum long-run average cost and that there are no excess profits. If all firms were making only normal profits in the long-run in what sense might they gain a surplus? Currie *et al.* (1971, p. 757) answer this in the following way:

> ...the average costs of each firm...may include payments to factors which are in the nature of rents or surpluses – that is, loosely speaking, payments in excess of the minimum amounts necessary to elicit their services. While these are costs from the point of view of the firms, they are not real costs to society. The inevitable question is whether the relevant area above a competitive industry's supply curve represents these rents. The answer is 'yes if the supply curve, as well as being an average cost curve including rents, is also a marginal cost curve excluding rents'.

These complicated conditions may be thought of as being met for agriculture where there is a fixed supply of land.

Land is of varying qualities and hence of varying productivities. The best quality land may be capable of yielding several times more grain than marginal cereal growing land, even when the same quantities of seed, fertiliser, fungicides, labour and machinery are employed per hectare. At a low grain price only the best, most fertile land will be brought into cultivation, since only on that land will returns be sufficient to meet the full costs of production and prevent the land being used for some other purpose or left idle. As the cereal price increases more and more land will be drawn into production; that is the supply curve of land to cereal production is upward sloping. If Fig. 10.8 is reinterpreted as showing the

Fig. 10.8. Producer surplus.

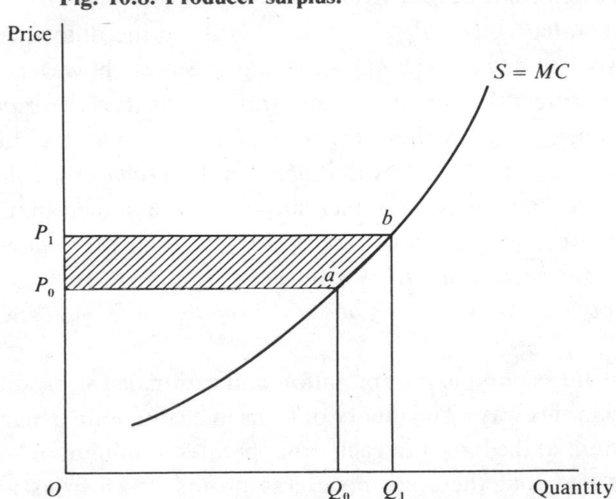

supply curve of cereal growing land, then price P_0 is just sufficient to draw the Q_0th hectare of land into production (that is to fully cover the *opportunity cost* of not employing it in some alternative activity, including idling it). It follows that at P_0 those hectares of land 'further down' the supply curve, closer to the origin, are obtaining returns in excess of that needed to secure their commitment to cereal growing. This excess return is a *pure surplus* to the farmers owning the land and is what the nineteenth century English economist David Ricardo, who first presented this analysis, called *economic rent*. The point is reinforced by considering the effect on the owner of the Q_0th hectare of an increase in the cereal price to P_1. The extra return $P_1 - P_0$ is a pure surplus to the Q_0th hectare since its owner incurs no additional direct (*i.e.* variable) costs to obtain it. If in this sense the supply curve can be defined as the marginal cost curve excluding rents then the shaded area in Fig. 10.8 is the increase in pure surplus or economic rent according to the owners of land from the price increase from P_0 to P_1.

In empirical studies of agricultural supply it is unlikely that the estimated supply curves correspond exactly to an industry marginal cost curve excluding rents. A significant number of farmers are tenants and may be eventually forced to pass on additional economic rents to landlords, retaining for themselves only the normal rate of return required to induce them to stay on as tenants. Moreover in agriculture as in other industries it may take many years for full adjustment to product price changes (for an exploration of this see Chapter 7). For these and other reasons empirical supply functions for, say, one year output responses to price changes are short-run functions. For such functions the estimated producer surpluses corresponding to the shaded area in Fig. 10.8 are best described as *quasi-rent*. This signifies that while production at a particular level involves a temporary surplus, maintenance of that production in the long-run will involve higher costs for some factors of production and smaller annual surpluses in the long-run. Put in another way, long-run supply curves may be expected to have a lesser upward slope than short-run curves, and attention must be paid to selecting the appropriate length-of-run supply curve if estimates of producer surplus are not to be biased.[7]

10.6 *The problem of the second best*

As explained in Section 10.2 there are three conditions (exchange efficiency, production efficiency, and output efficiency) which have to be simultaneously achieved if a market equilibrium is to be a Pareto-optimum or *first-best* solution. If for some reason a market imperfection exists in only one of the (factor or product) markets affecting the economy then at least one of these conditions will not be met and only a *second-best optimum* can be achieved. The imperfection may be thought of as a constraint preventing the attainment of the first best solution. Such a constraint may arise because of monopoly in a key production sector, from union monopoly in the labour market, from tariff and non-tariff barriers effected by other countries in export markets, or from constraints imposed by governments by such means as setting minimum wages or operating policies to guarantee minimum income or consumption levels. The question of policies to optimise social welfare in these individual circumstances was addressed by a number of economists, and led Lipsey and Lancaster to draw their findings together in a seminal paper 'The General Theory of Second Best' in 1957. In this the authors sought to establish what, if any, *general* policy principles could be applied to achieve a second best social optimum if the first was ruled out for one or other of the reasons above. As Ritson (1977, p. 248) states: 'Now, it would be most convenient if the attainment of a second best optimum required the application, wherever possible, of the same optimising rules with respect to production, distribution and output efficiency as those required for a first best optimum.' Unfortunately following the work of Lipsey and Lancaster, it emerges that theory does not support this; it also transpires that there may be several second best policies; because there is an imperfection or policy constraint in one market it does not necessarily follow that adopting free trade and encouraging competition in all other markets will lead to a second best optimum. As Mishan (1962) pointed out, however, this does not mean that pursuing competitive norms in all other markets would not in practice prove to be the optimal policy. But there can be no general presumption that this is so, and in some specific cases theory reveals that, where competition is distorted in one sector, the optimal second best policy is to introduce countervailing distortions in other sectors.

Illustration of the nature of the problem is most easily achieved by referring to some examples cited in the literature. Lipsey and Lancaster (1956, p. 16) considered as one of several examples, the case where a major part of the economy is rigidly controlled by central authority while the remaining sections are virtually uncontrolled. Since this implies impediments to allocation of resources between the controlled and uncontrolled sectors it implies misallocation of resources and economic inefficiency when measured against the Pareto-optimality standard. Lipsey and Lancaster characterise the policy debate on how to improve efficiency as follows: 'One faction argues that more control over the uncontrolled sector is needed, while another faction pleads for a relaxation of the degree of control exercised in the public sector. The principles of the general theory of second best support that *both sides* in the controversy may be advocating a policy appropriate to the desired ends. Both of these policies will move the economy in the direction of some second best optimum position.' This is so because both solutions will bring about an equilibrium in which the marginal relationship between output prices and marginal costs of production are the same in both sectors. Decontrol of the regulated sector will allow output levels and input use to adjust until output price equals marginal cost at the same input costs prevailing in the competitive sector. Alternatively, bringing the competitive sector under central control would enable (*in principle*) an allocation of resources *closer* to that which would be obtained in a freely competitive economy. The phrase *in principle* emphasises a problem entailed in using the theory of the second best to argue for more policy action to neutralise the effects of existing distortions, rather than for the removal of the distortions; namely that it depends upon the analytical power of the policy making machinery and its flexibility in the face of changing market circumstances. But what this particular case illustrates is that *there may be more than one second best policy* for improving economic efficiency and social welfare. If for any reason the market imperfection is of domestic origin and cannot for some reason be removed (although it is difficult to see how this could be true where the distortion is due to state control of a key sector), then the theory of the second best rules that a second best policy will require countervailing intervention in other sectors of the economy. As Lipsey and Lancaster state it: 'If a constraint is introduced which prevents the attainment of one Paretian condition, the other Paretian conditions, although attainable, are, in general, no longer desirable.'

Problems of the second best emerge clearly in relation to trade theory. As discussed in the next chapter the first-best conditions are where all markets internationally are competitive and there are no policy-induced barriers to trade. However, these first-best conditions do not prevail in world trade, and a question which arises concerns the optimal policies of countries faced with obstacles to their exports. Is their optimal policy to refrain from creating trade barriers (tariffs or subsidies) and to allow open competition to determine their pattern of trade, or should they perhaps seek a customs union in which there is free trade with a restricted number of neighbouring countries? It can be shown that the optimal policy in these circumstances *may* be not to opt for a laissez-faire trade policy, but be to either impose certain import tariffs or export subsidies, or to enter into a customs union. In certain circumstances these can be shown to be the optimal responses in a second-best world. This underscores one important result namely that where there is an imperfection in one market it is not automatically the optimal policy to pursue laissez-faire policies of open competition in all other sectors; in Ritson's words above, attainment of a second-best optimum does not require the same optimising rules with respect to production, distribution, and output efficiency as those required for the first-best optimum. It is also the case, as exemplified in the theory of trade policy, that there is no general set of rules for operating and identifying a second-best policy. The optimal policy nearly always depends upon specific circumstances, as in the case of the optimal import tariff referred to in the next chapter.

Despite the negotiations in UNCTAD (the United Nations Conference on Trade and Development) and successive rounds of the GATT (General Agreement on Trade and Tariffs), major obstacles to international free trade exist. Also major imperfections and elements of state control exist in the markets within individual countries. Thus the conditions for first-best, Pareto optimal equilibria in general do not exist. Discovery of optimal, second-best, policies requires detailed analysis and in many instances would call for some form of offsetting policy intervention. This complicates matters considerably, especially since there may be no unique second-best answer, and it opens the way for serious debate and legitimate conflicts of view about policy. However, as Mishan (1962) argued there are some types of market imperfection which still favour adoption of a laissez-faire policy. Moreover, when the costs of administering policy are allowed for and the revealed imperfections of policy making and analysis are acknowledged, care must be taken not to use the theory of the second-best as a pretext to bend over backwards to reject competitive solutions to resource allocation in economic development.

10.7 *Conclusions*

Chapter 10 has laid the theoretical foundation for the economic welfare analysis of agricultural policy which is presented in Chapter 12. An integral part of that analysis is the measurement of changes in *consumer and producer surplus* resulting from policy actions. These are widely adopted by agricultural economists as monetary measures of changes in the welfare of farmers and food consumers, and at the very least readers need to carry forward some understanding of these two concepts.

In policy analysis, in the short-run certainly, where one group of people gain another group loses. It is true that the losers may be foreign citizens, but that does not mean that such losses should be discounted. The issue of how the losses arising from a change in policy may be compared with the gains, in order to arrive at an economic judgement of the worthwhileness of the policy, has been addressed in discussing the *Hicks–Kaldor compensation principle*; which is that one situation is superior to another if the gainers from moving to it *could* compensate the losers. This principle is applied in a direct way in Chapter 12 to the analysis of agricultural policy. It is applied there without making any interpersonal comparisons that benefits to one group should be given priority (a higher weight) over others; if the monetary value of losses to one group exceed that of the benefits to another the policy is stated to have a net social cost. This is as far as economists as professionals are prepared to go, although their personal feelings may incline them to weight benefits to one group more highly than disbenefits (costs) to another. That judgement is left to the political arena, where it may be perfectly appropriate to weight a dollar in the consumer's pocket more highly than in a farmer's, or vice versa.

The roots of the compensation principle are to be found in the concept of *Pareto-efficiency* which was explored in Section 10.2. It is an important concept in helping to understand why economic analysis generally establishes perfect (pure, or atomistic) competition as the standard for efficient markets. This standard carries over into the next chapter and into examination of the economics of trade. In that context the basic economic position is to establish that under certain assumptions the competitively determined free-trade equilibrium is superior to equilibria with no trade or with restricted trade. If those assumptions do not hold then there may be a case for policy interference with trade, much as intervention in agricultural markets may be justified on compelling humanitarian or political grounds.

10.8 *Summary points*

1. In precisely determined theoretical conditions *perfectly competitive markets* would lead to price, output and input combinations which are *Pareto-optimal*; that is they would be such that no one could be made better off without someone being worse off.

2. There are as *many Pareto-optimal equilibria* as there are possible *income distributions* in society. Hence any particular Pareto-optimum is not necessarily that which yields the maximum social welfare.
3. Society may wish to pursue policies to alter income distribution and the patterns of prices and production. There is therefore a *trade-off between equity and efficiency*.
4. The *theory of the second-best* considers the choice of an optimal policy in conditions where a Pareto optimal or first-best outcome is not achievable because of market imperfections.
5. There may be more than one second-best policy.
6. In circumstances where Pareto-optimality is unachievable there are no simple general rules for selecting an optimal second-best policy.
7. A principle devised to test whether a policy improves social welfare is the *Hicks–Kaldor compensation test*. According to this a policy is beneficial if the gainers could compensate the losers.
8. For the Hicks–Kaldor test to be applied it is necessary to be able to obtain monetary values for welfare changes. *Consumer surplus and producer surplus* are widely used measures in agricultural policy analysis to assess policy impacts upon consumer and producer welfare.
9. The *change in consumer surplus* resulting in a price change is equivalent to the *income effect* of that change. Reducing prices is equivalent to increasing consumers' incomes and vice versa.
10. Producer surplus is, with various qualifications, a useful monetary measure of the changes in economic rent accruing to producers as prices rise or fall.

Further reading

Readers seeking good introductory treatments of welfare economics could consult Chapter 14 of Begg, Fischer and Dornbusch (1984), Chapter 13 of Call and Holahan (1983, 2nd Edn) or Chapter 5 of Ritson (1977). For a comprehensive, but quite advanced, treatment of welfare economics against a background of agricultural policy, readers could profitably consult the book by Just, Hueth and Schmitz (1982). This book also provides a thorough explanation of the Hicks–Kaldor compensation principle, and it explains the concepts of consumer and producer surplus. Alternatively, Ng (1983) also provides an advanced but clear exposition of this branch of theory.

Students interested to pursue the implications of the second-best theory for LDC policymaking, might like to obtain a pragmatic perspective by reading the first chapter of the book, on Policy Economics by Killick (1981). Those concerned to probe to the roots of the debate about this problem should consult the papers by Lipsey and Lancaster (1956) and Mishan (1962).

11

Economics of trade

11.1 *Introduction*

No countries are entirely self-sufficient in the supply of goods and services. All of them are engaged in trade, whereby some goods and services are exported abroad and others are imported. That is, there is a situation of international specialisation which mirrors that at the individual level in which (for example) farmers sell food to feed those who produce the fertiliser, machines, insecticide etc. that farmers buy. While much international trade is arranged by the decisions of individuals and firms, the State (particularly in LDCs) may exert considerable control over what is traded and upon what terms. While State interference is frequently criticised by economists (see Section 11.6 below), the fact that it is so widespread reflects the great importance countries attach to the economics of trade. Indeed at the current time there are major trade and economic issues on which LDCs are highly critical of the policies of DCs, and others on which international banks and international bodies such as the International Monetary Fund (IMF) are in turn critical of LDCs.

Stated in rather simplistic terms the IMF and World Bank, reflecting the dominant views emanating from western industrial countries and from a large group of economists, are generally in favour of 'free-trade'; that is in their dealings with LDCs they are generally opposed to measures which protect LDC producers and consumers and which reduce trade. The preference is to leave decisions about resource allocation and the distribution of products to individual market forces. This position to a large extent reflects acceptance of the theoretical arguments about the benefits of free-trade sketched out in this chapter, and of the argument presented in the previous chapter that policy intervention in a market (by means of a tariff, subsidy or other trade-restricting measure) results in economic inefficiency and a static welfare loss to society. Arguments in favour of 'free-trade' are further bolstered up by views that many attempts by governments to control markets have proved to be misguided and excessively costly, even where there appear to be acceptable reasons for intervention. Views of this type have been forcefully stated by amongst others Lal (1983) and Little (1982, see particularly Ch. 4).

There are, however, a number of limitations to the theory which do point to a case for trade restricting policies in certain cases. These are briefly touched upon in Section 11.5.3 below. More influential politically is the body of *structuralist* thought according to which markets do not work in the smoothly efficient way portrayed in neoclassical economic theory, and that, far from being beneficial, international trade is an inequalising force through which rich and powerful countries exploit poorer ones. The origins of this school are to be found in work by Prebisch (1950), Singer (1950) and Lewis (1954). The essence of their challenge was a rejection of the appropriateness of the standard assumption in trade theory that product and factor markets were purely competitive in both the Centre (industrialised countries) and the Periphery (LDC's). Whereas (see Box 11.3) neoclassical economic theory suggests that, where competition exists, technological changes which result in increased total factor productivity will lead to reduced product prices, Prebisch initially argued that this process only operates at the Periphery, competing down prices to the benefits of consumers at the Centre. At the Centre, it was argued, more monopolistic forces operate, particularly in the labour market where union power is seen as extracting the gains from increased productivity in the form of higher wages, and in the product market where firms are seen as having sufficient market power to pass on higher wage costs through higher prices to consumers at the Periphery and at the Centre. This line of reasoning has been reinforced by the perception that agricultural and other primary markets tend to be more competitive than industrial product markets which are seen as being influenced by monopolistic elements. Thus it was argued that, as a result of differences in competitive structure, the prices of primary exports from the Periphery are depressed relative to those of imported manufactured items (*i.e.* the LDCs' *commodity terms-of trade* will be depressed – see Section 11.5 below), and that trade will act as an 'exploitative' force on behalf of the Centre.

While in its most elementary form the Prebisch/Singer theory of deteriorating terms-of-trade has been strongly criticised (see Spraos, 1983, Chapter 2), the notion that trade can perpetuate and deepen inequality has endured, and indeed has been more forcefully stated in Emmanuel's book *Unequal Exchange* (1972) and later writings. As Edwards (1985, p. 295) states it:

> Emmanuel's argument went beyond that of Lewis and Prebisch. Whereas the latter had argued that unequal exchange applied only to *primary product exports* in which the Third World traded, Emmanuel generalised it to *all* commodities. Emmanuel argued that labour in the south was paid less, after taking into account differences in productivity, than labour in the north because in all sectors it was less organised and had less bargaining power. Thus, he argued, the rate of exploitation of all labour in the south was higher than in the north.

Again critics (e.g. Spraos 1983, Ch. 2) point to theoretical flaws in Emmanuel's theories. But it is not the purpose of this book to present an in-depth review of all aspects of the debate about the relationship between trade and development; although this brief introduction does acknowledge and point to the existence of a vigorous debate among economists. Rather the much more restrictive objective in this chapter is to provide readers with an understanding of basic neoclassical economic theory of free-trade in competitive markets. Following Meier (1980, p. 13), the theory presented can be said to address three major questions: One of these is '*what commodities will a country export and import under free-trade*'? A second is '*what determines the terms-of-trade of a country*'?, an issue which is (as already noted above) intimately concerned with the third question '*what are the gains from trade and who gains*'? The last of these questions can perhaps be rephrased in the context of the economics of developing countries, as *should LDCs pursue policies of free trade*? Understanding the theoretical answers presented in this chapter to these questions provides the foundation required to appreciate and participate in the broad policy debate about trade and development; much of that debate employs the economic terms and concepts used in this chapter.

11.2 *Trade theory*

11.2.1 *Theory of comparative advantage*

It was David Ricardo (1817) who first proposed the *principle of comparative advantage* to explain how trading partners could mutually benefit from specialisation in production and trade. Comparative advantage is defined to exist where the relative cost of producing different items differs between countries. Taking the simplest case of two countries and two commodities, comparative advantage would exist if the marginal opportunity cost of producing one good in terms of the other differed between the two countries. In this case (as explained fully below) each country would have a comparative advantage in one of the two goods and would gain by specialising in production of that good and trading some of its output for the other good. Each country would gain, because trade and specialisation enable countries to achieve higher consumption levels.

The key assumptions which underlie the Ricardian theory of comparative advantage are that:

(1) There is a fixed bundle of resources in each country which can be considered as a single input (labour) and which determines the maximum combinations of goods which can be produced.
(2) There are differences in production technique which lead to different relative production costs in different countries, *i.e.* there are differences in relative labour productivity.
(3) There are no economies of scale so that unit production costs do not vary with the quantity produced.
(4) The bundle of resources is fully employed.
(5) There are no transport or other transactions costs in trade.
(6) Markets are competitive.

Assumptions (3) and (5) are not *necessary* to demonstrate the principle of comparative advantage, but (3) is commonly used and most presentations of the analysis accept (5) for the sake of simplicity.

BOX 11.1
Countries as trading units

It is a common shorthand form of expression, which is used throughout this chapter, to talk of countries as if they produced and traded commodities, and were the beneficiaries from trade. It is of course firms and self-employed individuals (or households such as those in farming) within countries which are responsible for production decisions. Similarly, it is individuals and firms which arrange the export sales and import purchases which are recorded as a country's exports and imports; except in cases of centrally planned economies, or of special state trading organisations, trading decisions are made by private operators, working within the framework of state regulations of trade, on the basis of their profitability.

Furthermore, although we will talk of the gains from trade as if they accrued to countries they do in fact accrue to consumers via lower prices and to producing and trading firms in the form of higher returns. That is the gains

from trade may be thought of as taking the forms of increased *consumer* and *producer surpluses*, as explained in the previous chapter.

It would be tedious to spell this out fully in each case, hence this chapter employs the shorthand of saying that countries specialise in production and obtain the benefits of trade.

To illustrate the operation of the principle of comparative advantage consider the case of two countries which we will call the USA and Kenya. The USA can produce 100 m tonnes of wheat or 50 m tonnes of sugar, as shown by the *production possibility frontier*, *AB*, in Fig. 11.1(*a*), while Kenya can produce 40 m tonnes of sugar or 40 m tonnes of maize as shown by the production possibility frontier *CD* in Fig. 11.1(*b*).

In the absence of trade the opportunity cost of one tonne of maize in the USA is $\frac{1}{2}$ a tonne of sugar (since 100 m tonnes of maize can be substituted by 50 m tonnes of sugar), while in Kenya the opportunity cost of 1 tonne of maize is 1 tonne of sugar. (Note that this opportunity cost is equal to the marginal rate of transformation *in production* of sugar for maize.) Thus the USA has a *comparative advantage* over Kenya in maize production since it only has to give up $\frac{1}{2}$ a tonne of sugar to gain an extra tonne of maize whereas in Kenya 1 tonne of sugar has to be sacrificed. Looked at from the opposite side of the coin Kenya has a *comparative advantage* over the USA in sugar production since to gain an extra tonne of sugar entails a cost (sacrifice) of only 1 tonne of maize, whereas in the USA it is 2 tonnes.

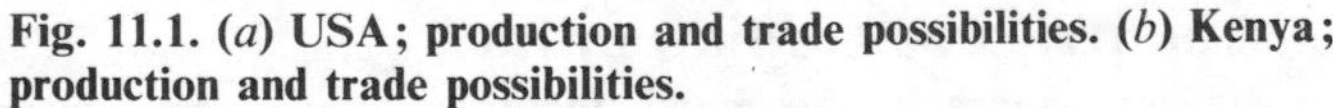

Fig. 11.1. (*a*) USA; production and trade possibilities. (*b*) Kenya; production and trade possibilities.

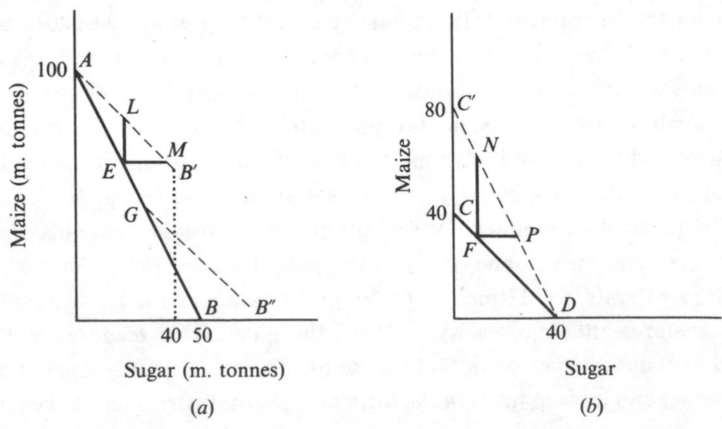

In the absence of trade it may be assumed that demand conditions are not such than Kenyans eat all sugar and no maize or that the converse is true in the USA. Rather, it may be assumed that consumption in the USA would entail a combination of maize and sugar such as that denoted by *E* in Fig. 11.1 (*a*); likewise consumption in Kenya might be at a point such as *F* in Fig. 11.1 (*b*).

It is clear that, in the absence of transactions and transport costs, both the USA and Kenya would benefit from trade. In Fig. 11.1 (*a*) the line *AB′* denotes the outer limit *consumption possibility curve* which the USA (when completely specialising in maize production) could achieve by exporting maize and importing Kenyan sugar. Kenya would gain from trade provided that for each tonne of sugar exported more (irrespective of how little more) than 1 tonne of maize was received in exchange. Suppose, for sake of argument, that exporters in Kenya were prepared to export each tonne of sugar for 'infinitesimally' more than one tonne of maize imported from the USA, then the USA could by exporting fractionally more than 40 million tonnes of maize buy the whole of the Kenya sugar crop of 40 million tonnes enabling it to consume at point *B′* (in Figure 11.1 (*a*)), which represents a consumption level of just less than 60 m tonnes of maize and 40 m tonnes of sugar. Any consumption point along *AB′* would be feasible for the USA on such advantageous *terms of trade*. Note that by consuming at points between *L* and *M* the USA would be able to consume more of both maize and sugar than would be possible without trade.

There is however no reason why the terms of trade should be so favourable to the USA, since, based on the marginal rate of substitution in the USA of two tonnes of maize to each tonne of sugar, USA importers should be prepared to export maize provided they receive anything (however little) more than 1 tonne of sugar for each 2 tonnes of maize exported. Thus for Kenya there is an outer bound *consumption possibility* represented by line *DC′* in Fig. 11.1 (*b*). *D* can be achieved without trade, *C′* (infinitesimally less than 80 m tonnes of maize) is the maximum which can potentially be obtained for consumption by exporting all Kenya's 40 m tonnes of sugar production in exchange for nearly 80 m tonnes of maize.

In practice the exchange price or *commodity terms-of-trade* need not lie at either of the extremes represented by the consumption possibility curves, *AB′* and *DC′*, but may lie somewhere inside them. (We will consider a simple theory of this commodity terms-of-trade later, but for the moment let us simply note that the theory of comparative advantage does not tell us where the exchange price will lie between the extremes represented by the marginal rates of substitution in production in the two trading countries.) What is certain is that trade will enable both trading partners to shift to consumption possibility curves which lie above their production possibility curves. Thus the theory of comparative advantage leads unambiguously to the conclusion that there are mutual welfare gains from trade, even though one trading partner may benefit more than another.

In Fig. 11.1(*a*) and 11.1(*b*) the production possibility curves have been assumed to be linear. That is, the marginal rates of transformation of one product into another (the opportunity costs of products) are assumed to be constant in each country. This tends to lead to the conclusion that countries should opt for *complete specialisation*, as in the case of Kenya in Fig. 11.1(*b*). If more than one tonne of maize can be obtained per tonne of sugar exported, Kenya will always be better off by producing the maximum amount of sugar (at *D*) and exporting some of it in exchange for maize. If, however, Kenya produced 30 m tonnes of sugar and 10 m of maize, then as Fig. 11.2 shows, the consumption possibility curve would be *VW*, which everywhere lies to the left of *DC*′, signifying (if production possibility curves were linear) that *incomplete specialisation* would involve lower levels of consumption than Kenya could achieve from complete specialisation.

In the case of our hypothetical example in Fig. 11.1(*a*) the USA may not be able to engage in complete specialisation simply because Kenya's

Fig. 11.2. Kenya, production and trade possibilities.

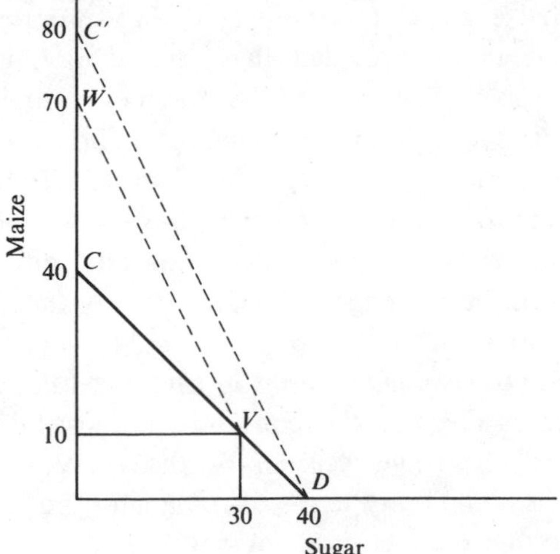

sugar output is only sufficient to extend the USA's consumption possibility by the segment *AB′*, where *B′* represents the situation which *could* theoretically be reached if the USA imported the full 40 m tonnes of sugar which Kenya can produce. Only if demand in the USA dictates an optimal consumption point somewhere on *AB′* should the USA completely specialise in maize production. The optimal solution might be incomplete specialisation at point *G* on the production possibility frontier in order to achieve consumption along *GB″* (where *GB″* also reflects the possibility of trading one tonne of USA maize for just less than one tonne of Kenyan sugar).

It is true that only a few countries produce civil and military aircraft, and that there are many countries which produce no oil, coffee, gold or tea. This apparent tendency to complete specialisation does not rest upon the linearity of production possibility frontiers, but upon the extremely high costs of extraction or production in many countries. Tea and coffee could be grown in Western Europe, but the opportunity cost of doing so is prohibitive. Similarly gold is found in many, if not all, countries, but its concentration in ore bearing rocks is so small that the opportunity cost of extraction is excessively high for most of them. Thus in general any observed tendencies to complete specialisation are less likely to be due to the linearity of production possibility frontiers, rather than due to large differences in relative production/extraction costs. More generally *production possibility curves will be non-linear and concave* as portrayed in Fig. 11.3. In this situation the optimal position on the production

Fig. 11.3. Incomplete specialisation in production.

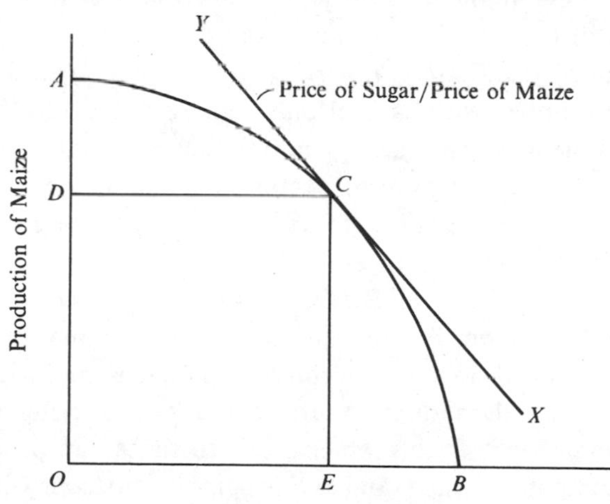

possibility curve will be at the point of tangency, *C*, with the free-trade price ratio. As can be seen this entails *incomplete specialisation* and the production of *D* tonnes of maize and *E* of sugar. (The higher the price of sugar to that of maize the more sugar will be produced and vice versa.)

Note in relation to Fig. 11.3 that, if the country has a comparative advantage in maize production its consumption possibility curve will lie along *CX*, whereas if its comparative advantage is in sugar production its outer bound consumption possibilities will lie on *CY*.

Note also that these results depend solely upon the existence of *comparative advantage*, *i.e.* differences in domestic opportunity costs. This must not be confused with *absolute advantage*, which exists when one country can produce all goods more cheaply than another. If Fig. 11.1 (*a*) and 11.1 (*b*) were to represent the production possibilities of two countries with workforces of identical size then the country labelled USA would have higher labour productivity in both goods than the country labelled Kenya, since the same number of workers could produce both more sugar and more maize. In that sense the USA would be more efficient at producing both products and would have an absolute advantage. Nevertheless, insofar as the domestic opportunity cost ratios are different, the principle of comparative (or relative) advantage still holds and the potential gains from trade are those which have been shown to exist; it is according to comparative (not absolute) advantage that free trade is argued to take place and to be mutually beneficial.

11.2.2 *Heckscher–Ohlin theory of trade*

The Heckscher–Ohlin theory of trade is so-named because it derives from the work of two Swedish economists of those names.[1] This theory is frequently called the *Factor Proportions or Factor Endowment theory of trade*. It is also linked with Samuelson's name since he added a logical extension of the theory to embrace the notion that trade will bring about an equalisation of prices paid to factors of production; *i.e.* Samuelson's (1948) extension suggests that trade should bring wage levels, land prices, etc. in different countries together.

The theory primarily differs from the Ricardian version by *abandoning the assumptions* (1) that there is one factor of production and (2) that there are intrinsic differences in production technique between countries. Instead the theory starts from the assumption that countries have different factor endowments, and that it is this which leads to the adoption of different production techniques, which (and at this point it converges with the Ricardian theory) in turn results in the existence of comparative advantage, of profitable trade and of mutually beneficial gains from trade.

If, as Meier (1980, p. 29) states, it is assumed that each individual factor of production is of identical quality in all countries, if there are no economies of scale and if the pattern of demand is the same in every country (such that, at each price ratio, all goods are consumed in the same proportions at comparable levels of real income per head in each country), *then* the existence of different relative factor endowments is a sufficient condition for the adoption of different production techniques under *autarky* (i.e. in the absence of trade with each country completely self-sufficient) and for the existence of comparative advantage. Since clearly there are very large differences in factor endowments this then appears an eminently reasonable basis for asserting the benefits of trade.

A country with a relative abundance of labour to other factors of production (land, capital, mineral resources) will have a low wage rate relative (i) to land prices and rents, and (ii) to interest rates on capital borrowing. At the prevailing wage to interest rate ratio it is optimal to adopt labour-intensive rather than capital-intensive techniques in agriculture, mineral extraction and industry to the extent that a choice of technique is available. (For it has to be recognised that for some products, such as say glass bottles, packaging materials, precision tools, there may be only limited scope for substituting labour for capital, whereas in crop production or furniture making there may be considerable opportunity to substitute labour for capital.) Conversely in countries with a relative abundance of capital to skilled labour the ratio of wages to interest on capital will be high and this should lead to an optimal choice of relatively capital-intensive techniques.

In the absence of trade the price ratio of labour-intensive goods to capital-intensive goods will be lower in the labour abundant country than in the one with abundant capital. Introducing trade according to comparative advantage into this situation would mean that the labour abundant country would export labour intensive goods in exchange for those with a higher capital intensity. This is equivalent to exporting labour in exchange for capital, while the capital abundant country would be exporting capital in return for labour. Thus according to the Heckscher–Ohlin theory trade will involve countries in exporting (in the form of goods) their abundant factors of production in exchange for scarce ones. From the standpoint of any one country therefore trade will have the effect of increasing demand for the abundant factor, thus bidding up its price, and increasing supply of the scarce factor thereby reducing its price. It is in this way that trade could be expected to reduce factor price differences between countries: under specific assumptions, indeed, full equalisation of *factor* prices must result from free trade in *commodities*.

11.2.3 *Vent-for-surplus*

It was Adam Smith who first proposed the idea that trade might act as a *vent-for-surplus*, but it was Myint (1958) who subsequently re-established it as a theory relevant to the trade of post-colonial Africa and South Asia. It is therefore rather different from the previous theories discussed in that it purports to have particular significance for less-developed countries (LDCs). It is for this reason that Gowland (1983, p. 24) views it as being more relevant as a theory of development than of trade.

The essence of the theory is that some LDCs were (and some still are) operating at a point inside their production possibility frontiers, signifying that some resources are unemployed. The introduction of (or greater exposure to) international trade provides the opportunity for them to shift to the production frontier, to draw unemployed resources into production, and also to obtain the further consumption gains available through trade. A problem with this theory is, however, to find acceptable explanations of why an LDC should operate inside its production possibility frontier and thereby leave resources (including labour) unemployed. (Here, it should be remembered that the Heckscher–Ohlin and comparative advantage theories have assumed full-employment of resources.)

Findlay (1970) has reviewed several hypotheses for underemployment of factors and proffers, as the most plausible, one in which the terms-of-trade between sectors are such that workers in the dominant food sector prefer to consume some available work time as leisure, rather than in the form of the additional simple goods they could obtain by working and exchanging extra food output with the 'handicraft' sector. To the extent that leisure is chosen, both some labour and land remain unused. It is then argued that the introduction of foreign manufactured goods through trade (as substitutes for domestically produced 'handicrafts') might provide the stimulus for food sector workers to increase labour input and shift onto the production possibility curve in order to produce a food surplus for international exchange. In this way trade might provide the (once-for-all) stimulus to bring surplus resources into production *i.e.* it is a vent-for-surplus.

Findlay's rationale for the existence of surplus resources does, however, raise several difficulties. It requires the assumption that for some reason factors are immobile and will not shift between sectors. Also it raises questions about how the production possibility frontier is to be defined. Is the labour supply at which potential production is assessed that which is actually made available in a specific period *or* is it based on the labour which would be made available if (as a result of integration into the world economy) marginal wage rates were higher? Only if is the latter can Findlay's use of leisure to explain the failure of an economy to work at full employment be accepted. But certainly the simple versions of the comparative advantage and Heckscher–Ohlin theories have not been presented on this basis, for that would require that production frontiers under self-sufficiency would differ from those with trade; real incomes and marginal returns to labour and land would differ under autarky and trade, which would signify different labour supplies and hence production possibility frontiers.

A more plausible rationale for the existence of untapped surplus resources in LDCs is that provided by Myint (1958). This is that there are serious institutional weaknesses and market imperfections, *i.e.* the assumption of efficient and competitive markets may be invalid. In such situations opening the economy to trade can strengthen market institutions and price signals so that unutilised resources are drawn into production and underutilised factors are more efficiently allocated, thus raising factor productivity.

The vent-for-surplus theory leads us away from the comparative static theory of the previous two sections into consideration of trade in a dynamic general equilibrium context in which changes are occurring in technological possibilities and in institutions. Is free trade always best in these circumstances, or are there circumstances in which protection of domestic industry and other trade restrictions are justified? Do, and would, poorer nations invariably gain from free trade? These are questions briefly addressed in Section 11.6.3.

11.3 *Trade equilibrium with no transport costs*

Using the *two-country, two-commodity model,* in which the production possibility frontiers of both countries are concave, it is possible to provide a useful and illuminating simple theory of the quantities of commodities which will be traded at equilibrium and the prices at which they will be exchanged. In Fig. 11.4(*a*) and 11.4(*b*) the *without-trade* (*autarky*) *equilibria* for our countries named the USA and Kenya are shown as points *A* and *D* respectively. These solutions are determined by the interaction of supply and demand for the two commodities within each country[2] and are characterised by sugar and maize prices such that domestic supply exactly equals demand for each commodity.

For the USA the equilibrium price ratio of sugar to maize is PS_U/PM_U, and in Fig. 11.4(*a*) this is shown as resulting in equilibrium quantities of maize and sugar equal to QM_U and QS_U respectively. Supply and demand within the USA would be exactly equal at these quantities and there would be no trade. Similarly, for Kenya, the *without-trade equilibrium* is shown in Fig. 11.4(*a*) as occurring at sugar to maize price ratio PS_K/PM_K resulting in equilibrium quantities of sugar and maize of QM_K and QS_K.

It will be noted that Figs. 11.4(*a*) and 11.4(*b*) have been drawn to reflect the assumption that Kenya has a *comparative advantage* in sugar production and the USA in maize production. This is reflected in the shapes of the production possibility frontiers, and in the assumption that, in the absence of trade the equilibrium price ratio of sugar to maize would be lower in Kenya than in the USA ($PS_K/PM_K < PS_U/PM_U$). In these circumstances, if trade occurs it would be expected to reflect the principle of comparative advantage and to entail Kenya exporting sugar in exchange for maize. In Kenya this would cause the sugar price to rise (as a result of demand from abroad) and the price of maize to fall (because of imported supplies); thus the sugar to maize price ratio in Kenya would increase towards the USA level. Conversely, in the USA trade would act to reduce the sugar to maize price ratio from the high level PS_U/PM_U. The *without-transport-cost* trade equilibrium for the two-commodity, two-country system would occur when the price ratio is identical in both countries and supply and demand is in balance for the system as a whole.

Fig. 11.4. (*a*) USA-production and consumption under autarky and free trade. (*b*) Kenya-production and consumption under autarky and free trade.

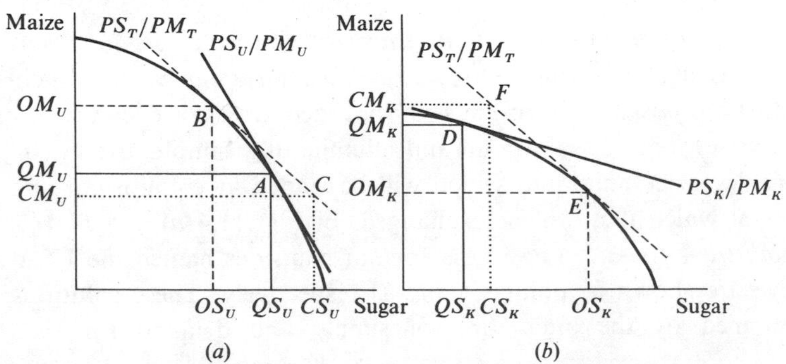

To see this consider what would happen if the possibility for trade at a price ratio PS_T/PM_T is introduced into Figs. 11.4(*a*) and 11.4(*b*). (*Note* the PS_T/PM_T is drawn as lying between the two countries' respective no-trade price ratios). In the USA this price ratio would result in a shift in production from point *A* to point *B* on the production possibility curve; USA output of maize would be OM_U and of sugar OS_U. However,[3] trade opens up the possibility that consumption in the USA could be at any point along the *consumption possibility curve* PS_T/PM_T. Let us assume that demand conditions in the USA are such that at this particular trade price ratio equilibrium consumption would settle at a point such as *C* where consumption of sugar exceeds the autarky level by a good margin but that of maize is reduced. Note that the with-trade consumption combination could lie between *B* and *C* in such a way that consumption of both commodities is higher. At *C*, USA consumption of maize is CM_U and of sugar CS_U.

Similarly in Fig. 11.4(*b*) Kenyans are also shown as enjoying increased consumption of both commodities as a result of trade occurring at price ratio PS_t/PM_T. Instead of production and consumption being at *D*, as would be the case without trade, there is increased specialisation in sugar production as domestic supply moves to point *E* on the production possibility curve. Trade, however permits consumption to move to a point such as *F* on the consumption possibility curve PS_T/PM_T.

From the analysis just conducted it is possible to derive each country's *export supply* and *import demand* curves as functions of the sugar to maize price ratio. Consider Kenya first. According to Figure 11.4(*b*) at PS_K/PM_K domestic supply exactly balances demand for both commodities at

Fig. 11.5. Import demand, export supply and trade equilibrium.

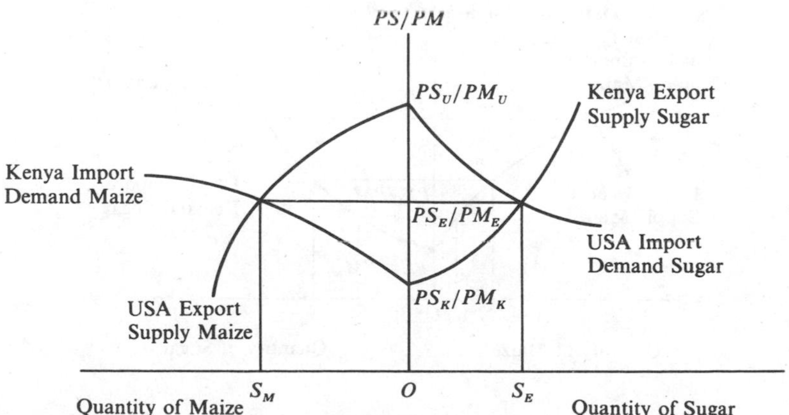

point D; thus, at this price ratio, export supply and import demand is zero for both commodities. This is shown in Fig. 11.5 where, at PS_K/PM_K on the vertical axis Kenya's export supply *and* maize import demand is shown as zero. From Fig. 11.4(*b*) we have that at price ratio PS_T/PM_T production will be at E and consumption at F. For this to happen exports of sugar from Kenya will have to equal $OS_K - CS_K$ and maize imports will be $CM_K - OM_K$. Thus at PS_T/PM_T Kenyan export supply of sugar is $OS_K - CS_K$ which can be plotted as a point on the sugar export supply curve, and import demand for maize $CM_K - OM_K$ can be plotted on the maize import demand curve. By plotting Kenya's sugar exports and maize imports for all price ratios above PS_K/PM_K the sugar export supply and maize import demand curves in Fig. 11.5 can be derived.

In complementary fashion the USA's maize export supply and sugar import demand curves can be derived using Fig. 11.4(*a*). At PS_U/PM_U USA markets are in a self-sufficient equilibrium such that maize export supply and sugar import demand are zero. As the price ratio falls – sugar price falls and maize price rises – below PS_U/PM_U USA maize export supply and sugar import demand will progressively rise in the manner shown in Fig. 11.5.

Equilibrium in this two-country, two-commodity (2 × 2) market will occur when import supply and export demand is simultaneously balanced in both commodity markets. In Fig. 11.5 this occurs at price ratio PS_E/PM_E, which is associated with a traded quantity of sugar equal to S_E and of maize equal to M_E.[4]

The relationships contained in Fig. 11.5 for the 2 × 2 case can be portrayed in a more concise and readily manipulatable form, namely in the form of *offer curves*. To understand what these are and how they may

Fig. 11.6. Derivation of Kenya's offer curve.

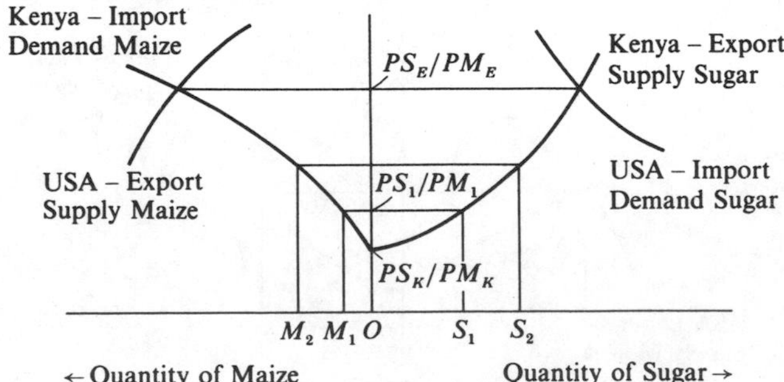

be derived, Fig. 11.6 (which is an enlarged version of the lower part of Fig. 11.5) may be used to obtain Kenya's offer curve of sugar for maize.

As repeated in Fig. 11.6, at PS_K/PM_K Kenya is self-sufficient and traders are not willing to offer any sugar in exchange for maize. Thus at this price ratio Kenya's offer curve in Fig. 11.7 passes through the zero trade point (the origin, O). At a higher relative price for sugar, PS_1/PM_1, Fig. 11.6 reveals that Kenyan traders would offer to exchange a relatively large quantity of sugar, S_1, in exchange for a relatively small quantity of maize, M_1. This *offer* is shown as point 1 on Kenya's offer curve in Fig. 11.7. Similarly at an even higher price ratio PS_2/PM_2 the offer would be S_2 of sugar for M_2 of imported maize – shown as point 2 in Fig. 11.7. By plotting the exchange offer for each alternative price ratio *greater than* PS_K/PM_K Kenya's full offer curve can be obtained. (Readers may construct the USA offer curve in a manner analogous to that used in Fig. 11.6 by considering all price ratios *below* PS_U/PM_U.)

Only at the price ratio PS_E/PM_E does the export offer of Kenyan sugar in exchange for M_E of imported maize just match the USA offer. At this price ratio therefore the export supply and demand curves for both maize and sugar simultaneously intersect in Fig. 11.6 which is reflected by the intersection of the offer curves in Fig. 11.7 at equilibrium point L.

Fig. 11.7. USA and Kenya offer curves and trade equilibrium for maize and sugar.

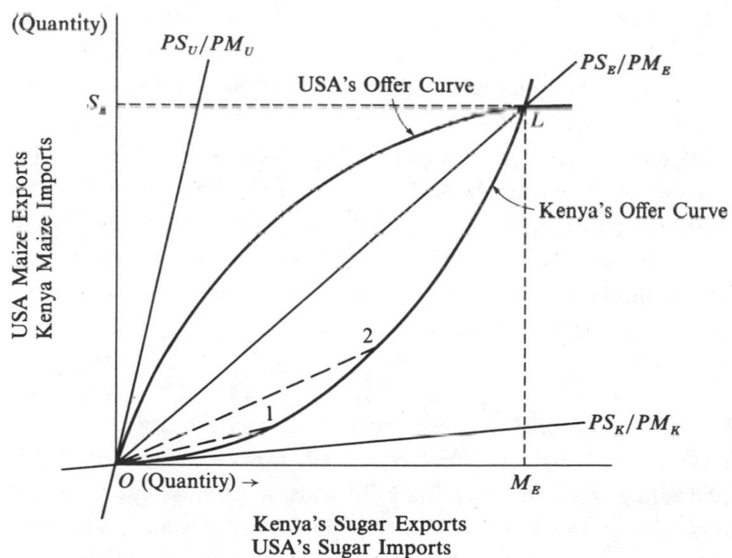

Offer curves are particularly helpful in analysing the economics of trade because of the amount of information that they convey. To see this consider just what is implied (lies behind) the point of intersection of the two offer curves at L in Fig. 11.7:

(1) Kenyan plus USA production of sugar (maize) exactly equals USA plus Kenyan demand for sugar (maize).

(2) No possibilities exist for reallocating resources in either country from one commodity to another in a way which increases profits.

(3) Consumers in both countries achieve maximum attainable satisfaction, given their income, its distribution and any other relevant factors.

(4) It is implied, although we do not explore it here, that both countries balance export earnings with import expenditures and that there is an equilibrium exchange rate between the two currencies which is simultaneously determined along with the volume of trade.

Thus an equilibrium generated by intersecting offer curves carries with it the information that the trade solution is the outcome of simultaneous equilibrium in all the input, product, and currency markets which influence the volume and pattern of trade.

Finally, in relation to Fig. 11.7, it should be noted that the slope of a line from the origin to any point on an offer curve can be interpreted as indicating the (sugar to maize) price ratio which would lead to that exchange offer. Only lines of lesser slope than PS_U/PM_U cut the USA'S offer curve indicating that no maize will be exported in exchange for sugar unless the price ratio is below PS_U/PM_U. Similarly all points on the Kenyan offer curve imply price ratios higher than PS_K/PM_K. As the diagram is drawn the equilibrium price ratio at which the two curves cross is almost halfway between PS_U/PM_U and PS_K/PM_K.[5] This equilibrium price ratio can be interpreted as the free-trade *commodity terms-of-trade* for the two-commodity case. It indicates the trade rate of either commodity in terms of the other.

11.4 *Trade with international transport and handling charges*

In reality, of course, international trade is not costless but entails transport, handling and insurance costs. This section builds upon the last and employs offer curves to explore the implications of such costs upon the pattern and volume of trade. The principal result which emerges is, as intuition might suggest, that high trade costs reduce the volume of trade. On its own this might seem a comparatively trivial result, except for the fact that it links up with several important issues in trade policy for LDCs.

Many, particularly of the smaller developing countries do not have firms owning ships for transporting bulk products in international trade, so that the international freight charges for both imports and exports accrue in large measure to firms in other countries. Nor do small LDCs have insurance firms to earn the rewards for insuring international cargoes. More important, however, is the fact that for small LDCs transport costs may be so high in relation to international market prices that the potential for trade is drastically reduced and the potentials for price instability and 'food insecurity' are greatly increased. Some exceptional cases of this nature are discussed in Box 11.2, where the international transport and handling cost may be almost as great as the international price of the commodity.

The sub-Saharan African cases referred to in Box 11.2 are extreme, but they do underline the need to consider trade equilibria in the presence of trading costs. Take the hypothetical case of a small trading nation, call it Zambia, unable to influence world prices, exporting sugar to the EEC and reciprocally importing wheat. Suppose the transport and other costs of moving a tonne of wheat from the EEC to Zambia is $80 and that it costs $70 to transport a tonne of raw sugar from Zambia to the EEC. Suppose also that in the EEC the price of raw sugar is $150 per tonne and that of wheat $120. For every tonne of sugar exported to the EEC for $150, Zambian exporters would have to pay $70 for transport, leaving a return of only $80 (the so-called *export parity price*) as foreign exchange earnings for Zambia. In contrast for every tonne of wheat imported from the EEC, the Zambian importers must pay $120 for the grain plus $80 in transport costs to give a total foreign exchange price (the so-called *import parity price*) of $200. From this hypothetical example it is apparent that, for a small country unable to influence international prices, high transport costs result in comparatively low returns for exports and high costs for imports. Lower transport costs would be extremely beneficial. Notice also that in the example, whereas with trade the price ratio of sugar to wheat in the EEC is 150/120, in Zambia it is only 80/200. Thus the existence of transport costs means that even when trade is in equilibrium the ratio of the sugar to wheat price differs (in the hypothetical case, very greatly) between trading partners.

To analyse the impact of transport costs let us rework Fig. 11.6 using

Samuelson's (1954) approach. Within the two-country, two-commodity model Samuelson's approach entails assuming that the countries exchange

---

BOX 11.2
Illustration of the importance of transport costs

In a study to *demonstrate the benefits of increased trade between neighbouring countries,* Koester (1986) estimated hypothetical *export* and *import parity prices* of major crops for selected locations in countries in the Southern African Development Coordination Conference (SADCC) on the assumption that all trade occurred with major markets outside Southern Africa. Since the bulk of trade of the countries concerned is with distant markets this is an informative exercise. *Import parity prices* were calculated as the price of supplies to the location from a major exporting country outside the SADCC area; that price includes the original purchase price plus all the transport and handling costs involved in delivery. Similarly, *export parity prices* are the return which would be left to suppliers at the location after all transport and handling costs had been deducted from the price obtained from exports to major international markets. Thus if transport and handling charges are denoted by T and the international commodity price in major markets by P the import parity price of the commodity equals $P+T$ and its export parity price $P-T$.

Koester's estimates of the two sets of prices for 1983/84 are presented in Table 11.1. It can be seen that there is a remarkable divergence between the two prices, signifying that transport costs between major international commodity markets and the individual locations in Southern Africa are equivalent to a very high proportion of the international price P. To illustrate this consider the most extreme example of sorghum at Rhumpi in Malawi; the figures infer that transport costs, T, between the USA and this location are \$134.5 per tonne and that the international price is \$139.5 per tonne; thus in relation to the international price the *import parity price* is \$274 = 139.5 + 134.5 while the *export parity price* is \$5 = 139.5–134.5.

It must be emphasised that these prices are artificial in the sense that there is no likelihood of sorghum being exported commercially from, say, Rhumpi to the USA – it certainly would not be profitable; also the import parity price from that source is so high that imports from the USA are also unlikely. But, what the estimates do indicate is the degree to which high transport costs effectively cut locations with poor transport links off from major international markets in bulk commodities. For, the low export parity prices in Table 11.1 almost certainly reflect the poor returns these countries

could obtain from exporting grain to any major importing country outside Southern Africa in competition with major exporters such as Australia, Canada, the EEC, and the USA. Moreover, they also indicate just how costly it is for such countries to obtain bulk grain supplies from outside southern Africa.

These are precisely the points that Koester's calculations aim to show, namely, that there are large potential benefits from expanding intra-regional trade, in this case between neighbouring African countries. This has been hindered appreciably by the poor rail and road links between some of these countries and the fact that transport routes inherited from colonial times were orientated largely to countries outside Africa. (Matters have also been greatly aggravated by the frequent guerilla attacks on the railway network, in Mozambique in particular.) Improvement of intra-regional transport networks with attendant cost reductions would stimulate trade within the region. If through such trade Tanzania were to obtain more maize from Malawi at the expense of USA or EEC maize, the import parity price of maize to Tanzania will fall and the export parity price to Malawi will rise. Thus there are potentially large trade benefits to be obtained from *trade diversion*, whereby neighbouring countries expand intra-regional trade at the expense of trade with other regions.

Finally, it is also worth noting that high transport costs are not conducive

Table 11.1. *Import and export parity prices for maize, sorghum, and wheat for selected locations in the SADCC region ($/ton)*

	Maize		Sorghum		Wheat	
	Import parity price	Export parity price	Import parity price	Export parity price	Import parity price	Export parity price
			(1983/84)			
Maun, Botswana	270	39	255	24	277	46
Maseru, Lesotho	227	82	212	67	234	89
Rumphi, Malawi	289	20	274	5	296	27
Lichinga, Mozambique	256	53	241	38	263	60
Manzini, Swaziland	199	110	184	95	206	117
Tabora, Tanzania	220	89	205	74	227	96
Lusaka, Zambia	254	55	239	40	261	62
Ndola, Zambia	265	44	250	29	272	51
Harare, Zimbabwe	214	95	199	80	221	102
Bulawayo, Zimbabwe	226	83	211	68	233	90

Source: U. Koester (1986), Table 18.

to achieving high standards of *food security*. This is so because high transport costs are almost always associated with slow delivery times, congested ports, and low volume-carrying capacity routes. If there is a drought and serious food shortage in areas isolated by high transport costs it may take months to ship in supplies from North America or Australia, whereas if intra-regional transport links were improved and costs lowered speedy and effective use might be made of stocks held in neighbouring countries.

---

their imports and exports at some midway international market. An international exchange ratio (*the commodity terms-of-trade*) is set at this midpoint. The transport costs involved in trade are represented by a fraction of the commodities being used up in the process of trade. Thus more commodity leaves the exporting country than arrives at the midway exchange point, the fraction of each commodity 'lost' being equivalent to the amount paid for its transport cost.

The *without-transport-cost* equilibrium portrayed in Fig. 11.7 using offer curves is re-presented at the heart of Fig. 11.8; since there are no 'commodity losses' in trade the offer curves at the USA and Kenyan borders are exactly reflected in the midway exchange market. *With transport costs* there are, however, commodity losses between country borders and the midway exchange market, such that the commodity exchange rate is less favourable to both trading countries at their own borders than it is in the exchange market. That is to say that at their

Fig. 11.8. Comparing trade equilibrium with and without transport costs.

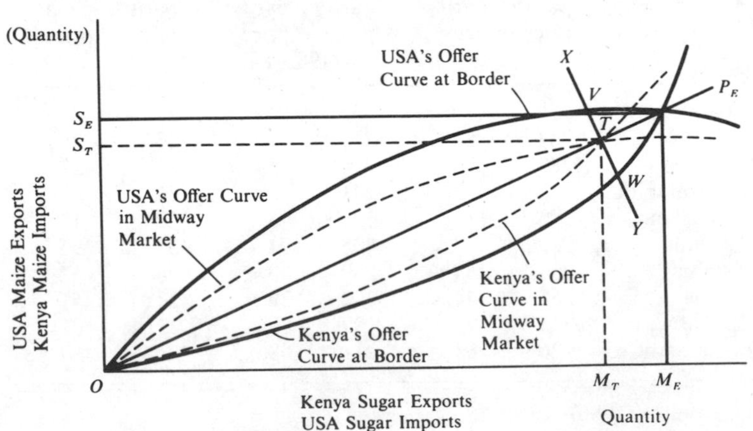

borders countries have to offer more export commodity for less imports than is the case in the midway exchange market, after transport costs are allowed for.

In Fig. 11.8 this is revealed in the relationship between the border level offer curves drawn in solid lines and their dotted line counterparts (after deducting transport costs) in the midway exchange market. For sake of convenience it is assumed that the counterpart offer curves do intersect at the price ratio P_E (which would have occurred in the absence of transport costs), although it is unlikely that introducing or changing transport costs would leave the equilibrium price ratio unaffected. Thus the trade equilibrium with transport costs occurs at point T where the counterpart offer curves intersect. It is therefore clear that the introduction of transport costs causes a reduction in the equilibrium quantities traded in the midway exchange market, of maize from M_E to M_T and of sugar from S_E to S_T.

The implications of transport costs for the border terms-of-trade of the two countries, are revealed by the intersection of the line XY (drawn at right angles to the equilibrium price ratio line from the trade equilibrium point T) and the solid line (border) offer curves of the two trading countries. XY cuts the USA border offer curve at V; the line from the origin to this point has a steeper slope than P_E signifying, as anticipated, that the sugar to maize price ratio in the USA exceeds that in the midway exchange market. Conversely, the point of intersection between XY and the Kenyan border offer curve at W indicates that the Kenyan sugar to maize price ratio will at equilibrium lie below P_E.[6] Thus, the border terms-of-trade of the two countries are not the reciprocal of one another.

Finally, it is worth noting that the effects of imposing import tariffs or export subsidies will in several key respects be much the same as increasing transport costs.[7] They will cause the internal commodity price ratio of trading partners to move further apart, and will reduce the quantities of commodity traded. According to the static two-country, two-commodity trade model, imposing border tariffs would normally be expected to reduce the welfare of both trading countries. However, as is explored in Section 11.6, there are theoretical conditions in which a country may improve its welfare by charging an import tariff.

11.5 *Terms-of-trade*

The theory of trade presented above has examined import and export supply and demand for commodities in relation to the relative price of one commodity (sugar) to another (maize). This price ratio has been defined as the commodity terms-of-trade. However, as will become apparent, this is just one of several alternative measures of the terms-of-trade. Each of the alternatives conveys different information about the conditions of exchange between one country or set of commodities and others. Because of the importance (in debates about development policy) which attaches to terms-of-trade measures, and in order to help avoid misinterpretation of the alternative measures which readers may encounter in official publications and books, this section explains the definition of the alternative terms-of-trade measures as well as the interpretation which may be placed upon them.

11.5.1 *Measuring terms-of-trade*

In the context of the two-country, two-commodity (2 × 2) model already explored, the terms-of-trade are readily identified in terms of the amount of one good which will be required to exchange for a fixed amount of the other. In the absence of trade there will still be exchange between specialist producers of the different goods within countries; in that case one can talk of the intersectoral terms-of-trade. With international trade the focus of interest for each separate country will be upon the amount of exported commodity required to purchase a fixed amount of imported commodity.

Consider an equilibrium solution to our 2 × 2 model *in the absence of transport costs* in which the USA exports 1.5 tonnes of maize in exchange for 1 tonne of sugar. This would imply that the price ratio of maize to sugar by weight is 1 : 1.5, *i.e.* sugar costs 1.5 times as much as maize.

The *commodity terms-of-trade* (CTT) are defined in general as the *ratio of the price of one bundle of commodities to the price of some other bundle.* Thus if we choose, in this case, as our bundles 1 tonne of sugar versus 1 tonne of maize the CTT for maize in terms of sugar are 0.666 (i.e. 1 : 1.5), while those for sugar in terms of maize are 1.5.

Note the following points in connection with these measures of the commodity terms-of-trade:

(a) If (as in reality) trade involves transport and handling costs, then the USA's terms-of-trade for maize in terms of sugar *will not* be the reciprocal of Kenya's terms-of-trade for sugar in terms of maize. (This follows directly from the analysis in Fig. 11.8, which shows the slope of the border exchange price ratio for the USA, *OV*, to be greater than that for Kenya, *OW*.)

(b) The fact that Kenyan prices are denoted in Pounds and the

USA's in Dollars, *i.e.* that there are different currencies, does not in any way affect the preceding points. Kenya's terms-of-trade for sugar in terms of maize will be 1.5 (or whatever their with-transport-cost value might be) irrespective of whether the exchange rate is £1 = \$2 or £1 = \$1.

In general, in measuring CTT interest focuses on bundles consisting of more than one commodity, and is also concerned with changes in the terms-of-trade over time. For example, there might be interest in changes in the terms of trade of food commodities relative to minerals or to manufactures. A key step towards measurement is therefore to define the contents of the bundles of commodities to be compared. This is done by choosing a *set of weights*, which can be interpreted as the proportion (in terms of value) of the bundle assigned to individual commodities, e.g. 20% maize, 5% butter, 10% rice, etc. The choice of weights can, and should, be adjusted to reflect different perspectives on trade, in the sense that the commodity bundles of relevance to any particular Western European country may differ substantially from those of a given West African or Latin American country.

Given the selected weights for each commodity and time-series of prices for each of them, the commodity terms-of-trade of bundle *A* in terms of bundle *B* is simply the weighted sum of the prices of commodities in bundle *A* divided by the sum of weighted prices in bundle *B*. That is[8]

$$CTT_t - \frac{PA_t}{PB_t}$$

Country interest may focus not upon some *CTT* measure but upon the performance of the prices of its exports relative to those of its imports. In that case it may well want to measure its *net barter terms-of-trade* (*NBTT*). The principles of measurement are the same as for the *CTT*, except that the comparison is made between the price of a bundle of exports PX_T and that of a bundle of imports PM_T, i.e. the measure is PX_T/PM_T. In constructing such an index for a particular country, not only should the weights chosen relate to that country, but the price series should be selected to reflect the f.o.b. (free-on-board) prices of exports and the delivered c.i.f. (cost-insurance-freight) prices of imports.

An NBTT measure conveys some useful information about a country's (or group of countries') changing conditions of trade, but it can be augmented to add more information. For example, a decline in a country's NBTT could be caused by a rapid expansion of export supply pushing down prices; if export volume increases more rapidly than *NBTT* declines, the country's import purchasing capacity will have increased. Thus the net barter terms-of-trade may be multiplied by a volume index of exports, Qx, to produce a measure of the *income terms-of-trade* (*ITT*), where

$$ITT = NBTT \cdot Qx$$

Growth of export volume may result from productivity growth in the exporting economy, and such increases in productivity would be expected typically to result in lower export prices.

BOX 11.3
Effect of increased factor productivity upon the terms-of-trade

The effect of increases in factor productivity on the terms-of-trade and volume of trade are portrayed in Fig. 11.9(*a*) and 11.9(*b*) for our 2×2 example. In Fig. 11.9(*a*) an increase in productivity in maize production is shown as causing a shift upwards in the USA offer curve, signifying that the USA will be prepared to increase the amount of maize it is willing to exchange for any given quantity of sugar. The impact of this is shown to be that the amount of maize traded increases from *A* to *B* and the amount of sugar from *C* to *D*. Following the earlier analysis in Section 11.1, this expansion in trade in the 2×2 Case reflects an improvement in consumer welfare in *both countries*; it involves new consumption possibility curves and the option for increased consumption of both commodities in both countries.

Fig. 11.9. (*a*) Effect of increased productivity in USA maize production upon trade equilibrium. (*b*) Effect of increased productivity in Kenyan sugar production upon trade equilibrium.

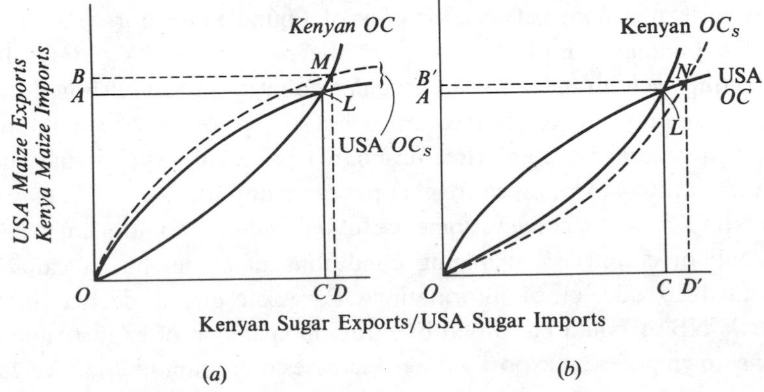

Thus through trade both countries benefit from productivity increases in one of them. It is also shown that the equilibrium commodity terms-of-trade will move in favour of sugar (since the slope of *OM* is higher than *OL*), which may be presumed to be caused by a fall in the maize price. Comparably, Fig. 11.8(*b*) analyses the effect of a rise in productivity in Kenyan sugar production. In this case also the amount traded of both commodities is shown as increasing, while the commodity terms-of-trade for sugar decline (the slope of *ON* is less than *OL*).

Where labour (or other factor) productivity improvements are responsible for a decline in export prices it is in principle of considerable interest to assess whether the import purchasing power of labour has nevertheless risen. This would occur if the decline in the relative prices (*NBTT*) is less than the rise in labour productivity. To allow for this the *single factoral terms-of-trade* (*SFTT*) are defined as

$$SFTT = NBTT \cdot \pi x,$$

where πx is the labour productivity index in export production. An improvement in this index indicates that the import purchasing capacity of one unit of labour employed in export production has increased.

Insofar as it is of interest to adjust the terms-of-trade for changes in export productivity it is also possible in principle to adjust for changes in labour productivity abroad in the production of imports, πM. Thus the *double factoral terms-of-trade* (*DFTT*) are defined as

$$DFTT = NBTT \cdot \frac{\pi x}{\pi M}$$

An increase in this measure would signify that a unit of labour employed in producing exports can purchase, through trade, more units of labour in the form of imports.

11.5.2 *Interpreting measures of the terms-of-trade*

As already discussed much of the debate about unequal exchange, associated with the names of Prebisch and Emmanuel, revolves around hypotheses as to why the terms-of-trade of LDCs should decline – particularly of those LDCs heavily dependent upon primary commodity exports. Hence, various statistics for terms-of-trade have been (and are) subjected to intense analysis to uncover what they reveal about this issue. Moreover such statistical series are frequently (but often inappropriately) interpreted as if they directly embody information about the welfare gains from trade. Given the key positions which terms-of-trade measures play in debates about development economics, it is, therefore, important to consider how to interpret alternative published series and to assess what welfare implications, if any, can be drawn from them.

Where terms-of-trade statistics are presented they are usually confined to the commodity and net barter terms-of-trade (as in Box 11.4), and it is seldom the case that the single or double factoral terms-of-trade are calculated. This is significant in that, as Spraos (1981) elaborates, the rationale for these latter measures is that they come closer to being measures of changes in economic welfare arising from trade than do the former. However none of the measures is truly a measure of welfare change, and the CTT and NBTT measures can be interpreted as only the simplest of proxies of welfare change.

All that the CTT measures is changes in the amount of one fixed quality bundle of commodities which can be acquired in exchange for another, while the NBTT indicates changes in the amount of a fixed quality bundle of imports obtainable for a bundle of exports; only indirectly can these be considered as welfare measures. The weights chosen for the construction of such series are conventionally base weights relating to bundles of commodities, imports or exports, which were traded some (often quite considerable number of) years previously. Weights used in contemporarily published series may well relate to 1980 or even before. To the extent that the composition of imports and exports changes over time, indices based on fixed weights have an imperfect relationship to what might be called the 'true' terms-of-trade. This will be especially so if, as economic theory leads us to believe, countries will tend to reduce their import demand for items which have become relatively more expensive and will try to expand exports of those which have become relatively highly priced. In other words the normal continuous operation of competitive market forces are directed at improving the terms-of-trade or limiting their decline.

BOX 11.4
Statistical series for terms-of-trade

Table 11.2 presents a selection of terms-of-trade series for 1969 to 1984 which have been assembled from international publications. The term assembled is well chosen since the series have been 'chained' together by linking data published over time. This chaining procedure can introduce arbitrary errors and may result in one researcher producing a somewhat

Table 11.2. *Changes in the terms of trade*

	Commodity terms of trade for primary[a] *products (1969 = 100)*				*Net barter terms of trade for developing*[b] *countries (1969 = 100)*		
	All primary ÷ manufactured	Food ÷ manufactured	Ag. non-food ÷ manufactured	Minerals ÷ manufactured	All developing	Major oil exporters	Non-oil exporters
1969	100	100	100	100	100	100	100
1970	98	100	93	100	99	98	99
1971	103	101	92	113	100	114	93
1972	111	107	101	116	100	117	94
1973	134	131	138	129	110	137	100
1974	186	141	129	291	154	331	96
1975	164	120	101	271	146	321	86
1976	170	123	111	279	155	340	90
1977	176	131	114	281	156	321	98
1978	155	115	107	248	150	305	93
1979	173	113	111	300	168	382	91
1980	233	120	107	453	201	523	86
1981	257	113	104	544	207	616	79
1982	249	103	93	531	205	607	76
1983	237	105	105	493	209	561	78
1984	243	104	115	500	210	562	78

[a] Calculated using data in the UN Monthly Bulletin of Statistics, September and December issues.
[b] *Source:* OECD, 1974 Review, *Development Cooperation*, Table II-3, Paris, November 1974, International Financial Statistics, and International Monetary Fund Annual Reports.

different series to another from basically the same data. Nevertheless the series presented provide an essentially correct picture of some major changes in relative commodity and trade prices in recent years.

The series show substantial fluctuations plus underlying trends over time. It may be surprising to readers to note that between 1969 and 1984 the commodity terms-of-trade (CTT) of all major classes of primary commodities rose relative to manufactures. In the case of foods the overall increase was negligible although there was a sharp improvement in 1973 and 1974. The most striking change was however in the CTT of minerals to manufactures, which was due largely to the dramatic increases in oil prices in 1973 and then 1980. This 'oil effect' is clearly reflected in the net barter terms-of-trade (NBTT) for oil exporting developing countries which had improved dramatically in the period shown (only to decline sharply in 1985 for which series are not yet available at the time of writing). Improvement of the NBTT of this group of countries was, in turn, responsible for pulling up the NBTT of all developing countries as a group. The non-oil exporting countries' NBTT did however decline sharply and seriously, because the adverse price effect of their oil, food and manufactured imports outweighed any increases in the nominal prices of their exports.

Another reason for rejecting a simplistic welfare interpretation of terms-of-trade indices relates to the 'quality factor'. A tonne of wheat or bauxite remains of much the same quality in terms of productive services (and hence of the welfare generated) irrespective of its year of production. The same is not true of manufactured items such as motor vehicles, textile machines or refrigerators. These have changed markedly in quality over time in the sense of providing improved services per unit cost. If, therefore, the CTT between, say, wheat and motor cars remained constant over time, wheat producers would become progressively better off in terms of motor car services. In this situation, even declining wheat-to-car prices would not rule out a welfare gain to wheat exporters.

As a final qualification, care should be taken not to draw inappropriate inferences about the behaviour of any particular country's terms-of-trade on the basis of indices measured for some other country. There are large variations between countries in the composition of their trade flows, and there are substantial inter-country differences in transport costs involved in trade. These can make it quite inappropriate to assume that the terms-of-trade of, say, East Asian countries all move in the same way, or that a net barter terms-of-trade index for the sub-Saharan African countries is a close approximation of Botswana's NBTT.

Indeed the divergence in the composition of the imports and exports of differing LDCs virtually assures that the terms of trade of countries will behave differently. This is certainly the finding of a recent comprehensive study by Scandizzo and Diakosavvas (1987). They conclude (pp. 159 and 160) that '...there is no basis to believe that a general deterioration has occurred in the welfare position of developing countries because of a declining trend in relative prices of primary commodities', but that 'there is, however, every reason to suspect that a 'selective' deterioration has affected some commodities and some LDCs for specific sub-periods'.

11.6 *Trade intervention*

Despite the theoretical arguments in favour of free trade all countries operate certain barriers to trade. Such barriers may be classed as *tariff barriers* (the effects of which are analysed in Section 11.6.1, or as *non-tariff barriers* which are briefly discussed in Section 11.6.2. Possible reasons for such restrictions to free trade are then considered in Section 11.6.3.

11.6.1 *The effects of imposing import tariffs on trade*

Import tariffs may be of the *fixed* variety (*i.e.* charged at £x per unit imported) or they may be *ad valorem* (*i.e.* charged as a certain percentage of the c.i.f. import price). Typically the importing agency or firm will pay the tariff as a tax to the government of the importing country. In order to recoup the cost of the tariff the importer will therefore have to charge customers a price at least equal to the import price plus the tariff. Thus, because of the tariff, the domestic price of the imported item will be higher than it would have been with free trade.

There are a number of methods for analysing the effects upon consumption, production and trade of imposing import tariffs. In this section, where we are dealing with trade from the standpoint of whole economies assumed to be producing two goods only, offer curves will continue to be used. In Section 11.6.2 and Chapter 12, in the context of analysing the effects of different agricultural policy instruments (including import tariffs), a single commodity approach is adopted for convenience. Readers checking ahead will observe that the two approaches give consistent results.

To analyse the effects of an import tariff it is simplest to take a two-commodity case for a small country which has a trade volume too small to influence international prices. That is the country is a price taker, such that its commodity terms-of-trade are unaffected by the amount of either its imports or exports; the price ratio of exports to imports is therefore in effect fixed by world markets. This can be represented as in Fig. 11.10, as a situation in which the international offer curve is a straight line equal to a fixed P_2/P_1, where P_2 is the price of the exported commodity and P_1 the price of the imported one.

Imposition of a tariff on imports of commodity 1 by such a 'small' country can be represented by an inward shift of its offer curve as shown in Fig. 11.10(*a*). The tariff will cause the domestic price of the imported commodity to rise. This will have several effects: (i) domestic demand for the imported commodity will fall, (ii) some domestic resources will be switched from production of the exported commodity, 2, to enable domestic production of 1 to increase and substitute for imports, (iii) lower production of commodity 2, will lead to reduced exports. In trade terms, therefore, the expected cumulative effect of imposing an import tariff will be a decline in both imports and exports; this is shown in Fig. 11.10(*a*) as a shift in the trade equilibrium, from point *M* to point *N*. From the standpoint of consumer welfare this diminution of trade as a result of a tariff is the converse of the effect that factor productivity increases have in expanding trade. The reduction of imports reflects a restriction of consumption possibilities and, in a purely competitive economy, in a loss of consumer welfare.

If a 'large' country which imports a significant proportion of the total

Fig. 11.10. The impact of an import tariff on trade.

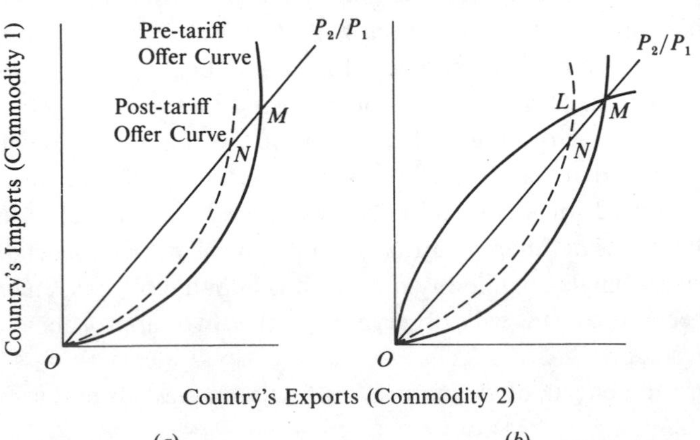

traded amount of a commodity were to impose an import tariff it would be expected that the terms of trade would tilt somewhat in its favour. Reduced demand for the imported commodity would lead to a reduction in the international price; this might also be accompanied by an increase in the price of exports caused by reduced export supply availability from the 'large' country. To the extent that the tariff results in improved terms-of-trade, the welfare loss (to the country imposing the tariff) and trade reduction will be less than if there was no responsiveness in international prices.[9] This is clearly revealed in Fig. 11.10(*b*) which portrays the situation of a 'large' country faced by an international offer curve which signifies that prices are responsive to the trade offer of the 'large' country. In this case the imposition of a tariff can be seen to cause the trade equilibrium to shift from *M* to *L*. This does represent a reduction of both imports and exports, but comparison of points *L* and *N* reveals that the reduction is less than if international prices were fixed and unresponsive. Notice also from Fig. 11.10(*b*) that the imposition of an import tariff on commodity 1 by the large country is shown as causing an improvement in the terms-of-trade; the pre-tariff export-to-import price ratio is P_2/P_1, the slope of the line from *O* passing through *M*; the post-tariff price ratio from *O* to *L* has a steeper slope.

It should be noted that *export subsidies* also distort patterns of trade and production and that for the purposes of analysis they can be treated in a complementary way to import tariffs. Instead of causing domestic resources to switch into import substituting production they switch resources into production for export, and instead of restricting trade they promote it. Given the information that an export subsidy could be represented as shifting the offer curve 'outwards' readers might like to check that they can demonstrate how the following probable outcomes would result: (a) trade volumes would increase, and (b) that (if anything) border terms-of-trade would worsen.

11.6.2 *Non-tariff barriers to trade*

Non-tariff barriers to trade exist in many forms. They may take the form of (a) import quotas, (b) 'voluntary' agreements by exporting countries to observe quantitative restrictions on their exports to key markets – an example of this is the Multi-Fibre Agreement under which many LDCs have accepted limits on their textile exports to Developed Countries; (c) health restrictions which ban imports of livestock and crop products on the grounds that disease may be spread; (d) use of import licences to control foreign exchange costs and the balance-of-payments;

(e) subsidies to protect domestic producers against foreign competition; (f) domestic consumption or production taxes; (g) multiple exchange rates, etc.

Some of these measures directly reduce the volume of trade, while others do so indirectly by causing adjustments in domestic resource allocation which in turn affect import demand or export supply. Consequently, non-tariff barriers to trade have similar adverse theoretical effects to tariffs upon social welfare. This can be most easily demonstrated by showing that a quota can have equivalent effects to a tariff.

In Fig. 11.11 (following Meier, 1980, p. 107) the domestic supply and demand curves are shown as *Sd* and *D* respectively. Supply from the rest of the world is assumed to be perfectly elastic at world price *Pw*, hence the import supply curve *Sw* is drawn horizontally. With competitive markets, in the absence of trade barriers, domestic supply would settle at *Q* and demand at *C*; the import quantity would be *C*–*Q*. Suppose now that an import quota, *q*, is imposed. This can be represented by defining a new 'with-quota' supply curve *Sd*+*q*, formed by adding *q* to the domestic supply at all prices above the world price *Pw*; thus at all prices above *Pw* total supply will equal that from domestic sources plus the import quota. This supply curve cuts the demand curve at *c* to the left of the free-trade equilibrium resulting in a higher domestic price *Pq*. At this price consumption will be less than before (at *C*′), domestic supply will rise to *Q*′, and imports will be cut to *C*′–*Q*′ equal to the amount of the quota, *q*. It can readily be seen that if an import tariff were to be imposed which raised the domestic price from *Pw* to *Pq* it would have precisely the same effect as the quota, namely that domestic output would rise to *Q*′,

Fig. 11.11. The equivalence of tariffs and quotas.

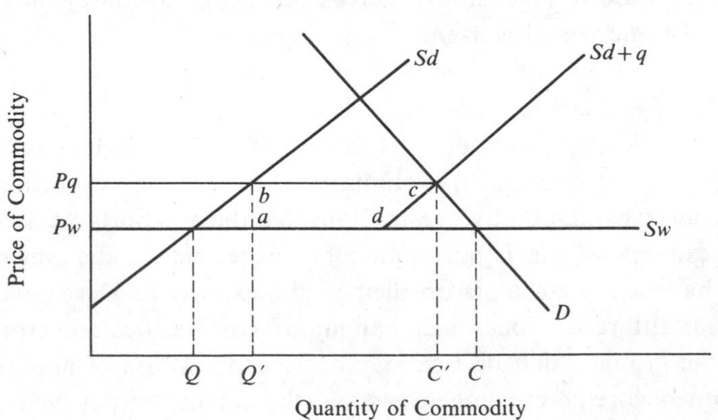

consumption fall to C', and imports would decline to $C'-Q'$. Thus $Pq-Pw$ may be said to be *equivalent tariff* to the quota q.

In certain other respects tariffs and quotas have different effects. Whereas a tariff would have raised government revenue equal to the imported quantity times the tariff (area *abcd* in Fig. 11.11), a quota would generate additional profits of the same value for those to whom the quotas were assigned, since they would be able to charge Pq for produce bought at Pw. However, in most basic respects trade restriction by non-tariff barriers will have equivalent welfare and trade effects to tariffs.

11.6.3 *Reasons for trade intervention*

As a basis for policy prescription the pure theory of trade is limited by its concern with the *static* gains in efficiency and welfare which can be achieved by liberalising trade. Economic policy decisions do, however, have to be made in a dynamic developmental context, and in this there are plausible reasons for restricting imports, at least in the short-run.

Economists would find it difficult to justify policies of import restriction which involve virtually permanent protection of inefficient (high cost of production) domestic industries. If there is no long-term prospect of a domestic industry competing successfully with imports, economists would generally agree that resources should be allowed to find alternative uses. Of course, if foreign countries are subsidising their export industries the difference between the home country's production costs and the import price will not reflect the true underlying competitiveness, and import tariffs could be justified on retaliatory grounds. Another acceptable argument for protection against imports relates to the *infant industry* case. This is the situation in which new industries require special measures of aid and protection if they are to develop to a competitively viable state. However, a skill in national economic management is to know when to wean infants from the breast of state support and to switch attention to younger infants; this is an argument for temporary rather than permanent support. Yet a further argument for short-term restriction of imports might be to avoid the damage to domestic industry which might arise from temporary very low import prices caused by random events. The danger with all of these arguments is that they may be used to justify the introduction of industry support/trade restriction measures which are unjustifiable in the long-term but prove impossible for politicians to dismantle. It is this which often leads to gross inefficiency in domestic resource allocation (in the sense of requiring massive state subsidies to bridge the gap between national and international prices), and which justifies the emphasis which economists place upon the virtues of free trade.

Nevertheless we can agree with Findlay (1970, p. 134) when he stated

> The formal theory of the gains from trade...is unfortunately restricted to a static context. Hence the vital contribution that the opportunity to specialise makes towards the dynamic transformation and development of an economy does not appear as one of the gains from trade, although this is of far greater significance than the mere pushing out of a utility-possibility curve. The gains from trade also go beyond the purely economic aspect of a nation's life since trading conditions and prospects greatly influence the social, political and cultural fabric of a nation as well. So far these aspects of the gains from trade have had to be left to the economic historians. It is to be hoped that the pure theory of the subject will advance sufficiently to take some account of these fundamental matters.

Thus we can agree that the pure theory of trade is an incomplete basis for the design of commercial policy. The Heckscher–Ohlin theory, in particular, has been the subject of intensive criticism faced with the manifest failure of the gap in wage rates between the rich industrialised countries and LDCs to close despite the growing importance of trade to LDCs. For a comprehensive survey of these criticisms see Edwards (1985, Ch. 2) on the 'rise and fall of the Heckscher–Ohlin theory'. Essentially, the fact is that the patterns of trade observed do not conform well to those expected by this theory, even given the appreciable fundamental difficulties that arise in measuring the relative abundance of capital and labour. The Ricardian theory of comparative advantage fares better, since it is a matter of elementary logic that if relative prices of products are sufficiently different in two locations then the principles of supply and demand ensure that both parties can gain by trade. However as Gowland (1983, p. 25) concludes 'The problem with comparative advantage may be that it is so flexible that it could explain anything.'

11.7 *Conclusions*

It should be recognised that the neoclassical case for free-trade, as conferring mutual benefits on trading partners, is a straight extension of the economic arguments in the last chapter in favour of market solutions generated by competitive markets. It will be recalled from Chapter 10 that it was shown that where competitive market equilibria exist they will be Pareto-optimal, in the sense that no-one could be made better off without someone being made worse off. However, any equilibrium which exists (in the framework of the analysis employed) depends upon the prevailing income distribution. To the extent that society is dissatisfied with that income distribution economic measures might be taken to effect some redistribution. Even though this redistribution may be achieved at the cost of some economic efficiency it may be judged that society's welfare is improved; there is almost certainly a *trade-off between equity and efficiency*.

In much the same way, even if it is accepted that competitive markets operating internationally would result in patterns of trade and resource allocation which are Pareto-optimal, there is still room for individual groups and countries to argue that they do not gain sufficiently from free-trade and to believe that their welfare would be increased by restricting trade in some way. In some instances advocacy of such a policy might be based upon a strong belief in the notion of trade as an inequalising force. In others it might rest upon the sort of generalised arguments for market intervention which were briefly set out in Section 11.6.3 above – these included the fact that markets might be felt to be too shortsighted,[10] that infant industries may need protection, or that monopoly and oligopoly elsewhere in the market system required the exercise of countervailing power.

In the light of these plausible arguments for trade intervention, the question for economists is *how successful have policies of trade intervention been at increasing economic growth, reducing income inequality and generally improving social welfare*? In a significant number of important cases a large body of economists (and politicians) have arrived at the conclusion that barriers to trade need to be reduced if not wholly dismantled, and that economic policy should be more closely attuned to price signals generated in international markets and by a movement to freer trade. Of course, some may argue it is not surprising that those economists schooled in neoclassical economics should arrive at such conclusions, and that they are hardly unbiased commentators. However it should be borne in mind that neoclassical economics provides a discipline for analysing and making decisions about such issues, and that the subject has developed precisely in order to provide a coherent response to them. But, it is better to leave readers to form their own judgements by instancing some of the major cases in which economists have been critical of trade restricting policies or where major political reforms to free trade have occurred.

At the top of any such list mention must be made of the economic reforms instituted in the People's Republic of China since the death of Mao Tse Tung in 1979. Essentially, prior to that date the economy of China had become a command economy, in which inter-regional trade was restricted by policies emphasising regional self-sufficiency (and also commune self-sufficiency within regions), and in which production quotas and targets over-rode the profit motive. The opportunity to exploit local and regional comparative advantage was stifled in such instances as where areas with a favourable environment for cotton growing had to grow their own basic foodstuffs rather than being allowed to export cotton in exchange for food. Since 1979 planning restrictions have been progressively removed, land has been returned to the management of individual households, and more and more elements of the economy have been opened up as competitive markets where prices are determined by the interaction of the individual decisions of many buyers and sellers. At the same time as much intra-national trade has been freed, so too have some restrictions on international trade. The results of all this have been rapid increases in the growth rate of agricultural output, of China's GDP and of incomes. Of course the PRC has not moved to complete free-trade, no countries have agreed to do that, but there is very strong evidence that freer trade and increased reliance on specialisation related to comparative advantage has brought considerable rewards. Other countries also, most noticeably the USSR, are also reducing the scale of bureaucratic control over the allocation of resources and distribution of products. Increasing emphasis is being placed upon competitive markets and the profit motive to improve the flexibility of the economy and promote growth and consumer satisfaction.

As regards agriculture in LDCs readers of this book should examine and form a view about the contents of Part II of the World Bank's *Development Report 1986*. There, attention is drawn to the problems which are perceived to have arisen from policies under which (a) farmers receive lower prices for products than they are worth on both domestic and international markets, (b) consumers pay lower prices for foodstuffs than government agencies pay to procure them, and (c) where currency exchange rates are overvalued so that exports earn less in local currency than they otherwise would do and imports cost more. (These topics will be specifically addressed in the next chapter). Again the policy prescription is to reduce bureaucratic/political interference with the operation of markets, and to rely more heavily upon price signals generated by competitive markets.

Another set of policies which have been subjected to considerable criticism, are the so-called *Import Substituting Industrialisation* (ISI) policies pursued particularly in Latin American countries in the 1960s and 1970s. Much inspiration for these policies derived from the influential school of economists starting with Prebisch, which espoused ideas of unequal exchange and of trade as a promoter of LDC dependency upon industrialised countries. The policies entailed erecting high tariff and non-tariff import barriers to protect and enable the development of new domestic industries to produce products which had previously been imported. A widespread consensus of opinion is that in the majority of cases these policies failed when matched against what other countries, particularly in East Asia, achieved with export-oriented policies which placed heavy reliance upon increasing trade. (It is not possible to review the complexities of this debate here, but for a comprehensive examination of ISI policies readers could consult Colman and Nixson, 1986, pp. 281–298).

The point to note about all the examples and issues referred to above is that in no case is totally unrestricted open competition and free-trade being advocated. It is accepted that there may be various good reasons for well designed market interventions. (This may take many forms, such as 'temporary' import tariffs, employment subsidies to encourage employment, publicly funded research programmes, temporary investment grants, special technical programmes, etc.). But what is suggested that it is likely to prove highly inefficient to persist in managing large sectors of the economy in ways which render them insensitive to international and national market signals. Thus free-trade and pure competition are benchmarks against which to evaluate government policies. What are the costs and benefits from restricting trade and competition? To answer this crucial question it is imperative to understand the case for and implications of free trade and pure competition as they have been set out in Chapters 9 and 10. Lal, an economist committed to the virtues of competitive markets puts it this way (Lal, 1983, p. 15):

> Given that the optimum is unattainable, the relevant policy problem becomes that of assessing to what extent particular government interventions may raise welfare in an inherently and inescapably imperfect economy. The Utopian construct of perfect competition then becomes relevant as a reference point by which

to judge the health of an economy, as well as the remedies for its amelioration.

Little, a very influential development economist of a neoclassical persuasion who was instrumental in establishing the foundations of social cost-benefit analysis, has written (1982, pp. 25, 26):

> no economist believes they (neoclassical models) are such exact explanations of reality that he need not look out for explanations of the workings of markets that include monopoly, oligopoly, and ignorance of both the present and the future, and be on the watch for policies that take account of such matters. Neoclassical economics can thus be described as a paradigm that tells one to investigate markets and prices, perhaps expecting them often to work well, but also to be on the watch for aberrations and ways of correcting them. Perhaps the single best touchstone is a concern for prices and their role.

11.8 *Summary points*

1. According to the *theory of comparative advantage* it can be shown that countries (i.e. their inhabitants) are better off by specialising in production and trading with other countries than by aiming for self-sufficiency.
2. According to the *Heckscher–Ohlin theory* international specialisation will be such that countries will produce and export goods which embody relatively large amounts of their most abundant factors of production and will import goods embodying relatively large amounts of their scarcest factors. Thus trade should tend to bring about *factor price equalisation* between trading partners.
3. High *transport costs* reduce the potential for trade and for obtaining the benefits of specialisation. Reducing transport costs by investing in roads, railways and harbours will stimulate trade and the benefits which derive therefrom.
4. While trade is mutually beneficial the *gains from trade are not necessarily shared equally between trading partners.*
5. *Deteriorating terms-of-trade* for LDCs are often cited in arguments claiming that LDCs obtain little benefit from trade. There are several alternative measures of the terms-of-trade, and it is shown that there are problems of interpreting these in the context of such arguments.
6. *Restriction of imports* (i.e. of trade) and protection of domestic

industry *can be justified in the short-run.* Long-run welfare gains from such a short-run policy could well be positive. But long-run, semi-permanent protection of industry through trade barriers is difficult to justify.

7. *Tariff and non-tariff barriers to trade* reduce the volume of trade, and in most cases reduce social welfare.

Further reading

A good basic textbook touching upon all the main aspects of trade theory and policy is that by Meier (1980). A shorter, but nevertheless comprehensive text is provided by Gowland (1983); this book contains a useful short critique of alternative theories of trade.

For a more extended comparison and evaluation of trade theories readers might like to consult the first five chapters of the book by Edwards (1985). In addition to a critique of the neoclassical theories reviewed in our book, Edwards devotes a chapter to theories of unequal exchange and another to Marxist theory and trade. Those wishing to explore in more depth theories of 'unequal exchange' might wish to refer to the book with that title by Emmanuel (1972) or to a book by Brown (1974) entitled *The Economics of Imperialism*. For a vigorous defence of open competition and free trade see Lal (1983) and Little (1982).

Given the frequency with which issues relating to the terms-of-trade surface in public discussion, the recent review of measurement and major empirical exercise by Scandizzo and Diakosavvas (1987) is a valuable reference point. An earlier, shorter work published by the Commonwealth Secretariat (1975) also contains an admirably clear empirical treatment of the terms of trade. For a more advanced theoretical treatment some readers may wish to consult Spraos (1983).

12

Food and agricultural policy

The principal purpose of this chapter is to show that many of the economic concepts presented in earlier chapters can be employed to develop an approach to the analysis and evaluation of agricultural policies. The approach is that of *partial equilibrium analysis* explained in Chapter 8, and it involves the manipulation of supply and demand curves for products and factors of production to identify the effects of different policy changes upon a whole range of variables including producer and consumer surplus, balance of payment costs, and budgetary expenditures. In this form of analysis any policy can be assessed by comparing its economic effects to those of any alternative policy. One alternative policy would be to have no purposeful intervention, and to leave all economic decisions to competitive market forces operating in conditions of free trade. The method provides a means of undertaking a form of *cost-benefit analysis* whereby the various benefits and costs of a particular policy can be assessed against competitive free trade or some other form of intervention.

Before proceeding to the analysis of selected agricultural policy instruments, Section 12.1 briefly examines the nature and principles of agricultural policy. This is crucial in establishing the broad policy context in which the subsequent analysis of specific policy instruments and individual commodity policies should be placed and interpreted. Section 12.2 starts with the *partial equilibrium analysis of policy instruments* which is the focus of the chapter. Coverage here is restricted to policy instruments which have not already been presented elsewhere in the book and (with one exception) to instruments of particular importance in LDCs. Arising out of this analysis sub-section 12.2.2 provides a classification, by general category, of the many impacts of policy intervention and underscores the desirability (in principle) of general equilibrium analysis.

Section 12.3 provides illustrations of how this form of analysis has been applied to a number of specific cases, both as a framework for numerically estimating the costs and benefits of policies and as a general basis for communicating economists' views about policies to policy makers. Two particular cases have been selected on the basis of their compactness and for the availability of numerical estimates of their costs and benefits. They are (1) the case of taxes imposed by Thailand on exports of rice, and (2) the case of Egypt's policy for subsidising consumption of wheat.

12.1 *Nature and principles of policy*

12.1.1 *The elements of policy*

Any country's policy towards the agricultural sector as a whole or towards one particular interest group such as food consumers, grain producers or fertiliser manufacturers can be characterised as consisting of three *sets* of elements, *(1) objectives, (2) instruments of policy, and (3) rules for operating instruments of policy*. That is to say, a policy is usually framed in terms of several simultaneous objectives, and involves several instruments which are applied according to specific rules devised in order to achieve the objectives. It is the way in which the rules are set for the operation of the instruments which determines the outcome of policy, and which thereby controls the extent to which the different objectives are individually achieved. Frequently what is actually achieved in terms of the balance between alternative objectives is substantially at variance with the rhetoric of official policy statements.

It is easiest for the authors to illustrate the above points by referring to the Common Agricultural Policy (CAP) of the European Economic Community (EEC). Article 39 of the Treaty of Rome establishes several objectives for the policy which may be summarised as being to support farmers' and farm workers' incomes, to increase efficiency and agricultural productivity, to stabilise markets, to guarantee regular supplies (which may be interpreted as signifying an attachment to achieving an unspecified degree of self-sufficiency in food supplies), and of ensuring reasonable prices to consumers. This main set of objectives is supplemented by others relating to assisting farming and rural communities in more remote and otherwise disadvantaged regions (what might be termed a regional dimension of policy), and to protecting specific habitats and landscapes (an environmental dimension). In pursuit of the whole set of objectives many different policy instruments are employed. These (which are explained more fully below) include variable import levies with minimum

---

BOX 12.1
Kenya's food policy

In 1981 the Kenyan Government (in Sessional Paper No. 4 of 1981) set out a statement of the National Food Policy. It provides a good example of the way in which policy objectives are stated, and also of the types of instruments to be employed.

The food policy *objectives* are stated as being to:

maintain a position of broad self-sufficiency in the main foodstuffs in order to enable the nation to be fed without using scarce foreign exchange on food imports;

achieve a calculated degree of security of food supply for each area of the country;

ensure that these foodstuffs are distributed in such a manner that every member of the population has a nutritionally adequate diet.

Thus the focus of the policy is to be upon nutritional objectives achieved as far as possible from domestic production, and upon minimising the burden of food imports on the balance of payments. This foreign exchange objective is further emphasised by the statement:

> **'As a general principle, there should be no diversification of land under export crops, the earnings from which are essential for national development, nor should there be further destruction of forests, which must be retained for ecological reasons.'**

It is made apparent that the food policy has to be integrated with other facets of national economic policy:

> **It is essential that the food policy be consistent, both internally and with the broad objectives of national development. This is important because it has implications for the attainment of other national objectives, such as high levels of employment, a more equitable distribution of income, optimal resource allocation and the maintenance of a sound balance of payments.**

As regards the *instruments* of price policy the policy document sets out the following details (and has corresponding statements about policy for agricultural inputs, research and extension and trade):

> **'Policy decisions on the pricing of the major food commodities will be among the most important factors determining whether the**

> nation achieves the rates of growth in food production necessary to recover to and maintain a position of broad self-sufficiency. To achieve this goal, government policy will be to provide incentives for the production of foodstuffs by relating producer prices at the farm-gate to import parity. Recognising the increasingly unstable nature of world grain markets, domestic producer prices will not be adjusted in reflect transitory world price movements, but will be based on longer-term parities. In order to provide a price incentive for increased production of drought-resistant food crops in arid and semi-arid areas for both human consumption and livestock feed, guaranteed minimum prices will be established for sorghum and finger millet and reviewed regularly as part of the Ministry of Agriculture's Annual Price Review.
>
> Consumer prices will generally be set at levels which cover the domestic producer prices plus processing and distribution costs.
>
> In the case of maize, the producer price will be based on the import parity price for yellow maize. When the nation is forced to import maize at prices above long-term import parity, the retail price will be subsidised in order to protect consumers.
>
> Given the erratic nature of the world market for powdered milk and consumer preference for fresh liquid milk, import parity pricing may be inappropriate. While the present substantial milk deficit remains, the aim of price policy will be to set producer prices at levels which will encourage the production of sufficient quantities of milk to meet consumption requirements for liquid milk throughout the year. To encourage greater production during the dry season, a seasonal pricing policy will be followed.

While this is not an absolutely clear statement of which policy instruments are to be applied it can be interpreted as indicating that there is to be some border instrument for insulating and protecting key domestic food prices from international price fluctuations; that consumer food subsidies will be of limited size; that there will be minimum producer prices for key crops presumably imposed by support-buying operated by a parastatal organisation for grains.

---

import prices, export subsidies, intervention buying to support prices, production quotas to control milk and sugar output, deficiency payments (for beef and sheep in the UK), production subsidies, investment grants, import quotas and tariffs, plus a range of measures to help dispose of and manage surplus production. As circumstances change so new instruments of policy are added, old ones scrapped, and the rules of operation changed so as to achieve a new balance between objectives.

Needless to say other countries have different objectives and emphasise different elements of policy. This is particularly so in LDCs where the aim has been less to support agricultural incomes, than to find ways of enabling agriculture to support other developing areas of the economy. In LDCs much more emphasis has been placed upon keeping food prices down (by subsidising consumers rather than producers), on stimulating agricultural exports to contribute to the balance of payments, and on securing indigenous cotton, sugar, vegetable oil and fibre output for local agricultural processing industries. (These points are all illustrated by the extracts relating to Kenya's Food Policy in Box 12.1.) Nevertheless the same pattern prevails, of many objectives and instruments.

In order to illustrate the significance attaching to the *rules of policy* a couple of simple examples will suffice. Sri Lanka has for many years operated a policy of subsidising the consumption of basic staples such as rice and cooking oil in order to promote equity, help control malnutrition and to contain pressure on wages. The policy was highly successful in these regards, but, because the amounts of subsidised food which consumers were entitled to were large in the early and mid 1970s, the budgetary and foreign exchange costs of the policy jumped sharply after the commodity price boom of 1973–74. In 1975 food imports amounted to a staggering 66% of Sri Lanka's total export earnings. In order to contain these costs the subsidised ration entitlement was progressively reduced by stages and has recently been further restricted to the most needy by limiting it only to those issued with food stamps;[1] *i.e.* the subsidy programme remains but the *way* it operates has been changed. In a parallel way the EEC has in recent years acted to control the budgetary cost of its intervention buying policy by progressively altering the rules; specific upper limits have been placed upon the amount of bread wheat which will be accepted into intervention, quality standards for acceptance have been raised, and for some commodities the period of availability of intervention has been shortened. Again the instruments of policy have been maintained, but their *effectiveness* has been reduced by adjusting the rules of operation.

12.1.2 *Classification of instruments of policy*

Policy makers have adopted a multitude of different means (instruments) of influencing the behaviour of the agricultural sector. As it is not possible to analyse all of them in full in this chapter, it will be helpful to attempt to produce a classification of instruments in order to highlight differences between major groups of instrument. There are, however, many alternative criteria for classification which have been proposed, but we choose to start (see Table 12.1a) by considering the level in the production and distribution system at which intervention is applied. Using this approach instruments are listed according to whether they are imposed (1) directly at the *farm level*, (2) at the national *frontier*, or (3) at some other point in the domestic *market*.[2]

The general significance of this three-dimensional classification is as follows: *Frontier-level instruments* alter the relationship between the domestic and international markets; that is to say they shift the relationships between domestic and international prices and the volume (and possibly direction) of trade flows from their free-trade levels. *Instruments applied at the farm level* permit the amount and type of economic activity in farming to be adjusted relative to the levels which would be dictated by competitive pressures from national and international markets. Instruments operated at what is here termed the

Table 12.1a. *Classification of selected policy instruments*

Level of imposition		
Farm	Market	Frontier
1. Deficiency payments	9. Parastatal trading and marketing boards; price discrimination	15. Import tariffs, levies or duties
2. Production subsidies	10. Intervention buying – public stock management	16. Export subsidies or taxes
3. Input subsidies/credit	11. Food subsidies to consumers	17. Import quotas
4. Investment grants	12. Excise taxes	18. Non-tariff barriers
5. Production or acreage quotas	13. Grants to industry	
6. Compulsory food requisition	14. Public investment in education, research, and infrastructure	
7. Land retirement/set aside		
8. Land reform measures		

Table 12.1b. *Brief definitions of selected policy instruments*

Farm level

1. *Deficiency Payment* – a variable subsidy paid per unit of output to compensate for the shortfall (deficiency) between the average market price and a higher, pre-announced guaranteed price.
2. *Production Subsidy* – a fixed or proportionate subsidy paid per unit of output.
3. *Input Subsidies/Credit* – subsidies per unit of a variable input used. Cheap credit offered for the purchase of inputs will have the same effect.
4. *Investment Grants* – subsidies for investment in medium and long term capital, such as machinery, irrigation systems, or land levelling.
5. *Production or acreage quotas* – where limits are imposed on total production or acreage of a crop, individual farms may either be allocated quota, or may be able to buy quota.
6. *Compulsory Food Requisition* – producers may be required to sell minimum quantities of grain to State trading organisations at below market prices.
7. *Land Retirement/Set Aside* – producers may be offered payments to reduce the acreage allotted to some use, provided they agree to restrictions on alternative use.
8. *Land Reform Measures* – legislative measures may be enacted to control landlords and tenants rights, or to reallocate land rights. Payments may be offered to promote land amalgamation or to encourage older farmers to retire.

Market level

9. *Parastatal Trading or Marketing Boards* – the State may authorise the creation of commodity trading bodies with a variety of powers. They may be constituted as monopolies or monopsonies to exercise market power in a variety of ways e.g. increase producer prices by discriminating monopoly pricing, tax producers by applying monopsony powers. (See Chapter 9 for analysis of monopoly and monopsony pricing.)
10. *Intervention Buying* – a parastatal organisation may be empowered to help place a *floor price* in the wholesale market by purchasing commodity at a pre-announced 'intervention price'.
11. *Food Subsidies to Consumers* – parastatal organisations may be used to manage the distribution of low price basic food supplies to consumers. Subsidies are required to finance the gap between the prices at which these organisations secure supplies and the lower prices charged to consumers.
12. *Excise Taxes* – taxes levied on the production or processing of goods.
13. *Grants to Industry* – subsidies, often in the form of investment grants, paid to industry. Alternatively there may be special tax concessions which are equivalent to subsidies.
14. *Public Investment in Infrastructure, Education and Research* – public sector investment in physical and human capital stimulates economic activity at all stages of the distribution chain, by making available the services or products of capital (roads, research findings, trained manpower) at no direct cost to firms.

Frontier level

15. *Import Tariffs, Levies or Duties* – taxes on imports may be charged in several ways. They may be as a fixed sum per unit, as a fixed proportion of

Table 12.1b. (*cont.*)

the value (*ad valorem*), or as a varying sum equal, say, to the difference between a fixed minimum import price and a variable international price.

16. *Export Subsidies or Taxes* – as the counterpart to import taxes, exports may be promoted by fixed, proportional, or variable subsidies. In some cases, however, exports have been taxed to discourage them.
17. *Import Quotas* – quantitative limits may be placed on imports to protect domestic industries. As Section 10.5.2 has shown an import quota can be interpreted as being equivalent to a certain import tariff or tax.
18. *Non-tariff Barriers* – a large number of legislated instruments may be used to impede imports. Health regulations, labelling requirements, and special technical requirements, which may be continuously changed are all used to restrict imports.

market level may be used in a variety of general ways; state marketing boards can use their powers to raise or lower prices received by farmers thus causing farm output to deviate from competitive levels, or they can be used as a vehicle to pass food subsidies to consumers thus raising consumption from the level it would otherwise be, or in conjunction with a frontier instrument they can be used to raise or lower prices to producers and consumers simultaneously. The full significance of these points may not yet be appreciated by all readers, but the analysis in Sub-section 12.2.1 and the case studies in Section 12.3 should make them clear.

Various other classifications of agricultural policy instruments have been proposed and are useful supplements or complements to that suggested above. One possibility is to partition instruments according to whether their point of impact is in agricultural *product or factor markets*; clearly import taxes or subsidies may be applied to items which are factor inputs into agriculture as well as to products, while others such as capital grants or acreage diversion operate specifically upon factors of production. In a related vein, Ritson (1977, Ch. 8), in considering policy instruments directed towards the interests of farmers only, subdivides them according to whether they *enhance revenue* or *reduce costs* – clearly instruments of the latter type nearly all operate through input markets. Alternatively instruments may be *classified* by *policy objectives*. McCalla and Josling (1985, p. 109) supplement their classification of instruments by level of intervention by recording the primary and secondary objectives which each instrument typically serves. This provides a basis for assessing the effectiveness (in terms of the costs of achieving any policy target) of instruments with such common objectives as, say, (1) increasing the food consumption of those with low incomes or (2) increasing the incomes and output of small farms. It can therefore be seen that the purpose of any classification is to focus attention on particular aspects of policy, and each separate aspect leads to selection (through classification) of a different set of instruments.

12.1.3 *Rules of policy*

A basic rule of economic policy is that *there must be at least as many instruments as there are objectives*. It is self-evident that where there is a *single objective* of policy, such as for example to increase grain output in a country by a specific amount above the level likely with free-trade, that *at least one policy* instrument would be required (*i.e.* rejection of freely competitive market solutions requires at least one form of intervention to be employed). The instrument chosen might be (1) one of several which would raise the price of grain received by producers, such as an import tax or a production subsidy, (2) an instrument to reduce the cost of grain production, such as an input subsidy or capital grant, or (3) it might, less plausibly, be an instrument which reduces returns to products which compete with cereals for land, thus causing substitution of resources into cereal production. It is in turn obvious, therefore, that *more than one instrument* (some combination of the above) may be simultaneously employed to pursue a *single objective*.

If there are two objectives the policy rule requires the activation of at least two instruments. Suppose that, in addition to the goal of raising grain supplies by a given amount, policy makers also support a distributional objective which is to raise the incomes of those with small farms by a notional percentage. It might be possible to achieve the target increase in grain production by paying a fixed subsidy per unit of output. Inevitably with such a policy those who have most land, and produce most, benefit most from the subsidy. This is perfectly justifiable in terms of economic efficiency, but the additional subsidy to those with little land may be too small to have much impact on their poverty. One way of helping to deal with this would be to add a second policy instrument which sets a maximum limit on the amount of subsidy that any producer could be paid. If this were combined with a higher rate of subsidy both the higher output and greater equity objectives might be achieved.[3]

This introduces an interesting point, which is that there is no basic difference between an objective of policy and a political constraint on policy. The immediately preceding case can be characterised in terms of setting a grain output target subject to a constraint on the distribution of farm incomes; to achieve the target and stay within the constraint necessitated the use of at least two policy instruments.

Another excellent example of this principle is to be found in the Common Agricultural Policy of the EEC. Here (as already referred to in Box 8.1) an important instrument for raising producer prices is intervention buying by agencies operated by the EEC. With this instrument producers and merchants only sell into intervention when the intervention price exceeds the market price paid by commercial users. If international prices were low relative to the authorised intervention price, and there were no restraint upon imports, produce could be imported and a profit made by selling to the EEC's intervention agencies. Without import restrictions the policy could end up supporting producers throughout the world (although the intention is only to support those within the Community) and could become vastly more costly than it already is. To prevent this the EEC operates its intervention buying instrument in conjunction with a high minimum import price (operated using a variable import levy instrument) to make it completely unprofitable to import produce for sale into intervention. There are two possible interpretations of this situation. One is that the intervention buying instrument operates subject to the constraint that it applies only to produce from the EEC and that this necessitates the use of a second, minimum import price, instrument. Alternatively it might be argued that the intervention-buying instrument cannot be operated without the use of other instruments. It is in fact common to find that policies operate using characteristic combinations of instruments; output price supports may be operated with output quotas or other measures to limit payments to producers; food subsidies to consumers cannot be operated without a high degree of centralised control over international trade and domestic distribution, and they are usually accompanied by some form of rationing. The significance of this is that ideally policy analysis should examine several instruments operating simultaneously, whereas most textbook treatments (and the following section of this book) analyse instruments individually.

12.2 *Analysing the effects of policy instruments*

12.2.1 *Partial equilibrium analysis*

In order to demonstrate how partial equilibrium analysis (as outlined in Chapter 8) can be used to assess the welfare costs and benefits of agricultural policy, five instruments of policy are considered in this section. They are, an input subsidy, food subsidies to consumers, deficiency payments, variable import taxes, and intervention buying (all as defined in Table 12.1b). For the purpose of simplicity it is assumed in each case that the country applying the instrument is a *small open economy* which has no influence upon *international commodity prices*. Hence world supply and demand for the commodity concerned is assumed to be perfectly elastic at a world price P_w.

(a) *Input subsidy* Subsidies are in widespread use in LDCs for inputs such as inorganic fertiliser, improved seeds and irrigation water. Some of the most important implications of such subsidies are revealed by the analysis in Fig. 12.1. In Figure 12.1(*a*) the domestic agricultural supply curve (without subsidy) is shown as *aS*, the domestic demand curve as *DD*, and the world supply curve as the horizontal line P_w. At a price equal to P_e domestic supply would equal demand and the trade volume would be zero; this is plotted as point *m* in Figure 8.1(b), which indicates zero imports at price P_e. At world price P_w domestic supply (without subsidy) would be q_s and demand q_d; imports would be $q_d - q_s = i$, which again is plotted in Fig. 12.1(*b*) as point *n*. Both *m* and *n* lie on the *import demand* or *excess demand curve*, *mnrs*. (Note that at prices above P_e supply exceeds demand, and it is *excess* or *export supply* which is available.)

Introducing a fertiliser subsidy reduces the marginal costs of production to farmers causing the supply curve to shift downwards to the right to *aS*′. In drawing the shift in this way certain assumptions have been made about the production function underlying the supply curve. Specifically, it assumes that higher output requires larger applications of fertiliser, so

Fig. 12.1. Input subsidy.

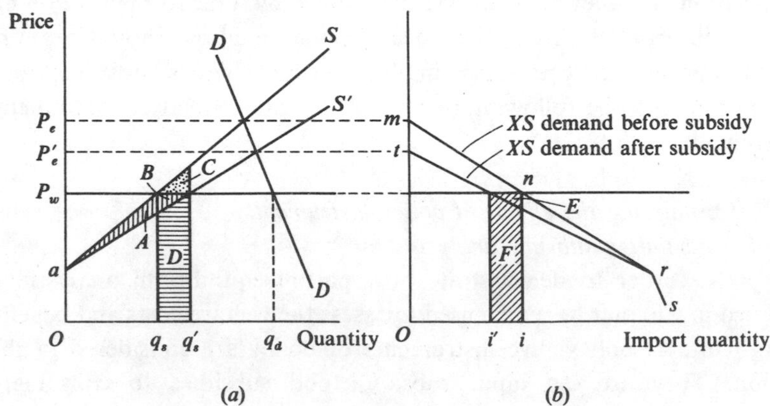

that the value of the input subsidy per unit of output increases linearly with output.

The subsidy causes no change in the market price of the product, which remains at P_w in this open-economy case. Thus demand remains unchanged at q_d, but domestic supply increases to q'_s. The *cost of the subsidy*, which represents the amount of producer costs which is borne by taxpayers, is the value equivalent of the shaded areas $A+B+C$ in Fig. 12.1(*a*). As a result of this subsidy, *producer surplus* increases by $A+B$.[4] A is clearly an addition to surplus since it represents a subsidy for resource costs which were already being met to produce q_s before the subsidy was introduced. Also B is an addition to surplus insofar as it represents an element of resource cost which is incurred to increase output from q_s to q'_s, but which is remunerated *twice*, once by the subsidy and again by the market since it is covered by the price P_w. Hence clearly producers do obtain an element of surplus equivalent to B. (C, however, is not a contribution to surplus; it is an element of resource cost required to expand output from q_s to q'_s which is not recovered in the market price P_w, but which is only recouped through the subsidy and which would not be employed if the subsidy were not available). The excess of the subsidy cost over the increase in producer surplus, C, is identified as the *welfare* or *deadweight economic loss* resulting from the input subsidy policy. In this connection it will be recalled (from Chapter 6) that all departures from competitive equilibrium are assumed to entail a loss of economic efficiency, and it is this which may be measured in C in this case. C may be interpreted as the value of resources overcommitted to producing the commodity under consideration, resources which could not be justified at the competitive market price P_w. It represents a loss of production efficiency arising from what the theory considers a competitive misallocation of resources.

Fig. 12.1 provides an alternative route for estimating the deadweight loss from the subsidy policy. As a result of the policy additional resources to the value of shaded areas $B+C+D$ are drawn into production; this is termed *the resource cost*. As a consequence output expands, imports decline by the same amount, and there is a *foreign exchange saving* of $B+D$ (which is equal to $F+E$ in Fig. 12.1(*b*)). Thus additional resources worth $B+C+D$ when valued at competitive international prices have been employed to achieve a foreign exchange saving for imports worth only $B+D$. Again this indicates a misallocation of resources equivalent in value to C. As will be seen from the ensuing analysis of other policy instruments, this form of partial equilibrium analysis always provides two alternative ways of calculating the welfare economic loss from market intervention. One calculation is based on analysis of the *monetary transfers* arising from the policy, the second on comparison of the value of changes in *resource and commodity flows*.

The results of this partial equilibrium analysis may therefore be summarised as follows in terms of the shaded areas in Fig. 12.1.

Subsidy Cost to Taxpayers = $A+B+C$;
Producer Surplus Gain = $A+B$;
Deadweight Economic Loss = C;
Resource Cost = $B+D+C$;
Foreign Exchange Gain = $B+D$.

It is through the explicit analysis of such trade-offs that this form of analysis provides a systematic framework for evaluating benefits in terms of costs. In the case of a fertiliser subsidy it may be that there are additional long-term benefits of relevance. The subsidy may induce new farmers to adopt inorganic fertiliser, so that even if the subsidy is later reduced or withdrawn fertiliser use and production are shifted to higher levels than would otherwise be the case.

Note that the analytical procedure used to identify the economic loss, C, is based on the principle (discussed in Chapter 10) for comparing the economic superiority of two alternative equilibria, namely '*can the gainers from the policy intervention potentially compensate the losers*?'. The answer in this and the subsequent cases is that, given the classes of gainers and losers considered, they cannot. In the case of input subsidies, the gainers from the foreign exchange saved *could not* fully compensate those who lose from the reallocation of resources, since the value of the resources diverted exceeds that of the foreign exchange saved. This point can be explained with even greater clarity in relation to the other instruments analysed, and it is re-examined below in relation to the impact of food subsidies.

(b) *Food subsidy* It is very common for LDCs to operate some form of food subsidy policy to consumers. There are many complex variants of this policy, but in the simplified analysis presented in Fig. 12.2 the policy may be thought of *either* as one in which every consumer pays less by a fixed amount per unit purchased than it has cost the seller to supply it and where government compensates the seller with a subsidy, *or* as one where for every unit purchased at the full market price (P_w) the consumer received a cash subsidy payment.

In the absence of a subsidy the operation of the market is described by domestic demand curve *DD*, supply curve *SS*, and the *excess* or *import demand curve* is *rstu*. Introducing a consumer subsidy causes a parallel upward shift in the demand curve to *D′D′*, such that the vertical distance between the two demand curves equals the amount of subsidy per unit; that is the subsidy equals $P_w - P_s$. Import demand also increases at all price levels and the excess demand curve shifts upwards to *vwxy*.

By contrast to the input subsidy case where all the domestic impact was upon supply (and taxpayers), a consumer subsidy can be seen to have no effect upon supply (in this open-economy case) but to have effects solely upon consumption and consumers (and taxpayers). It causes domestic demand to rise from q_d to q'_d and imports to rise by the same amount from i to i'. There is also an increase in *consumer surplus* by the amount $A+B+C+D$ of the areas in Fig. 12.2(*a*). The per unit subsidy on all units consumed, q'_d, entails a *subsidy cost to taxpayers* of $A+B+C+D+E$. The difference between the increased value of consumer surplus and the subsidy cost is E the *economic loss* resulting from the policy.

Consider again this method of calculating the economic loss as a test of the welfare economics principle '*could the gainers from the policy compensate the losers*?' In the case of a food subsidy the gainers are consumers and the losers are taxpayers, but the analysis reveals that (on a dollar-for-dollar or rupee-for-rupee basis) the gains are less than the losses by the value *E*, the economic loss. Thus the gainers could not fully compensate the losers.

The identical assessment of the economic loss emerges if the *foreign*

Fig. 12.2. Food subsidy/consumption subsidy.

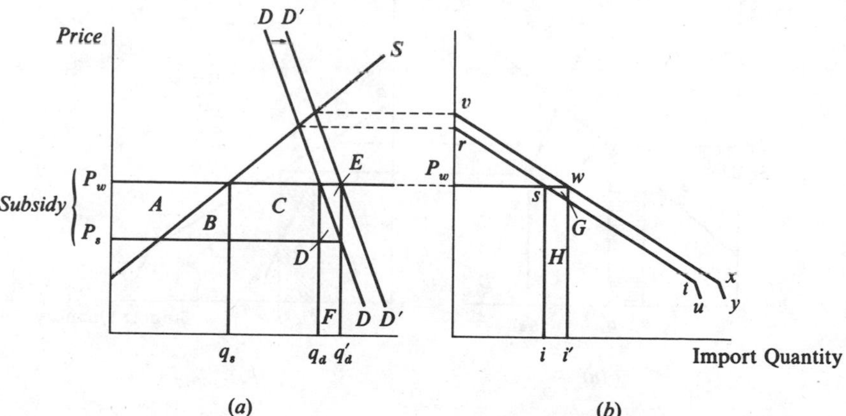

exchange costs of the food subsidy are compared to the *value of the extra consumption* which it stimulates. The foreign exchange costs are $D+E+F$, but the value of the extra consumption (valued under the original demand curve *DD*) is only $D+F$; again the difference is shown to be *E*, the social welfare loss.

(c) *Deficiency payment* The use of deficiency payments is relatively common in the policies of developed countries such as those in the EEC, and the USA. As stated in Table 12.1b it involves government paying a variable subsidy ($P_g - P_w$ in Fig. 12.3(*a*)) to producers to make up the difference between a supported guaranteed price and a fluctuating lower market price. In most essential respects, as revealed by Fig. 12.3 the effects are very similar to those of an input subsidy. Only the supply side of the domestic market is affected, supply being increased from q_s to q_s' and imports reduced by the same amount from *i* to *i′*. With this instrument domestic supply becomes completely unresponsive to market price changes below the guaranteed price. Producers know that whatever happens they will receive P_g per unit of output. This has a marked effect on the import demand curve at price levels below P_g; as Fig. 12.3(*b*) indicates the deficiency payment causes the excess demand curve to shift from *abcd* to *abe*. Thus import demand becomes much more inelastic *i.e.* unresponsive to price changes. The costs and benefits of applying this instrument can be summarised as follows in terms of the shaded areas of Fig. 12.3.

Fig. 12.3. Deficiency payment.

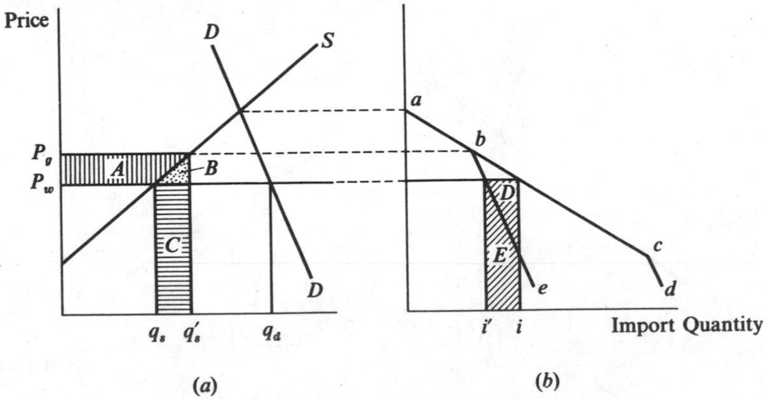

Subsidy Cost = $A+B$;
Producer Surplus Gain = A;
Deadweight Economic Loss = B;
Resource Cost = $B+C$;
Foreign Exchange Gain = C.

The deadweight economic loss in this case equals B. It can be calculated *either* as the subsidy cost minus the producer surplus gain, *or* as the resource cost minus the foreign exchange gain. It is most readily interpreted in terms of the second of these, which reveals clearly that domestic resources valued at $B+C$ have been re-allocated to save imports with a resource value of only C.

(d) *Variable import tax or levy* A variable import tax can be employed (as in the EEC) to prevent imports occurring below some politically determined minimum import price, P_m. In Fig. 12.4 a variable import levy imposed at the border is shown raising domestic prices from the international level P_w to P_m. Unlike the previous instruments, which operated either upon supply or demand, this instrument affects both. Domestic supply increases from q_s to q_s' and demand declines from q_d to q_d'. Thus this instrument affects the welfare of both producers and consumers, the former in a positive manner the latter negatively. Imports are reduced because of both the supply and demand effects, and they are in fact cut from q_d-q_s to $q_d'-q_s'$, or from i to i'. Indeed the variable import levy causes the excess demand curve to shift from *stuv* to *stw*. Thus it becomes completely inelastic at prices below P_m. This is because quite irrespective of what changes occur in world prices the price in the domestic market will not fall below P_m, provided that imports are still needed, making domestic supply and demand completely unresponsive to world prices below P_m.

In contrast to the instruments already considered this one does not involve a subsidy. In fact the import levy generates tax income of value C. It is domestic consumers who carry the main burden of price support in this case, with a loss of consumer surplus equal to $A+B+C+D$.

As partially analysed in Fig. 12.4 an import tax would have the following economic effects.

Consumer Surplus Loss = $A+B+C+D$;
Producer Surplus Gain = A;
Tax Revenue Gain = C;
Deadweight Economic Loss = $B+D$.

In this case the deadweight economic loss is equal to the consumer surplus loss minus both the producer surplus and the tax revenue gains. The resulting amount $B+D$ comprises precisely the same two triangular areas, representing production efficiency loss and consumption allocation efficiency loss respectively, which have constituted the economic loss incurred by the previous instruments analysed.

Application of the import tax can be seen from Fig. 12.4 to generate a foreign exchange saving of $E+F=G$. This however is achieved at a resource cost of $E+B$ and a loss of consumption value under the demand level of $F+D$. Again, subtracting the foreign exchange gain from the resource cost plus loss of consumption value leaves $B+D$, the deadweight economic loss.

Fig. 12.4. Variable import tax (VIT).

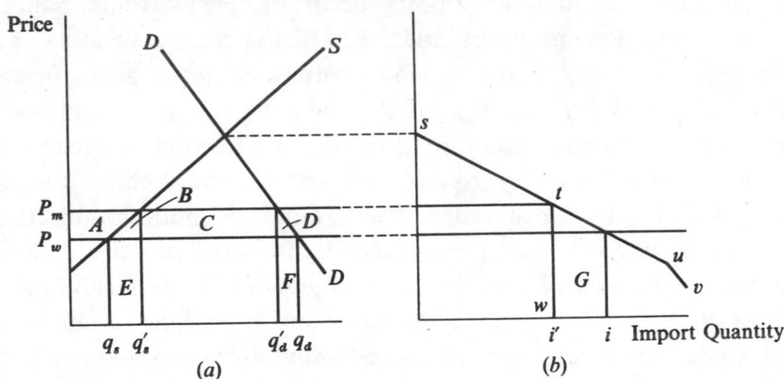

(e) *Intervention buying* It is common for parastatal trading corporations to undertake support buying operations to support market prices for key commodities, namely grains. In LDCs such operations usually only operate intermittently in periods of unanticipated excess supply to prevent prices falling to levels which would undermine the livelihood of small farmers and discourage future production. In developed countries such as the USA (through the Commodity Credit Corporation) or the EEC (through the national Intervention Boards) support buying occurs with much greater frequency with the overt objective of raising prices above normal competitive free-trade levels. Unlike all the instruments previously analysed which operate against the background of a domestic deficit of supply, intervention buying only occurs when domestic supply exceeds demand. For the sake of simplicity, however, we assume in Fig. 12.5 that the domestic market would just be in balance at the world price and that it is the support price P_i set by the intervention authority which stimulates excess supplies. As already noted operating a policy along these lines necessitates setting a minimum import price in order to prevent the commodity being imported to sell into intervention.

The social costs of state purchasing are greatly influenced by the management and terms for disposal of the stocks purchased by the authorities. In the summary of benefits and costs which follows nothing is included for storage and handling costs by the intervention authority, and in addition it is assumed that the stocks acquired can be disposed of at world prices so that the costs of organising intervention are simply equal to $B+C+D$, which is equivalent to an export subsidy of P_i-P_w (intervention price minus world price). That is to say, it is assumed that the portion $E+F$ of cost involved in taking $q'_s-q'_d$ into public ownership can be recovered as export receipts. In reality the storage costs incurred by intervention authorities are high, and frequently public stocks acquired for market support purposes can only be disposed of at prices substantially below P_w because they have deteriorated in quality during prolonged storage. Any costs incurred in these ways would add directly to the deadweight economic loss from operating such a policy.

It should be noted that this is a policy instrument which forces consumers to pay some of the costs of price support, so that there is a loss of consumer surplus equal to $A+B$. This arises because the intervention authority is a source of competition with consumers for supplies which only becomes active when prices fall to P_i. In effect, it is a demand agent which enters the market only when prices drop to the official support price.

Fig. 12.5. Intervention buying.*

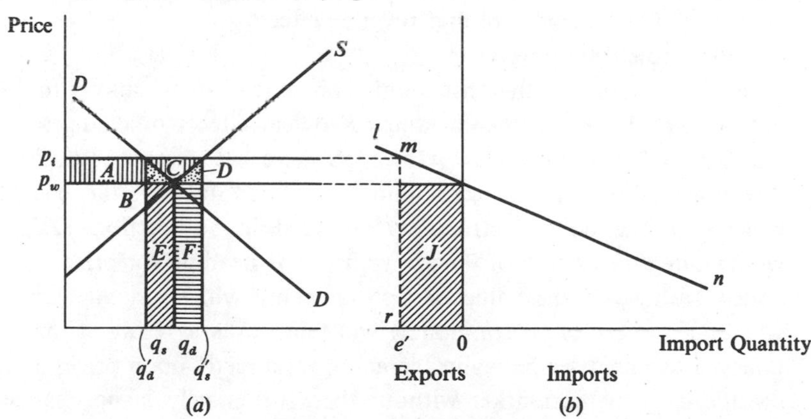

* In the absence of intervention buying the excess demand function is *lmn*. With intervention buying there is an excess supply curve *lmr*.

As analysed in Fig. 12.5 the following costs and benefits arise from a policy of intervention buying:

Consumer Surplus Loss = $A+B$;
Intervention Purchase Cost[5] = $B+C+D$;
Producer Surplus Gain = $A+B+C$;
Deadweight Economic Loss = $B+D$.

The deadweight economic loss of applying this policy instrument, $B+D$, is exactly comparable to that which was shown to arise from an import levy. It can be calculated (as above) by subtracting the value of producer surplus gain from the costs in terms of consumer surplus and intervention purchases. In parallel with the previous instrument examined it can also be calculated by subtracting the foreign exchange saving from the resource cost plus the loss in consumption value under the demand curve, where:

Resource Cost = $F+D$;
Consumption Value Loss = $E+B$;
Foreign Exchange Saving = $E+F = J$.

12.2.2. *Classifying the effects of agricultural policy*

Using an extended version of the list devised by Corden (1971, p. 7) in relation to import tariffs, the economic effects of market interventions can be classified under the following headings:

1. Price effects.
2. Production or protection effects.
3. Consumption effects.
4. Trade or balance-of-payments effects.
5. Public expenditure and revenue effects.
6. Redistribution effects.

In some contexts this list might be extended to allow for such *externalities* as environmental and ecological effects or changes in the number and size of farms. However, here we restrict ourselves to categories of measurable economic effect. Certainly all the costs and benefits of the policy-instruments analysed in Sub-section 12.2.1 fall within categories 2 to 6 of the above list. The heading for price effects is added because of the value of distinguishing which prices (farm-gate, wholesale, retail, or international) will change as a result of an act of policy. In some cases policy instruments act directly upon prices at some specific level in the market without there necessarily being changes at other levels. An example of this would be a deficiency payment policy for producers, which raises (guarantees) the farm-gate price but (in a small, open economy) leaves prices to consumers unchanged. In other cases, such as intervention buying, competitive market forces ensure that if intervention prices are raised so too are prices to both producers and consumers. How many separate effects are considered in each of the six categories depends upon how narrow or partial is the analytical procedure used. In the case of the five instruments examined in Section 12.2.1 the approach used was an extremely narrow (partial) one in which the focus was restricted to a single product market in a small, open economy such that international prices are unaffected by any adjustment in the domestic market. In many cases a more *general equilibrium* approach needs to be taken (refer to Section 8.2.1) which recognises the linkages running from one product market to others, from product to input markets, and also linkages through trade to international prices and even currency exchange rates. It is never realistic to undertake general equilibrium analysis in the ultimate sense of trying to allow for the fact that 'everything depends upon everything else'. It is, however, important that significant linkages should be allowed for. If a maize price rise which causes maize production to increase also results in a largely offsetting fall in sorghum production this *substitution* relationship should be allowed for in the measurement of production effects; likewise any important complementarity relationship in production, as for example between milk and beef, should be included. Where changes in output cause large adjustments in demand (quantity and/or price) of inputs, or in the volume of activity in the agricultural processing industry these too should be included among the measured production effects, and any significant implications that these linked effects have for *trade* should be considered under that heading.

In measuring consumption effects it is likely to be particularly necessary to allow for substitution between commodities, and in rarer instances for complementarity. The limitations of both income and appetite mean that substitution of one good for others is generally observed and should be allowed for.

It is a matter of judgement as to how many commodities in production, consumption and trade should be allowed for in analysing any particular problem. But it is important that all major linkages should be allowed for, particularly where these involve substitution relationships or offsetting changes in input prices. For, these effects operate to counteract the primary impacts of policy measures upon target commodities or sectors, and failure to allow for them would result in overestimation of the total net effects of policy.

The last two categories of effect (5 and 6) are fairly self-explanatory.

Governments are highly sensitive to the public expenditure costs and to any revenues arising from the operation of policy. Indeed they may be more influenced by these than by the redistributional outcomes, despite the fact that it is the latter which will reflect the main stated objectives of policy. For it is under the heading of redistributional effects that the impacts upon consumer and producer surplus will fall; who are the beneficiaries and who bears the cost? To answer these questions fully may require separate analysis of the impact of policy upon narrowly defined groups of producers and consumers; producers might be classified by

Table 12.2. *Domestic effects of five selected agricultural policy instruments*[a]

	Input subsidy	Food subsidy	Deficiency payment	Variable import tax	Intervention buying
Domestic Economic Effects					
Output Price Effects					
Producer Price			+	+	+
Wholesale Price				+	+
Retail Price		−		+	+
Production Effects					
Output	+		+	+	+
Quantity of inputs	+		+	+	+
Price of inputs	[d]		+	+	+
Consumption Effects					
Consumption		+		−	−
Trade Effects					
Net imports[b]	−	+	−	−	−[e]
Balance of payments[c]	+	−	+	+	+[e]
Public Expenditure Effects					
Budgetary cost	+	+	+		+
Tax revenue				+	
Redistribution Effect					
Producer surplus	+		+	+	+
Consumer surplus		+		−	−
Taxpayer cost	+	+	+	−	+

Notes:
[a] A positive sign denotes an increase (or a reduction in the case of budgetary and import costs). A negative sign denotes a decrease (or an increase in the case of budgetary and import costs).
[b] A negative (positive) sign signifies a decrease (increase) in imports (exports).
[c] A positive (negative) sign denotes an improvement (worsening) of the balance of payments.
[d] The input price to farmers will fall, but input suppliers may charge higher prices than before the subsidy because of increased input demand. Both are simultaneously possible because of the subsidy – in other words input suppliers may capture part of the subsidy.
[e] Under the conditions assumed in the text intervention buying will increase the exportable surplus.

regions, by size of farming operation, and by combination of products; consumers might be separated by income class, by family size and age. This could be necessary because the focus of policy was upon the food consumption of poor families with young children, or with the viability of small farms producing a particular mix of crops in remote areas. Thus, as with all the categories, a detailed set of effects might require enumeration.

A simple indication of the way in which this classificatory approach to the effects of policy may be used is displayed in Table 12.2. There, a qualitative summary is presented of the analysis of the five policy instruments from Section 12.2.1, with positive signs denoting increases or improvement in the values of variables and negative signs the converse. An interesting point which emerges from this summary is that whereas certain instruments (variable import taxes, and intervention buying) are shown as influencing all variables and participants in the market, the effect of the others is confined to specific target groups. For example an input subsidy is shown as having no effect upon output prices or consumption. This is a direct result of assuming that the reduction in product imports which results is too small to influence international prices. If that assumption were abandoned the fall in import demand would cause international and hence domestic prices of the product to decline causing increases in consumption and consumer surplus. To the extent that these '*feedback effects*' from the international market would be small in the majority of cases, the simplifying assumption of no change in import price is an acceptable one, since the impact of an input subsidy on producers would indeed dominate that on consumers. The same general argument applies to the results relating to deficiency payments and food subsidies.

12.3 *Economic analysis of selected agricultural policies*

12.3.1 *Export taxes for Thai rice*

As stated by Tolley *et al.* (1982, p. 76), 'Since World War II Thailand has been one of the few developing countries fortunate enough to have large surpluses of a food crop, rice, for example. Unlike many developing countries that incur large bills for food imports, Thailand has earned foreign exchange by exporting its rice. The dependence on rice exports, however, has also posed problems. The international market for rice is highly unstable with widely fluctuating prices. Since rice constitutes a high percentage of the national income of Thailand and is also the main staple for consumption, the government has understandably tried to insulate the domestic economy from world price fluctuations. The *taxation of rice exports* has been an important means of generating government revenue, and it was believed that the export tax, when varied continuously, could also serve as an instrument for stabilising the domestic price of rice in the face of world price fluctuations.'

Thailand has employed three separate forms of rice export taxation (Trairatvorakul, 1984, p. 16). Firstly there is a straightforward system of *ad valorem export taxes*. Secondly there is the *rice premium*, which is a fixed rate tax per ton, the level of which is changed continuously in order to help stabilise domestic rice prices. Thirdly there is the system of *rice reserve requirements*; using this instrument the government has from time-to-time compelled rice exporters to sell a proportion of the quantity of exported rice to the government at below market prices; the supplies obtained by this form of export taxation have been used to provide rice to urban areas at retail prices lower than those for normal commercial supplies.

Fig. 12.6. Export tax on Thai rice.

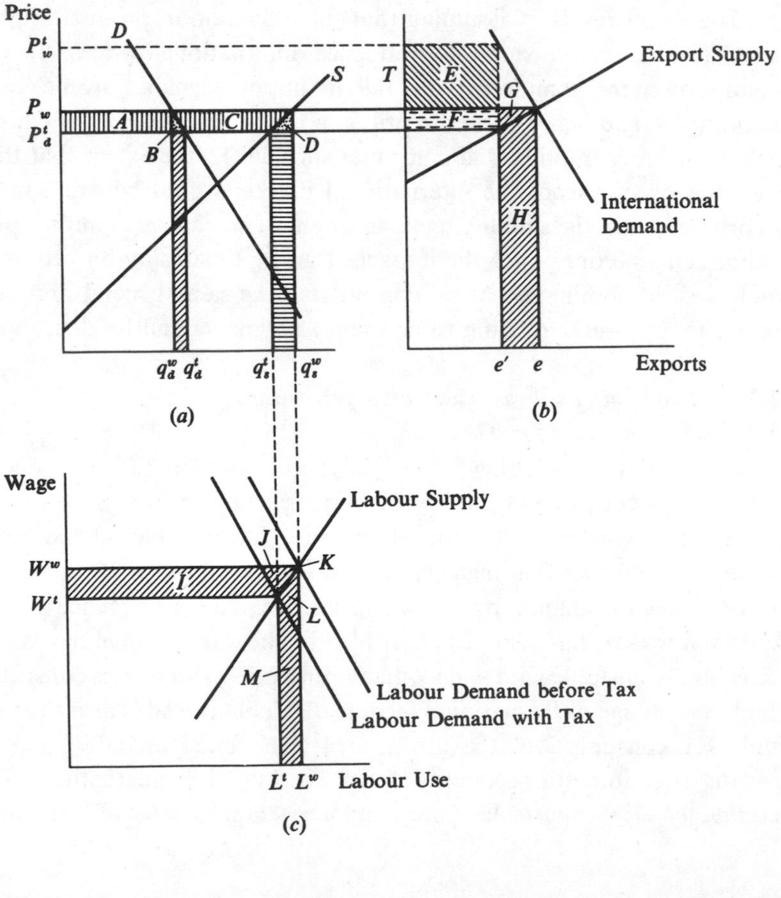

Because Thailand is a dominant exporter in the world market and is assumed to have an element of monopoly power, it would be inappropriate to assume that the international price is unaffected by changes in the export availability of Thai rice. Consequently, in the diagrammatic analysis of the export tax in Fig. 12.6, the international demand curve for Thai rice is shown as downward sloping (rather than horizontal as in Figs. 12.1–12.5). In this analysis, which follows Trairatvorakul (1984, p. 40), the three different forms of export tax are combined and treated as a single tax (T) per unit of exports. Another element which is examined in panel c of this analysis is the demand for labour for rice production. Demand for labour for work on the rice crop is an important determinant of the incomes of landless and near landless households, and changes in it have a significant impact upon the alleviation or worsening of rural poverty. Any policy which affects rice supply is, therefore, likely to have a direct impact on the welfare of poor rural households, and it is appropriate that the partial equilibrium analysis be extended to encompass this.

In the absence of an export tax, Fig. 12.6 indicates that the international and domestic Thai market price for rice would be P_w. At that price Thai producers would supply q_s^w which, with domestic demand at q_d^w, would lead to an exported surplus $e = q_s^w - q_d^w$. At that level of domestic production L^w of labour would be employed at a wage W^w. The imposition of an export tax T per unit of exports would cause a drop in domestic supply, since domestic producers would bear part of the tax. In fact the domestic price is shown as falling to P_d^t, a drop which entails a fall in producer surplus equal to the value of the shaded areas $A+B+C$. This fall in rice prices is of course of benefit to Thai consumers who are shown as enjoying an increase in consumption, from q_d^w to q_d^t, and an increase in consumer surplus of $A+B$. Thus producers lose and consumers gain. Labourers, however, also lose since the drop in production causes a fall in labour demand, from L^w to L^t, as well as a drop in the wage rate from W^w to W^t. Labour income equivalent to the shaded areas in panels ($I+J+K+L+M$) is lost. To some extent this loss is offset by the fact that the price of rice, the staple food, has declined. But the overall effect of the tax will be a welfare loss to both farmers and rural labourers.

Part of the cost of the tax is shown to be borne by foreign consumers who now pay, P_w^t, a higher price for rice from Thailand. This leads to a drop in export demand to e' which is consistent with the reduction in available export supplies. This in turn entails a *decline* in foreign exchange earnings, which is of the order $G+H-E$. Government revenues, however benefit by the amount $E+F$ as a consequence of levying the tax T on each unit exported. Component F of this export tax revenue is in effect paid by producers and exporters since it is generated by a lowering of the domestic market price from P_w to P^t_d. Component E, however, represents a tax on foreigners since it arises from the fact that foreigners are now having to pay the higher price P^t_w for the Thai rice they consume. This component represents a gain of resources to the Thai economy which therefore represents a partial offset to the deadweight loss $B+D$, where this loss is evaluated at the original world price P_w. Clearly an export tax is a useful measure for raising government revenue, and is employed by many LDCs, but as the analysis shows costs are borne domestically by agricultural producers and labourers, and there is also a deadweight loss of $B+D$ in terms of economic efficiency measured at the world price.

The distribution of the costs and benefits arising from this export tax policy are dependent (among other things) upon the slope of the international demand curve for Thai rice. If instead of a downward sloping demand function in panel *b* of Fig. 12.6 the international demand curve were horizontal (as in earlier figures), then world price would be unaffected by the tax, and the full burden of it would fall on domestic producers and exporters. In contrast if the international demand curve were vertical, totally inelastic, all the burden of the tax would be borne by foreign consumers. (Readers should check these results for themselves.) This is well illustrated by the results of the empirical analysis undertaken by Wong (1978) as republished in Tolley, Thomas and Wong (1982). Wong undertook an econometric estimation exercise which enabled him to estimate the cost and benefit transfers arising from the Thai rice export premium. His results presented in Table 12.3, are calculated in relation to the average rice export premium between 1961 and 1970, and vary according to the degree by which international prices change in response to the tax.

If, case 1, international prices are unaffected by the tax then the results confirm that there is no 'tax' cost to foreigners but that transfers from farmers were considerable. If the responsiveness of international price were higher (as in cases 2 to 4 progressively) the burden of the tax is seen to be switched from farmers to foreigners. If, in case 4, international price had risen by 25% of the export tax premium transfers from foreigners would, it was estimated, have amounted to 462 m baht as against a total deadweight economic loss at the 'without-tax' international price of 794 m baht. Thus at 25% international price responsiveness the net social cost of the tax to Thailand would have been only 332 m baht as opposed

Table 12.3. *Estimated long-run effects of the Thai export rice premium, 1961–70 average (million baht)*

				Deadweight economic loss			
Case	Rise in international price as percentage of premium	Producer[a] surplus loss	Foreign[b] exchange loss	Production[c] efficiency loss	Consumption[d] efficiency loss	Transfer[e] from foreigners	Net economic[f] loss to Thailand
	(1)	(2)	(3)	(4)	(5)	(6)	(7)
1	0	−5565	−9499	−1007	−545	0	−1552
2	5	−5239	−8021	−909	−364	45	−1228
3	15	−4602	−6843	−728	−291	134	−885
4	25	−2303	−1005	−567	−227	462	−332

Sources: Wong (1978), p. 71; Tolley, Thomas and Wong (1982), p. 170.
[a] Equivalent to areas $A+B+C$ in Figure 12.6
[b] Equivalent to areas $G+H-E$ in Figure 12.6
[c] Equivalent to area B in Figure 12.6
[d] Equivalent to area D in Figure 12.6
[e] Equivalent to area E in Figure 12.6
[f] This (in absolute value) is calculated as the deadweight losses in columns (4) and (5) minus the transfer from foreigners in column (6). The deadweight economic losses are valued at the free-trade equilibrium price P_w; since the tax has caused international prices to rise some of the deadweight economic loss is passed on to foreigners, and is not borne by Thailand.

to 1552 m. for the same average level of tax if international prices were totally unaffected.

The details of how the costs presented in Table 12.3 were obtained are explained by Wong in the source publications, and reflect the procedures generally applied in this form of analysis. They will not be explained here, but it is appropriate to make some general points. Readers will note that all the lettered shaded areas in Figs. 12.1–12.7 are either rectangles or are rectangles cut diagonally (i.e. are right-angled triangles). One side of each rectangle is a quantity level or quantity difference and the other is a price level or price difference. Once these differences or changes in price and quantity are estimated it is a simple matter to calculate the monetary values of the areas by multiplying the two differences together (and dividing the product by two in the case of the triangles). Consider an area such as *A* in Fig. 12.6; this is the numerical product of the quantity which would be consumed at international price P_w multiplied by the difference between P_w and the domestic price P_d^t which results from imposing the tax. To obtain P_w and P_d^t requires that the domestic supply and demand curves be known (and hence the export supply curve) as well as the international demand curve for Thai rice. Similarly area *B*, which equals half the product formed by multiplying $P_w - P_d^t$ by the change in Thai domestic rice demand caused by the price change, depends upon the same knowledge about the slopes of the demand and supply curves. The values used for these key slope values are obtained by statistical processes for measuring economic relationships known as *econometrics*. It is there that the fusion of economic theory and statistical methods occurs. Economic theory provides a structure within which statistical methods are employed to estimate such things as demand and supply functions, and it also supplies the framework for using the statistically estimated functions to calculate the probable effects of economic policy upon various groups in society domestically and internationally.

12.3.2 *Egypt's wheat procurement and distribution policy*

Agricultural policy in Egypt has involved extensive state controls over prices and trade by the General Authority for Supply Commodities (GASC), and has involved massive subsidies to consumers for basic foodstuffs such as wheat flour, bread, rice, sugar and cooking oil. In the late 1970s and early 1980s food subsidies accounted for between 10% and 17% of total government expenditure and were a major factor in the growth of Egypt's foreign exchange debts.[6] The complete system is far too complex to consider fully here. Instead we draw upon that part of the study by von Braun and de Haen (1983) which deals with an aggregate analysis of wheat procurement and subsidisation policy. Von Braun and de Haen summarise the policy in terms of a diagram reproduced here as Fig. 12.7. What is interesting about this piece of partial equilibrium analysis is that it combines the effects of several policy instruments into one diagram.

The main element of Egyptian food policy is that of subsidising basic foodstuffs. The price (P_s) at which consumers could buy subsidised forms of wheat was generally below 50% of its import price (P_w) from 1965 to 1980 (see Table 12.4) and in 1980 was as little as 28.4% of P_w. Subsidies for rice and other commodities were on a similarly generous scale. In order to try and control the public expenditure costs of these subsidies several supplementary policy instruments have been necessary. Procurement quotas were imposed whereby producers had to sell an amount of wheat to the GASC at a low procurement price, P_r. As Table 12.4 shows this procurement price has usually been set below the open market price, P_m, which producers could obtain for commercial sales, but above the subsidised consumer price, P_s. The vigour with which the wheat procurement quota has been enforced has varied considerably; it was most stringently applied in periods of budgetary shortage (such as 1974 and 1975). Nevertheless government procurement accounted for 7–19% of the crop in the period 1965–80. The balance of the domestic wheat crop was sold on the open market at prices, P_m, held well below the import parity price, P_w, of commercial imports. In fact there are no private commercial imports. All imports are made by the GASC and are on a sufficient scale

Fig. 12.7. Egypt's wheat procurement and distribution policy.

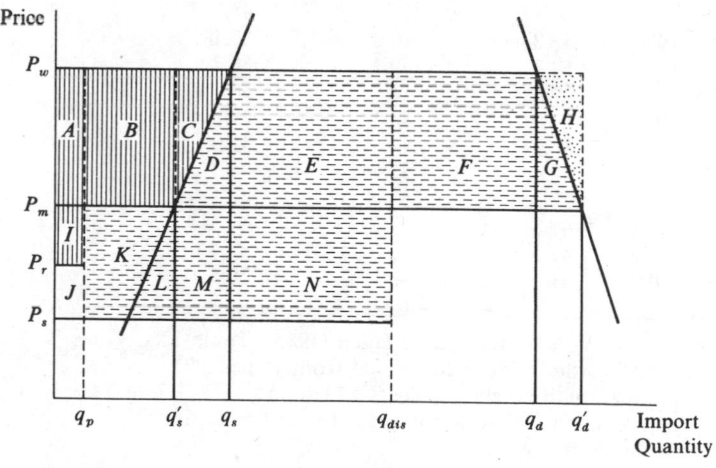

such that (in terms of Fig. 12.7) a total wheat supply (domestic plus imports) of q'_d is made available leading to the market clearing price, P_m, well below the import price P_w. Some of the imported supplies obtained by the GASC are at concessional prices, particularly from the USA under Public Law 480 provisions, although no explicit recognition of this is given in Fig. 12.7.

It can be seen from Fig. 12.7 that consumers have benefited on a massive scale. Without the combination of policy instruments outlined it may be assumed that q_d would have been consumed at a price of P_w. Instead consumers have been able to obtain a large quantity q_{dis} of wheat flour and bread distributed under the subsidy program at the very low price of P_s, plus the balance of their consumption (equal to $q'_d - q_{dis}$) at the low market price P_m. Thus consumer surplus has been increased by the

Table 12.4. *Relationship of Egyptian policy prices for wheat to international prices*

	Share of international price		
Year	Procurement price	Open market producer price	Fixed consumer price
	(percent of border price)[a]		
1965	36.9	49.4	42.6
1966	43.4	61.5	43.7
1967	44.4	75.6	45.8
1968	50.4	92.0	58.1
1969	48.1	66.6	53.5
1970	50.1	65.2	48.3
1971	57.2	70.0	56.1
1972	58.3	69.1	56.7
1973	29.6	41.5	30.0
1974	29.0	38.5	29.6
1975	35.3	43.8	31.9
1976	39.4	45.7	36.7
1977	53.2	66.6	47.1
1978	49.8	77.2	44.4
1979	45.5	48.6	32.4
1980	41.5	45.7	28.4

Source: Von Braun and de Haen (1983), Table 12.
[a] The border price is calculated from values of imports, with marketing costs added and corrections made to account for the overvaluation of the currency.

sum of all the marked areas except *H*, and consumption has been raised from q_d to q_d'. Wheat producers have lost heavily as consequences of the reduced market price and very low procurement price – although apparently they have received partial compensation via input subsidies. Production will have been reduced, from q_s to q_s' at the prevailing market price P_m and there will have been a loss of producer surplus equal to the sum of shaded areas $A+B+C+I$. The area *I* being lost as a result of the government's procurement policy.

On balance therefore it can be seen that the combination of instruments has caused a large transfer from producers to consumers. The scale of this can be gauged from the estimates which are presented in Table 12.5 from the study of von Braun and de Haen (1983). For example in 1980 it appears that wheat producers 'lost' 72 million Egyptian pounds (LE),

Table 12.5. *Estimated costs and benefits of Egypt's price and subsidy policies for wheat (million 1975 Egyptian pounds)*

	Producer[b] losses	Consumer gains	Changes in[a] the budget
1965	58	183	21
1966	49	130	15
1967	47	135	20
1968	26	68	−6
1969	33	151	−5
1970	44	184	6
1971	37	101	1
1972	32	115	3
1973	122	395	131
1974	149	485	196
1975	119	376	143
1976	84	310	80
1977	28	190	39
1978	25	237	59
1979	65	376	290
1980	72	438	328

Source: von Braun and de Haen (1983), pp. 52, 53.
[a] These are the budgetary costs estimated using the economic model, rather than from the official figures of budgetary costs.
[b] An element of input subsidy has been deducted in calculating producer losses. These subsidies are in part a deliberate attempt to offset some of the adverse effect of lower prices upon producers.

whereas consumers 'gained' LE438 million. The other large debit item has been in terms of budgetary cost, which for 1980 was estimated by von Braun and de Haen at LE328 million. This arises both from the domestic and import procurement policies. The subsidy cost of domestic procurement has been modest and is equivalent to area J in Fig. 12.7. For imports, without allowing for any concessional and aid supplies, the cost has been considerable. The quantity imported, q_m is equivalent to the difference between total demand q'_d and domestic supply q'_s. The total quantity sold by the GASC at subsidy prices is equal to procured domestic supplies, q_p, plus imported supplies, i.e. $q_{dis} = q_p + q_m$. Or alternatively $q_m = q_{dis} - q_p$. Thus the potential[7] subsidy cost associated with imported procurement appears in Fig. 12.7 as the sum of the areas $B+C+D+E+K+L+M+N$; and the potential total foreign exchange cost as $P_w(q_{dis} - q_p)$.

Von Braun and de Haen pursue the analysis further and extend it to other key commodities. What is important here however is that a partial equilibrium analytical framework constructed using supply and demand curves and concepts of producer and consumer surplus provided the basis for an empirical study of the costs and benefits of policy which has helped shape changes in Egyptian agricultural policy. For in the light of this and other studies there has been an improved understanding of economic impacts, and most particularly of the costs of policy, which has led the Egyptian authorities to try and reduce food subsidies, and raise domestic market prices relative to the import parity price, P_w. This should help increase domestic supply, and reverse the trend of declining food self-sufficiency, as well as to reduce import and budgetary costs.

12.4 *Conclusions*

Markets in agricultural commodities conform particularly well to the assumptions made in presenting the theory of supply, demand and markets (in Chapters 2–7). There are many producers and consumers and, although the number of food processors and wholesalers are not as numerous, agricultural markets can therefore appropriately be described as competitive. In addition there are well defined markets in relatively homogeneous commodities such as barley, maize, beef, sugar or bananas, for which well established statistics exist on prices, trade, supply and consumption. This has permitted and stimulated numerous empirical studies to estimate agricultural supply and food demand functions for both developed and less-developed countries. Indeed agricultural economists have been at the forefront of developing and applying quantitative techniques and economic theory to supply and demand estimation. Markets for manufactured products often prove less easy to analyse since they are usually more complex and conform less closely to the concepts in basic economic theory. There is a greater incidence of oligopoly in industrial markets, and they are frequently characterised by strong brand differentiation (e.g. for motor cars, televisions or refrigerators), with individual brands varying appreciably in quality and price.

The comparatively ready availability of data on agricultural markets (partly because pervasive intervention by government policies has necessitated careful monitoring of the sector), and the consequent feasibility of estimating the parameters of supply and demand curves, has permitted agricultural economists to undertake the sort of 'welfare analysis' of policy which has been explored in this chapter. It has meant that welfare economics (Chapter 10) has come to be of particular importance to agricultural economists and that they have been much concerned with the theoretical development and interpretation of this branch of economics.[8]

The sort of partial equilibrium welfare analysis of policy explored in this chapter has enabled economists to make constructive and important contributions to debates on agricultural policy. (Any reader doubting this should read Chapter 4 of the World Bank's *World Development Report 1986*, which puts great emphasis on the economic efficiency losses associated with different agricultural policies, and emphasises the importance of adjustment to freely competitive allocation of resources and products.[9]) It represents a distinctive contribution to such debates from an economics standpoint, but care needs to be taken not to interpret it too mechanically. In Chapter 10, dealing with welfare economics, it was emphasised that there is a trade-off between distributive and economic efficiency objectives. That is not something which has been explicitly considered in this chapter. For example the deadweight economic loss associated with a food subsidy policy was stated to be the amount by which taxpayer cost exceeded the increase in consumer surplus. Calculating things in this way assumes that one rupee in the average taxpayer's pocket has no more value than one rupee of extra food consumption to the average consumer. If the poor do not pay taxes the average taxpayer will be richer than the average food consumer, and readers might wish to argue that the consumer's rupee is worth more than the taxpayer's. Economists are not insensitive to this argument and are well aware of the implications of valuing a rupee in the consumer's pocket as being of equal value to one in the pocket of the average food producer or taxpayer. Nevertheless decisions about redistributive weights are ones for society (ideally through democratic processes) and it is not for economists to say what differential weighting *should* be applied. What economists can do using the sort of analysis presented in this chapter is to draw society's attention to different effects upon different groups which arise from policy, in order to allow better informed judgements to be made by politicians. It enables economists to make a special contribution to policy debates, which draws heavily upon the economic theory set out in this book as well as upon the associated econometric techniques required to quantify supply and demand functions.

12.5 *Summary points*

1. A policy may be characterised as consisting of a set of *objectives*, *instruments* for achieving those objectives, and *rules* for operating the instruments.
2. The *rules* of policy determine precisely how, where and when an instrument functions, and they control the impact of the instrument.
3. Agricultural policy extensively employs instruments which intervene in markets through subsidies, taxes or quantitative controls. Such *instruments typically affect many parameters* of the market, not only those which are the focus of policy objectives.
4. The theory of markets combined with welfare economics provides a valuable framework within which the major effects of agricultural policies can be evaluated. Among the *effects which can be measured are the welfare losses and gains arising from policy*.
5. In empirical policy analysis the effects of many instruments can be analysed *simultaneously* by means of a *mathematical model* of the relevant agricultural system and markets.
6. Because of the weighting scheme adopted whereby a dollar gained by one party is assumed to be exactly cancelled by a dollar lost by another party, all market intervention policies are shown as resulting in *net welfare losses* to society. Giving higher weights to dollars gained than to dollars lost could reverse this result, but decisions about such weights cannot be imposed by economists, they are the matter of politics.
7. Economic analysis directs policy makers attention to effects of policy which might otherwise be overlooked, and facilitates attempts to quantify these.

Further reading

For a more comprehensive view of the economics of agricultural policy there are several sources that readers could usefully consult. In a recent book Houck (1986) provides a basic treatment, unadorned by any case material, of the welfare economic analysis of the major policy instruments from a developed country perspective.

In this chapter, with the exception of the Thai rice example, analysis has been confined to the case of a small open economy. Hill and Ingersent (1977, pp. 187–96) present analysis of a variety of instruments from the standpoint of countries large enough to influence international prices. This is also done more extensively by McCalla and Josling (1985) who consider the impacts of the same sort of policy instruments for (1) a closed economy, (2) a small open economy, and (3) a large open economy. Some readers may find parts of this book rather advanced, but its overall coverage and approach to policy are ones which we consider particularly useful.

There is a relative paucity of books dealing explicitly with agricultural pricing policies in LDCs. The book by Tolley *et al.* (1982) is one such; it is a very useful book for those with a sound theoretical and quantitative training which explores four particular policy cases for Bangladesh, Korea, Thailand and Venezuela. Another by Timmer, Falcon and Pearson (1983) provides an overview of Food Policy Analysis with developing countries in mind, which is a useful complement to the present volume.

Finally readers might find it very useful to start by consulting the World Bank's, *World Development Report, 1986*; Chapters 4 and 5 are devoted to an overview of agricultural pricing policies in developing countries and Chapter 6 to those of developed countries. Readers consulting this will perceive just how strong an impact the sort of analysis presented in this Chapter has had upon the Bank's thinking; this underlines the relevance of this type of economic analysis in contemporary policy debates.

Notes

Chapter 1

1 In contrast, 'macroeconomics' utilises highly aggregated concepts such as total consumption, national output, investment etc. Recently some studies (e.g. Timmer *et al.* (1985)) have noted that macroeconomic policies and adjustments can have a major impact on the agricultural sector. A great deal of research on these macroeconomic linkages remains to be done and we have chosen not to elaborate on the topic here.

2 Rao (1986) provides a critical review of neoclassical, neo-Marxian and structuralist approaches to the study of agriculture in development.

3 The recent reassertion of the neoclassical approach in development economics reflects to some degree the disillusionment with the results of centralised planning and control in general developing countries in the 1960s and 1970s. See Killick (1978).

Chapter 2

1 For a discussion of this, see Ghatak and Ingersent (1984, Chapter 3).

2 Empirical work however cannot be conducted at this level of generality and so in quantitative analysis a specific mathematical form of the production function must be assumed. A popular choice in agricultural economics has been the Cobb–Douglas function: $Q = aX_1^{b_1} X_2^{b_2} \ldots X_n^{b_n}$ where $a, b_1, b_2, \ldots, b_n$ are production parameters to be estimated.

3 The terms *output* and *product* are used interchangeably. By convention the concepts of the theory are expressed in terms of 'product', as in total product, average product and marginal product. Similarly the terms *input* and *factor* (for factor of production) are interchangeable.

4 This ratio is known as the *partial derivative* in calculus

i.e. $MP_{X_1} = \dfrac{\partial Q}{\partial X_1} = \lim\limits_{\Delta X_1 \to 0} \dfrac{\Delta Q}{\Delta X_1}$.

5 $AP_{X_1} = \dfrac{OQ_0}{OX_1^0} = \dfrac{AX_1^0}{OX_1^0}$ = slope of the line OA.

6 Apart from labour, all inputs, including the size of farm, are assumed fixed.

7 It can be shown that the marginal rate of substitution of X_1 and X_2 equals the ratio of the marginal product of X_1 (i.e. $\partial Q/\partial X_1$) to the marginal product of X_2 (i.e. $\partial Q/\partial X_2$). Given that on an isoquant $\mathrm{d}Q = 0$, we can write

$$\mathrm{d}Q = \mathrm{d}X_1 \frac{\partial Q}{\partial X_1} + \mathrm{d}X_2 \frac{\partial Q}{\partial X_2} = 0.$$

and by rearranging

$$\frac{\mathrm{d}X_2}{\mathrm{d}X_1} = (-)\frac{\partial Q}{\partial X_1}\bigg/\frac{\partial Q}{\partial X_2}.$$

See Koutsoyiannis (1979, Chapter 21).

8 A common example of this case is where the two inputs are tractors and tractor drivers.

9 For example, if X_1 denotes fertiliser usage, the magnitude of *MRS* would depend on whether X_1 is measured in cwt. or kg.

10 In Fig. 2.6, the production-possibility curve bulges outward i.e. it is concave to the origin. This shape is related to the law of diminishing marginal returns, when the commodities are produced with different factor intensities and constant returns to scale are assumed. The concavity would be more pronounced if there were decreasing returns to scale.

11 Economists define *profit* as the excess of revenues derived from the sale of output over the full opportunity costs of all the factors used in production. Hence the cost of inputs is measured by the value which could have been generated if the inputs were used in alternative ways.

12 Models of the firm which do not rely on the profit maximisation objective are discussed in detail in Koutsoyiannis (1982).

13 The formal derivation is given in Chapter 3.

14 The cost outlay is typically computed in terms of the monetary costs to be expended on purchased inputs, but where unpaid labour is used it may be relevant to calculate the *opportunity costs* of labour of the producer and any of the producer's family engaged in production.

15 The same equilibrium condition would be derived if we had specified the problem as one of maximising output for a given cost outlay.

Chapter 3

1 In other words 'other things remaining constant'. Much economic analysis rests on the *ceteris paribus* assumption.

2 There is a third form of uncertainty, namely that surrounding the prices and quality of inputs. This and other aspects of risk and uncertainty are discussed more fully in Chapter 4.

3 See also Ghatak and Ingersent (1984, Chapter 7).

4 The subject of econometrics concerns the application of mathematical and statistical techniques to economic problems.

Chapter 4

1 Interested readers should refer to Schultz (1978) and Da Silva *et al.* (1985).

2 'Capital' is defined as material assets other than land.

3 This is the view expressed by Russell and Young (1983) on which much of this section is based.

4 Strictly, this is 'Hicks-neutral' technological change, since it corresponds to the definition of neutrality suggested by Hicks (1946).

5 Rosenberg (1982, Chapter 6) presents the 'learning by using' concept with reference to the 'consumer goods industry'.

6 A technology package is divisible if it can be implemented on any scale of operation.

7 As more and more farmers take up the new technology and expand output, the product price will fall. This decline in price may prompt those farmers who have not yet adopted the technology to do so, in order to avoid losses. However it may also bear heavily on those farmers who are unable to adopt the technology because of the topographical or climatic conditions under which they operate.

8 We are not choosing to draw a distinction between the terms 'risk' and 'uncertainty'. Both terms are used to describe situations in which complete information or perfect knowledge is absent.

9 Farmers may also face uncertainty regarding the quality of inputs, particularly capital, and agricultural policy e.g. the timing of announcements of the degree of market support in the production period.

10 The objective is denoted as maximise $E\ U(\Pi)$, where $U(\Pi)$ is the utility function in which profit is a parameter. The form of the utility function is determined by the producer's attitude to risk. Utility functions are presented in more detail in Chapter 5.

11 Formally this is written as minimise $Pr\ \{\Pi < \Pi_0\}$, where Pr denotes probability and Π_0 is the disaster level.

12 For other examples, see MacLaren (1983).

13 More generally, they could be thought of in terms of a *transformation function* describing the maximum sets of values of multiple outputs producible from alternative quantities of many inputs. It is easier to explain the basic principles with respect to a production function in which there is a single output and many inputs.

14 For a one unit change in the use of fertiliser, $\Delta TVC = p_F$, the price of fertiliser, and ΔQ = marginal product (MP) of fertiliser. Hence, using the definitions of Chapter 2,

$$MC = \frac{\Delta TVC}{\Delta Q} = \frac{p_F}{MP},$$

and $$AVC = \frac{TVC}{Q} = \frac{p_F \cdot F}{Q} = \frac{p_F}{AP}$$

where F = units of fertiliser used.

Debertin (1986, Section 9.5) discusses duality between production and cost relationships for the case of multiple variable inputs.

15 The conditional input demand functions, $X_i = g_i(p_1, \ldots, p_n, Q)$ are found by taking the partial derivatives,

$$\frac{\partial \tilde{C}}{\partial p_i} i = 1, \ldots n.$$

16 Specifically, taking the partial derivative, $\partial\tilde{\Pi}/\partial P$ yields the supply function and the negative of the partial derivative, $\partial\tilde{\Pi}/\partial p_i$, gives the *i*th input demand equation.

Chapter 5

1 Some authors prefer the term *effective demand* to emphasise the role of actual market behaviour.
2 The indifference curve, which depicts combinations of goods yielding the same level of satisfaction is analogous to the isoquant in production theory which indicates the combinations of factors of production yielding the same level of output.
3 In setting up the budget constraint (that expenditure cannot exceed income), we are implicitly assuming that there is no saving or that saving can be treated as an item of expenditure.
4 The slope of the budget line is given as $(-)(M_0/P_2)/(M_0/P_1) = (-)P_1/P_2$.
5 By consuming Q_1^* and Q_2^*, the consumer maximises satisfaction given the budget constraint. Since there are no forces which would induce him or her to change this consumption pattern, the consumer is said to be in *equilibrium*.
6 This discussion follows Deaton and Muellbauer (1980) who present additional examples of unconventional budget constraints.
7 Recall that a similar decomposition was effected in Chapter 3. There the impact of an input price change was divided into a substitution effect and an expansion effect.
8 In the unlikely event that the income effect of a change in price of an inferior good is so strong as to outweigh the substitution effect, the total effect will be positive. In other words as price falls, the demand for the product decreases. This special case is termed a *Giffen Good.*

Chapter 6

1 We will give a precise definition of a market in Chapter 9.
2 The Lorenz coefficient or Gini coefficient (as it is more commonly portrayed) is a standard measure of inequality; a definition can be found in Colman and Nixson (1986, p. 86).
3 In fact it can be shown that the demand curve between *A* and *B* is elastic ($\varepsilon_{ii} > (-)1$), at *B* (the midpoint of the curve) is unitary elastic ($\varepsilon_{ii} = (-)1$), and between *B* and *C* is inelastic ($\varepsilon_{ii} < (-)1$).
4 This point is discussed in greater detail in Chapter 9.
5 Note that this factor is closely related to the availability of substitutes.
6 Since by definition, $E_i = P_iQ_i$, then it can be shown that $(\partial E_i/\partial M)\ (M/E_i) = (\partial Q_i/\partial M)\ (M/Q_i) + (\partial P_i/\partial M)\ (M/P_i)$. If there are

no significant quality differences in the product then the last term in this equation would be set to zero.

7 This is evidence that income distribution at a given time will be an important determinant of demand for food products.

8 The formal derivation is complex and need not concern us here. The interested reader can refer to Phlips (1983) or Deaton and Muellbauer (1980).

9 Young (1980) estimated an asymmetric demand function for coffee in Great Britain. His results imply that coffee demand is price elastic (−1.17) with respect to price falls but inelastic (−0.69) with respect to price increases.

Chapter 7

1 If a good at its current price is inefficient in the provision of characteristics (i.e. for a given outlay, it provides less of one characteristic and no more of any other characteristic than other market goods) it will not be consumed, irrespective of the distribution of consumer preferences.

2 By valuing household time at the market wage, the time and income constraints can be collapsed into a single 'full income' constraint:

$F = wT = w\Sigma t_j + \Sigma P_j Q_j$.

3 The compensated demand functions are analogous to the cost minimising input demand functions of Chapter 4. In that case, input demand was determined by input prices and the level of output, i.e. keeping the firm on the same isoquant.

4 Since $Q_i = h_i(P_1, \ldots, P_n, U^*) = \partial C/\partial P_i \quad i = 1, \ldots, n$.

5 The demand functions which are estimated are specified with budget shares as the dependent variables and with prices and total expenditure as explanatory variables. See Deaton and Muellbauer (1980).

6 By using 'Roy's Identity', $Q_i = -(\partial U^*/\partial P_i)/(\partial U^*/\partial M)$.

7 Thomas (1987) neatly summarises two well-known empirical models based on specific indirect utility functions, namely Houthakker's *Addilog* model and the flexible functional form developed by Christensen, Jorgenson and Lau.

Chapter 8

1 For example, wheat may be sold to a miller who produces flour which is subsequently sold to a baker who makes bread.

2 In the latter the product traded would be labour services and the product price would be the wage rate. As the wage rate increases in the lower range of wages, the individual worker is willing to supply more labour services. Since the opportunity cost or 'price' of leisure has increased, the *substitution effect* induces more work to be undertaken and less leisure to be enjoyed. On the other hand in the upper wage range, further increases in the wage rate may bring forth less labour services. This is because the *income effect* of the wage

change on the demand for leisure outweighs the substitution effect. For a full analysis see, for example, Hirshleifer (1976).

3 It should be stressed that this discussion is confined to price regulation in a competitive product market. If there are market imperfections, some modifications to the analysis are required (see Chapter 9).

4 For example some surplus milk has been removed by subsidising the use of milk powder by animal feed compounders, and some milling wheat has been 'denatured' and sold to farmers to use as animal feed.

5 Clearly we are assuming that the product in question is a normal good.

6 Since short run supply of most agricultural products is price inelastic any shifts in demand which may occur in the short term, will also produce large price variation.

7 Just (1977) surveys some of the pertinent issues.

8 See Tomek and Robinson (1981).

9 For example, in the developed countries, health concerns may induce some consumers to reduce their purchases of red meats, dairy products, and sugar.

10 The empirical work is usually conducted with reference to the 'terms of trade'. In other words the price of an agricultural product or set of (usually export) agricultural products, relative to a price of a bundle of other goods (usually imports) is the variable of interest. The 'terms of trade' are discussed in more detail in Chapter 11.

11 This approach was suggested by Walras in the late nineteenth century.

12 This process may be represented as $\mathrm{d}P/\mathrm{d}t = \lambda(QD\text{-}QS)$, with the constant $\lambda \geqslant 0$. In a static model, price does not vary over time and so in that case, $\lambda = 0$.

13 If the product can be stored from one crop year to the next, then expectations of price levels in the subsequent season must be taken into account and there may be occasions when these expectations justify some 'carryover'.

14 Tomek and Robinson (1981) discuss the limitations of the simple model at some length.

15 The wage rate represents the opportunity cost of time spent at leisure rather than at work. It can thus be thought of as the price of leisure.

16 The basic model can be extended in a number of directions. For example, multiple products, borrowing, government deficits, and risk are among the issues considered in Singh *et al.* (1986a).

17 Consider the demand function for the agricultural good (8.20 above). The total effect of a price change will be:

$$\frac{\mathrm{d}Q_a}{\mathrm{d}P_a} = \frac{\partial Q_a}{\partial P_a} + \frac{\partial Q_a}{\partial Y^*}\frac{\partial Y^*}{\partial P_a}$$

or in elasticity form:

$$\frac{\mathrm{d}Q_a}{\mathrm{d}P_a}\frac{P_a}{Q_a} = \frac{\partial Q_a}{\partial P_a}\frac{P_a}{Q_a} + \frac{\partial Q_a}{\partial Y^*}\frac{Y^*}{Q_a}\cdot\frac{\partial Y^*}{\partial P_a}\frac{P_a}{Y^*}.$$

The first term on the right hand side is the standard own-price elasticity. The second term measures the profits effect.

Chapter 9

1 $TR = P \times Q$. Note that price (P) is now a function of quantity sold and so

$$MR = \frac{\partial TR}{\partial Q} = P\frac{\partial Q}{\partial Q} + Q\frac{\partial P}{\partial Q} = P + Q\frac{\partial P}{\partial Q}$$

$$= P\left(1 + \frac{Q}{P}\frac{\partial P}{\partial Q}\right) = P\left(1 + \frac{1}{\varepsilon}\right)$$

where

$\varepsilon = \frac{\partial Q}{\partial P}\frac{P}{Q}$, the price elasticity of demand.

2 If elasticity is infinite, $1/\varepsilon$ approaches zero in the limit and $P = MR$.

3 In other words, total revenue would decrease if output were increased.

4 Another form of price discrimination, which will not be discussed here, occurs when the same consumer is faced with a price schedule in which the per unit price varies with quantity purchased. This form, sometimes termed 'multi-part pricing', is common in the telephone and electricity services industries.

5 See Currie and Hoos (1979).

6 Another type of marketing board is established to provide funds for general economic development. This is considered in Section 9.2.

7 For example, the Citrus Marketing Board of Israel has full monopoly control in the domestic market but must compete in its export markets with the citrus products of other countries. In order to reduce this competition, the Board has tried to develop a brand image for its products.

8 See, for example, Masson and Eisenstat (1980).

9 Marginal cost pricing is of particular interest because it is a condition for a social optimum. See Chapter 10.

10 If there are few producers in product markets and few buyers in factor markets, we refer to *oligopoly* and *oligopsony* respectively. These forms of economic organisation, lying between pure monopoly and pure competition, call for different economic models. See Koutsoyiannis (1979).

11 It should be noted that just as the monopolist's marginal cost curve could not be taken to be the supply curve, the monopsonist's marginal revenue product curve is not strictly the firm's demand curve for the input.

12 Bardhan (1984) discusses, in more detail, the question of monopsony in agricultural labour markets in developing countries.

13 It should perhaps be stressed that our analysis is *partial*, in that we are assuming there are no interactions with other input markets, and

static, in that all dynamic effects, such as the impact on expectations, are ignored.

14 Strictly, the *MFC* curve is discontinuous in the range *FG*.

15 See Livingstone and Ord (1981).

16 A market in which a single buyer (monopsonist) is confronted by a single seller (monopoly) is termed *bilateral monopoly*. The precise price and output levels at which trade takes place are however indeterminate and will depend *inter alia* upon relative bargaining power.

17 Typically an export marketing board is the sole buyer of the specific crop but must face competition when the product is sold on world markets.

18 It should be noted that whereas the payment of low producer prices inhibits the expansion of production and reduces farm income, other sections of society may benefit from the disposition of the board's surpluses. The latter is not taken into account in the analysis above but is explained in the policy cases analysed in Chapter 12 below.

19 In reality there is no reason why this margin should be the same for all points on the derived demand curve, but it is helpful for a graphical presentation of this analysis. Readers who wish to test this should experiment with primary and derived demand curves which are not parallel. In an algebraic analysis it is easy to relax this strong assumption.

Chapter 10

1 The original form of the concept was introduced by Pareto in his book *Cours d'Economie Politique* published in 1897.

2 Equation 5.2 stated this as *MRS* of Q_1 for Q_2.

3 This possible result, known as the Scitovsky Paradox is concisely explained by Ng (1983), pp. 60–1.

4 Very readable reviews of the debate have been published by Currie *et al.* (1971) and by Just *et al.* (1982) Chapters 4 and 6. The debate about consumer surplus is also well presented by Ng (1983), Chapter 4.

5 Just *et al.* (1982), pp. 88, 89.

6 Those who wish to study the subject in greater detail should consult Currie *et al.* (1971), pp. 753–65, or Just *et al.* (1982), Chapters 4 and 7.

7 See Just *et al.* (1982), pp. 64–7 for further details about the appropriate approach.

Chapter 11

1 Their original works dated 1933 and 1919 respectively are reprinted in English in Ellis and Metzler (1949).

2 These equilibrium solutions, *A* and *D*, can be visualised as being determined by the tangency of the relevant indifference curves to the production possibility curves. At equilibrium, the relative price of

sugar to maize will equal (i) the marginal rate of transformation in production of maize for sugar, and (ii) the marginal utility to consumers of sugar relative to that of maize.

3 This employs the logic discussed in connection with Fig. 11.1(*a*) and 11.1(*b*).

4 Note that in Fig. 11.4(*a*) and 11.4(*b*) there is no suggestion that the trade price ratio PS_T/PM_T is the equilibrium ratio. It is simply one price ratio (lying between PS_K/PM_K and PS_U/PM_U) at which trade would be expected to occur.

5 This draughtsmanship is a matter of convenience. The equilibrium price ratio will be determined by market forces and could be anywhere between PS_U/PM_U and PS_K/PM_K.

6 Notice also in comparing *W* to *T* that more maize is exported from the USA than arrives at the central market, and that less sugar arrives in the USA than was dispatched from there. Comparably, comparing *V* to *T*, reveals that some sugar is 'used up' en route from Kenya to the central market as is some maize during transfer in the opposite direction. These losses reflect the transport costs.

7 One difference is, of course, that the tariff revenue accrues to government, while transport costs are earned by transport firms. To the extent that government uses its revenue differently than transport firms there will be differences in the macro-economic implications.

8 $$\frac{PA_t}{PB_t} = \frac{\left(\sum_{i=1}^{n} PA_{it} \cdot WA_{it}\right) \Big/ \sum_{i=1}^{n} WA_{it}}{\left(\sum_{j=1}^{m} PB_{jt} \cdot WB_{jt}\right) \Big/ \sum_{j=1}^{m} WB_{jt}} =$$

$$\frac{(PA_{1t} \cdot WA_1 + PA_{2t} \cdot WA_2 + \ldots + PA_{nt} \cdot WA_n)/(WA_1 + WA_2 + \ldots + WA_n)}{(PB_{1t} \cdot WB_1 + PB_{2t} \cdot WB_2 + \ldots + PB_{mt} \cdot WB_m)/(WB_1 + WB_2 + \ldots + WB_m)}$$

where

PA_{it}, PB_{jt} = the price series (or index) of commodity *i,j*

WA_i, WB_j = the weight assigned to commodity *i,j*

$t = time = 1, 2, \ldots, T,$

(Note it is normal to adjust the terms-of-trade series calculated in the above way, by multiplying it by a constant so that its value is set at 100 in some chosen *base year*.)

9 Indeed if the country concerned had sufficient monopoly power in trade it is theoretically possible that it might be able to increase the welfare of its citizens by imposing an export tariff – an outcome which would of course entail a loss of welfare to other countries. There are few instances of countries possessing the necessary degree of monopoly power, although the dominant position of the OPEC countries in the world oil market between 1973 and 1980 does provide an example. In this circumstance economic theory suggests there is an

optimum export tariff which will maximise the exporting country's welfare. The optimum will be where the marginal welfare gain from improved terms of trade is just equal to the marginal welfare loss from the reduction in trade volume. A readable explanation of the *optimum tariff* and its counterpart the *optimum subsidy* is provided by Meier (1980, pp. 90–101). As Meier (p. 85) emphasises in a world of the *second best* from the standpoint of a country or group of countries 'the only first best economic argument for protection is the optimum tariff. All other arguments for protection should really be arguments for some form of government intervention in the domestic economy, and the use of tariffs in these cases would be sub-optimal policy'.

10 One version of this would be the case of 'trade-pessimism' whereby the view would be held in politically influential quarters that export prospects for current major exports were poor. Plans might therefore be made to orientate production and trade towards a future in which the expected relative prices of commodities are significantly different to current ones. This entails a bold act of faith in the forecasting ability of the trade pessimists.

Chapter 12

1 Food stamps are a form of money exchangeable only for certain foods, they are used by those issued with them to buy food. The shop owner can then exchange stamps paid by customers for cash from the appropriate government agency.

2 McCalla and Josling, (1985, pp. 108–109) adopt a classification based on five levels – (1) frontier, (2) consumption or retail level, (3) product market, (4) input markets, (5) fixed factors.

3 It is true that for smaller producers operating below the maximum subsidy threshold, the subsidy benefit would still be proportional to output. However, by paying the higher subsidy rate and preventing large farmers from receiving more than the upper limit in subsidy receipts there would be an improvement in equity.

4 Refer to Section 10.5 for the definition of producer surplus.

5 The purchase cost $E+F$ is assumed to be recouped by the intervention authority as revenue from the sale of exports.

6 For more details of the scale and costs of these policies see Scobie (1981) and Alderman *et al.* (1982).

7 Without allowing for concessional supplies.

8 Excellent examples of this are the already cited works by Currie *et al.* (1971) and Just *et al.* (1982).

9 There are many other publications which could be referred to for a similar message, but the importance of the World Bank's views makes the position stated in the World Development Report particularly noteworthy.

References

Alderman, H., J. von Braun, and Sakr Ahmed Sakr (1982). *Egypt's Food Subsidy and Rationing System: A Description*, International Food Policy Research Institute, Research Report 34.

Arrow, K. J. and T. Scitovsky (eds.) (1969). *Readings on Welfare Economics*. Allen and Unwin.

Askari, H. and J. T. Cummings (1976). *Agricultural Supply Response: A Survey of the Econometric Evidence*. Praeger.

Bardhan, P. K. (1984). *Land, Labour and Rural Poverty. Essays in Development Economics*, Oxford University Press.

Barker, R. and R. W. Herdt, with B. Rose (1985). *The Rice Economy of Asia*. Resources for the Future.

Beattie, B. R. and C. R. Taylor (1985). *The Economics of Production*. John Wiley.

Begg, D., S. Fischer and R. Dornbusch (1984, British Edn). *Economics*, McGraw-Hill.

Blandford, D. (1979). 'West African marketing boards', Chapter 6 in Hoos (1979), *loc. cit*.

Brown, M. B. (1974). *The Economics of Imperialism*, Penguin Books.

Call, S. T. and W. T. Holahan (1983, 2nd Edn). *Microeconomics*, Wadsworth Publishing Co.

Caves, R. E. and R. W. Jones (1977). *World Trade and Payments: An Introduction*, Little, Brown.

Colman, D. (1983). 'A Review of the arts of supply response analysis'. *Review of Marketing and Agricultural Economics*, **51**, (3).

Colman, D. and F. Nixson (1986, 2nd Edn). *Economics of Change in Less-Developed Countries*, Philip Allan.

Commonwealth Secretariat (1975). *Terms of Trade for Primary Commodities*, Commonwealth Economic Papers No. 4.

Coppock, D. J. (1977). *International Trade Instability*. Saxon House.

Corden, W. M. (1971). *The Theory of Protection*, Oxford University Press.

Currie, J. M., J. A. Murphy and A. Schmitz (1971). 'The concept of economic surplus'. *Economic Journal*, **LXXXI** (324).

Currie, J. M. and S. Hoos (1979). 'Marketing boards: a comparative summary', Chapter 12 in Hoos (1979), *loc. cit.*

Da Silva, J. A. B. B. (1984). *Measuring the effects of Government Policies on Brazilian Agriculture, with Particular Emphasis on the Beef and Dairy Sectors.* Unpublished Ph.D. thesis, University of Manchester.

Da Silva, J. A. B. B., T. Young and W. B. Traill (1985). 'Market distortions in Brazilian agriculture: an analysis of the effects of government policy on the beef and dairy sectors'. *Journal of Agricultural Economics*, **XXXVI** (3).

Dalrymple, D. G. (1986). *Development and Spread of High-Yielding Wheat Varieties in Developing Countries.* Bureau for Science and Technology. Agency for International Development.

Deaton, A. and J. Muellbauer (1980). *Economics and Consumer Behavior*, Cambridge University Press.

Debertin, D. L. (1986), *Agricultural Production Economics*, Macmillan.

Doll, J. P. and F. Orazem (1984, 2nd Edn). *Production Economics. Theory with Applications.* John Wiley.

Edwards, C. (1985). *The Fragmented World.* Methuen.

Eicher, C. K. and J. M. Staatz (ed.) (1985). *Agricultural Development in the Third World.* Johns Hopkins University Press.

Ellis, F. (1987). *Peasant Economics: Farm Households and Agrarian Change*, Cambridge University Press.

Ellis, H. S. and L. A. Metzler (eds.). (1949) *Readings in the Theory of International Trade*, Irwin.

Emmanuel, A. (1972). *Unequal Exchange.* New Left Books.

Emmanuel, A. (1982). *Appropriate or Underdeveloped Technology.* John Wiley.

Epp, D. J. and J.W. Malone Jr (1981). *Introduction to Agricultural Economics.* Macmillan.

F.A.O. (1983). *Income Elasticities of Demand for Agricultural Products.* ESC/M/83/7.

F.A.O. (1985). *Agricultural Price Policies*, Conference of FAO, 23rd Session, C85/19.

Farrell, M. J. (1957) 'The Measurement of Productive Efficiency'. *Journal of the Royal Statistical Society*, **Series A, 120**

Feder, G., R. Just and D. Zilberman (1985). 'Adoption of Agricultural Innovations in Developing Countries: A Survey', *Economic Development and Cultural Change*, **33** (2).

Fei, J. C. H. and G. Ranis (1964). *Development of the Labour Surplus Economy: Theory and Policy.* Irwin.

Findlay, R. (1970). *Trade and Specialisation*, Penguin Books.

Ghatak, S. and K. Ingersent (1984). *Agriculture and Economic Development.* Wheatsheaf.

Gowland, D. (1983). *International Economics*, Croom Helm.

Green, H. A. J. (1976, revised Edn). *Consumer Theory*, Macmillan.

Griffin, K. (1979, 2nd Edn). *The Political Economy of Agrarian Change: An Essay on the Green Revolution.* Macmillan.

Hayami, Y. and V. W. Ruttan (1985, 2nd Edn). *Agricultural Development: An International Perspective.* Johns Hopkins University Press.

Haughton, J. (1986) 'Farm price responsiveness and the choice of functional form. An application to rice cultivation in West Malaysia' *Journal of Development Economics*, **24**, 203–23.

Hazell, P. B. R. and J. R. Anderson (1986). 'Public policy toward technical change in agriculture', in P. Hall (ed.) *Technology, Innovation and Economic Policy.* Philip Allan.

Heathfield, D. F. and S. Wibe (1987), *An Introduction to Cost and Production Functions.* Macmillan.

Henry, C. M. (1985). 'Technological change for agricultural development. An econometric analysis.' *Oxford Agrarian Studies*, XIV.

Herdt, R. W. and C. Capule (1983). *Adoption, Spread and Production Impact of Modern Rice Varieties in Asia*. International Rice Research Institute.

Hicks, J. R. (1940). 'The valuation of the social income', *Economica*, **7** (26).

Hicks, J. R. (1941). 'The rehabilitation of consumer's surplus', *Review of Economic Studies*, **8**.

Hicks, J. R. (1943). 'The four consumers' surpluses', *Review of Economic Studies*, **11**.

Hicks, J. R. (1946, 2nd Edn). *Value and Capital*. Oxford University Press.

Hill, B. E. and K. A. Ingersent (1977). *An Economic Analysis of Agriculture*, Heinemann Educational Books.

Hill, B. E. (1984). *The Common Agricultural Policy: Past, Present and Future*, Methuen.

Hirshleifer, J. (1976). *Price Theory and Applications*. Prentice Hall.

Hoos, S. (ed.) (1979). *Agricultural Marketing Boards – An International Perspective*, Ballinger Publishing Co.

Houck, J. P. (1986). *Elements of Agricultural Trade Policies*, Macmillan.

Johnson, D. G. (1979). 'Food reserves and International trade policy', in J. S. Hillman and A. Schmitz (eds.). *International Trade and Agriculture: Theory and Policy*. Westfield Press.

Just, R. E. and D. Zilberman (1986). 'Does the Law of Supply Hold Under Uncertainty'. *Economic Journal*, **96** (382).

Just, R. E., D. L. Heuth and A. Schmitz (1982). *Applied Welfare Economics and Public Policy*. Prentice-Hall.

Just, R. E. (1977). 'Theoretical and Empirical Possibilities for Determining the Distribution of Welfare Gains from Stabilization', *American Journal of Agricultural Economics*, **59** (5).

Kaldor, N. (1939). 'Welfare propositions in economics'. *Economic Journal*, **XLIX** (2).

Killick, T. (1978). *Development Economics in Action: A Study of Economic Policies in Ghana*. St Martin's Press.

Killick, T. (1981). *Policy Economics; a textbook of applied economics on developing countries*. Heinemann.

Koester, U. (1986). *Regional Cooperation to Improve Food Security in Southern and Eastern African Countries*, International Food Policy Research Institute, Research Report 53.

Kohls, R. L. and J. N. Uhl (1980, 5th Edn). *Marketing of Agricultural Products*. Collier Macmillan.

Koutsoyiannis, A. (1979, 2nd Edn). *Modern Microeconomics*. Macmillan.

Kuznets, S. (1961). 'Economic Growth and the Contribution of Agriculture: Notes on Measurement'. *International Journal of Agrarian Affairs*, Vol. 3. Reprinted in C. K. Eicher and L. W. Witt (eds.) (1964) *Agriculture in Economic Development*, McGraw-Hill.

Labys, W. C. (1973). *Dynamic Commodity Models*, Lexington Books.

Laidler, D. (1981, 2nd Edn). *Introduction to Microeconomics*. Philip Allan.

Lal, D. (1983). *The Poverty of Development Economics*. Hobart Paperback 16, Institute of Economic Affairs.

Lancaster, K. (1971). *Consumer Demand: A New Approach*. Columbia University Press.

Lau, L. J. and P. A. Yotopoulos (1971). 'A test of relative efficiency and application to Indian agriculture'. *American Economic Review*, **61** (1).

Levi, J. and M. Havinden (1982). *Economics of African Agriculture*. Longman.

Lewis, W. A. (1954). 'Economic development with unlimited supplies of labour'. *Manchester School*, **22** (2).

Lipsey, R. G. and K. Lancaster (1956). 'The general theory of second best', *Review of Economic Studies*, **24** (1).

Lipsey, R. G. (1983, 6th Edn). *Introduction to Positive Economics*, Weidenfeld and Nicolson.

Little, I. M. D. (1982). *Economic Development Theory, Policy and International Relations*. Basic Books.

Livingstone, I. and H. W. Ord (1981). *Agricultural Economics for Tropical Africa*. Heinemann.

Low, A. (1986). *Agricultural Development in Southern Africa: Farm Household Economics and the Food Crisis*. James Currey.

MacLaren, D. (1983). 'The output response of the risk averse firm: some comparative statics of agricultural policy'. *Journal of Agricultural Economics*, **XXXIV** (1).

Marshall, A. (1927, 7th Edn). *Principles of Economics*. Macmillan.

Masson, R. T. and P. M. Eisenstat (1980). 'Welfare impacts of milk orders and the antitrust immunities for cooperatives', *American Journal of Agricultural Economics*, **62**, (2).

Matthews, A. (1985). *The Common Agricultural Policy and the Less Developed Countries*. Gill and Macmillan.

McCalla, A. F. and T. E. Josling (1985). *Agricultural Policies and World Markets*. Macmillan.

McInerney, J. P. (1978). 'The technology of rural development'. *World Bank Staff Working Paper*, No. 295.

McInerney, J. P. and G. F. Donaldson (1975). 'The consequences of farm tractors in Pakistan'. *World Bank Staff Working Paper* No. 210.

Meier, G. M. (1980). *International Economics: The Theory of Policy*. Oxford University Press.

Mellor, J. W. (1963). 'The use and productivity of farm family labour in early stages of agricultural development'. *Journal of Farm Economics*, **XLV** (3).

Mellor, J. W. (1966). *The Economics of Agricultural Development*. Cornell University Press.

Mellor, J. W. (1985). 'Determinants of rural poverty: the dynamics of production, technology and price', in J. W. Mellor and G. M. Desai, *Agricultural Change and Rural Poverty: Variations on a Theme by Dharm Narain*. Johns Hopkins University Press.

Michael, R. T. and G. S. Becker (1973). 'On the new theory of consumer behaviour'. *Swedish Journal of Economics*, **75** (4).

Ministry of Agriculture, Fisheries and Food (MAFF) (1985). *Household Food Consumption and Expenditure*. Annual Report of the National Food Survey Committee. HMSO.

Mishan, E. J. (1962). 'Second thoughts on second best'. *Oxford Economic Papers*, **14** (3). Reprinted in Mishan (1969). *Welfare Economics: Ten Introductory Essays*, Random House.

Myint, H. (1958). 'The classical theory of international trade and the undeveloped countries', *Economic Journal*, **68** (270).

Nakajima, C. (1970). 'Subsistence and commercial farms: some theoretical models of subjective equilibrium', in C. R. Wharton Jr (ed.) *Subsistence Agriculture and Economic Development*. Frank Cass.

National Fertiliser Development Centre (1984, Fiscal), 'annual fertiliser report – stagnant demand, price distortions and short term demand projections', by R. M. U. Sulesman. *Review Report 3*.

Nerlove, M. (1958). *The Dynamics of Supply: Estimation of Farmers' Response to Price.* Johns Hopkins University Press.

Newbery, D. M. G. and J. E. Stiglitz (1981). *The Theory of Commodity Price Stabilisation: A Study in the Economics of Risk.* Clarendon Press.

Ng, Y-K. (1983, revised Edn). *Welfare Economics: Introduction and Development of Basic Concepts.* Macmillan.

Pareto, V. (1897). *Cours d'Economie Politique.*

Pasour, E. C. Jr (1981). 'A further note on the measurement of efficiency and economics of farm size'. *Journal of Agricultural Economics,* **XXXII** (2).

Phlips, L. (1983, 2nd Edn). *Applied Consumption Analysis.* North Holland.

Pinstrup-Anderson, P. (1982). *Agricultural Research and Technology in Economic Development.* Longman.

Pitt, M. M. (1983). 'Farm-level fertiliser demand in Java: a meta-production function approach'. *American Journal of Agricultural Economics,* **65** (3).

Prebisch, R. (1950). *The Economic Development of Latin America and its Principal Problems,* U.N.: Economic Committee for Latin America.

Quandt, R. E. (1978). 'Tests of the equilibrium vs. disequilibrium hypotheses'. *International Economic Review,* **19** (2).

Rao, J. M. (1986). 'Agriculture in recent development theory'. *Journal of Development Economics,* **22**.

Ricardo, D. (1817). *On the Principles of Political Economy and Taxation,* Sraffa edn, Cambridge University Press (1951).

Ritson, C. (1977). *Agricultural Economics: Principle and Policy.* Granada.

Rizzo, M. J. (ed.) (1979). *Time, Uncertainty and Disequilibrium.* Lexington.

Rosenberg, N. (1982). *Inside the Black Box: Technology and Economics.* Cambridge University Press.

Roy, A. D. (1952). 'Safety first and the holding of assets'. *Econometrica* **20** (3).

Russell, N. P. and T. Young (1983). 'Frontier Production Functions and the Measurement of Technical Efficiency'. *Journal of Agricultural Economics,* **XXXIV** (2).

Sadan, E. (1979). 'Milk and dairy marketing boards', Chapter 9 in Hoos (1979), *loc. cit.*

Saleh, H. and D. Sisler (1977). 'A note concerning the effect of income distribution on demand'. *Journal of Agricultural Economics,* **XXVIII** (1).

Samuelson, P. A. (1948). 'International trade and the equalisation of factor prices'. *Economic Journal,* **58** (2).

Samuelson, P. A. (1954). 'The transfer problem and transport costs: analysis of effects of trade impediments'. *Economic Journal,* **64** (254).

Samuelson, P. A. and W. D. Nordhaus (1985, 12th Edn). *Economics,* McGraw-Hill.

Scandizzo, P. L. and D. Diakosavvas (1987). *Instability in the terms of trade of primary commodities, 1900–82.* FAO Economic and Social Development Paper 64, Food and Agriculture Organisation of the United Nations.

Schultz, T. W. (1964). *Transforming Traditional Agriculture.* Yale University Press.

Schultz, T. W. (ed.) (1978). *Distortions of Agricultural Incentives.* Indiana University Press.

Schumacher, E. F. (1974). *Small is Beautiful.* Abacus.

Scitovsky, T. (1976). *The Joyless Economy. An Inquiry into Human Satisfaction and Consumer Dissatisfaction.* Oxford University Press.

Scitovsky, T. (1978). 'Asymmetrics in economics'. *Scottish Journal of Political Economy,* **25**, (3).

Scobie, G. M. (1981). *Government Policy and Food Imports: The Case of Wheat in Egypt*, International Food Policy Research Institute, Research Report 29.

Sen, A. K. (1966). 'Peasants and dualism with or without surplus labour'. *Journal of Political Economy*. **74** (5).

Sidhu, S. S. and C. A. Baanante (1981). 'Estimating farm-level demand and wheat supply in the Indian Punjab using a translog profit function'. *American Journal of Agricultural Economics*, **63** (2).

Sidhu, S. S. (1974). 'Relative efficiency in wheat production in the Indian Punjab'. *American Economic Review*, **64** (4).

Singer, H. (1950). 'The distribution of gains between investing and borrowing countries'. *American Economic Review*, **40** (2).

Singh, I., L. Squire and J. Strauss (eds.) (1986*a*). *Agricultural Household Models*. Johns Hopkins University Press.

Singh, I. *et al.* (1986*b*). 'A survey of agricultural household models: recent findings and policy implications'. *The World Bank Economic Review*, **1**, No. 1.

Smith, A. (1776). *Wealth of Nations*.

Smith, S. and J. Toye (1979). 'Three stories about trade and poor countries', *Journal of Development Studies*, **15** (3).

Spraos, J. (1981). *Inequalising Trade*, Oxford University Press.

Stewart, F. (1978, 2nd Edn). *Technology and Underdevelopment*. Macmillan.

Thirtle, C. G. and V. W. Ruttan (1987), *The Role of Demand and Supply in the Generation and Diffusion of Technical Change*. Harwood Academic Publishers.

Thomas, R. L. (1987). *Applied Demand Analysis*. Longman.

Thomas, W. J. (ed.) (1972). *The Demand for Food*. Manchester University Press.

Timmer, C. P., W. P. Falcon and S. R. Pearson (1983). *Food Policy Analysis*. Johns Hopkins University Press.

Tolley, G. S., V. Thomas and Chung Ming Wong (1982). *Agricultural Price Policies and the Developing Countries*, Johns Hopkins University Press.

Tomek, W. G. and K. L. Robinson (1981, 2nd Edn). *Agricultural Product Prices*, Cornell University Press.

Traill, W. B., D. Colman and T. Young (1978). 'Estimating irreversible supply functions'. *American Journal of Agricultural Economics*, **60** (3).

Trairatvorakul (1984). *The Effects of Income Distribution and Nutrition of Alternative Price Policies in Thailand*. International Food Policy Research Institute, Research Report 46.

Von Braun, J. and H. de Haen (1983). *The Effects of Food Price and Subsidy Policies on Egyptian Agriculture*. International Food Policy Research Institute, Research Report 42.

Wharton, C. R. Jr (ed.) (1970). *Subsistence Agriculture and Economic Development*, Frank Cass.

Wong, Chung Ming (1978). 'A model for evaluating the effects of Thai Government taxation of rice on trade and welfare'. *American Journal of Agricultural Economics*, **60** (1).

World Bank (1982). *World Development Report*. Oxford University Press.

World Bank (1986). *World Development Report*. Oxford University Press.

Young, T. (1980). 'Modelling asymmetric consumer responses, with an example'. *Journal of Agricultural Economics*, **XXXI** (2).

Ziemer, R. F. and F. C. White (1982). 'Disequilibrium market analysis: an application to the U.S. fed beef sector'. *American Journal of Agricultural Economics*, **64** (1).

Index

Page references in *italics* refer to figures; those in **bold** type to tables.